Dōgen's Manuals of Zen Meditation

Dōgen's Manuals of Zen Meditation

CARL BIELEFELDT

University of California Press

Berkeley, Los Angeles, London

To Yanagida Seizan

University of California Press
Berkeley and Los Angeles, California

University of California Press, Ltd.
London, England

© 1988 by
The Regents of the University of California

Library of Congress Cataloging-in-Publication Data
Bielefeldt, Carl.
    Dōgen's manuals of Zen meditation Carl Bielefeldt.
        p.   cm.
    Bibliography: p.
    ISBN 978-0-520-06835-3 (pbk.)
        1. Dōgen, 1200–1253.   2. Meditation (Zen Buddhism)   3. Sōtōshū-
Doctrines   4. Dōgen, 1200–1253 . Fukan zazengi.   I. Title.
BQ9449.D657B53 1988
294.3'443—dc19   87-12527
                                                                        CIP

11 10 09 08
 9   8   7   6

Contents

Acknowledgments

I should like to thank the Japan Foundation and the Social Science Research Council for grants in support of the initial research for this work; the Center for Japanese Studies, University of California, Berkeley, and the Center for Research in International Studies, Stanford University, for support of the writing; Professors Kajiyama Yūichi and Yanagida Seizan, of Kyoto University, for assistance during the initial research; and the Kuroda Institute and the University of Hawaii Press for permission to reprint here a revised version of my article "Ch'ang-lu Tsung-tse and the 'Secret' of Zen Meditation."

Abbreviations and Conventions

DNBZ	*Dai Nihon bukkyō zensho* 大日本仏教全書. 150 vols. Tokyo, 1912–22.
DZZ	*Dōgen zenji zenshū* 道元禅師全集. Ed. by Ōkubo Dōshū 大久保道舟. 2 vols. Tokyo, 1969–70.
IBK	*Indogaku bukkyōgaku kenkyū* 印度学仏教学研究, Tokyo.
KDBGKK	*Komazawa daigaku bukkyō gakubu kenkyū kiyō* 駒沢大学仏教学部研究紀要, Tokyo.
KDBGR	*Komazawa daigaku bukkyō gakubu ronshū* 駒沢大学仏教学部論集, Tokyo.
KDKK	*Komazawa daigaku kenkyū kiyō* 駒沢大学研究紀要, Tokyo.
SK	*Shūgaku kenkyū* 宗学研究 (Komazawa Daigaku), Tokyo.
SKKKK	*Sōtō shū kenkyū in kenkyū sei kenkyū kiyō* 曹洞宗研究員研究生研究紀要, Tokyo.
SSZ	*Sōtō shū zensho* 曹洞宗全書. 20 vols. Tokyo, 1929–38.
T	*Taishō shinshū daizōkyō* 大正新修大蔵経. 85 vols. Tokyo, 1924–33.
ZZ	*Dai Nihon zoku zōkyō* 大日本続蔵経. 750 vols. Kyoto, 1905–12.

Citations of T take the following form: volume: page, column, (line); hence, e.g., T.46:470b12 indicates volume 46, page 470, column b, line 12. The notation T.# indicates T document number.

Citations of ZZ take the form: section, (part), case: page, column, (line); hence, e.g., ZZ.2B,1:362c6 indicates section 2 (*daini hen*), part B (*otsu*), case

1, page 362, verso column 1, line 6. (For those referring to editions with consecutively numbered volumes, section 2 begins at vol. 96, part B at vol. 128.)

Citations of SSZ take the form: section, volume: page, column, (line); hence, e.g., SSZ.Shiden,2:21a15 indicates the historical and biographical section, volume 2, page 21, column a, line 15.

Transliteration of Japanese terms appearing in Dōgen's writings follows, where possible, the readings in Katō Shūkō, ed., *Shōbō genzō yōgo sakuin*, 2 vols. (1962–63).

Introduction

The Zen school is the Meditation school, and the character of Zen can be traced in the tradition of its meditation teaching. Historians have shown us that the origins of the school in China are considerably later and more complicated than the traditional account of the lineage of Bodhidharma would have it and that the early history of the school is in fact a history of the teachings and traditions of several Buddhist meditation communities of the seventh and eighth centuries. If the masters of these communities did not yet see themselves as members of a Ch'an, or Meditation, school, and if—as is clear from their own reports—they did not always agree on their interpretations of Buddhism, still they were bound together by a common concern for the immediate, personal experience of enlightenment and liberation and, hence, by a common emphasis on the cultivation of spiritual techniques conducive to that experience. To this extent they may be spoken of as participants in a single reform movement, which sought to cut through the scholastic elaborations of the medieval Chinese Buddhist church and to translate the yogic traditions of north China into a popular modern idiom acceptable to the T'ang Buddhist community.

By the end of the eighth century the Ch'an reformation had established itself as a distinct Buddhist school, complete with its own history, literature, and dogma. Nevertheless, the emphasis on practice and immediate experience remained a hallmark of the faith. Indeed some scholars have held that it was precisely this emphasis that allowed the school to weather the persecutions of the late T'ang and emerge as the sole surviving form of Chinese monastic Buddhism. On several counts such a view is probably overdrawn; but, if the number of Ch'an books from the late T'ang and Sung suggests that there was considerably more to Ch'an religion in those days than simply "seeing one's nature and becoming a Buddha," there is much in the content of these books to indicate that the ground of the religion continued to be the meditation hall and the daily round of the monastic routine.

Again, historians may rightly question the common claim that it was the school's practical bent and ascetic rigor that account for the subsequent adoption of Zen by the medieval Japanese warrior class; but there is no need to doubt that, quite apart from its obvious cultural appeal as the dominant form of Sung Buddhism, the Ch'an traditions of monastic discipline and meditation practice made the religion an attractive option for those in the spiritual turmoil of Kamakura Japan who sought concrete means to the direct experience of Buddhist enlightenment. Even today in the midst of our own turmoil these same traditions continue to characterize the school and attract adherents both in Japan and abroad.

Given the centrality of meditation to the school, it is hardly surprising that the interpretation of the practice should have formed a major—perhaps the major—issue of Ch'an and Zen doctrine, and that when the school has bothered to argue over doctrine, it has tended to do so in terms of this issue. We may recall that the most famous such argument, that between the "Northern" and "Southern" factions of the eighth century, revolved around the supposed differences between two accounts of the meditative path— one describing a "gradual" mental cultivation, the other emphasizing a "sudden" spiritual insight. Again, in the twelfth century, the well-known dispute between the Lin-chi and Ts'ao-tung houses of Ch'an was cast in terms of two competing meditation styles—one recommending the investigation of the *hua-t'ou*, or *kung-an*, the other advocating something known as "silent illumination" (*mo-chao*). This latter dispute was carried over to Japan, where to this day it remains—albeit in somewhat altered forms—the primary ideological rationale for the separation of the two major Japanese schools of Rinzai and Sōtō.

Throughout the long and sometimes stormy history of Ch'an and Zen meditation teaching, probably no single figure has been more closely identified with the practice than the Zen master Dōgen (1200–1253), a pioneer in the introduction of the religion to Japan and the founder of what is today the largest of its institutions, the Sōtō school. For Dōgen, seated meditation, or *zazen*, was the very essence of the Buddhist religion—what he called "the treasury of the eye of the true *dharma*" (*shōbō genzō*) realized by all the Buddhas and handed down by all the Patriarchs of India and China. The practice of this *zazen* was not simply an important aid to, nor even a necessary condition for, enlightenment and liberation; it was in itself sufficient: it was enough, as he said, "just to sit" (*shikan taza*), without resort to the myriad subsidiary exercises of Buddhist spiritual life. Indeed (at least when rightly practiced) *zazen* was itself enlightenment and liberation: it was the ultimate cognition, the state he called "nonthinking" (*hi shiryō*) that revealed the final reality of things; it was the mystic apotheosis, "the sloughing off of body and mind" (*shinjin datsuraku*), as he said, that released man into this reality. Such practice then (at least when rightly understood) was its own end, as much the expression as it was the cause of transcendence: it was "practice based on enlightenment" (*shōjō no shu*); it was the activity of Buddhahood itself (*butsugyō*). As such, this was, ultimately speaking, no mere human exercise: it was participation in the primordial ascesis (*gyōji*) of being itself, that which brought forth matter and mind, heaven and earth, the sun, moon, stars, and constellations.

Few Buddhists, whether of the Zen or other persuasions, would disagree with Dōgen that, since the days of Śākyamuni, meditation has been, in one form or another, a core element of the religion—though most might question whether it is in itself sufficient to gain the final religious goal. Few Zen Buddhists, whether of the Sōtō or other denominations, would be surprised by Dōgen's claim that (at least when rightly understood) the practice of Zen is itself the direct realization of the enlightened Buddha mind within us all, but many would doubt that the meaning of this claim is best interpreted through the concrete exercise of seated meditation. Dōgen was not unaware of these questions and doubts. The true vision of the *shōbō genzō*, he held, was always the minority view, handed down in each generation through a unique line of transmission (*tanden*) from Śākyamuni and preserved in his own day only in the person of his Chinese master, the Ts'ao-tung teacher T'ien-t'ung Ju-ching (1163–1228). As for the rest—the benighted adepts of the Hīnayāna, the word-counting scholars of the Mahāyāna, and the self-styled masters of the other houses of Ch'an (especially of the Lin-chi house that had come to dominate Sung China)—they blasphemed *zazen* or paid it lip service without real understanding or authentic practice.

In our own day Dōgen's vision of the *shōbō genzō* has become recognized as one of the major monuments in the history of Zen thought; yet even now the blasphemy continues. In the first volume of his *Studies in the History of Zen Thought*, the great Rinzai scholar D. T. Suzuki attacked Dōgen's doctrine of "body and mind sloughed off" as mere negativism and his practice of "just sitting" as mere mental stasis. *Shikan taza*, he complained, failed to capture the vital spirit of Zen religious practice: like his forebears in the Chinese Ts'ao-tung school, Dōgen taught a form of quietistic Zen meditation—a version of the old "silent illumination" (*mokushō*)—that tended to put philosophy before experience and to ignore the dynamic aspect of Zen wisdom in favor of stillness and stagnation. For his part, Suzuki preferred the psychological power and spiritual insight of the *kōan* practice developed by his own forebear, the famed Sung Lin-chi master Ta-hui Tsung-kao (1089–1163).[1]

---

1. *Zen shisō shi kenkyū* I (1943), repr. in *Suzuki Daisetsu zenshū*, vol. 1 (1968), 1–344; for his treatment of Dōgen, see especially 57–83, and 161–98, where he is more critical of later Sōtō interpretations than he is of Dōgen himself and proposes a revisionist account of Dōgen's Zen.

No one did more than D. T. Suzuki to bring Zen studies into the modern world, but here (as is often the case in his work) he is also carrying forward the old world of the eighteenth century and the ideological origins of contemporary Japanese Zen sectarianism. It is the world of Hakuin Ekaku (1686–1769), who fixed the orthodox Rinzai *kōan* practice and attacked what he called "dead sitting in silent illumination" (*koza mokushō*) as counter to the Buddhist path and disruptive of social ethics; and it is the world of Mujaku Dōchū (1653–1744), who established modern Rinzai scholarship and dismissed Dōgen's Zen as "pitiable." This Zen, said Mujaku, simply clung to the notion that the deluded mind was itself Buddhahood (*mōjin soku butsu*) and ignored the transformative experience of awakening (*satori*). Dōgen "never even dreamt" of the state of *satori* that was the meaning of the advent of the Buddha, the purpose of Bodhidharma's mission to China, and the message of the patriarch of *kanna*, or *kōan* Zen, Ta-hui.[2]

It is not surprising that Hakuin and Mujaku should have failed to appreciate Dōgen's brand of Buddhism. In modern times his rare vision of *zazen* has become the sacred centerpiece of Sōtō ideology, but it was not always so, and for some half a millennium after his death, his *shōbō genzō* was ever in danger of extinction even in his own school. In the eighteenth century the chief architect of modern Sōtō dogmatics, Menzan Zuihō (1683–1769), lamented the precarious history of the founder's Zen. Only the Sōtō house, he said, preserves the teaching that sitting itself is the "treasury of the eye of the true *dharma* and the mystic mind of *nirvāṇa*" (*shōbō genzō nehan myōshin*); the practitioners of *kanna* have "never even dreamt" of it. Even within the Chinese Ts'ao-tung tradition, by the end of the Sung, only T'ien-t'ung Ju-ching still taught it; and, throughout the Yüan and Ming, the masters of Ts'ao-tung and Lin-chi alike have been wholly given over to Ta-hui's *kanna*. In Japan as well, only the founding ancestor, Dōgen, proclaimed it; and after several generations the Sōtō monks went to study in the five Zen "mountains" of Heian and Kamakura, took up the style of Rinzai practiced there, and lost the *dharma* of their own house.[3]

There are many religious practices, said Menzan, that go by the name *zazen*, from the meditations of Taoism, Confucianism, and Shintō to the contemplative exercises of the Buddhist *sūtras* and *śāstras*; and, in Zen, at least since the decline of the orthodox transmission of Bodhidharma's practice, individuals have made up their own techniques, like the *kanna* Zen so

---

2. *Shōbō genzō senpyō*, cited in Yanagida, "Dōgen to Rinzai," *Risō* 513 (2/1976), 84. Mujaku's interpretations of Dōgen have recently been treated at some length by Shibe Ken'-ichi, in "Shōbō genzō senpyō no ichi kōsatsu," SK 24 (3/1982), 72–77; and "Shōbō genzō senpyō to Edo ki shūgaku no kanren," SK 25 (3/1983), 246–61. Hakuin's remarks appear in the first letter of his *Orategama*. (*Hakuin oshō zenshū* 5 : 128–29; see also his criticisms of the "dead *dharma* of the burned out mind and spent wisdom" [*keshin minchi*], in *Yabu kōji* [ibid., 331].)

3. *Eiso zazen shin monge*, SSZ.Chūkai,3 : 40b.

popular even today. But Dōgen's *zazen* has nothing to do with any of these.[4] For Menzan and his church, Dōgen's *zazen* is like no other: it is the practice of "nonthinking," a subtle state beyond either thinking or not thinking and distinct from traditional Buddhist psychological exercises of concentration and contemplation; it is "just sitting," a practice in which, unlike the *kōan* exercise of Rinzai Zen, "body and mind have been sloughed off" and all striving for religious experience, all expectation of *satori* (*taigo*), is left behind. This *zazen* is nothing but "the mystic practice of original verification" (*honshō myōshu*), through which from the very start one directly expresses the ultimate nature of the mind.

The eighteenth-century movement of which Menzan has proved the most influential representative sought to return Sōtō faith to the religion of its founder, and in fact many of the premises behind the sort of interpretation of his *zazen* that we see here can be found in Dōgen himself. In theoretical terms this interpretation begins, like Dōgen's own, from a version of the "sudden practice" (*tonshu*) of the supreme vehicle (*saijō jō*), the venerable Ch'an ideal of a transcendental religion, beyond the expedients (*hōben*) of ordinary Buddhism, in which the spiritual exercise is brought into perfect accord with the ultimate principle of inherent Buddhahood. Again, as in Dōgen's own presentation of the theory, the assertion of such a transcendental religion is accompanied by a strong emphasis on two equally venerable historical corollaries to it: (1) that the full revelation of the religion is not given in the writings of ordinary Buddhism but is only "transmitted from mind to mind" (*ishin denshin*) through the generations of the enlightened Patriarchs; and (2) that in any given generation such revelation must occur "all at once" (*tongo*) in the Patriarch's accession to the transmission. There is not, then, in this style of presentation properly speaking any such thing as an intellectual history of Ch'an and Zen, either of the tradition as a whole or of the thought of any of its authentic representatives.

In one form or another, something akin to these three hermeneutical principles—of the higher unity of practice and theory, of the historical continuity of esoteric tradition, and of the inner integrity of spiritual experience—still guides the presentation of what is often called "Dōgen Zen" in the halls of Eihei ji, the chief monastery of the Sōtō school, and the classrooms of Komazawa, the university that now trains most of its academics. The principles can be seen at work throughout the religious writings of such influential modern masters as Nishiari Bokusan and Kishizawa Ian and even find their way into much of the historical and textual work of the modern "sectarian studies" (*shūgaku*) represented by such eminent scholars as Etō Sokuo and Ōkubo Dōshū. Yet, if such principles go back beyond Dōgen to the very origins of Ch'an tradition, so too of course do the disagreements

---

4. *Fukan zazen gi monge*, SSZ.Chūkai,3:4b.

within the tradition over their implications for the understanding of Ch'an history and practice; and, if the principles continue to work in Sōtō theology today, there is no doubt that they have often brought "Dōgen Zen"—like Zen tradition in general—into conflict with the assumptions of modern secular philological and historical method.[5]

Even in Menzan's day, for example, the notion that the unity of theory and practice entailed a form of Zen distinct from Rinzai *kōan* study was dismissed by prominent Sōtō masters like Tenkei Denson (1648–1735); and in our own day Tenkei's tendency to accommodation with Rinzai has been preserved among a small but active faction of Sōtō popularized especially by such modern masters as Harada Sogaku (1870–1961) and Yasutani Hakuun (1885–1973).[6] Much more important of course have been the intellectual developments outside the school that have challenged the Sōtō historical claims about the continuity of its tradition and of Dōgen's place in it. The discovery of this Zen master's thought by prewar philosophers like Watsuji Tetsuro and his subsequent treatment by historians like Ienaga Saburo, Buddhologists like Tamura Yoshiro, literary historians like Karaki Junzō, and so on, have led to a wide range of new interpretations of his Buddhism, all of which, whatever their obvious differences, tend to treat it as the product of an independent, Japanese religious thinker and, hence, inevitably to undermine the conviction that Dōgen merely served as a conduit for the orthodox *shōbō genzō* of his master Ju-ching and the Chinese Ts'ao-tung Patriarchs.[7] Finally, the rapid development over the last few decades of the new Zen studies of scholars like Yanagida Seizan, based as they are on the critical use of historical documents, has forced a general rethinking of the old sacred histories of the school and, in the case of a figure like Dōgen for whom the documentation is rather rich, has replaced the old sacred biography with more modern, secularized accounts of the his-

    5.   The *shūgaku* style of presentation is still current in much of the writing on "Dōgen Zen": the former president of Komazawa University, for example, has recently twice reissued a representative sample of the style; see Kurebayashi Kōdō, "Dōgen zen no kihon teki seikaku," in the same author's *Dōgen zen no honryū* (1980), 11–32; and in *Dōgen*, ed. by Kawamura Kōdō and Ishikawa Rikizan, *Nihon meisō ronshū* 8 (1983), 76–96; the piece was originally published in two parts in SK 3 (3/1961), and 4 (3/1962). In a companion to the second anthology here that is otherwise largely devoted to representative historical studies, the same editors have seen fit to reissue a polemical piece in this style by a noted professor of Kurebayashi's university on the superiority of *shikan taza* to Hakuin's *kanna* practice; see Sakai Tokugen, "Zen ni okeru henkō," in *Dōgen zenji to Sōtō shū*, ed. by Kawamura and Ishikawa, *Nihon bukkyō shūshi ronshū* 8 (1985), 22–41; originally published in SK 2 (1/1960).
    6.   Harada's efforts to spread a broader version of Zen meditation that accommodated the *kōan* can be seen, for example, in his early popular tract, *Zazen no shikata* (1927); Yasutani's *kōan* style has been made famous in the West through the publication of Philip Kapleau's *Three Pillars of Zen* (1966).
    7.   For examples of these scholars' treatments, see Watsuji's pioneering "Shamon Dōgen," in his *Nihon seishin shi kenkyū* (1926), Ienaga's *Chūsei bukkyō shisō shi kenkyū* (1947), Tamura's highly influential *Kamakura shin bukkyō shisō no kenkyū* (1965), and Karaki's *Mujō* (1965).

torical circumstances of his ministry and the historical development of his thought.[8]

Clearly the Sōtō system of interpretation is now experiencing many of the sort of intellectual challenges to its faith with which we have been familiar for over a century. As in our own case, the most conspicuous developments have occurred in the area of historical understanding, and the larger, more difficult question of how such understanding should affect our reading of Dōgen's religion has inevitably lagged behind and has not yet, it is probably fair to say, received systematic attention. In particular the topic of his meditation, perhaps precisely because it lies so close to the heart of Zen tradition and especially of Dōgen's religion (and somewhat outside the most immediate interests of both the historian and the philosopher) has tended to remain insulated from the effects of the new scholarship. One of the purposes of the following study is to begin to break down this insulation by bringing to bear on Dōgen's meditation manuals some of the methods and findings of recent Zen studies. In this way I hope the work will serve not only as an introduction of these manuals to the Western literature on the school but also as one sort of prolegomenon to the rethinking of the traditional historical and theoretical principles of their interpretation. The study will seek, therefore, on the one hand simply to review what is now known about the manuals and on the other to raise certain questions, to locate problem areas, and to suggest possible new paths of inquiry. To this latter end, it will at times intentionally play the role of what we might call Māra's advocate, and it will in general be less concerned with completing a new model of Dōgen's Zen than with calling attention to the fact that our present model may be rather less complete than is often assumed.

Dōgen was a prolific author, who produced, over the quarter century of his active career, a sizable and varied corpus that ranged from formal treatises in *kanbun* (i.e., Chinese) to delicate Japanese verse. His work includes popular tracts on Zen practice, esoteric commentaries on Zen *kōan*, records of his lectures to monks, and detailed rules of monastic ritual and routine. Given the centrality of *zazen* to his religion and the breadth of (at least the more abstract of) his definitions of it, this entire corpus is in some sense concerned with meditation; and, in fact, references to the practice abound in almost all of his writing. Still, there are certain of his texts that deal specifically with *zazen* and that have been central to the interpretation of his teaching on the topic. Some years ago the Educational Division of the Sōtō administrative headquarters, concerned that the modern school might

---

8. Yanagida's seminal *Shoki zenshū shisho no kenkyū* has become, since its publication in 1967, rather like the bible of the new Zen historians; though the book itself deals only with the historical texts of early Ch'an, its methodological influence has spread over a much wider field, and in fact in more recent years Yanagida himself has devoted considerable attention to Japanese Zen, including Dōgen.

lose sight of its essential message (*shūshi*) of *shikan taza*, brought out a sourcebook of what it considered the prime sacred texts (*seiten*) on the subject to be used in the education of Sōtō adherents. The book contains eight texts by Dōgen. One of these, the *Shōbō genzō zazen gi*, is a practical manual of *zazen* included in the famous collection of his Japanese essays, the *Shōbō genzō*; others are more theoretical, like the *Shōbō genzō zanmai ō zanmai* or the *Shōbō genzō zazen shin*; still others, like the *Bendō wa* and *Gakudō yōjin shū*, combine both of these characteristics. Among this last type is by far the most famous and important of Dōgen's works on meditation, the *Fukan zazen gi*, or "Universal promotion of the principles of seated meditation."[9]

The *Fukan zazen gi* is a brief tract, in one roll of roughly 800 graphs, composed in a florid *kanbun* style and devoted to an explanation of both the theory and the procedures of *zazen* practice. It is generally held to represent Dōgen's first Zen teaching, promulgated immediately following his return to Japan after the pilgrimage to Sung China that culminated in his great awakening to the *dharma* of Ju-ching. As the opening act of his ministry, intended to reveal the very essence of the message he sought to bring to the Japanese Buddhist community, its composition is widely regarded as marking the historical origin of his Sōtō school. It was, the school would later say, the very "dawn of Buddhism in Japan."[10] This historical significance for the tradition, coupled with the work's intrinsic importance as the primary textual source for the tradition's characteristic form of meditation, has given the *Fukan zazen gi* a central place in the literature of the Sōtō school. Indeed it has been taken into the litany of the church and is still recited daily at the close of evening meditation in the school's monasteries throughout Japan.[11]

Like much else in modern Sōtō Zen, the place of the *Fukan zazen gi* was largely fixed by Menzan, who first singled out the work for special attention in his *Fukan zazen gi monge*, published in 1757. Thereafter, from the *Fukan zazen gi funō go* of Menzan's contemporary Shigetsu (1689–1764), to the commentaries of the present day, the little manual has been used by many masters of the church as a vehicle for transmitting the way of *zazen*. In this

---

9. For the sourcebook, see *Ryōso daishi zazen seiten*, ed. by Sōtōshū Shūmuchō Kyōikubu (1959). (Most of the work of annotation was done by Kurebayashi Kōdō; on the purposes of the book, see the afterword, following p. 203.) Also included here is a brief note by Dōgen, the so-called "Fukan zazen gi senjutsu yurai," and two texts by the "Second Founder" of Sōtō, Keizan Jōkin: the *Zazen yōjin ki* and *Sankon zazen setsu*. The book omits one significant document that I shall be using in this essay: Dōgen's *Bendō hō*, a work devoted to the rules of the meditation hall.

10. Preface to *Fukan zazen gi monge*, SSZ.Chūkai,3:1a.

11. A practice prescribed in the modern handbook of church ritual (see *Shōwa teiho Sōtō shū gyōji kihan* [1967], 40). The handbook also permits the substitution of Keizan's *Zazen yōjin ki*, which itself draws on the *Fukan zazen gi*. Both manuals were included in one of the first modern "bibles" of Sōtō (actually a liturgical reference book), the *Zenshū Sōtō seiten*, compiled by Yamada Kōdō at the end of the Meiji period and reprinted many times during Taishō.

century it has also been the subject of numerous historical and doctrinal studies in the religious and academic journals of Sōtō and, in recent decades, has several times been translated into modern Japanese and Western languages.[12] Yet for all its current reputation and wide public dissemination, in intellectual terms, the *Fukan zazen gi* has barely escaped the walls of the monastery: while outside those walls the academic study of Dōgen and of the history and teachings of Ch'an and Zen Buddhism in general has been making remarkable advances, the interpretation of this text and of its author's message has tended to circle narrowly within the confines of the religious concerns of sectarian tradition. In the following study I explore some of the contours of these confines and the ways they have circumscribed our understanding of the origins, intellectual background, and religious character of Dōgen's meditation teachings.

Though the monks who chant the *Fukan zazen gi* each day may do so in the conviction that it represents the founding document of their faith, in terms of the history of its author's own faith, the version of the work current in the modern church is rather late, probably dating from the last decade of his life. There is, however, an earlier version, preserved in an ancient manuscript thought to be in Dōgen's own hand, which describes a form of meditation seemingly somewhat different from that now celebrated in the Sōtō literature. The existence of this manuscript has been known for decades, but, apart from several technical articles, it has received surprisingly little attention, and its implications for our understanding of the origins and development of Dōgen's religion have not been taken very seriously. For this reason I begin my study here with a reexamination of the historical provenance of the two versions of the *Fukan zazen gi*, along with Dōgen's other major writings on *zazen*, bringing together what is now known or can be inferred about the circumstances of their composition and going on to suggest how this information might affect the way we are used to reading his texts and interpreting the inspiration of their message. At issue for the tradition here is the question of the relationship between the facts of Dōgen's new, secularized biography and the Sōtō faith in his enlightenment and accession to the Patriarchate as the primary and constant determinant of

---

12.   Menzan's *Monge* can be found at SSZ.Chūkai,3: 1–33; Shigetsu's *Funō go*, published in 1759, at ibid., 47–53. For samples of the continuing commentarial tradition, see, for example, *Fukan zazen gi teiji roku* (1911), which records the teachings of the influential Meiji master Nishiari Bokusan (1821–1910), as edited by Kishizawa Ian; Harada Sogaku, *Fukan zazen gi kōwa* (repr. 1982); Ōbora Ryōun, *Gendai kōwa Fukan zazen gi* (repr. 1982); Uchiyama Kōshō, *Shūkyō toshite no Dōgen zen: Fukan zazen gi ikai* (1977). Some years ago the chief monastery of the Sōtō school, Eihei ji, devoted two special issues of its journal to the text: see *Fukan zazen gi no sankyū*, *Sanshō* 372 (9/1974), 373 (10/1974). Perhaps the most recent modern Japanese translation has been done by Yanagida Seizan, in *Shisō dokuhon: Dōgen*, ed. by Yanagida (1982), 176–79; of the several English translations, see especially Norman Waddell and Abe Masao, "Dōgen's Fukanzazengi and Shōbōgenzō zazengi," *The Eastern Buddhist*, new series 6, 2 (10/1973), 115–28.

his life and thought; and, in order the better to bring out this issue, I adopt here a somewhat "positivistic" treatment of the biography that may at times seem as alien to some recent styles of historiography as it is to the tradition itself. Whether or not it is the proper job of the historian to uncover "the facts" of the past, the sensitivity to such facts has separated modern Zen studies from the tradition, and for this reason we must begin with them. By the nature of both the method and the material here, the argument of Part I will sometimes involve considerable historical and bibliographic detail, and casual readers—or those interested more in meditation than the particulars of Dōgen's life and writings—will be excused if they prefer to skim over some of this detail with an eye for the larger points behind it.

Though many modern interpreters may rightly hold up Dōgen's *zazen* teachings as a seminal moment in the Zen meditation tradition, they have often tended to treat these teachings in isolation from the larger tradition, preferring to focus on the internal structure of Dōgen's system and looking up from the system only long enough to establish its pedigree or dismiss its competitors. Yet, if Dōgen's *Fukan zazen gi* is the first and most famous work of its kind written in Japan, it is also (as he himself emphasizes) deeply indebted to the heritage of the Buddhism its author sought to introduce from China. In fact, it is now well known to students of the text that it draws heavily on a Northern Sung Ch'an manual much read in Dōgen's day. Interestingly enough, elsewhere in his writings, he himself dismisses this earlier work as failing to convey the orthodox tradition of *zazen*. This ambivalence toward his own sources reminds us of the need to pay more careful attention to the literary and intellectual background of Dōgen's work and to the place of the work in the long history of Ch'an discourse on meditation. To this end, in Part II, I turn from the detail of Dōgen's biography to the larger frame of this history and try to sketch at least the outline of what I take to be its major features. Chapter 3 deals with the history of the Ch'an meditation literature before and during Dōgen's day; Chapter 4 discusses some of the religious issues that characterize this literature and set the stage for Dōgen's own presentation of *zazen*. While my treatment of these broad subjects, spanning as it does fully half a millennium of religious history, will necessarily often skim lightly over some of the most complex topics and vexed issues of Zen studies, I trust that some of what I have to say here will prove entertaining not only to students of Dōgen but to those with interest in the history and character of the Zen tradition as a whole.

These chapters present one version of the sort of "intellectual history" of Ch'an that is now heavily impinging on the more traditional sacred history of the *shōbō genzō* and that has raised many questions about the meaning of Zen transmission and the spiritual continuity of the Patriarchate. Where traditional treatments preserved the model of the *shōbō genzō* by explaining the discontinuities of Ch'an and Zen history apparent in its various factional disputes as the ongoing struggle between the true *dharma* and its heretical interpreters, some modern treatments have tended in effect to explain away these disputes as mere theological decoration on what was "really" political and social competition. My own approach here tries to avoid both these forms of reductionism and seeks rather to view the discontinuities in terms of the recapitulation, under various historical circumstances, of certain continuing tensions inherent in the Ch'an teachings themselves—tensions, for example, between exclusive and inclusive visions of the school's religious mission, between esoteric and exoteric styles of discourse, and especially between theoretical and practical approaches to its meditation instruction.

The recurrent "debates" over the interpretation of meditation that mark the history of Ch'an and Zen are justly famous and regularly receive due notice in accounts of the school. Yet there remains a sense in which we have not fully come to grips with the historical character and the religious problematic of the meditation tradition in which they occur. We are often told, for example, that Zen Buddhism takes its name from the Sanskrit *dhyāna*, or "meditation," and that the school has specialized in the practice, but we are rarely told just how this specialization is related to the many striking disclaimers, found throughout the writings of Ch'an and Zen (including Dōgen's own), to the effect that the religion has nothing to do with *dhyāna*. It is the gap between these two poles that serves as the arena for the debates and creates the kind of tension between Zen theory and its practice that is supposed to be resolved in the school's characteristic notions of the transcendental sudden practice (and in Dōgen's famous doctrines of enlightened *zazen* and just sitting). The supposition of such a resolution, whether valid or not, has had the effect of focussing our attention—like that of the tradition itself—on its various novel permutations and of limiting the degree to which we have taken the continuing historical tension seriously. In fact our treatment of Dōgen's *shikan taza* and our notices of the earlier debates of the Meditation school rarely seem to extend to discussion of the actual techniques of meditation that may (or may not) have been at issue, and we are not often told in concrete terms just how Dōgen and the other monks of the school actually went about their specialization. As a result, we are hardly in a very good position to consider what—if any—implications the school's meditation discourse may have had for the religious experience of its adherents.

To attempt to get "behind" the discourse to the experience is not, for more than one reason, an unproblematic exercise—particularly in the case of something like Zen meditation. The general tendency of Buddhist scholarship to favor the study of theory over practice, whatever else it may say about the discipline, is surely in part the reflection of an inherent difficulty in getting at information on what actually took place in the meditation halls (let alone in the heads) of premodern Buddhists. To be sure, there have been Buddhists—like the famed sixth-century scholar and meditation teacher T'ien-t'ai Chih-i (538–97)—who left detailed and historically influential models of their spiritual exercises; but, by the nature of the case, the physical and psychological techniques of meditation are doubtless better learned through personal contact with an instructor than through books; and, in fact, despite (or perhaps because of) its abiding interest in meditation, the Ch'an and Zen tradition—with its emphasis on direct oral transmission from the master and its habit of making a virtue of ambiguity—has often been more loath than most to record the concrete details of its practice. Dōgen, for all his fame as a meditation teacher, is by no means the least delinquent in this regard. Still, if he shares a preference for the higher discourse of metaphysical interpretation, unlike most of the famous masters of classical Ch'an, he did write at length on practice; hence there is somewhat more room in this writing than we have hitherto exploited to ask him about the actual techniques of "just sitting" and to reflect on their relationship both to what we know of earlier descriptions of meditation and to the more theoretical levels of his and earlier Ch'an teaching.

This last issue—the relationship between the practical and theoretical levels of Ch'an discourse—provides the dominant theme of my treatment of the tradition and serves as the ground for Part III, where I deal with Dōgen's own teachings. Here I adopt a more analytic approach and try, through a close reading of selected passages of the *Fukan zazen gi* and related works, to reconstruct what Dōgen said (and also what he did not say) about Zen meditation, reflecting along the way on how some of this material is related to earlier accounts of the subject. Focussing first on the older, autograph version of the work, I use it to explore his teachings on the concrete techniques and historical tradition of *zazen*; I then turn to the revised, vulgate text to consider Dōgen's famous theory of enlightened practice and the knotty problem of how this theory both reveals and obscures the historical character of his practice. Finally, in my conclusion I step back a bit from Dōgen's texts and the ideological issues of Zen tradition that are the primary concern of this book to suggest very briefly what I think might prove a fruitful course for further study. In the back matter I have included for the reader's convenience a comparative table of translations of Dōgen's various meditation manuals, together with their Chinese predecessor, as well as translations of two other documents that figure in the discussion.

Part I

Texts

1

The Earliest Manual and the Origins of Dōgen's Zen

According to traditional histories, Japanese Sōtō Zen began in 1227. On this date the young Dōgen, fresh from his enlightenment on Mt. T'ien-t'ung, returned to his native soil. Such was the strength of his new conviction and the urgency of his new mission that, almost immediately upon disembarking, he proclaimed the gospel of Sōtō Zen and set to work transmitting to his countrymen the teachings of its Chinese Patriarch, his master, Ju-ching. To this end his first act was the composition of a Zen meditation manual, the *Fukan zazen gi*, in which he enunciated the characteristic Sōtō doctrine of enlightened practice and described the unique Sōtō meditation of non-thinking in which that practice is realized.

This tradition that the *Fukan zazen gi* directly reflects the religion of Ju-ching and represents its initial statement in Japan is based on the theory that the work was written within months of Dōgen's return from the continent, and that, therefore, it should be read as a manifesto of the Buddhism he had brought back from Mt. T'ien-t'ung. Apart from its larger assumptions about the nature of Ju-ching's religion and its transmission to Dōgen, the theory rests on the evidence of two passages in the latter's writings, both of which seem to indicate an early date for the text. One of these passages occurs in the *Bendō wa*, a well-known tract in Japanese from 1231. At the conclusion of the work, in the course of explaining his reasons for writing it, Dōgen adds, "The procedures of meditation should be carried out in accordance with the *Fukan zazen gi*, composed during the Karoku era [1225–27]."[1]

---

1. DZZ.1:746, 763.

The second passage appears in a brief, untitled manuscript in Chinese, apparently in Dōgen's own hand, discovered during the Edo period at Eihei ji. In this note, after lamenting the fact that no meditation manual had yet been transmitted to Japan, Dōgen says, "When I returned to my country from the land of the Sung in the Karoku era, there were students who asked me [to compose a *zazen gi*]; and so, I felt obliged to go ahead and compose one."[2]

Since the Karoku era ended within a few months of Dōgen's return to Japan, the manual he mentions here must have been composed almost immediately upon his arrival.[3] The relationship of this manual, however, to the extant texts of the *Fukan zazen gi* remains problematic. Prior to the twentieth century, it was assumed that the text referred to in these passages was the vulgate version of the *Fukan zazen gi* in use in Sōtō monasteries; but the discovery, at the beginning of this century, of a second version of the work has shown that assumption to be false.

This new version is preserved in an ancient manuscript belonging to Eihei ji. It first came to the attention of the scholarly community in 1922, when it was put on public display at Tokyo Imperial University.[4] The document, in one roll, is in a remarkable state of preservation. Its mounting, which appears to date from the late Edo period, bears a colophon identifying the manuscript as an authentic example of Dōgen's calligraphy (*shinpitsu*) and stating that it was donated (presumably to Eihei ji) by the calligraphy

---

2. DZZ.2:6. For a translation of the full text, see Document 1. The manuscript is badly deteriorated and was already difficult to decipher in the eighteenth century when it was studied by Menzan. The phrase in brackets in the translation here is illegible in the original and follows Menzan's interpolation. (See DZZ.2:6, note.) Given the context, there seems little reason to question his reconstruction.

3. Early sources for Dōgen's biography do not agree on the exact date of his return from China, and the issue has long been a subject of dispute. We know, however, from the certificate of transmission (*shisho*) Dōgen received from Ju-ching that he was still at T'ien-t'ung shan during the third year of the Chinese Pao-ch'ing era (1227). (DZZ.2:287.) On the fifth day of the tenth month (November 15) of this year, he wrote a brief note in Japan, entitled "Shari sōden ki," concerning the delivery of his teacher Myōzen's remains to one of the latter's disciples. (DZZ.2:396.) Hence Dōgen must have reached Japan in the third year of Karoku (1227), sometime prior to the tenth month. On the basis of seasonal patterns in the ship movements between the continent and Japan, many scholars now place the date in the eighth month. (See, e.g., Takeuchi Michio, *Dōgen*, Jinbutsu sōsho 88 [1962], 183–85. The sources for, and theories regarding, the date of Dōgen's return have been discussed at some length in Ōkubo Dōshū, *Dōgen zenji den no kenkyū* [rev. ed., 1966], 174–90.) On the tenth day of the twelfth month (January 18, 1228), the Japanese era name was changed from Karoku to Antei. We may assume, then, that Dōgen's Karoku manual was composed sometime during the latter half of 1227.

4. See Ōkubo Dōshū, *Dōgen zenji goroku*, Iwanami bunko 2211–12 (1940), 214. In 1925, Ōkubo reproduced the manuscript in collotype facsimile in his *Zen'en bokka*, vol. 1 (repr., 1974), and in 1930, the text was published in SSZ.Shūgen,2:11–12. Ōkubo's edition of the text can be found at DZZ.2:3–5; a supplement to this collection, *Dōgen zenji shinpitsu shūsei* (1970), 1–15, provides a photocopy of the manuscript.

expert Kohitsu Ryōhan (1827–53).[5] Unfortunately, we have no information on the earlier history of the document or on how it fell into Ryōhan's possession. Its state of preservation would indicate that it was apparently little handled over the centuries and lay largely unstudied in some private or institutional library. There is no evidence in the literature of the Sōtō school that its contents were known to the tradition.

The manuscript is written on elegantly illustrated paper, thought to be of Sung manufacture, in a *kaisho* script following the Sung style; the calligraphy as well as the signature (*kaō*) accord well with other manuscripts attributed to Dōgen. Thus, there is every reason to believe that the inscription on the mounting is correct in its assessment of the document's authenticity. In 1941 and again in 1952, it was judged an autograph and designated a National Treasure (*kokuhō*) by a commission of the Japanese government.[6]

This autograph version of the *Fukan zazen gi* shows quite a few interesting differences from the vulgate text. We shall consider some of these in detail later on; here it is sufficient simply to note that the comparison of the two texts has left little doubt that the vulgate is a later, edited version of the autograph. This means that the manual Dōgen wrote in 1227 could not have been the vulgate *Fukan zazen gi*, since the autograph manuscript is clearly dated in the first year of Tenpuku (1233). Faced with this fact, modern scholars have been forced to abandon the traditional date for the vulgate text; but, in doing so, they have also had to surrender the primary historical evidence for the traditional understanding of Dōgen's earliest Zen teachings. Perhaps to salvage what they could of that understanding, they have turned instead to the autograph version, arguing that it was this work that Dōgen must have written immediately upon his return from China.

The meditation teachings of the Tenpuku manuscript do not quite correspond to those of the vulgate *Fukan zazen gi*, let alone to the "orthodox" interpretation of Dōgen's Zen. Still, in other respects, the work does introduce certain themes characteristic of his later writings and central to Sōtō doctrine. Of these, perhaps the most conspicuous is the emphasis on the historical and philosophical tradition of the Ch'an school. As we shall see when we take up the content of the text, Dōgen's description of meditation practice is closely integrated with his advocacy of this tradition. Though he

---

5. An inscription on the lid of the box in which the manuscript is preserved indicates that the donation was made in September 1852. See Yokoi Kakudō, "Fukan zazen gi goshinpitsu bon ni tsuite," SK 11 (3/1969), 79–81.

6. Yokoi, "Fukan zazen gi goshinpitsu bon ni tsuite," 79. For a discussion of the style of the calligraphy, see ibid., 81–84. As might be expected, there is considerable difference of opinion on which of the many manuscripts attributed to Dōgen are authentic. Some of the more widely accepted have been reproduced in Ōkubo, *Dōgen zenji shinpitsu shūsei*, but Furuta Shōkin has recently questioned this selection. (See his *Shōbō genzō no kenkyū* [1972], 17–43.) In this same paper (33–34), he reaffirms the authenticity of the *Fukan zazen gi* manuscript on the basis of its signature.

does not use the term itself here, he leaves little doubt that the practice he recommends is derived from, and leads to the realization of, the *shōbō genzō*, the ancient wisdom of the Buddha handed down solely by the Ch'an Patriarchs.

Whatever else we may say of this theme as a religious teaching, its historical claim to a unique tradition of Buddhism, ultimately validated by Śākyamuni himself, gives the Tenpuku *Fukan zazen gi* a decidedly polemical cast. Indeed the work has been described as Dōgen's "declaration of independence" from the established schools of Japanese Buddhism, and as what amounted to a "declaration of war" with the most powerful of these schools, the Tendai organization on Mt. Hiei; it has also been seen as the opening move in Dōgen's attempts to reform the contemporary Ch'an school and restore what he took to be the original character of the tradition. There is undoubtedly some truth in both (and especially, perhaps, in the former) of these characterizations of the autograph *Fukan zazen gi*, but there is little justification for using either as direct evidence for the kind of Buddhism Dōgen might have brought back from China. Quite apart from the question of whether its content can be traced to Ju-ching, the frequent claim that the Tenpuku manuscript is merely a copy of a text originally composed immediately upon Dōgen's return from the Sung does not rest on very firm ground. Since this claim is crucial to current interpretations of the origins of Dōgen's Zen, it is worth considering in some detail.[7]

We have seen that there are two sources for our knowledge of the missing Karoku manual. In the *Bendō wa* passage the manual is explicitly identified as the *Fukan zazen gi*; ordinarily this would seem sufficient reason for concluding that the extant text, though dated later, is a copy of the earlier work. In this case, however, both the value and the implications of the evidence are open to question. The *Bendō wa* is a notoriously problematic text, the authenticity of which has long been the subject of controversy. The discovery in this century of an early manuscript has done much to allay doubts regarding the provenance of the work, and few scholars today would seriously question its attribution to Dōgen. Nevertheless, the many significant differences between this manuscript and the vulgate version strongly suggest that the text has undergone considerable revision during the course of its transmission. Indeed one scholar recently has suggested that the

---

7. The notion that the Tenpuku manuscript is but a fair copy (*seisho*) of the Karoku work has been current in Dōgen scholarship since Ōkubo proposed it in his influential study of the text in *Dōgen zenji goroku*, 207–14. (Slightly revised versions of this study subsequently appeared in his *Dōgen zenji den no kenkyū*, 299–305, and in the introduction to his revised edition of *Dōgen zenji zenshū*, vol. 2 [1970], 519–22.) For examples of the use of the autograph text to support the traditional view that, immediately upon his return from China, Dōgen declared the independence of Sōtō Zen from both Japanese Tendai and Chinese Lin-chi, see Imaeda Aishin, *Chūsei zenshū shi no kenkyū* (1970), 19–22; and Akishige Yoshiharu, "Fukan zazen gi kō," *Tetsugaku nenpō* 14 (1953), 460–63.

passage on the Karoku *zazen gi* represents such a revision, and that it was not included in Dōgen's original version.[8]

Even if we choose to accept the authenticity of the *Bendō wa* reference to the *Fukan zazen gi*, we have not established the identity of the Karoku and Tenpuku texts. Dōgen's other works indicate that he was in the habit of editing and revising his writings, and we cannot rule out that possibility here. In fact, as we know, the two extant texts of the *Fukan zazen gi* show marked divergences; similar or greater differences could certainly separate the Karoku and Tenpuku manuals. Nor would it be surprising if the 1233 manuscript reflected something of its author's experience during the six years since his return to Japan—years in which, as we shall see, his situation underwent marked change. Under the circumstances, then, it would seem rash to identify the Karoku and Tenpuku texts simply on the basis of an identity of title.[9]

Even greater problems confront us in the case of our second source. This document is now commonly referred to as the "Fukan zazen gi senjutsu yurai" [Origin of the composition of the *Fukan zazen gi*], but in fact it has no title and nowhere refers to that work.[10] The notion that the note was written in reference to the *Fukan zazen gi* is based, rather, on its content. After mentioning his Karoku *zazen gi*, Dōgen goes on to criticize the understanding of meditation found in the *Tso-ch'an i* of Tsung-tse's *Ch'an-yüan ch'ing-kuei*, the inadequacies of which he felt made it necessary for him to compose his own meditation manual. Tsung-tse's work and Dōgen's doubts about it will be discussed in detail in subsequent chapters; here it is sufficient simply to indicate that the text of the Tenpuku manuscript does indeed

---

8. See Furuta Shōkin, *Shōbō genzō no kenkyū*, 34. The *Bendō wa* seems to have been unknown to Edo scholars prior to the discovery of several texts late in the seventeenth century—hence, the doubts regarding its authenticity. In the 1930s, Ōkubo Dōshū discovered a manuscript at the Shōbō ji in Iwate prefecture that bears a colophon dated 1515 and purports to be a copy of a 1332 manuscript. (See DZZ.1:763. For a discussion of this and other texts of the *Bendō wa*, see Etō Sokuō, *Shōbō genzō josetsu: Bendō wa gikai* [1959], 29–37.) While the Shōbō ji text varies considerably from the vulgate version, the passage on the *Fukan zazen gi* is almost identical. This passage seems somewhat out of place in its context and may have been added as an afterthought, though this does not, of course, rule out the possibility that it was written by Dōgen himself. Furuta (*Shōbō genzō*, 34) suggests that it was added by some later editor on the basis of our second source for the Karoku manual.

9. We may note in this regard the view of Nagahisa Toshio, who doubts that Dōgen would have dated the colophon of his manuscript in Tenpuku if he had actually composed it in Karoku. He points out that the verb *sho*, appearing in the colophon, is regularly used by Dōgen in the sense "to compose" (rather than "to copy") and suggests that it should be understood in that sense here. Thus he takes the colophon as evidence that the Tenpuku text was sufficiently different from the Karoku manual for Dōgen to have considered it a new work. (See his "Fukan zazen gi no kenkyū," SK 5 [4/1963], 11.)

10. Menzan, in his commentary on the *Fukan zazen gi*, assumed that the note represented a postface to the manual (*Fukan zazen gi monge*, SSZ.Chūkai,3:33); the title by which it is now usually cited was supplied by Ōkubo when he originally published the text in *Zen'en bokka* (see his *Dōgen zenji den no kenkyū*, 176). The manuscript has been photocopied in Ōkubo, *Dōgen zenji shinpitsu shūsei*, 16, and described at ibid., 3.

represent a revision of the *Tso-ch'an i* and, hence, would seem to accord with Dōgen's stated purpose in writing his manual. Therefore, the argument has gone, we can safely assume the identity of this text with the Karoku work referred to in the "Senjutsu yurai." [11]

Here again, the argument obviously suffers from an excluded middle term: even if we grant that the Karoku *zazen gi*, like the Tenpuku manuscript, was a revision of Tsung-tse's manual, we cannot necessarily conclude that the two works were identical. The fallacy is painfully conspicuous in this case, where we have a total of four extant meditation texts by Dōgen, all of which represent greater or lesser revisions of the *Tso-ch'an i*. If the argument from content were valid, we should expect all of these texts to be the same. In fact, of course, they are not. This formal weakness, moreover, is only one of the problems with the argument: of greater interest is the fact that it is based on what seems a questionable reading of the "Senjutsu yurai."

The passage on the composition of the *zazen gi* that I quoted earlier is widely cited as evidence for the original date of the *Fukan zazen gi*. Unfortunately, it is almost always cited in isolation, and surprisingly little attention has been paid to the context of the passage or to the historical character of the "Senjutsu yurai" itself. Consequently, the *zazen gi* mentioned in this passage is generally assumed to be the work for which the "Senjutsu yurai" was intended as an explanation. This assumption stands behind the notion that the Karoku *zazen gi* was critical of Tsung-tse's *Tso-ch'an i*. Yet a careful reading of the text reveals that, in fact, it was not necessarily written for the Karoku manual, nor does it explicitly connect that manual with the Chinese work.

The "Senjutsu yurai" informs us that Dōgen returned to Japan in the Karoku era, was asked about meditation, and, therefore, felt obliged to write a manual of *zazen*. It then goes on to praise the T'ang figure Po-chang Huai-hai (749–814), famed as the author of the first Ch'an monastic code, and to criticize Tsung-tse for his failure to transmit Po-chang's meditation teachings faithfully. Finally, it closes with the statement "Now I gather the true arcana I have myself seen and heard, [offering them] merely as a substitute for what is received in the mind's expression." [12]

Although the date of the "Senjutsu yurai" is unknown, given the fact that the document mentions Dōgen's return to Japan in the Karoku era, the date must be put sometime after the end of that era. The last sentence clearly seems to indicate that the note was written on the occasion of the composition of the work for which it was an explanation. Thus it is not certain that the text of this work was the same as that of the original Karoku *zazen gi*. On the contrary, there may well be two distinct texts: one (the

---

11. This argument was first proposed by Ōkubo Dōshū, in his *Dōgen zenji goroku*, 108–9.
12. DZZ.2:6.

Karoku *zazen gi*), which Dōgen says at the beginning of the note he composed just after his return; and another (unidentified), alluded to in the final sentence, for which he is now writing the "Senjutsu yurai." According to this reading, this latter work would seem to be the one offered as a correction of Tsung-tse's manual. Presumably, it was also intended to improve on Dōgen's own earlier efforts at a *zazen gi*; otherwise, there would have been no need to compose it. Indeed this presumption is strengthened by the rather apologetic tone Dōgen strikes in referring to his Karoku work, which he wrote, as he says, only out of a sense of obligation. The "Senjutsu yurai," then, does not indicate that Dōgen's first *zazen gi* was critical of Tsung-tse; far from establishing the identity of the Tenpuku and Karoku texts, in fact, it suggests the possibility that the two may have been quite different.

Since the "Senjutsu yurai" lacks both title and date, we cannot say with any certainty for which of Dōgen's *zazen gi* it was written. The two most likely dates for the note are (1) 1233, on the occasion of the composition of the Tenpuku *Fukan zazen gi*; and (2) sometime in, or shortly after, 1243, when, as we shall see, Dōgen composed his *Shōbō genzō zazen gi* and probably also his revised version of the *Fukan zazen gi*. Internal evidence would appear to support the former. The "Senjutsu yurai" opens with a lament over the fact that "the special transmission outside the scriptures, the treasury of the eye of the true *dharma*" (*kyōge betsuden shōbō genzō*) has hitherto been unknown in Japan. In 1241, Dōgen wrote the *Shōbō genzō bukkyō*, a work devoted largely to a severe criticism of the famous Ch'an dictum of a "special transmission outside the scriptures." One doubts that soon thereafter he would make use of the dictum in the "Senjutsu yurai" to describe his own tradition.[13]

---

13.   For the dates of the *Shōbō genzō bukkyō*, see DZZ.1:314; Dōgen's criticism of the notion of *kyōge betsuden* appears at 306–8. My point here, I must admit, is somewhat vitiated by one of Dōgen's poems, written in the winter of 1247–48 during his visit to Kamakura, on the theme *kyōge betsuden* (DZZ.2:412). Prof. Yanagida Seizan has called my attention to the fact that the "Senjutsu yurai," in emphasizing fidelity to the monastic code of Po-chang, reflects a sentiment appearing at the end of the Tenpuku *Fukan zazen gi* in the line, "Honor the rule of Po-chang and everywhere convey the circumstances of Shao-lin"—a line that does not appear in any of Dōgen's later manuals.

In opposition to a Tenpuku date, we have the opinion of Furuta Shōkin, to the effect that the calligraphic style of the "Senjutsu yurai" is "more mature" than that of the Tenpuku manuscript. He suggests that it was written around 1243, as an explanation of the *Shōbō genzō zazen gi*. (See his *Shōbō genzō no kenkyū*, 33.) The question of the relative maturity of Dōgen's calligraphy must be left to the experts in such matters; but the specific association of the note with the *Shōbō genzō* text seems unlikely, since one would hardly expect Dōgen to offer a formal explanation in Chinese of a vernacular work apparently first composed as a lecture. Still, Furuta's suggestion is an interesting one, because it leads him to speculate that the Karoku text was, in fact, an early version of the *Shōbō genzō* manual, not of the *Fukan zazen gi*. In one sense this is implausible, since, as we shall see in our discussion of this text, the manual in the *Shōbō genzō* presupposes material much later than 1227. If, however, his suggestion is intended only to indicate that the Karoku text, like the later *Shōbō genzō* work, may have been simply a practical manual on the procedures of meditation, then it appears to be well taken.

Whatever the true date of the "Senjutsu yurai," its evidence does not allow us to read into Dōgen's earliest meditation manual the teachings of the Tenpuku manuscript. If, as the text informs us, he was asked to teach *zazen* after he returned from China, Dōgen was presumably looked upon, at least in some quarter, as knowledgeable in meditation. This would hardly be surprising, since he had just completed four years of training in Chinese monasteries. There was obviously much interest in the Sung Ch'an movement among Japanese Buddhists at this time, and anyone of his background and social prominence would probably have been eagerly approached for information. Under the circumstances he might well have "felt obliged" to compose a work on the *zazen* practice he had studied abroad. This work could easily have been simply a practical manual, giving concrete instructions on meditation technique; it need not have shared the ornate literary character of the *Fukan zazen gi* or its "revolutionary" political and doctrinal implications.

In regard to the question of the Karoku text's relationship to the *Tso-ch'an i*, we can only speculate. There is every reason to believe that Dōgen was familiar with Tsung-tse's work when he composed his first manual. It was well known in China, and indeed there is some evidence that it was recommended to Dōgen by Ju-ching himself. Portions of its text, moreover, had previously appeared in Japan in Yōsai's *Kōzen gokoku ron*, a work with which we may presume Dōgen was acquainted even before he left for the mainland.[14] As we have noted, all four of Dōgen's extant works on meditation practice make use of the *Tso-ch'an i*, and it seems reasonable to suppose that the Karoku *zazen gi* was no exception. We know that by 1233, when he wrote the Tenpuku manuscript, Dōgen had already begun to modify Tsung-tse's presentation of Zen practice, but whether he did so in his first manual is not clear. Particularly if the Karoku work—like the *Tso-ch'an i* and unlike the *Fukan zazen gi*—was intended solely as a practical guide, he might well have been content simply to restate the kind of basic instructions on contemplative technique found in this popular Ch'an meditation text. Indeed this would explain why his subsequent criticism of Tsung-tse obliged him to rewrite his own manual.

I have considered the question of the missing Karoku *zazen gi* at some length here because these doubts about its content have a significant effect on the broader issue of how we are to interpret the origins of Dōgen's Zen and the development of his ministry. If, as it appears, we cannot identify the work with the text of the *Fukan zazen gi*, then neither can we use this text to show what Dōgen thought about Zen when he left Ju-ching. Put the other way, if Dōgen's earliest extant meditation manual cannot be dated before

---

14.   See T.80: 12a,14–27. As we shall see, Yōsai's text is apparently based only indirectly on Tsung-tse's manual. Although this work must be used with some caution, in the *Hōkyō ki*, Ju-ching is reported to have recommended the *Tso-ch'an i* to Dōgen. (DZZ.2: 386.)

1233, our reading of it must take into account not only its author's experience in China but also the events of the half-decade and more that had passed since his return to Japan. Let us briefly review here what we know of these two historical factors.

The traditional story of the young Dōgen's search for the true *dharma* is well known, and its details need not long detain us here.[15] The son of a powerful Heian aristocratic family, he is said to have entered the Tendai order on Mt. Hiei at the age of thirteen and subsequently to have studied under the important Tendai prelate Kōin (d. 1216), then abbot of Onjō ji, one of the two major centers of the school. Following the death of Kōin, he moved to Kennin ji, the monastery in Heian recently founded by Yōsai (1141–1215) for the practice of the new Zen tradition that the latter sought to introduce from China. There Dōgen became the disciple of Yōsai's student Myōzen (1184–1225), with whom, in 1223, he undertook his pilgrimage to the Southern Sung.[16]

When the two Japanese monks arrived on the continent, they made for the Ching-te monastery on Mt. T'ien-t'ung. There they studied under the current abbot, a Lin-chi master by the name of Wu-chi Liao-p'ai (1149–1224), who had been a student of Ta-hui Tsung-kao's influential disciple Fo-chao Te-kuang (1121–1203). Although on several occasions this abbot acknowledged his enlightenment, Dōgen remained dissatisfied with his own understanding and unconvinced by Wu-chi's brand of Buddhism. After something over a year at T'ien-t'ung, therefore, he set out in search of another master. On nearby Mt. Aśoka, he visited the monastery of A-yü-wang, like T'ien-t'ung, one of the five great "mountains" (*wu shan*) of Ch'an recognized by the government of the Southern Sung; but he could find no one there of substance. He went north, to the first of the five mountains, Wan-shou ssu on Mt. Ching; here he had an interview with the master Che-weng Ju-yen (1151–1225), another of Te-kuang's disciples, but again he came away empty-handed. He went south, as far as Mts. T'ien-t'ai and

---

15. The most detailed and influential single study of Dōgen's biography is Ōkubo's *Dōgen zenji den no kenkyū*; for an English account of the early years, see James Kodera, *Dōgen's Formative Years in China: An Historical Study and Annotated Translation of the Hōkyō-ki* (1980).

16. Dōgen is usually said to be the son of the minister Minamoto no Michichika (d. 1202), of the Koga branch of the Murakami Genji; but the early sources on his parentage disagree, and the current theory has recently been questioned in favor of Michichika's son Michitomo (1170–1227). (See Kagamishima Genryū's review of Kawamura Kōdō, *Shohon taikō Eihei kaisan Dōgen zenji gyōjō Kenzei ki*, KDBGR 6 [10/75], 141–46.)

Menzan states that Dōgen first visited Kennin ji in 1214, while he was still studying on Hiei zan (*Teiho Kenzei ki*, SSZ.Shiden,2:16), and Ōkubo has devoted an entire chapter to arguing for this date and for the tradition that Dōgen had an interview with Yōsai on this occasion (*Dōgen zenji den no kenkyū*, 83–109); but here again the theory is certainly open to question. (See Kagamishima's review of Kawamura.) There is considerably better evidence to suggest that Dōgen visited the monastery in 1217, a few years after Yōsai's death, but we cannot be sure that he remained in residence thereafter until his departure with Myōzen.

Yen-tang; along the way, he was offered (and declined) *dharma* transmission by a certain Lin-chi master Yüan-tzu, abbot of Wan-nien monastery, and had an inconclusive meeting with the master P'an-shan Ssu-cho, also a descendant of Ta-hui.

By now Dōgen despaired of finding a true teacher in China and was ready to return to Japan. At this point there appeared an old monk, who told him of the new abbot of T'ien-t'ung, the venerable master Ju-ching. Dōgen headed straight back to the mountain, arriving just in time for the summer meditation retreat of 1225. Ju-ching, we are told, was a strict abbot, who turned away most applicants to his monastery; but fortunately for the Japanese pilgrim, his arrival had been foretold by no less than Tung-shan Liang-chieh (807–69), the founder of the Ts'ao-tung house, who appeared to the abbot in a dream the night before Dōgen's arrival. Under the circumstances, Ju-ching welcomed the new disciple, comparing their meeting to the first transmission of the *shōbō genzō* on Vulture Peak. Thus encouraged, Dōgen threw himself into the practice of meditation; before long, upon hearing Ju-ching speak of the practice as "the sloughing off of body and mind," he attained the great awakening.

Ju-ching immediately acknowledged Dōgen's enlightenment and, indeed, invited him to become his personal attendant. The Japanese disciple declined the honor on the grounds that a foreigner's appointment to such a post would reflect poorly on the qualifications of Chinese monks. He preferred, rather, to continue his meditation practice and prepare himself for his coming mission. In 1227, he expressed his desire to return to Japan. He was given a certificate of succession, a robe, a portrait of the master, and other insignia of *dharma* transmission; with these, he took his leave of Ju-ching.

By this traditional account, Dōgen's four-year sojourn on the continent was divided into two distinct phases, punctuated by his encounter with Ju-ching. The first phase was spent in the concerted quest for a true teacher; the second, in enlightened practice under such a teacher. Put in other terms, the first half of his pilgrimage was devoted to training in the *k'an-hua* Ch'an of the Lin-chi school; the second half, to the Ts'ao-tung practice of just sitting with body and mind sloughed off. Thus, as he studies under, and rejects, a series of teachers of the Ta-hui tradition, Dōgen—rather like Śākyamuni before him—masters and transcends the prevalent religion of his contemporaries, until he finally arrives at the ancient wisdom of the Buddhas. Perhaps this is what happened, but the account I have summarized here depends heavily on the hagiographic literature of early Sōtō. This literature includes considerable material not confirmed by earlier sources and introduces many fanciful elements into its story of Dōgen's life. Though modern biographers now reject at least the most obvious of these latter, they have yet to question seriously the basic account of Dōgen's itinerary in China.[17]

Though Dōgen himself, at least in his later life, would probably have appreciated the church's version of his travels in the Sung, his own recollections of those travels do not necessarily lend it much support. Indeed, if we limit ourselves to his own reports, our knowledge of his China years is sketchy at best. He seems to have arrived on the mainland in the fourth month of 1223 and, in the seventh month, to have followed Myōzen to Ching-te ssu, the Ch'an monastery on Mt. T'ien-t'ung, near the coast of modern Chekiang.[18] This was the institution at which their predecessor Yōsai had studied for two years, under its then abbot, the Huang-lung master Hsü-an Huai-ch'ang (dates unknown), and it is probably for this reason that the two Japanese pilgrims made it their base while in China. Myōzen apparently remained on T'ien-t'ung until his death there in the spring of 1225. What Dōgen did is not very clear.

According to his later writings, he made a visit to A-yü-wang in the autumn of 1223, probably within a few weeks of his arrival at Ching-te ssu.[19] Such an outing would hardly be surprising, since Mt. Aśoka is only a short distance from T'ien-t'ung, and its famous relic of the Buddha had previously attracted Yōsai. Apart from this episode, we have no firm evidence that Dōgen ever left Mt. T'ien-t'ung prior to the death of its abbot and of Dōgen's own master, Myōzen. The tradition of his wanderings in search of a true teacher seems to be based solely on his passing reference to a trip to the region of Mt. T'ien-t'ai sometime during the Pao-ch'ing era (1225–27). This mountain, a little to the south of T'ien-t'ung, was, of course, the traditional seat of the T'ien-t'ai order and one of the most popular spots on the Japanese pilgrim circuit. It was also the site of the Wan-nien monastery, where Yōsai had first studied with Huai-ch'ang. We do not know what Dōgen was doing

---

17. The most influential of these hagiographic works is the *Kenzei ki*, by the fourteenth abbot of Eihei ji, Kenzei (1415–74). The extant manuscripts of the work, which vary considerably in content, have been collected in Kawamura Kōdō, *Shohon taikō Eihei kaisan Dōgen zenji gyōjō Kenzei ki* (1975). Kenzei dutifully records the standard miracles and prodigious powers associated with the careers of Buddhist saints: at the time of Dōgen's birth, a voice in the sky predicts his future greatness, and he bears all the signs of a sage (ibid., 3); by the age of three, he has read the *Li Chiao tsa yung*, by eight, the *Abhidharma-kośa* (p. 4), and by seventeen, the entire Buddhist canon twice over (p. 10); during his quest in China, he meets and overcomes a wild tiger (p. 18); in later life, when he lectures at Eihei ji, flowers fall on the entire assembly (p. 55); for months, a marvelous fragrance pervades his temple (p. 70), and mysterious bells are heard to chime (p. 76). Like some of the earlier biographies on which he drew, Kenzei also enhances his account with verbatim reports, of dubious origin, of Dōgen's conversations with various masters, including his first teacher, Kōin (p. 10), Che-weng and P'an-shan (p. 18), and Ju-ching (p. 24). For a general discussion of the *Kenzei ki* and other early sources for Dōgen's biography, see Ōkubo, *Dōgen zenji den no kenkyū*, 20–35.

18. *Shōbō genzō senmen*, DZZ.1:431, 442; *Tenzo kyōkun*, DZZ.2:299.

19. *Shōbō genzō busshō*, DZZ.1:26.

there or how long he stayed; he mentions his meetings in that district with Yüan-tzu and P'an-shan but does not say whether he actually studied with either man. In any case, since we know that he was in the area of T'ien-t'ung in the winter of 1224 and the summer of 1225, this excursion to the south may well have taken place sometime after he had begun to study with Ju-ching.[20]

Whatever the intensity of his inner search during this time, as a physical pilgrimage, Dōgen's quest for the true *dharma* in China seems a rather desultory one. Even by traditional accounts, he never looked beyond eastern Chekiang province, and his tour of monasteries there lasted no more than a few months; from his own report, there is still less to suggest that he actively sought, as he later said, "to investigate the dark import of the five houses" of Ch'an. On the contrary, as he himself remarks at one point, he did little wandering through the Ch'an "groves" but only studied with Ju-ching;[21] in fact, he may have simply remained on Mt. T'ien-t'ung with his master, Myōzen, and then, following the latter's death in the fifth month of 1225, became a disciple of the new abbot of the monastery.

In Dōgen's writings (and in much of the modern literature based on them), the new abbot of Ching-te ssu appears as a lofty and luminous peak rising above the otherwise drab spiritual landscape of the Southern Sung. In a degenerate age, when Ch'an monasteries were run by unprincipled and ambitious men, Ju-ching alone stood upright and firm; in a benighted age, when unlettered monks wandered in the darkness of heresy, Ju-ching alone illumined the ancient way of the Patriarchs. In short, in an age when Ch'an was dominated by the followers of Ta-hui, only Ju-ching preserved the true tradition of the *shōbō genzō*. For Dōgen, he is "the old Buddha," "the Buddha among Buddhas," not to be compared with any of his contemporaries. He alone in all of China has understood the true significance of "just sitting" as "the sloughing off of body and mind"; he alone in the last half-millennium has thoroughly attained "the eye of the Buddhas and Patriarchs." With this eye, he sees the shallowness and corruption of the other Ch'an masters of his day and laments the sad decline of the *dharma*. Clearly, in Dōgen's own eye, his former master was unique. What is less clear is the extent to which that

---

20.   In the *Shōbō genzō menju*, Dōgen dates his first meeting with Ju-ching on the first day of the fifth month of the first year of Pao-ch'ing (DZZ.1:446); elsewhere, we learn that he was still in the T'ien-t'ung area during the tenth month of the preceding year (*Shōbō genzō kesa kudoku*, DZZ.1:643; *Shōbō genzō den'e*, DZZ.1:298). On the assumption that the encounter with Ju-ching represented the culmination of Dōgen's quest and, hence, put an end to his wanderings, his biographers have been obliged to squeeze his visits to other monasteries between these two dates. Dōgen's reference (in the *Shōbō genzō shisho*, DZZ.1:344) to his T'ien-t'ai trip does not indicate that he was seeking a teacher there but only that, while there, he had the opportunity to see some Ch'an certificates of succession (*shisho*). Shibata Dōken, though he accepts the tradition of Dōgen's wanderings in China, is almost alone in suggesting that they took place during his study with Ju-ching; see Shibata's *Zenji Dōgen no shisō* (1975), 203.

21.   For these remarks, see *Shōbō genzō butsudō*, DZZ.1:380; *Eihei kōroku*, DZZ.2:18.

uniqueness lay beyond the beholder, since there is little evidence elsewhere that would set Ju-ching apart from other Ch'an teachers of his time.[22]

As Dōgen himself complains, his master's greatness seems to have gone largely unappreciated in China, and the standard histories of Ch'an pass him by with little notice. We do have, however, a collection of his recorded sayings, compiled by his Chinese students and preserved in Japan; yet the Ju-ching of this text bears scant resemblance to the man Dōgen recalls as his "former master, the old Buddha" (*senshi kobutsu*). Nowhere here do we find a sign of the uncompromising reformer of contemporary Ch'an or the outspoken critic of its recent developments; nowhere do we find any particular assertion of the Ts'ao-tung tradition or doubt about the rival Lin-chi house. Neither, indeed, do we find mention of any of the central terminology of Japanese Sōtō: "the treasury of the eye of the true *dharma*," "the unity of practice and enlightenment," "sloughing off of body and mind," "nonthinking," or "just sitting." Instead what we find is still another Sung master, making enigmatic remarks on the sayings of Ch'an, drawing circles in the air with his whisk, and, in what is almost the only practical instruction in the text, recommending for the control of random thoughts concentration on Chao-chou's "*wu*," the famous *kung-an* that was the centerpiece of Ta-hui's *k'an-hua* Ch'an.[23]

The fact that Dōgen's "former master, the old Buddha" fails to appear in Ju-ching's collected sayings does not, of course, necessarily mean that the Japanese disciple made him up; Ju-ching's Chinese editors must have had their own principles of selection and interpretation around which they developed their text. Moreover, what they have recorded is largely restricted to rather stylized types of material—sermons, lectures, poetry, and the like—that by its very nature would be unlikely to yield at least some of the teachings Dōgen attributes to Ju-ching. This kind of material must have been quite difficult for Dōgen to follow, given his limited experience with the spoken language; perhaps most of what he understood of his master's Buddhism, he learned from more intimate, perhaps private, remedial instruction. Indeed Sōtō tradition preserves a record of such instruction that does contain several sayings similar to those Dōgen attributes to Ju-ching elsewhere. Unfortunately, this text, known as the *Hōkyō ki*, or "Record from

22. For more detail on this and the following discussion of Ju-ching, see my "Recarving the Dragon: History and Dogma in the Study of Dōgen," in *Dōgen Studies*, ed. by William LaFleur, Studies in East Asian Buddhism 2 (1985), 21–53.

23. See *Nyojō oshō goroku*, T.48:121–33, and *Tendō san Keitoku ji Nyojō zenji zoku goroku*, T.48:133–37; Chao-chou's famous *kung-an* appears at 127b. A Kamakura manuscript of Ju-ching's record has recently been discovered at Sōji ji and published at *Dōgen zenji shinseki kankei shiryō shū* (1980), 309–418. For a recent detailed study of the life and teachings of Ju-ching, together with a translation of his *Goroku*, see Kagamishima Genryū, *Tendō Nyojō zenji no kenkyū* (1983); especially on 105–33, the author argues for sharp differences between the teachings of Dōgen and his Chinese master.

the Pao-ch'ing era," is not very reliable as a historical source; it was discovered only after Dōgen's death by his leading disciple, Koun Ejō. Hence we cannot say with any certainty even how much of the extant text is Dōgen's work, let alone how much accurately records the words of Ju-ching.[24]

It would be easier to dismiss our doubts about Dōgen's claims for his master and to accept the traditional account of the origins of his Zen were it not for the fact that these claims do not appear in his writings until quite late in his life. Not until the 1240s, well over a decade after his return from China and at the midpoint of his career as a teacher and author, does Dōgen begin to emphasize the uniqueness of Ju-ching and to attribute to him the attitudes and doctrines that set him apart from his contemporaries. Prior to this time, during the period when one would expect Dōgen to have been most under the influence of his Chinese mentor, we see but little of Ju-ching or, indeed, of some of those teachings now thought most characteristic of Dōgen's Zen. We shall return to this important point further on, when we consider the later development of Dōgen's thought; it is enough here to recognize that, had Dōgen written nothing between the ages of forty and forty-five, we should now have a very different picture both of what he professed and of how he came to profess it. He did not stop writing at forty, and what he wrote thereafter gives us considerable information on how he himself came to understand the sources of his Zen; but the date of this material, its contrast to his earlier teachings, and its often polemical character make it difficult to use with confidence as evidence for the historical origins of Dōgen's religion.

In sum, then, while it is certain that, when Dōgen returned to Japan in 1227, he brought back a certificate verifying his inheritance of the *dharma*

---

24.   For the text of the *Hōkyō ki*, see DZZ.2 : 371–88. The report of Ejō's discovery appears in the colophon of his autograph manuscript, ibid., 388. Mizuno Yaoko, among others, has recently been making the argument that, whatever records Dōgen may have kept of his master's instruction, the text of the *Hōkyō ki* was compiled near the end of Dōgen's life as a summation of what he then considered Ju-ching's most helpful teaching; see her "Hōkyō ki to jūni kan Shōbō genzō," SK 21 (3/1979), 27–30; and "Hōkyō ki," in *Dōgen no chōsaku, Kōza Dōgen* 3, ed. by Kagamishima Genryū and Tamaki Kōshiro (1980), 218–40.

In any case, even in this text, the evidence for Dōgen's fidelity to Ju-ching is mixed. In one of the most famous passages of the text, the Chinese master is quoted as saying,

To study Ch'an [*sanzen*] is to slough off body and mind [*shinjin datsuraku*]; it is only attained when you just sit [*shikan taza*], without reliance on offering incense, making prostrations, reciting the name of the Buddha [*nenbutsu*], practicing repentence or reading *sūtras.*

Ju-ching goes on to define the sloughing off of body and mind as seated meditation (*zazen*). Interestingly enough, however, the reason he gives is that "when one just sits in meditation [*shikan zazen*], he gets free from the five desires [*goyoku, pañca-kāma*] and removes the five hindrances [*gogai, pañca-nivaraṇa*]." When Dōgen rightly objects that this explanation is nothing but the sort of thing said by the scholastics (*kyōke*) and reduces *zazen* to the kind of practice common to both Hīnayāna and Mahāyāna, he is rebuked by his master for criticizing the two vehicles and denying the holy teaching of the Tathāgata. (DZZ.2 : 377–78.)

of the abbot of T'ien-t'ung, it is much less certain what such inheritance meant at the time either to the Chinese abbot or his Japanese disciple. Nor does the little information we have on Dōgen's first years back in Japan throw much light on this question. It is possible, of course, that immediately upon reaching his native land, he set about broadcasting a new Zen doctrine among the people. Indeed, in the *Bendō wa*, he describes the heavy burden of responsibility he felt on his return for "spreading the *dharma* and saving beings." Yet the same passage goes on to say that he had decided to await more favorable conditions before embarking on the dissemination of his message; and, in fact, aside from his references to the Karoku manual, we know of no significant writings by Dōgen until the *Bendō wa* itself in 1231.[25]

If we have no information on Dōgen's earliest views on Zen, we have only little more on his earliest activities. He himself tells us merely that, after returning to Japan, he spent several years at Kennin ji. For one supposed to have declared war on the Tendai school and to have rejected the teachings of Rinzai Zen, this choice of residence is a curious one. Kennin ji at this time remained under the jurisdiction of the nearby Tendai headquarters on Mt. Hiei, and the Zen practiced there was the Rinzai tradition introduced by the founder, Yōsai. Under these circumstances it was probably one of the least likely places in Japan from which to launch a Sōtō Zen reformation. We do not know why Dōgen returned there rather than take an independent course. Given his social connections, it could hardly have been a matter of economic necessity. On the contrary, he may have expected his connections, and his status as a descendant of Yōsai, to win for him a position of prominence in this government-supported monastery in the capital.[26]

Our only other source on Dōgen's activities during this period is an entry in the *Hottō kokushi gyōjitsu nenpu*, a chronology of events in the life of Shinchi Kakushin (1207–98), traditionally regarded as the founder of the Fuke, or Komu, sect of Rinzai. The entry records the fact that, on the fifteenth day of the tenth month (November 25) of 1227, Dōgen participated, along with the renowned Kegon master Myōe Kōben (1173–1232), in the opening of

---

25. The only earlier document is the note on Myōzen's relics mentioned earlier. For the *Bendō wa* passage, see DZZ.1:729–30, 747.

26. Dōgen refers to his stay at Kennin ji in the *Tenzo kyōkun*, DZZ.2:300, and again in Ejō's *Shōbō genzō zuimon ki*, DZZ.2:438. Kennin ji, in the present Higashiyama ward of Kyoto, had been built for Yōsai by the second Kamakura shōgun, Minamoto no Yoriie (1182–1204). During his second trip to China (1185–91), Yōsai had received transmission in the Huang-lung branch of Lin-chi and; after his return, had sought to introduce Zen practice to Japan. For this, he was attacked by the Tendai church. Nevertheless, he himself remained a Tendai monk and—like the Tendai founder, Saichō, before him—interpreted the Zen tradition as but one element in a larger Buddhist synthesis. Hence Kennin ji was put under the administration of Hiei zan and furnished with cloisters for the study of both Tendai and tantra. Its later status as an independent Zen institution is generally thought to have begun in the second half of the thirteenth century, under the influential abbots Enni (Ben'en) (1202–80) and Lan-ch'i Tao-lung (Rankei Dōryū, 1213–78).

Saihō monastery at Yura in Kii province.[27] We do not know how Dōgen became associated with this monastery, but the fact of the association is interesting because it places him, immediately after his arrival in Japan, within a politically prominent Buddhist circle surrounding Yōsai's leading Zen disciple.

Saihō ji (later known as Kōkoku ji) was built by a monk named Ganshō (d. 1275), formerly Katsurayama Kagetomo, a follower of the third Kamakura shōgun, Minamoto no Sanetomo (1192–1219). Sanetomo was an ardent and romantic Buddhist, with a deep fascination for things Chinese. Toward the end of his brief life, he made plans to sail to the continent, there to experience directly the spiritual culture of Sung Buddhism. When these plans failed, he dispatched in his stead his loyal retainer Kagetomo. The latter proceeded to Yura, where he began preparations for the crossing; before they could be completed, Sanetomo was assassinated. In his grief Kagetomo climbed Mt. Kōya and took Buddhist vows from Taikō Gyōyū, of the Cloister of the Vajra-samādhi (Kongō Zanmai in). Thereafter, he returned to his fief in Kii and began the construction of Saihō ji as a memorial (*bodai ji*) to his departed lord.

Ganshō's master, Gyōyū (1163–1241), was the most successful of Yōsai's disciples. Originally a Shingon monk from Kamakura, he converted to Yōsai when the latter first visited the *bakufu* capital to found the Jufuku monastery there. He soon rose to a position of prominence and, following in his master's footsteps, served as the abbot of Jufuku ji, Kennin ji, and the Kongō Zanmai in on Mt. Kōya. In these important posts he taught such notable early Zen figures as Daikatsu Ryōshin (dates unknown), later abbot of both Kennin ji and Jufuku ji; Enni (Ben'en) (1212–80), founding abbot of Tōfuku ji and restorer of Kennin ji; and Shinchi Kakushin, who served as head monk (*daiichi za*) at Kongō Zanmai in and later became founding abbot of Ganshō's Kōkoku ji. Ganshō's choice of Gyōyū as his preceptor is not surprising, since this monk had long been the personal teacher of Sanetomo's mother, the politically powerful Hōjō Masako (1156–1225), to whom he had also given the tonsure many years before. It was this Masako who had sponsored the construction of both Jufuku ji and Kongō Zanmai in.[28]

The brief notice in Kakushin's chronology tells us very little about Dōgen's relationship to this circle, but his participation in the ceremonies at Saihō ji forms a suggestive link with certain other facts in his biography. For example, while in China, Dōgen was close to a disciple of Yōsai named Ryūzen, who was also studying on Mt. T'ien-t'ung. After his return to Japan, this monk seems to have succeeded Gyōyū as abbot of Kongō Zanmai

---

27. Quoted in Ōkubo, *Dōgen zenji den no kenkyū*, 177; the text can be found in *Zoku Gunsho ruijū* 9A:348.

28. For a recent study of Gyōyū, see Hanuki Masai, "Kamakura bukkyō ni okeru Yōsai monryū no ichi: Taikō Gyōyū to sono shūhen," *Bukkyō shigaku kenkyū* 20, 2 (3/1978), 1–29.

in and to have appointed Kakushin as head monk.[29] We also know that Kakushin himself, after the death of Gyōyū, sought out Dōgen and received from him the Bodhisattva precepts.[30] It has been suggested, moreover, that one of Dōgen's early supporters, a nun named Shōkaku, may have been Sanetomo's wife, Nobuko, who also took Buddhist vows from Gyōyū after her husband's death and established a memorial monastery for Sanetomo in Heian.[31] Finally, though the source is a late one, we have the text of a letter from Dōgen to his patron Hatano Yoshishige in which he states that he considered his own monastery a memorial to Sanetomo and Hōjō Masako.[32] On the basis of such connections, more than one scholar has recently proposed that Dōgen's trip to China was supported by Ganshō and Sanetomo's followers in Heian, and that for this reason, immediately upon his return from the trip, we find him participating in ceremonies at the late shōgun's memorial temple.[33]

Whatever the nature and import of Dōgen's association with Gyōyū's followers, it did not seem to have helped him at Kennin ji; by 1231, he was on his own, living at what was probably a rather dilapidated monastery on the outskirts of the capital. Why he left Kennin ji is unclear. Unfortunately, we know very little about the monastery during this period or about the succession of Yōsai's disciples that seem to have controlled it. Some years later Dōgen would complain that discipline at Kennin ji had declined greatly since the days of the founder, and perhaps he simply did not like the place. For some reason he failed to find a place among Yōsai's other followers

---

29. See Harada Kōdō, "Nihon Sōtō shū no rekishi teki seikaku (2): Dōgen zenji to Ryūzen Kakushin to no kōshō o megutte," KDBGR 5 (12/1974), 1–16.

30. *Hottō Enmyō kokushi no engi*, quoted in Ōkubo, *Dōgen zenji den no kenkyū*, 244; see also "Ju Kakushin kaimyaku," DZZ.2:291. The bestowing of the precepts took place in 1242; in 1249, Kakushin proceeded to China, where he studied with the famous Lin-chi master Wu-men Hui-k'ai (1183–1260).

31. Ōkubo Dōshū, *Dōgen zenji den no kenkyū*, 208–11. Nobuko's biography in the *Azuma kagami* does not identify her Buddhist name, but in the *Sanshū meiseki shi*, it is given as Hongaku. Whether or not Ōkubo is correct in identifying her with Dōgen's patron Shōkaku, it is clear that the latter was a woman of considerable means; for it seems that, when Dōgen built his new monastery in Fukakusa, she personally funded the construction of the lecture hall. (See *Kenzei ki*, SSZ.Shiden,2:21; *Eihei ji sanso gyōgō ki*, SSZ.Shiden,1:3.)

32. Preserved in Menzan's edition of the *Kenzei ki*; for the text, see "Hatano Yoshishige ate shojō," DZZ.2:407. The letter is undated and the monastery in question unidentified. Most writers have followed Menzan in assuming that it relates to Eihei ji, which we know was supported by Yoshishige; but Moriya Shigeru has recently suggested that it refers to Dōgen's earlier Kōshō ji in Fukakusa and should be dated around 1237. (See "Fukakusa Kōshō ji no kaiki Shōkaku ni ni tsuite," IBK 26, 1 [12/1977], 55–60; reprinted [together with a related piece, "Dōgen to Minamoto no Sanetomo Hongaku ni no kotodomo,"] in Moriya, *Dōgen zenji kenkyū: Kyōto shūhen ni okeru Dōgen to sono shūmon* [1984], 42–54.)

33. See Moriya, "Fukakusa Kōshō ji no kaiki Shōkaku ni ni tsuite"; and Sugio Gen'yū, "Minamoto no Sanetomo no nyū Sō kito to Dōgen zenji," SK 18 (3/1976), 41–46. In connection with this theory, it should be noted that, when Kagetomo was dispatched to China, his destination was supposed to have been Wan-nien monastery, and that, when Kakushin left for China in 1249, Kagetomo requested that he inter Sanetomo's remains on Yen-tang shan. It may be more than a coincidence that both of these spots appear on Dōgen's itinerary during his trip to Mt. T'ien-t'ai.

and did not see a future for himself there. In any case, from this time forth, Dōgen would be an outsider, living apart from the major centers of the nascent Japanese Zen movement and without the support that the Kamakura government was providing them.[34]

When Dōgen left Kennin ji, he appears to have taken up residence at a place called An'yō in, said to be on the grounds of an old monastery at Fukakusa, in the present Fushimi ward of Kyoto. This monastery, known as Gokuraku ji, had been founded in the ninth century by Dōgen's Fujiwara ancestors, and he was apparently invited there by an influential relative, Kujō Noriie (dates unknown). When Dōgen arrived, the site seems to have been relatively unused; within a few years, he had taken over the entire complex and turned it into a Zen monastery, the first independent such institution in Japan. He would call it Kōshō Hōrin ji, a name that evoked both Pao-lin ssu, monastery of Hui-neng (638–713), the famous Sixth Patriarch of Ch'an, and Hsing-sheng ssu, the first of the five official Ch'an monasteries in the Sung. Clearly, he had high aspirations for the place.[35]

---

34. In his *Tenzo kyōkun* (DZZ.2:300), Dōgen states that he spent "two or three years" at Kennin ji. The *terminus ad quem* for his move is provided by the "Shi Ryōnen dōsha hōgo," a brief teaching presented to a female disciple, which was composed in the seventh month of 1231 at An'yō in, in Fukakusa. (See Ōkubo, *Dōgen zenji den no kenkyū*, 354; DZZ.2:162n.) According to tradition at Kennin ji, following the founder's death, the abbacy passed to Taikō Gyōyū and then through a series of five lesser-known disciples of Yōsai. Dōgen's dissatisfaction with the monastery is expressed in the *Tenzo kyōkun* (DZZ.2:300) and in the *Shōbō genzō zuimon ki* (DZZ.2:461).

There is some evidence that Dōgen did not leave Kennin ji voluntarily but was forced from the monastery by the Tendai church. This evidence comes from a fragment of what appears to have been a letter written on the back of a manuscript of the *Hyōhan ki*, copied by Fujiwara no Teika (1162–1241), which reports that the "mountain monks" (i.e., of Hiei zan) were angry at Buppōbō (i.e., Dōgen) and had decided to destroy his residence and drive him from the capital. (See Ōkubo, *Dōgen zenji den no kenkyū*, 185–90.) Recent biographers have been quick to accept this evidence, and to suggest that the cause of the mountain monks' anger was the doctrine of the *Fukan zazen gi*. (See, e.g., Imaeda Aishin, *Chūsei zenshū shi no kenkyū*, 19–23; Takasaki Jikidō, "Mukyū no butsugyō," in *Kobutsu no manabi [Dōgen]*, ed. by Takasaki and Umehara Takeshi, *Bukkyō no shisō* 11 [1969], 59.) In the light of our ignorance of the Karoku manual, however, this suggestion remains highly speculative. Moreover, Ōkubo's argument (*Dōgen zenji den* 188–89) to the contrary notwithstanding, it remains uncertain that the *Hyōhan ki* letter dates from Dōgen's years at Kennin ji rather than from his later Kōshō ji period, when we know that he was under pressure from Hiei zan.

35. The identification of An'yō in with Gokuraku ji was proposed long ago by Menzan (*Teiho Kenzei ki*, Kawamura, *Shohon taikō Kenzei ki*, 33) but has never been definitely established. Noriie was the brother of the powerful court figure Kujō Michiie (1193–1252); in 1225, he took Buddhist vows and henceforth was known as Guzei in Jikan. According to the *Kenzei ki* (SSZ.Shiden,2:21), this man was one of Dōgen's early supporters and donated the main altar (*hōza*) for the *dharma* hall (*hattō*) of Kōshō ji. The establishment of Kōshō ji is usually dated at 1233, when Dōgen seems to have moved to larger quarters at a place called Kannon Dōri in. His new monastery was built on this site, the formal opening of the monks' hall taking place in the winter of 1236. The historical significance of Kōshō ji as the first Japanese monastery to isolate Zen from Tendai and Shingon was early recognized by Enni's disciple Mujū Dōgyō (1226–1312): in his *Zōtan shū*, he singles it out as the first place to provide facilities for formal Zen meditation in the traditional Chinese style. (Yamada Shōzen and Miki Sumito, *Zōtan shū*, Chūsei no bungaku 1:3 [1973], 257.)

At this point, after his withdrawal from the established Zen center at Kennin ji and at the outset of his efforts to create what he hoped would be a new center at Fukakusa, Dōgen composed the autograph *Fukan zazen gi*. The manuscript bears a colophon indicating that it was written on the fifteenth day of the seventh month (August 21) of 1233. This date corresponds to the day known as *gege*, the end of the traditional Buddhist three-month summer meditation retreat (*ango*). Although in 1233 the Gokuraku ji complex still lacked the lecture hall (*hattō*) and monks' hall (*sōdō*) necessary for formal Zen training, Dōgen apparently observed the retreat, in some form at least, during this year. Presumably, therefore, his manual was connected with this retreat and reflects his meditation teachings during the preceding months.[36]

We do not know for whom the *Fukan zazen gi* manuscript was written. Unfortunately, we have no information on the names or the number of those attending the 1233 *ango*. Over the years Kōshō ji seems to have grown into a considerable community, but for this early date, there is little evidence to suggest that there were many monks in residence. Indeed at this point in his career, Dōgen is unlikely to have had any very close disciples. On the other hand, his activities at Kōshō ji were supported by some influential members of the Heian aristocracy, and the content both of the *Fukan zazen gi* itself and of his other writings from this time suggests that his teaching was directed less to an intimate congregation of committed Zen practitioners than to the larger Buddhist community, lay as well as clerical. Given this content, the quality of its paper, and the obvious care with which it was copied (and perhaps also the excellent state of its preservation), it is tempting to speculate that the *Fukan zazen gi* manuscript was presented to one of the more important persons participating in, or supporting, the 1233 summer retreat.[37]

It is in this historical setting, then, that we find Dōgen's first extant meditation manual. Within this setting the work can be read as, in part, a political piece, intended to advertise the newly imported Zen tradition as a historically distinct and religiously valid form of Buddhism, and to promote the newly established Zen community that Dōgen hoped would become a center of that tradition in Japan. To this extent it probably does represent

---

36. The dates of the Buddhist retreat (*varṣa*) differ according to the source. (For a summary discussion, see *Hōbōgirin: Dictionnaire encyclopédique du Bouddhisme*, fasc. 1, s.v. "ango.") It was the practice of the Chinese Ch'an school to keep the retreat from the sixteenth of the fourth month to the fifteenth of the seventh month, and we know that Dōgen followed this tradition. (See his *Shōbō genzō ango*, DZZ.1:576, 580.) Reference to Dōgen's 1233 *ango* appears in the colophon of his *Shōbō genzō maka hannya haramitsu* (DZZ.1:13). The condition of Gokuraku ji is mentioned in his "Uji Kannon Dōri in sōdō kenritsu kanjin sho," an appeal for donations for the construction of the monks' hall, composed in 1235 (DZZ.2:400–401).

37. We may note in passing here that the *Genjō kōan*, a work written just after the *Fukan zazen gi*, seems to have been presented to a lay disciple from Kyūshū named Yō Kōshū. (See DZZ.1:10.)

a declaration of independence, though not necessarily the independence of the Sōtō school. On the contrary, the immediate model for the work—both for its conception and for the Zen practice it sought to promote—was not the teachings of Ju-ching but the popular meditation manual by the Yün-men monk Ch'ang-lu Tsung-tse.

In its themes, and sometimes in its very phrasing, the *Fukan zazen gi* mirrors other texts from the earliest phase of Dōgen's writing—texts like the *Bendō wa*, from 1231; the *Gakudō yōjin shū*, a *kanbun* tract probably from early 1234; and also (though it differs in historical character) the *Shōbō genzō zuimon ki*, the collection of talks supposed to date from the Katei era (1235–38). In these texts we see Dōgen perhaps more as popular Zen preacher and pamphleteer than as sophisticated Zen master. He seems to be addressing the Japanese Buddhist community at large and focussing on the basic, practical question of how a Buddhist can best go about cultivating the faith. He singles out Zen mental training as the answer to this question—an answer that is at once the very core of the religion and yet accessible to all, an answer that has been the centerpiece of the tradition in the great kingdoms of India and China and has now finally been transmitted to the remote islands of Japan. This phase of teaching would not last long: within a few years Dōgen would turn to a more technical style and more esoteric subjects, and his focus would narrow to the Sōtō tradition and the monastic community.

2

The Vulgate Manual and
the Development of Dōgen's Zen

Despite its historical interest and the attention it has attracted from contemporary scholars, the Tenpuku text of the *Fukan zazen gi* seems to have had no impact on the development of the Sōtō school. Until its rediscovery in this century, it apparently remained unstudied by the Sōtō masters; in its place, another, somewhat different version of the *Fukan zazen gi* gained currency in the school. This version—usually referred to as the *rufu*, or vulgate, text—alone has been the subject of study and commentary by the tradition. The differences in content between the two versions will be discussed in detail later; in what follows here, I shall limit myself to consideration of some historical questions, including the provenance of the vulgate text and the circumstances surrounding its composition.

The existence of the Tenpuku manuscript indicates that Dōgen originally intended the *Fukan zazen gi* as an independent treatise on the theory and practice of meditation, and in modern times the essay is always treated as such. The fact is, however, that we have no early manuscripts of the vulgate text and, indeed, no definite evidence that it was ever transmitted as a separate work prior to the eighteenth century. The modern treatment of the *Fukan zazen gi* seems to originate with Menzan's influential commentary, the *Fukan zazen gi monge*. Menzan's text for the commentary was a meditation manual embedded in the *Eihei kōroku*, the "extensive record" of Dōgen's Zen teachings, compiled in Chinese by several of his disciples. This manual, known as the *Kōroku* text, became the basis for all later printings of the *Fukan zazen gi*. To understand the provenance of the version of the *Fukan zazen gi* in common use today, therefore, we must review something of the textual history of the work from which it was drawn.

It is not entirely clear when or by whom the record of Dōgen's teachings was put together. Some of the *Eihei kōroku* may reflect Dōgen's own editing, but the final work was presumably done shortly after his death by his chief disciple and *dharma* heir, Koun Ejō (1198–1280), and/or by the other disciples to whom the compilation of the individual fascicles is attributed.[1] We cannot entirely rule out the possibility that the edited text of the *Fukan zazen gi*, which appears in fascicle 8, reflects, at least in part, the editorial work of Ejō and the other disciples responsible for this section of the *Eihei kōroku*; but there is reason to think that this is not the case, and that the tradition is justified in attributing the vulgate *Fukan zazen gi* to Dōgen himself. First, there is considerable doubt as to whether the manual was actually included in the compilation of the *Eihei kōroku* worked on by his disciples; second, and more importantly, there is internal evidence to suggest that it originally belonged to a group of meditation texts composed during the last decade of his life. Let us, then, consider these two points in turn.

The standard modern version of the *Eihei kōroku*, and the one used by Menzan, is an edition published in 1673 by Menzan's teacher, Manzan Dōhaku (1636–1715). According to the preface, it is based on several manuscripts and corrects the various mistakes and corruptions that its editor felt had crept into the work during the course of its transmission.[2] Unfortunately, we know little of Manzan's sources, but his edition shows considerable differences from the earliest extant version, a manuscript, known as the Monkaku text, that dates from the end of the sixteenth century.[3] Some of the differences undoubtedly reflect Manzan's editorial decisions, but they are sufficiently pronounced to indicate that there were at least two separate textual traditions of the *Eihei kōroku*. It has been suggested that both go back to the time of Dōgen, and that the Monkaku manuscript preserves an early draft of the *Eihei kōroku* subsequently revised—possibly by Dōgen himself—in the "ur-text" of the tradition favored by Manzan.[4] Given the present

---

1. Of the ten fascicles, seven are devoted to a record of Dōgen's formal lectures (*jōdō*) presented at Kōshō ji (*kan* 1), Daibutsu ji (*kan* 2), and Eihei ji (*kan* 3–7); the remaining three rolls preserve his informal teachings (*shōsan* and *hōgo*, *kan* 8), verse appreciations of Ch'an sayings (*juko*, *kan* 9), and poetry (*geju*, *kan* 10). According to the colophons of these fascicles, the first was compiled by Senne (dates unknown), *kan* 2–4 by Ejō, 5–7 by Gien (d. 1314), 8 by Ejō and others, and 9–10 by Senne and others.

2. SSZ.Shūgen,2:43.

3. Also known as the Sosan text, it is named after the twentieth abbot of Eihei ji, Monkaku (d. 1615), who had several of his disciples copy it out from unidentified manuscripts in his possession. The text has been published at DZZ.2:7–200, with textual notes on the variants in the Manzan edition.

4. See Itō Toshimitsu, ed., *Eihei kōroku chūkai zensho*, vol. 1 (1961), 10; Kagamishima Genryū, "Eihei kōroku to Ryakuroku," KDKK 15 (3/1957), 64. Kagamishima has more recently abandoned this position in favor of the view that Dōgen never edited the work, and that the Manzan text has no early precedent; see his "Eihei kōroku kō," *Shūkyō gaku ronshū* 8 (12/1977), 147–60; revised in Kagamishima, *Dōgen zenji to sono shūhen*, Gakujutsu sōsho: Zen bukkyō (1985), 247–365.

state of our knowledge of the *Eihei kōroku*, this suggestion remains rather speculative; and we should not rule out the possibility that the differences between the two extant versions are the result of radical alterations in the texts during the course of their transmission. Indeed it would appear that it is just such an alteration that accounts for the inclusion of the *Fukan zazen gi* in the collection.

Whatever their other differences, both the Monkaku and Manzan versions contain the text of the *Fukan zazen gi* at the end of fascicle 8. On the surface this might seem to lend support to the view that both textual traditions originally included the manual, but, in fact, a closer reading of this fascicle suggests the opposite. For example, commentators have pointed out that the treatise on meditation seems out of place in this section of the *Eihei kōroku*, which is otherwise devoted to Dōgen's informal talks and writings (*shōsan* and *hōgo*), and that there are signs in the texts themselves that the *Fukan zazen gi* may represent a later appendix to the section.[5] Perhaps most telling is the fact that, whereas the two redactions of the *Eihei kōroku* show many textual differences throughout this fascicle, their versions of the *Fukan zazen gi* are identical. This anomaly strongly suggests that the textual history of the manual is different from that of the remainder of the fascicle, and that both redactions are relying on a common separate source for their text of the *Fukan zazen gi*. We know, in fact, that such a source was available, since long before Monkaku and Manzan, the *Fukan zazen gi* had appeared in a little book known as the *Eihei Gen zenji goroku*.

Although the oldest extant manuscripts of the *Eihei kōroku* are fully three and a half centuries after Dōgen's death, the antiquity of some version of his recorded sayings is testified to by the *Eihei Gen zenji goroku*, first published in 1358 by the sixth abbot of Eihei ji, Donki (dates unknown). The origin of this collection, commonly known as the *Ryakuroku*, or "abbreviated record," is explained in a postface to the work, dating from 1264 and written by a Chinese monk named I-yüan (dates unknown), one of the disciples of Dōgen's master, Ju-ching. According to this document, Dōgen's disciple Giin (1217–1300) took a copy of his teacher's "extensive record" to China and asked I-yüan to edit the text. The resulting work amounts to only about one-tenth of the present *Eihei kōroku* and, moreover, shows many textual

---

5. See Ōkubo Dōshū, *Dōgen zenji goroku*, 213–14; ibid., *Dōgen zenji den no kenkyū*, 303–4. Ōkubo notes that, whereas in the Manzan edition, the *Fukan zazen gi* is followed by Dōgen's "Zazen shin," this poem does not appear in the Monkaku manuscript, a fact that suggests to him that the content of *kan* 8 was not fixed, and that the fascicle as we now have it may be the result of accretions to an original core. Itō Toshimitsu has further pointed out that, in the Monkaku manuscript, the words "end of *hōgo*" appear both before and after rhe text of the *Fukan zazen gi*, which suggests to him that *kan* 8 may once have ended with the *hōgo*, and that some copyist, confronted with the appended text of the *Fukan zazen gi*, inadvertently duplicated the words originally intended to signal the end of the fascicle. (*Eihei kōroku chūkai zensho*, vol. 3, p. 196, notes.)

differences from both the Monkaku and Manzan redactions. The reasons for these differences are not clear: some may derive from the Chinese editor himself or from later alterations in the text of the *Eihei kōroku*, but it is also quite possible that I-yüan worked with a collection of Dōgen's recorded sayings different from either of the known traditions. In any case, what is most important for our purposes here is that, immediately following its selection of *hōgo*, the *Ryakuroku* contains a text of the *Fukan zazen gi* identical with the *Kōroku* version.[6]

If, as seems likely, the *Eihei Gen zenji goroku* provided the source for the *Kōroku Fukan zazen gi*, it might well be asked whether the differences between the vulgate text and the Tenpuku manuscript are not the result of I-yüan's editing. In fact, though scholarship once flirted with the question, this is highly improbable. Whatever he may say in his postface, we need not imagine that I-yüan actually spent much effort in the close editing of the sayings of his master's Japanese disciple. Indeed there are probably passages within the *Ryakuroku* version of the *Fukan zazen gi* itself that would hardly have escaped the eye of a conscientious Chinese editor. More importantly, as we shall shortly see, all the major innovations of that version are closely related both in content and phrasing to passages occurring in Dōgen's vernacular *Shōbō genzō*, a work obviously inaccessible to the Chinese. Hence, even if I-yüan did see the *Fukan zazen gi*—and this is by no means certain—there is little call to take seriously the notion that he had a hand in its revision.[7]

The true story of the vulgate *Fukan zazen gi* may never be known. A more precise understanding of its origin and early transmission can be achieved only in the light of a clear textual history of the *Eihei kōroku*. In the absence of a detailed analysis of the various redactions of that work, we cannot say whether such a history can be established. For the present, apparently, we

---

6. The text of the *Eihei Gen zenji goroku* can be found at SSZ.Shūgen,2:27–42. The date of I-yüan's work on the text is inferred from his preface, ibid., 27; for the date of Donki's printing, see ibid., 41. Extant xylographs of the work date only from the mid-seventeenth century, but it is mentioned in medieval sources. Several scholars have noted that Manzan's text of the *Eihei kōroku* is closer to that of the *Ryakuroku* than is the Monkaku manuscript, and it has been suggested that he relied on the abbreviated record in his editing of the work. The possibility that I-yüan's text is based on a collection different from either of the extant traditions has been suggested by Kagamishima Genryū, who points out that the *Ryakuroku* contains five *jōdō* not found in either Monkaku or Manzan. (See his "Eihei kōroku to Ryakuroku," 60.) This possibility is rejected by Itō at *Eihei kōroku chūkai zensho*, vol. 1, p. 12.

7. The possibility that the *Kōroku Fukan zazen gi* was edited by I-yüan was first raised by Ōkubo Dōshū (see *Dōgen zenji goroku*, 223); but, in his later works, he himself abandoned the idea in favor of the view that Dōgen had edited the text himself (see *Dōgen zenji den no kenkyū*, 304). The question of the extent to which I-yüan actually worked over the text of the *Eihei kōroku* is the subject of disagreement. Although his postface says that he was asked by Giin to "edit and correct" (*kōsei*) the work, Menzan suggests that he simply selected passages to form the *Ryakuroku*, without making substantial changes in the text. Kagamishima has pointed out an obvious mistake in I-yüan's text, which suggests that he did not go over the work carefully. (See his "Eihei kōroku to Ryakuroku," 62.)

must restrict ourselves to the following tentative chronology. (1) The vulgate *Fukan zazen gi* was probably composed by Dōgen as an independent treatise. (2) It was probably not originally included in either of the traditions of the *Eihei kōroku* that have come down to us in the Monkaku and Manzan redactions. (3) The vulgate *Fukan zazen gi* was included in the *Eihei Gen zenji goroku* sometime prior to the latter work's publication in 1358, but we cannot say by whom this was done. Given our present knowledge, three possibilities seem most likely: (a) that the *Fukan zazen gi* was included in the collection of Dōgen's sayings used by I-yüan; (b) that it was added to the *Ryakuroku* by Giin; or (c) that it was added by Donki at the time he printed the *Ryakuroku*.[8] (4) Sometime between 1358 and 1598, the *Ryakuroku* text of the *Fukan zazen gi* was appended to the Monkaku (and possibly also the Manzan) tradition of the *Eihei kōroku*.[9] (5) With the publication of Menzan's *Fukan zazen gi monge* in the eighteenth century, the *Fukan zazen gi* was once again separated from the *Eihei kōroku* and circulated as the independent work we know today.

If we are correct in the assumption that the authorship of the vulgate *Fukan zazen gi* is rightly attributed to Dōgen himself, then we can only conclude that he wrote two rather different versions of his manual—one preserved in the Tenpuku manuscript, the other in the *Eihei kōroku*. This conclusion raises the question of the chronological relationship between the two. Unfortunately, the *Kōroku* text is undated, and apparently we cannot say precisely when it was composed. Nevertheless, internal evidence does allow us to narrow down the range of probabilities. First, and most importantly, a comparison of the two texts leaves little doubt that the *Kōroku* version represents a revision of the Tenpuku work and, therefore, must be dated sometime after 1233. Second, we have several dated documents, closely related in content and phrasing to the *Kōroku* text, that give us grounds for placing the *Fukan zazen gi* in the period between 1242 and 1246. The most important of these is the *Shōbō genzō zazen shin*.

In the *Eihei Gen zenji goroku*, the text of the *Fukan zazen gi* is accompanied

---

8. Possibility (a) is not widely defended, but, if we accept the suggestion that I-yüan worked with a text different from either of the extant traditions, it must be given serious consideration. Possibility (b) was the suggestion of Ōkubo, who speculated that Giin might have taken a copy of the Tenpuku *Fukan zazen gi* to China, received I-yüan's corrections, and then included it in the *Ryakuroku* (*Dōgen zenji goroku*, 223); if we dismiss—as Ōkubo himself later did—the likelihood of I-yüan's editing the *Fukan zazen gi*, this view would seem to have little to recommend it. Possibility (c) was proposed early on by the fifteenth-century Rinzai master Unshō Ikkei, in his *Untō shō* (cited in Kagamishima, "Eihei kōroku to Ryakuroku," 57); it is supported by Itō Toshimitsu, at *Eihei kōroku chūkai zensho*, vol. 1, p. 15.

9. Itō (*Eihei kōroku chūkai zensho*, vol. 1, p. 15) assumes that it was Manzan himself that, following the lead of the *Ryakuroku*, added the *Fukan zazen gi* to his version of the *Eihei kōroku*. Since, however, the manual had already found its way into the Monkaku tradition, we ought not rule out the possibility that it was also included in one or more of the texts with which Manzan worked.

by a brief verse entitled "Lancet of Meditation" (*Zazen shin*). This piece is based on a work of the same name by the famed Sung-dynasty Ts'ao-tung figure Hung-chih Cheng-chüeh (1091–1157).[10] Dōgen's verse appears elsewhere in his writings as the conclusion to a discussion of the Chinese original in the *Zazen shin* fascicle of the *Shōbō genzō*. In this essay, as in most of the vernacular *Shōbō genzō*, Dōgen presents his views on Zen in the form of Japanese commentary on several passages from the literature of the school— in this case, passages dealing with the meaning and goal of meditation practice. The commentary treats some of his favorite themes, and what he has to say there represents, along with the *Fukan zazen gi* itself, one of our most important sources for understanding Dōgen's interpretation of *zazen*.

No one familiar with the vulgate *Fukan zazen gi* can read the *Shōbō genzō zazen shin* without immediately noting the close relationship between the two. Moreover, if one then compares these two texts with the Tenpuku manual, he or she can see that the major innovations in the vulgate occur precisely in those passages that most closely parallel the teachings of the *Zazen shin*. Such a comparison has, in fact, been worked out in detail by Akishige Yoshiharu, and there is no need to repeat it here. In brief, his argument begins by isolating five key passages in which the Tenpuku and *Kōroku* texts of the *Fukan zazen gi* differ; he then proceeds to show that in each case the version of the latter is relying on one of the five major sections into which the *Zazen shin* can be divided. From this, he concludes that the *Kōroku* manual represents a revision based on the *Shōbō genzō* commentary.[11]

Akishige's argument was originally intended to refute the notion that the vulgate *Fukan zazen gi* might have been the result of I-yüan's editing. While we may not wish to accept all the details of his argument, he has surely made his point—although he has not quite shown that it was Dōgen himself who used the *Zazen shin* to edit the *Fukan zazen gi*. In any case he has given us a *terminus a quo* for the *Kōroku* text, since we know that the *Zazen shin* fascicle was composed in April 1242 and subsequently presented as a lecture (*jishu*) in the winter of the following year.[12] Akishige himself suggests

---

10. The "Zazen shin" verse (SSZ.Shūgen,2:39b) seems even more out of place than the *Fukan zazen gi* in kan 8 of the *Eihei kōroku*; as we have noted, it is not found in the Monkaku redaction, and it may well be that, like the meditation manual, it was not included in the original compilation of Dōgen's sayings. Hung-chih's "Tso-ch'an chen" is preserved in fascicle 8 (on poetry) of his *Kuang lu* (T.48:98a–b).

11. "Fukan zazen gi kō," 459–80. This article, published more than thirty years ago, deserves more attention than it seems to have received. Its basic argument has since been repeated—without reference to (and with considerably less elegance than) Akishige's work—in Kinoshita Jun'ichi, "Fukan zazen gi no kenkyū," SK 7 (4/1965), 132–37; and in Furuta Shōkin, *Nihon bukkyō shisō shi no sho mondai* (1964), 137–44.

12. The former date appears in the body of the text itself (DZZ.1:100); the latter (appearing in the colophon at DZZ.1:101) does not seem to be found in manuscripts prior to the Edo.

the latter date as the more likely one for the *Fukan zazen gi*. He does so on the basis of the *Shōbō genzō zazen gi*, another of Dōgen's meditation texts, which is usually dated around the end of 1243.

The *Shōbō genzō zazen gi* is a brief manual in Japanese. No doubt originally written, like the more famous *Fukan zazen gi*, as an independent work, it came at some point to be included with Dōgen's other vernacular writings in the *Shōbō genzō* collection. The text represents a reworking of the central section of the *Fukan zazen gi*, which deals with the actual technique of meditation. Thus it omits the lengthy and elegant discussion of the meaning of Zen training that occupies such a prominent place in the *kanbun* work; at the same time it adds several concrete details on the preparation for, and procedures of, *zazen*. What is important to note here is that the many passages that do parallel the *Fukan zazen gi* are much closer to the *Kōroku* version than to the Tenpuku manuscript. Indeed so exact is the correspondence in certain crucial phrases that there can be no doubt that one of the texts is relying on the other.[13]

On the basis of the close relationship between these two documents, Akishige concludes his discussion of the composition of the *Kōroku* manual by suggesting that Dōgen edited the *Fukan zazen gi* "around the time" that he wrote his Japanese version. In the end prudence may dictate that we content ourselves with this somewhat vague suggestion; yet we cannot but wish for some solution to the question of the relative chronology of these two documents. If it can be established that the Japanese *zazen gi* is derived from the *Kōroku* text, this would finally lay to rest any lingering doubts regarding Dōgen's authorship of the vulgate *Fukan zazen gi*. And, in fact, there does seem to be some internal evidence to suggest that the Japanese text was written with reference to the *Kōroku* manual, not vice versa.

We have seen that the *Kōroku Fukan zazen gi* and *Shōbō genzō zazen gi* share certain key passages not contained in the Tenpuku manuscript. In some of them, the Japanese coincides exactly with the Chinese text; in others, however, the two versions diverge. Careful comparison of these latter cases leaves one with the distinct impression that in each case the vernacular version represents a refinement of the passage in question. Moreover, there are also cases in which the Japanese *zazen gi* has modified passages shared by the two versions of the *Fukan zazen gi*. Both these features suggest that the *Shōbō genzō* text is more distant from the Tenpuku original and represents an elaboration of the revisions made in that original by the *Kōroku* manual.

---

13. The conscientious reader may wish to consult here the comparative table of texts appended in Document 2. Note especially the following important innovations in FKZZG (B) that have parallels in the Japanese manual: "Do not intend to make a Buddha, much less be attached to sitting." "Sitting fixedly, think of not thinking. How do you think of not thinking? Nonthinking." "*Zazen* is not the practice of *dhyāna*."

This would imply, of course, that the *Kōroku Fukan zazen gi* preceded the Japanese work and would allow us to place its composition sometime between the *Zazen shin* and the *Shōbō genzō zazen gi*.[14]

Let me hasten to admit that this argument for the relative dates of the two manuals is quite subjective. The passages in question are few, and their evaluation is complicated by the fact that they were written in different languages. I must finally leave it to the reader to examine the texts for himself or herself and decide whether the evidence justifies the conclusion. Whether or not it does, it should be pointed out, before we leave this matter of dates, that there still remains some doubt about the absolute date of the vulgate *Fukan zazen gi*. While Akishige follows the accepted practice of assigning the *Shōbō genzō zazen gi* to the end of 1243, there is some early manuscript evidence to indicate that it was composed—or perhaps revised —as late as 1245 or 1246. Unless we choose to dismiss this evidence, we shall have to extend our *terminus ad quem* for the *Fukan zazen gi* and be content to date its composition sometime in the period 1242–46.[15]

Aside from its obvious importance for establishing the authenticity of the work, the question of the date of the vulgate *Fukan zazen gi* is more interesting than it might at first appear; the period in which the manual seems to have been composed was the most volatile and dramatic of Dōgen's career—a time that witnessed a severe crisis in his ministry and a considerable revolution in his teaching. To understand the new historical and intellectual circumstances surrounding his revision of the *Fukan zazen gi*, we need to go back and briefly review the developments that had taken place in the decade or so since the composition of the original Tenpuku text.

If Dōgen's ministry was still in its infancy in 1233, it was not long before his Zen community at Kōshō ji began to develop. We have seen that even in these early days he had some significant lay support. In 1235, he was able to launch a successful campaign for major construction at his monastery, and, in the following year, he held the formal opening of what was then the only fully independent Zen institution in the country. Already by this time he had attracted the man who would become his leading disciple and *dharma*

---

14. As examples of the innovations in the Japanese manual, note especially the introduction of such "Dōgenesque" locutions as the following: "Good is not thought of; evil is not thought of. It is not mind, intellect or consciousness; it is not thoughts, ideas or perceptions." "Cast off sitting." "Having thus regulated body and mind...." "[*Zazen*] is the undefiled practice and verification."

15. According to the colophon of the *Zazen gi* manuscript in the 75-*kan* Kenkon in *Shōbō genzō* collection, the work was "presented to the assembly" (*jishu*) in the eleventh month of 1243 at Yoshimine shōja in Echizen (*Eihei Shōbō genzō shūsho taisei*, vol. 1 [1975], 146). Surprisingly, the 60-*kan* Dōun ji *Shōbō genzō*, which ordinarily supplies very good information on the date and place of composition, lacks this colophon (ibid., vol. 6 [1979], 98); and both the 83-*kan* Rurikō ji and 75-*kan* Kōun ji redactions associate the *Zazen gi* with Daibutsu ji, the monastery to which Dōgen moved after his stay at Yoshimine (ibid., vol. 3 [1978], 57; vol. 5 [1978], 514). Dōgen's Daibutsu ji period covered two years, from the autumn of 1244 to the summer of 1246.

heir, Koun Ejō. This former Tendai monk had previously studied Zen under a certain Butchi Kakuan (dates unknown), a disciple of the pioneering Japanese Zen figure Dainichibō Nōnin (dates unknown). Ejō seems to have entered Kōshō ji in 1234, and within a few years he became head monk (*shuso*) of the monastery. In 1241, he was joined by another of Kakuan's students, Ekan (d. 1251?), who brought with him quite a number of his own disciples. By this time, then, Dōgen was the master of a sizable group of Zen monks and the abbot of an established Zen monastery. During 1242–43, he was being invited to the Rokuhara district of the capital to give lectures at the residence of his lay supporter, the influential *bakufu* figure Hatano Yoshishige.[16]

Dōgen's success was not without its costs, however, since it brought him to the attention of the Buddhist establishment, and he soon found himself embroiled in a dispute with the Tendai headquarters on Mt. Hiei. Exactly what caused the trouble, we do not know. Perhaps, given the climate of the times, trouble was inevitable for anyone who, like Dōgen, sought to strike out on his own without compromising with the establishment or winning the protection of the government. But Dōgen's problems may have been exacerbated by the company he kept; for his most prominent disciples—Ejō and the other descendants of Dainichibō Nōnin—belonged to a lineage of Buddhist outcasts, whose version of Rinzai Zen had once been proscribed by the court and rejected by Yōsai, and whose teachers had been hounded by the ecclesiastical establishment in both Heian and Nara.[17]

While Dōgen was thus engaged in a struggle with Tendai, he soon faced another challenge from within the Zen movement itself. Hard by the site of his monastery in Fukakusa, the powerful minister Kujō Michiie began the

---

16. See the colophons of *Shōbō genzō zenki*, DZZ.1:205; *Shōbō genzō toki*, DZZ.1:209; *Shōbō genzō kobusshin*, DZZ.1:81. The absorption of the disciples of Kakuan and Ekan—Gikai (1219–1309), Giin, Gien, Gijun (dates unknown), and others—clearly had a major impact on the development of Dōgen's movement: Ejō, of course, was to become the leader of the movement after Dōgen's death; and Gikai and Gien, both of whom succeeded him in this role, were to father the two major branches of the Sōtō church.

17. Nōnin's teaching was proscribed by the court in 1194, in response to a petition from the Tendai headquarters on Mt. Hiei. His contemporary Yōsai, who was himself under pressure from Tendai, was careful to distinguish his own brand of Zen from what was apparently seen as an antinomian tendency in Nōnin's approach to Buddhism. Whether or not the tradition is true that the latter was assassinated by his relative Taira no Kagekiyo, we do know that his followers continued to suffer persecution. In 1227 and 1228, Kakuan's center at Tōnomine, in Yamato, was destroyed by the monks of Kōfuku ji, and his disciple Ekan was forced to take refuge in Echizen. Nōnin's tradition, often now known as the Japanese Bodhidharma school (Nihon Daruma shū), though largely ignored in many standard histories of Japanese Zen Buddhism, has recently become the focus of much attention. Its impact on Dōgen's ministry and the early Sōtō church was originally emphasized by Ōkubo (*Dōgen zenji den no kenkyū*, 406–46) and has since been taken up by Imaeda Aishin, Furuta Shōkin, Yanagida Seizan, and quite a few others. For a helpful survey of some of the burgeoning literature on the school, together with a discussion of several issues in its interpretation, see Nakao Ryōshin, "Dainichibō Nōnin no zen," SK 26 (3/1984), 221–35.

construction of a great Zen monastic complex. Called the Tōfuku ji, it was intended to rival the ancient Nara institutions of Tōdai ji and Kōfuku ji from which it took its name. The complex, which was constructed along the lines of the famous Ch'an monasteries of the Southern Sung, was to serve as the centerpiece of the new Zen religion in the capital. But Dōgen, the abbot of neighboring Kōshō ji, was not invited to head this major monastery; instead Michiie chose the Rinzai monk Enni (1202–80), who had only just returned from study in China.[18]

These two pressures reached their climax in the years 1242–43, during which Dōgen was compelled to defend his Buddhism in a formal apologia to the throne, and his Zen rival, Enni, arrived in the capital to take up his duties as founding abbot of Tōfuku ji. Perhaps partly for this reason, in the summer of 1243, Dōgen suddenly abandoned Kōshō ji and the Japanese capital and led his followers into the isolated and mountainous province of Echizen, along the coast of the Japan Sea. It was just over a decade since he had walked out of Kennin ji to become an independent Zen master, and he was now on the move again.[19]

During his first year in Echizen the erstwhile abbot of Kōshō ji had no monastery to call his own. The colophons of his works from this period indicate that Dōgen spent his time commuting between two local, and probably rather obscure, temples known as Yoshimine shōja and Yamashi bu. But by March of 1244, even as the deep snows of Hokuriku were melting away, he had already begun work on a new establishment, which would be called the "Temple of the Great Buddha" (Daibutsu ji). In August, though it would yet be many months before the major buildings were completed, he took up residence as founding abbot. One year later, in July of 1246, Dōgen decided to change the name of his monastery to Eihei ji, after the Yung-p'ing era of the Han, during which Buddhism was said to have been introduced to China.[20]

Dōgen's remaining years were spent almost wholly within the bosom of

18. The impact of Tōfuku ji on Dōgen's mission has been emphasized by Furuta Shōkin, in *Nihon bukkyō shisō shi no sho mondai*, 145–60; I have summarized his views in my "Recarving the Dragon."

19. The evidence for Dōgen's apologia comes from the *Keiran shūyō shū*, which informs us that, during the reign of Gosaga (1242–46), Dōgen defended his views in a petition to the throne entitled "Gokoku shōbō gi." The official assigned to the case decided that these views were heretical, and the petition was denied. (T.76:539c–540a; the text is quoted and discussed in Ōkubo, *Dōgen zenji den no kenkyū*, 191–96.) According to the *Kenzei ki* (SSZ.Shiden,2:23), Dōgen left Kōshō ji for Echizen on the sixteenth of the seventh month (August 3), a date verified by the colophons of his works from this period (see DZZ.1:336, 357). Several factors may have been involved in his choice of Echizen: it was the domain of his lay patron Hatano Yoshishige; it was Ekan's base and the center of the Nihon Daruma school; and, as Imaeda Aishin has emphasized, it was the territory of the Hakusan Tendai order, centered at Heisen ji, which may have offered some refuge from the power of the Hiei zan order (see Imaeda's *Dōgen: Zazen hitosuji no shamon* [1976], 146–47).

20. For these dates, see *Kenzei ki*, SSZ.Shiden,2:24–25. Yoshimine dera (also known as Kippō ji) and Yamashi bu are thought to have been located several miles east of the later site

his community at Eihei ji, far from the centers of political power and religious culture. Except for a final journey to Heian, he seems to have descended from the mountains only once—for a brief visit to Kamakura in 1247–48. According to traditional accounts, he went at the invitation of the shōgun Tokiyori, on whom he bestowed the *bodhisattva* precepts and by whom he was asked to found a temple in the city. Why Dōgen undertook this trip, we do not know. We do know that, if he had political ambitions in the new *bakufu* headquarters, they remained unfulfilled; after only a few months he was back at Eihei ji, where he would remain until his final days, when failing health drove him to seek medical aid in the capital. He died there shortly after his arrival.[21]

Over this period Dōgen's literary activities have a distinct rhythm that closely follows the historical developments. In the early years of his ministry, years devoted to establishing himself as a teacher, he wrote several tracts on Zen that—like the Tenpuku *Fukan zazen gi*—sought to introduce the new religion to the Japanese Buddhist community, to argue for the supereminence of its historical tradition and spiritual benefits, and to urge the adoption of its approach to the cultivation of the mind. Once he had established himself, rather different kinds of writing began to appear. Following the dedication of Kōshō ji in 1236, his attention seems to have turned first to the regulation of his growing community; over the next three years, he composed a series of pieces—like his well-known *Tenzo kyōkun*, on the practice of the monastery cook—that dealt with monastic ritual and routine.[22] Then, beginning in 1240–41, he entered into a radically new—and by far his most important and productive—phase of work.

In 1235, Dōgen seems to have put together a collection of three hundred

---

of Eihei ji. (For a convenient map of the area, see Imaeda, *Dōgen: Zazen hitosuji no shamon*, 147.) Their origin and history are unknown, but apparently they were already established when Dōgen arrived. The exact location of Daibutsu ji is uncertain. According to tradition, it was situated several miles from the present site of Eihei ji, to which it was moved by the fifth abbot, Giun. (The question is discussed at Ōkubo, *Dōgen zenji den no kenkyū*, 217–22; and Shibata Dōken, *Zenji Dōgen no shisō*, 302–7.)

21. Dōgen's Kamakura trip is one of the most problematic elements in his biography. It is reported first in the fifteenth-century *Kenzei ki* (SSZ.Shiden,2:27a) and gets no mention in the *Azuma kagami* or other earlier historical sources, but it seems to be substantiated by several references in the *Eihei kōroku*. Speculation on Dōgen's motives for the trip have varied widely—from the fanciful notion that he sought the restoration of imperial rule, through more obvious suggestions that he went at the bidding of his *bakufu* patron, Yoshishige, or of family members in Kamakura, to the recent playful piece by Yanagida Seizan, which begins by imagining that Dōgen had a love affair with Tokiyori's wife and ends by dismissing the entire tradition of his trip as itself a product of the pious imagination of Dōgen's descendants. (See Yanagida's *Chūsei hyōhaku* [1981], 59–98. For a balanced discussion of the trip and its significance, see Notomi Jōten, "Dōgen no Kamakura kyōke ni tsuite," KDBGKK 31 [3/1973], 181–203; reprinted in Kawamura and Ishikawa, *Dōgen*, 276–308.)

22. DZZ.2:295–303. Also from this period are the *Shukke ryaku sahō* (DZZ.2:272–78), on the ordination ceremony; the *Jūundō shiki* (DZZ.2:304–7), on the rules of the monks' hall; and the *Shōbō genzō senmen* (DZZ.1:424–45) and *Senjō* (466–74), on the procedures for the monks' ablutions and use of the lavatory (*tōsu*).

Zen stories—"old cases" (*kosoku*) culled from the Chinese literature of the school. The practice of making such collections was, of course, a common one among Sung Ch'an authors, who used them as an opportunity to offer their own interpretations and appreciations of the wisdom of the elders. Indeed the fact that Dōgen styled his effort "*Shōbō genzō*" suggests that he had as his model a similar compilation of the same title by the most famous of Sung masters, Ta-hui Tsung-kao. Unlike the latter, Dōgen was content here simply to record the stories without interjecting his own remarks. A few years later, however, he embarked on a major project to develop extended commentaries on many of these and other passages from the Ch'an literature. The fruit of this project was his masterwork—the remarkable collection of essays known as the *kana*, or "vernacular," *Shōbō genzō*.[23]

It is difficult to exaggerate the literary and religious achievements of the *Shōbō genzō* essays. To be sure, they are of decidedly mixed quality. At their best, though, they rank with the best of Buddhist writing, and even at their worst, they represent a highly original form of Japanese religious literature. Though they vary somewhat in format (and indeed a number of the pieces in some redactions are clearly anomalous), the representative texts are obviously inspired by the Chinese Ch'an commentarial literature. As far as we know, Dōgen was the first of his country to enter deeply into this arcane literature and try his own hand at this difficult, highly specialized form of writing. Yet Dōgen was no slavish imitator of Sung letters. Unlike most of his contemporaries, who continued to depend on the language of the Middle Kingdom for saying things important, he opted to evoke the religious style of the Ch'an masters through the more intimate medium of his native tongue. The result is a unique form of Zen writing—a rich (and often

---

23. For Ta-hui's *Cheng-fa yen-tsang*, see ZZ.2,23:1–78. For Dōgen's *kōan* collection, popularly known as *Shōbō genzō sanbyaku soku*, see DZZ.2:201–52. The 1235 date of compilation is provided by the colophon of a preface purportedly by Dōgen himself. Opinion is divided on the question of whether the work was done simply as a reference for Dōgen's personal use or as a textbook for his students, but Kawamura Kōdō, the leading scholar of the work, has speculated from the characteristics of the two major textual traditions that Dōgen made redactions for both purposes. ("Kanazawa bunko shozō Shōbō genzō kanken," *Kanazawa bunko kenkyū* 17, 11 [11/1971], 1–9; 17, 12 [12/1971], 10–16; repr. in Kawamura and Ishikawa, *Dōgen zenji to Sōtō shū*, 54–74. For a discussion and comparative table of the extant manuscripts of the text, see the same author's "Mana Shōbō genzō no kenkyū," KDBGKK 30 [3/1972], 135–59; 31 [3/1973], 95–138; 33 [3/1975], 41–96; 34 [3/1976], 64–98. Ishii Shūdō has provided a detailed chart of the sources for Dōgen's old cases in "Mana Shōbō genzō no motozuku shiryō ni tsuite," SKKKK 3 [10/1974], 51–84.)

Although the modern 95-*kan* redaction of the vernacular *Shōbō genzō* incorporates almost all Dōgen's Japanese writings, including such early pieces as the *Bendō wa* and *Genjō kōan*, it is by no means clear how many of these works were originally intended as part of a single collection. There is evidence that Dōgen once envisioned such a collection, to consist of one hundred fascicles; but the same evidence indicates that he took up this project only toward the very end of his life, and that it was never brought to fulfillment. (See Ejō's postface to the *Shōbō genzō hachi dainin gaku*, DZZ.1:726.) What is clear, from the dates of the *Shōbō genzō* texts, is that it was around 1240 that Dōgen began to work in earnest in this new genre of vernacular commentary.

linguistically playful) mix of Chinese and Japanese, spun out in extended essays that draw on all, but have no exact precedent in any, of the standard genres of Ch'an commentary, lecture, poetry, and preaching. The style soars and dips: at times, it is clearly intended only for Dōgen's immediate audience and is filled with personal anecdote and practical admonition; at other times, it is just as clearly written for posterity and is carefully crafted and self-consciously elegant. The total effect is a striking example of the vital tension—seemingly so characteristic of Zen—between the immediate, raw power of the man and the timeless, pristine wisdom of the Buddha.

This tension seems lost on some of those modern interpreters who would read the *Shōbō genzō* simply as a treatise on metaphysics. Of course, much material in these texts can lend itself to formulation as universal philosophy, but it often requires truly heroic acts of abstraction to isolate such material and lift it from all that speaks directly only to Dōgen's immediate community (and perhaps to those of later generations who would count themselves among his spiritual descendants). Indeed, as in so much Zen literature, the *Shōbō genzō* has a strongly esoteric cast. This is not to say that the essays were intended to be secret (though they were, in fact, sometimes treated as such by subsequent tradition); rather, they tend to be technical—directed toward, and probably fully accessible only to, those steeped in the language, lore, and practice of Zen. This quality is probably latent in the very medium of the *kōan* commentary that is the primary purpose of the bulk of the *Shōbō genzō* essays, and it is clearly manifest in some of the particular religious themes developed there.

In Zen usage the "treasury of the eye of the true *dharma*" (*shōbō genzō*) may connote a timeless truth realized by all the Buddhas and Patriarchs, but it also denotes the esoteric knowledge historically transmitted only among the Buddhas and Patriarchs. If Dōgen's own *Treasury* brims with the universal wisdom of Buddhahood, it also bristles with his insistence on the historical limits of the Patriarchate. Already in his early writing, Dōgen had used the familiar Zen notion of the historical transmission to argue for the orthodoxy of the new school of Buddhism he was importing from China. But in his *Shōbō genzō*, this broader argument tends now to be taken for granted, and his vision narrows to the question of which among the various living lineages of the school actually preserves the transmission of the Patriarchs. Thus, as we have already seen, he comes to rediscover the historical significance of his master, Ju-ching, and through him, the ancestry of his Ts'ao-tung house.

The new emphasis on Ju-ching and the orthodoxy of Sōtō Zen in many of the *Shōbō genzō* essays may well be connected with some of the historical circumstances that occasioned their composition. Whether or not Dōgen's earlier *Shōbō genzō kōan* collection was prompted in part by the arrival of his new student, Ejō, it is probably no accident that he began serious work on his *kōan* commentaries just at the time that he adopted, en masse, Ejō's fellow descendants of Dainichibō Nōnin. As students of the Bodhidharma school, these men were experienced confederates in Zen, who offered Dōgen a new opportunity to exploit the technical literature of the tradition. But as members of a school that looked back to the Yang-ch'i house of Lin-chi, they were followers of Ta-hui's Zen, who presented Dōgen with the new challenge of pitting his understanding of the literature against the most famous master of the *kōan* and author of the original *Shōbō genzō*. And, if today Dōgen's understanding seems to stand on its own merits, within his own religious context, it could only be bolstered by a demonstration of its historical link to the orthodox transmission of the true *dharma*.[24]

In any case, in a number of the essays of the *Shōbō genzō*, and especially in those that date from the period around the time that Dōgen led his band of new disciples into the mountains of Echizen, alongside the bursts of poetic and philosophic genius there is a preoccupation with matters of orthodox lineage and esoteric transmission. In the midst of the exalted discourse on the ultimate enlightenment of all beings and the universal pervasion of the *buddha-dharma*, there are shrill attacks on the Lin-chi house—on its founder, on Ta-hui, and on his followers in contemporary China—and there are startling claims that the Ts'ao-tung lineage of Ju-ching represents the sole legitimate spiritual tradition.[25]

---

24. Although Nōnin himself never made the pilgrimage to the Southern Sung, he did send two disciples to the continent to request a certificate of succession from the abbot of A-yü wang, Fo-chao Te-kuang, a direct disciple of Ta-hui Tsung-kao. It is, perhaps, more than a coincidence that, in his *Shōbō genzō*, Dōgen rejects the possibility of such an indirect transmission of the *dharma* (*Menju*, DZZ.1:451–53) and contrasts the sincerity of his own master, Ju-ching, with the hypocrisy and ambition of Te-kuang (*Gyōji*, DZZ.1:158). That Dōgen's Daruma school disciples retained a strong sense of their original tradition is suggested by the fact that, despite his efforts to convert them, some continued for several generations following his death to identify themselves with the lineage of Ta-hui. For a discussion of the delicate relations of this lineage, and especially its "Fourth Patriarch," Gikai, to Dōgen's Sōtō school, see Tsugunaga Yoshiteru, "Nihon Sōtō shū ni okeru Dainichi Nōnin no Daruma shū no shōchō," *Shoryōbu kiyō* 18 (11/1966), 31–42; recently reprinted in Kawamura and Ishikawa, *Dōgen*, 346–64.

The question of the extent to which the religion of the Daruma school actually reflected the *kanna* practice of its Sung lineage is the subject of some disagreement. Several scholars have emphasized the Yang-ch'i heritage of the school and used it to explain Dōgen's own treatment of the Sung Ch'an literature; but recently published original documents of the school seem to indicate that it was little influenced by developments in the Southern Sung and relied rather on the earlier style of the T'ang. (See especially the *Kenshō jōbutsu ron* and *Jōtō shōkaku ron*, published in *Kanazawa bunko shiryō zensho*, vol. 1 [1974], 173–98, 199–206; and Ishii Shūdō's seminal study, "Busshō Tokkō to Nihon Daruma shū," *Kanazawa bunko kenkyū* 20, 11 [11/1974], 1–16; 12 [12/1974], 1–20. For the school's use of the collection of classical texts known as the "Three Treatises of the Great Master Bodhidharma" [*Daruma daishi sanron*], see Shiina Kōyū, "Shōshitsu rokumon to Daruma daishi sanron," KDBGR 9 [11/1978], 208–32. Most of the known sources on the school have been brought together in Takahashi Shū'ei, "Dainichibō Nōnin to Daruma shū ni kansuru shiryō," *Kanazawa bunko kenkyū* 22, 4 [6/1976], 14–16; 22, 7–23, 1 [12/1976–1/1977], 23–33.)

25. For an account of Dōgen's anti-Lin-chi polemic, together with some recent interpretations, see my "Recarving the Dragon."

During the years 1240–43, Dōgen seems to have devoted himself to his work on the *Shōbō genzō* essays with ever-increasing intensity.[26] The *Zazen shin* essay, composed in 1242 and apparently reworked in the following year at Yoshimine, stands at the very center of this period and well represents both the style and some of the themes of Dōgen's writing at the time—both the highly insightful, artistically fashioned commentary on the ancient Chinese Ch'an sayings and the sharp polemics against the contemporary Chinese Ch'an scene. In contrast, our other *Shōbō genzō* text, the *Zazen gi*, is one of those that seems out of place in this collection. It does not draw on the Ch'an literature but merely recasts, as we have seen, Dōgen's own writings; and it does not engage in any of the philosophical or historical discussion characteristic of the other essays. Indeed, though it is usually treated simply as a Japanese abbreviation of Dōgen's *kanbun* meditation text, its omission of all the theoretical discussion in this work and its exclusive concern with the description of *zazen* give it a character rather different even from the *Fukan zazen gi*. To put it plainly, it is a simple ritual manual; in this, it seems to point us toward the final phase of Dōgen's writing.

The gradual introversion of Dōgen's vision of the *Shōbō genzō* reached its climax in the period just following his withdrawal to Echizen. From this time he becomes increasingly focussed on the immediate community of monks that was to embody the transmission of the true *dharma*. Whereas in his early writings he had emphasized the universality of Zen and encouraged its practice by all, as he watched the construction begin on his mountain Temple of the Great Buddha, he was convinced that Zen lived only within the halls, and through the traditional forms, of the monastery. Preoccupied, no doubt, with preparations for the opening of the Temple, he broke off work on his vernacular commentaries; though he later returned to add several more commentaries, his interest had by now clearly shifted from *kōan* to cultus and from the wisdom of the masters to the rituals of the monk.[27]

The new interest in the forms of the monastic discipline is reflected not only in the late vernacular essays of the *Shōbō genzō* but in a new kind of text that represents the most important work of Dōgen's last years. In the spring of 1244, in preparation for the opening of Daibutsu ji, he composed a formal

26. Of the approximately ninety texts included in the various early redactions of the *Shōbō genzō*, only a handful were composed prior to 1240. In that year Dōgen wrote seven; in 1241, eleven; in 1242, sixteen; and in 1243, twenty-three. (For a convenient chronological table of the texts, see *Gendai yaku Shōbō genzō*, ed. by Zen Bunka Gakuin [1968], 224–25.)

27. In the first three months of 1244, Dōgen produced over a dozen *Shōbō genzō* essays. Thereafter, for the space of a full year, we see none at all; and, for the subsequent years until his death in 1253, we have only a handful of dated texts (though it is generally assumed that many of the undated pieces in the 12-*kan* redaction of the *Shōbō genzō* were produced during this time). The majority of these late essays are taken up with the forms and the spirit of monastic practice. For Dōgen's rejection of lay Buddhism, see especially *Shōbō genzō sanjūshichi hon bodai bunpō* (DZZ.1:511–13), composed in the third month of 1244, one week after the groundbreaking of the *dharma* hall of the Daibutsu ji.

kanbun document laying out for his monks sixty-two rules for proper decorum in dealings with superiors—rules that he called "the body and mind of the Buddhas and Patriarchs" and "the ultimate purport of the Great Vehicle."[28] Over the following few years, at Daibutsu ji and Eihei ji, he produced a series of similar works of monastic regulation—on the offices of the monastery, the rituals of eating, the rules and procedures of the kitchen, the common hall, the monks' hall, and so on. Taken together, these works represent the first Japanese Zen monastic code; and in fact most of them were later collected by the Sōtō school in the regulations now known as "The Eihei Code" (*Eihei shingi*).[29]

Of these new *kanbun* pieces on rule and ritual, the most important—both for the Sōtō school and for our purposes here—is undoubtedly the *Bendō hō*. This work on the practices of the meditation hall dates from Dōgen's Daibutsu ji period—possibly from the first half of 1245, when we know that the monks began to use the new *sōdō* of the monastery. Here we find detailed instructions on how the monks are to sit, sleep, move about in the hall, care for their robes and bedding, wash themselves, brush their teeth, and so on. Toward the end of these instructions is a section briefly describing the method of *zazen*.[30]

The discussion of meditation in the *Bendō hō* has much in common with that of the *Shōbō genzō zazen gi*. Like the Japanese manual, it is closely related to the central portion of the *Kōroku Fukan zazen gi* and includes material developed in the *Zazen shin*. Also like the *Shōbō genzō* manual, it contains passages not found in either version of the *Fukan zazen gi*. While some of these passages have no precedent in Dōgen's other descriptions of meditation, a few seem to correspond to innovations in the Japanese text. We have already seen that, although this latter is usually dated slightly earlier, some manuscript traditions assign it, like the *Bendō hō*, to the Daibutsu ji period; it may have been written (or revised) as an amplification of Dōgen's work on the rituals of the meditation hall.

One other feature of the *Bendō hō* throws some interesting light on all

28. *Tai taiko goge jari hō*, DZZ.2:308–12.

29. This collection was brought together by the thirtieth abbot of Eihei ji, Kōshō Chidō (d. 1670), and first published in 1667 under the title *Nichiiki Sōtō shoso Dōgen zenji shingi*. The current edition is based on a version brought out in 1794 by Gentō Sokuchū (1729–1807). In addition to the *Tai taiko goge jari hō*, it includes the *Tenzo kyōkun* (composed while Dōgen was still at Kōshō ji), the *Bendō hō* (described later), and three works from Dōgen's Eihei ji period: *Chiji shingi* (DZZ.2:320–46), from 1246; *Shuryō shingi* (DZZ.2:363–66), from 1249; and *Fu shukuhan pō* (DZZ.2:248–57), the date of which is unrecorded. (For a discussion of these texts, see Ōkubo, *Dōgen zenji shingi*, Iwanami bunko 2896–98 [1941], 271–85.)

30. DZZ.2:317–18. Like most of the works in the *Eihei shingi*, we have no early manuscripts of the *Bendō hō*; the Edo printings identify the place of composition as Daibutsu ji but, unfortunately, do not provide us with a date. For the suggested date of 1245, see Ōkubo, *Dōgen zenji den no kenkyū*, 342. We may note that the *Shōbō genzō ango*, which gives instructions on the procedures for the summer meditation retreat, was also composed during this period, on the thirteenth of the sixth month.

of Dōgen's later works on meditation. We have noted that the *zazen gi* embedded in this text includes several passages not found in any of the other manuals. Interestingly enough, some of them suggest the phrasing of Tsung-tse's *Tso-ch'an i*.[31] Readers may be excused if they find it a bit odd that in 1245 Dōgen was still referring to Tsung-tse's description of meditation in writing his own. After all, we know that the *Fukan zazen gi* was written, in part, to improve on the *Tso-ch'an i*, and that Dōgen explicitly rejected the Chinese work in his "Senjutsu yurai." From another perspective, however, Tsung-tse's possible influence on the *Bendō hō* is not so surprising. His manual was part of the *Ch'an-yüan ch'ing-kuei*, the standard monastic code in Dōgen's day. It was, of course, precisely such a code that Dōgen himself was engaged in creating through the *Bendō hō* and other works from this period; despite his dissatisfaction with its section on meditation, the *Ch'an-yüan ch'ing-kuei* remained his primary textual source for the correct organization and operation of the Zen monastery. Thus we know that he was regularly referring to Tsung-tse at the time that he wrote his description of *sōdō* practices, and it is by no means improbable that he should have reread the *Tso-ch'an i* for his account of *zazen*.[32]

This, then, is the context within which Dōgen produced the vulgate version of his *Fukan zazen gi*. Exactly where it falls chronologically and why Dōgen decided to revise his original version, we do not know. Since in some ways the refounding of his mission in Echizen was a recapitulation of the circumstances at Kōshō ji that had occasioned the Tenpuku manual, perhaps it is not surprising that he should have returned to that manual now in order to bring it up to date. If we see his subsequent Kamakura episode as an indication that, despite his decision to withdraw from the capital, he continued to seek wider dissemination of, or at least support for, this mission, we can speculate that—like other Zen manuals from Dōgen's day—the ultimate audience for the *Fukan zazen gi* still resided beyond the mountains in the Heian and Kamakura halls of power, perhaps in the halls of the shōgunate itself. In any case, whatever the exact date of, and historical occasion for, the work, the text reflects the new technical language of the *Shōbō genzō* commentaries and their reevaluation of Zen, and (despite its retention of the original title, "Universal Promotion of the Principles of Meditation"), it was written at a time when Dōgen was turning in toward

---

31. Note especially that for some reason Dōgen has here reverted to Tsung-tse's order of presentation in his description of the semi-cross-legged posture and the positioning of the hands, and that he has reintroduced variants of the latter's instructions on maintaining a straight spine and relaxing the abdomen.

32. Dōgen often cites the *Ch'an-yüan ch'ing-kuei* by name in the texts of the *Eihei shingi* and in the *Ango* and other essays of the *Shōbō genzō* from this period. A partial list of these citations can be found in Kagamishima Genryū, *Dōgen zenji to inyō kyōten goroku no kenkyū* (1965), 262–63. On the relationship between the *Ch'an-yüan ch'ing-kuei* and Dōgen's code, see Nishio Kenryū, "Sōdai Nitchū bukkyō kōryū shi," *Bukkyō shigaku kenkyū* 19, 1 (1/1977), 1–32.

his monastic community and focussing more narrowly on the preservation of the pristine form of the orthodox tradition. Probably both these new religious elements—the wisdom of the *kōan* literature and the ritual of the monastic tradition—played a part in the revision. I shall come back to them both when I take up the content of Dōgen's meditation teachings; first, though, to give us a broader perspective on the historical and intellectual place of these teachings, I want to explore something of their Chinese background and especially the Chinese manual that was the original model for all Dōgen's meditation texts.

Part II

Sources

3

Ch'ang-lu Tsung-tse and
the New Meditation Literature

In the preceding chapters I have sketched some of the historical setting for Dōgen's meditation teachings. Within such a setting the role of his Chinese master—and, indeed, of his Chinese experience in general—in the formation of these teachings becomes rather less clear than is usually maintained. In part, no doubt, this blurring of what we might call spiritual causality follows inevitably from the nature of the historical perspective taken; but a similar phenomenon seems to occur when we shift that perspective slightly from Dōgen's biography to the textual background of his meditation writings.

The ideological emphases on Dōgen's personal experience at T'ien-t'ung and on the direct transmission from Ju-ching that we find in the later *Shōbō genzō* and subsequent Sōtō teaching have served to isolate Dōgen's religion not only from the historical circumstances of his life but from the written sources of his inspiration. On the grounds, I suppose, that he did not learn his Zen from books, we have largely ignored the question of the books he read and the ways in which his own writings are related to those books. To be sure, Sōtō commentators from the eighteenth century on have duly noted at least the most obvious instances of quotation and allusion in Dōgen's works and have sometimes attempted to explore the uses of specific texts or passages, but few seem to have been interested in reading the founder as even partly a product of his sources.

Yet if Dōgen learned his Zen through spiritual practice, reading was certainly a part of that practice. Indeed for a Japanese pioneer of Zen studies with only four years on the continent, it could hardly have been otherwise.

And, if he taught that Zen wisdom goes beyond words and letters, he also emphasized that it is in words and letters—in the *sūtras* and the records of the masters—for those with eyes to see it. In fact, like many of his Sung predecessors, Dōgen was a man of letters, a man whose writings are deeply colored by his consciousness of the Zen literary tradition and his own place in it.[1]

Both this literary consciousness and our own lamentable tendency to ignore it are nowhere more obvious than in the case of the *Fukan zazen gi*. Dōgen scholars have long been aware of the parallels between this work and Ch'ang-lu Tsung-tse's *Tso-ch'an i*. They have also been somewhat discomfitted by these parallels, which tend to undermine established positions on both the origins of Dōgen's teaching and, in some cases, the interpretation of its content. Hence they have generally seen fit to ignore Tsung-tse's work—or, at best, to dismiss it lightly with a reminder that Dōgen himself was dissatisfied with it—and to read the *Fukan zazen gi* solely as an expression of its author's personal Sōtō convictions. Such an approach may have its own value, but it also has its obvious limitations: to treat the manual in isolation from its sources—or to focus, as is often done, on only what is new in it—not only runs the risk of distorting the nature and significance of its message but also overlooks the broader historical and religious context in which it was composed. Whatever the place of the *Fukan zazen gi* in the formation of Dōgen's religion and the structure of Sōtō ideology, in terms of the history of Ch'an and Zen literature, the work represents but one example of a new genre of popular meditation texts characteristic of the school at this time. As such, it is hardly surprising that it drew on Tsung-tse's *Tso-ch'an i*, since the latter was in fact the pioneer of this genre.

Thus to appreciate the historical character as well as the content (both original and borrowed) of the *Fukan zazen gi*, we need to understand the work that was its model. Despite its importance as the first and in some ways the most influential Ch'an meditation manual, this little tract has not enjoyed the attention it deserves. Perhaps the neglect is due in part to the somewhat pedestrian quality of the work, which may have disappointed modern scholars even as it did Dōgen; perhaps neglect is the fate of a work that does not fit neatly into either of the two Japanese traditions of Zen meditation that dominate modern scholarship. Yet, for an historical under-

---

1. In the *Shōbō genzō zuimon ki*, Dōgen is recorded on several occasions apologizing for his wide knowledge of Ch'an and other Chinese literature; he goes on to warn his listeners against studying books and claims that he himself has given up reading (DZZ.2:447–48, 449–50). This is perhaps best interpreted as an example of his *upāya-kauśalya*. In any case it is not surprising that he might have felt moved to apologize for the demands his many literary allusions and obscure Ch'an locutions must have placed on his students. Although Dōgen is usually grouped with the "popular" reformers of the Kamakura period, in fact, much of his writing, at least in the *Shōbō genzō*, must have gone over the heads of those unversed in the Ch'an literature.

standing of Zen, both these characteristics—the artlessness and the inno-
cence of later sectarian dogma—make the work quite revealing. Hence,
before we consider Dōgen's own uses of the text, I want to examine here in
some detail the origin of Tsung-tse's manual and its place in the literature
of meditation.[2]
    The provenance of the *Tso-ch'an i* is not entirely clear. It is usually
thought to have been composed as a section of the *Ch'an-yüan ch'ing-kuei*, the
Ch'an monastic code compiled by Tsung-tse in 1103. The content of the
work, however, suggests that—like the *Fukan zazen gi*—it was originally
written as an independent tract, and that it was intended less as a set of rules
for the meditation hall than as a popular primer, for both novice monk and
layman, on the basics of Ch'an meditation. Textual history seems to bear
this out. The association of the manual with Tsung-tse's code is based on its
inclusion in a revised and enlarged edition of the code published in 1202 by
a certain Yü Hsiang (dates unknown).[3] There is, however, a variant text of
the *Ch'an-yüan ch'ing-kuei* that does not contain the *Tso-ch'an i*. This text,
produced in Korea from blocks carved in 1254, is based on a Northern Sung
text printed in 1111. Thus it is by far the earliest extant version of Tsung-tse's
code, dating to within a decade of the composition of the work, and it
strongly suggests that Tsung-tse's original text of the *Ch'an-yüan ch'ing-kuei*
did not include the meditation manual.[4]
    If the *Tso-ch'an i* was not written as a part of Tsung-tse's monastic code,
we cannot be certain of its date or, indeed, of its authorship. Still, there is
reason to think that it belongs to the period—around the turn of the twelfth
century—in which Tsung-tse flourished. We know that the manual was in
circulation well before the publication of Yü Hsiang's edition, since an
abbreviated version of the text already appears in the "Dhyāna" section of
the *Ta-tsang i-lan*, the lengthy compendium of scriptural passages composed
by Ch'en Shih (dates unknown) sometime prior to 1157.[5] Ch'en Shih's

2.   Portions of my discussion of Tsung-tse in this and the following chapter have previously
appeared under the title, "Ch'ang-lu Tsung-tse's *Tso-ch'an i* and the 'Secret' of Zen Meditation," in *Traditions of Meditation in Chinese Buddhism*, ed. by Peter Gregory, Studies in East Asian
Buddhism 4 (1986), 129–61.
    3.   See *Chung-tiao pu-chu Ch'an-yüan ch'ing-kuei*, ZZ.2,16:438–71. For the original date of
Tsung-tse's compilation, see his preface, ibid., 438a. The *Zoku zōkyō* text is based on eighteenth-
century Japanese printings; earlier, somewhat variant traditions of Yü Hsiang's edition are
preserved in a Southern Sung printing from 1209 and a mid-Kamakura manuscript in the
collection of the Kanazawa bunko. (See Kagamishima Genryū, "Kanazawa bunko bon Zen'en
shingi ni tsuite," *Kanazawa bunko kenkyū* 14, 3 [3/1968], 1–6.)
    4.   A brief discussion of the significance of the Korean text and a comparison of its contents
with the Yü Hsiang edition can be found in Kozaka Kiyū, "Zen'en shingi no hen'yō katei ni
tsuite: Kōrai ban Zen'en shingi no kōsatsu o kaishite," IBK 20, 2 (3/1972), 720–24. For a
modern edition of the *Ch'an-yüan ch'ing-kuei*, with textual notes for all the early versions, see
Kagamishima Genryū et al., *Yakuchū Zen'en shingi* (1972).
    5.   See *Shōwa hōbō sō mokuroku* 3:1305a–b. On the date of this work, see Yanagida Seizan,
"Zenseki kaidai," in Nishitani Keiji and Yanagida, *Zenke goroku* 2, *Sekai koten bungaku zenshū*

quotation does not identify the author, but it does provide us with a *terminus ad quem* probably within a few decades of Tsung-tse's death. Yü Hsiang's version, moreover, contains a quotation from the Ch'an master Fa-yün Fa-hsiu (1027–90), the presence of which indicates that the text cannot be earlier than mid-eleventh century. This quotation is particularly significant, because, as Yanagida Seizan has pointed out, it lends some credence to the tradition of Tsung-tse's authorship of the *Tso-ch'an i.* Although little is known of Tsung-tse's life, we do know that he originally entered the order under Fa-hsiu. Hence the appearance here of this master's saying—words not recorded elsewhere—would seem to provide circumstantial evidence for the work's ascription to his student Tsung-tse.[6]

However the *Tso-ch'an i* originated, by the time Dōgen visited China in the thirteenth century, it had become an integral part of the *Ch'an-yüan ch'ing-kuei*; and it is clear from his "Senjutsu yurai" that Dōgen himself associated the manual with Tsung-tse's code. Since this code was widely regarded as an expanded version of the original Ch'an monastic regulations established by Po-chang Huai-hai (720–814), Dōgen may have been attracted to the manual partly out of a belief that it preserved something of the meditation teachings of this famous T'ang master. Indeed, as we have seen, in his "Senjutsu yurai," he takes Tsung-tse to task for failing to transmit Po-chang's teachings accurately.

In the *Ch'an-yüan ch'ing-kuei* there is a *Tso-ch'an i.* Though it follows Po-chang's original intention [*ko i*], it adds several new clauses by Master I [i.e., Tsung-tse]. For this reason, it is filled with many mistakes and misunderstandings.[7]

At first glance, Dōgen appears to be criticizing Tsung-tse on the basis of his own knowledge of Huai-hai's meditation teachings. Indeed the passage has given rise to speculation that he obtained and read the original Po-chang code during his stay in China.[8] If this were true, the differences between the *Tso-ch'an i* and the *Fukan zazen gi* might be at least partly the result of Dōgen's

---

36B (1974), 496. The *Ta-tsang i-lan* text is quite similar to Yü Hsiang's version but lacks several more or less parenthetical amplifications. It is possible, of course, that this earliest extant text of the *Tso-ch'an i* is closer to the original, and that the longer version represents a later expansion; but given the character of Ch'en Shih's work, it would hardly be surprising if he had quoted only the basic material of the manual.

6. See Yanagida's "Kaisetsu," in Kajitani Sōnin et al., *Shinjin mei Shōdō ka Jūgyū zu Zazen gi, Zen no goroku* 16 (1974), 225–38, especially 232–33. It should be noted that the *Ta-tsang i-lan* version does not include the reference to Fa-hsiu; but since this version is quite abbreviated, its absence there, while not helping, does not detract from Prof. Yanagida's argument. I shall come back later on to what little is known of Tsung-tse's biography; for the reference to his association with Fa-hsiu, see *Chien-chung ching-kuo hsü teng lu,* ZZ.2B,9:133c11–12.

7. DZZ.2:6. The "Senjutsu yurai" manuscript here accords with some other early sources in giving the second graph in Tsung-tse's name as *I* rather than *Tse.* For this question, see Kondō Ryōichi, "Chōro Sōsaku ni tsuite," IBK 4, 2 (3/1966), 280–83.

8. Ōkubo Dōshū, *Dōgen zenji shingi,* 8.

attempt to restore the original text of a meditation manual by Huai-hai. Yet almost certainly this is not the case. Had Dōgen known the content of Po-chang's famous code, he would surely have made use of it. As has now been demonstrated, however, all of his many quotations from Ch'an monastic regulations are traceable to the *Ch'an-yüan ch'ing-kuei* itself.[9] The apparent judgment of the "Senjutsu yurai" that Tsung-tse has added "new clauses" (*shinjō*) to Po-chang's text is not, in fact, a judgment but is simply taken from the preface of the *Ch'an-yüan ch'ing-kuei*.[10] The errors that Dōgen purports to find in the manual surely have nothing to do with textual questions: they concern the understanding of meditation practice; also, as is clear from the content of the *Fukan zazen gi*, Dōgen "corrects" them not by returning to Po-chang's text but by rewriting the manual—often in reliance on material that postdates Huai-hai. Indeed Dōgen himself makes clear the religious basis of his dissatisfaction with the *Tso-ch'an i* in the summation of his criticism of Tsung-tse: "He knows nothing of the understanding beyond words (*gongai shi ryōran*); who can fail to realize this?"[11]

If Dōgen is nevertheless able to discern in the *Tso-ch'an i* the "original intention" of Po-chang, we can only put this down to his own understanding beyond words; it is doubtful that either he or Tsung-tse had any record of the T'ang master's meditation teachings. Though Tsung-tse claims that his *Ch'an-yüan ch'ing-kuei* represents a revision of Po-chang's rules to fit the circumstances of his day, it is unlikely that he knew what those rules were. Despite Po-chang's fame as the founder of the independent Ch'an monastic system and repeated references in the literature to a Po-chang monastic code, there is little evidence that this monk actually produced a set of written regulations and still less that they survived to Tsung-tse's time.[12] In any case,

9. See Kagamishima Genryū, *Dōgen zenji to inyō kyōten goroku no kenkyū*, 188, 262–63. Kagamishima finds one example from the later *Ju-chung jih-yung ch'ing-kuei*. The possibility (raised by Kondō Ryōichi, "Hyakujō shingi to Eihei shingi," IBK 13, 1 [1/1965], 297–300) that some of these passages originated in the *Po-chang ch'ing-kuei* cannot be totally disproven, but unless we accept the dubious notion that the *Ch'an-yüan ch'ing-kuei* was almost identical with Huai-hai's text, the absence of any quotation not wholly traceable to the latter should certainly make us suspicious.

10. Kagamishima et al., *Yakuchū Zen'en shingi*, 3.

11. DZZ.2:6.

12. Our earliest source for Po-chang, the epitaph by Ch'en Hsü, written just after his death, in 818, makes no reference to a *Po-chang ch'ing-kuei* ("T'ang Hung-chou Po-chang shan ku Huai-hai ch'an-shih t'a-ming," *Ch'üan T'ang wen* 446:4b–7a); and in fact the tradition's knowledge of Po-chang's famous rule seems to have been limited to brief notices attached to his biography in the *Sung kao-seng chuan* (T.50:770c–771a) and *Ching-te ch'uan teng lu* ("Ch'an-men kuei-shih," T.51:250c–251b). It is no doubt because this is all he had on Po-chang's regulations that Tsung-tse felt it worth including the latter text, under the title "Po-chang kuei-sheng sung," at the end of his own code. (Kagamishima et al., *Yakuchū Zen'en shingi*, 340–52. For a brief discussion and partial English translation of the "Ch'an-men kuei-shih," see Martin Collcutt, *Five Mountains: The Rinzai Zen Monastic Institution in Medieval Japan* [1981], 139–41.) Ui Hakuju was of the opinion that the original *Po-chang ch'ing-kuei* was still preserved on Po-chang shan in the early fourteenth century (see his *Zenshū shi no kenkyū*, vol. 2 [1941],

given the radical changes in the Ch'an monastic system in the centuries between the mid-T'ang and the Sung, much in the *Ch'an-yüan ch'ing-kuei* would have been unfamiliar to Po-chang. Particularly when we turn to our text, the *Tso-ch'an i*, the connection with Huai-hai seems remote indeed. There is no evidence whatsoever that this T'ang master wrote a meditation manual; especially if, as appears likely, Tsung-tse's own manual was not originally composed as a part of the *Ch'an-yüan ch'ing-kuei*, there is no reason to think that it was based on Po-chang's teachings.[13]

Once we abandon the old assumption that Po-chang authored the prototype for the *Tso-ch'an i*, Tsung-tse's manual becomes the earliest known work of its kind in the Ch'an tradition. This is rather surprising. After all, Ch'an is the "Meditation school," and by Tsung-tse's day the monks of this school had been practicing their specialty for half a millennium. One might well expect them to have developed, over the course of these centuries, a rich literature on the techniques of their practice, but in fact they do not appear to have done so. Yet, if this is surprising, perhaps more curious is the fact that we have given so little attention to this issue and the obvious questions it raises about the character both of the Ch'an meditation tradition and of Tsung-tse's place in it. Why was the tradition so long silent? And why did Tsung-tse break that silence?

Part of the answer to the first question here may be simply that the Meditation school had little to offer on the subject of contemplative technique beyond what was already available to the Buddhist community in the many Indian and Chinese treatises. In Chapter 4, where I sketch a history of what I take to be the major features of the Ch'an meditation teaching, we shall see that the school did develop its own discourse on the subject. Some elements of that discourse have practical implications and suggest a characteristic Ch'an meditation style distinct from at least some of the traditional techniques of Buddhist contemplation, but much of it is purely theoretical and has to do with the definition of a characteristic Ch'an ideology of practice distinct from that of other schools. Under the influences

---

377–78), but his argument has been refuted by Kagamishima Genryū (*Dōgen zenji to inyō kyōten goroku no kenkyū*, 181–92). At the latest, we know that in 1335, when Te-hui composed his *Ch'ih-hsiu Po-chang ch'ing-kuei*, he was unable to find any trace of Po-chang's work in China. (See his postface, T.48:1159a–b.)

13.   That his contemporaries shared Dōgen's belief that the *Tso-ch'an i* was derived from Po-chang is indicated by a Kamakura manuscript of the work that identifies it as "Ch'an Master Po-chang's Principles of Seated Meditation" (*Hyakujō zenji zazen gi*) (see Ishii Shūdō, "Daie Sōkō to sono deshitachi [5]," IBK 22, 1 [12/1973], 291–95); similarly, Enni's follower Mujū cites the work as "Po-chang's Principles of Seated Meditation" (*Hyakujō no zazen gi*) (Yamada and Miki, *Zōtan shū*, 259). For examples of the changes in the monastic institution, see Kagamishima Genryū, "Hyakujō ko shingi henka katei no ichi kōsatsu," KDBGKK 25 (3/1967), 1–13; Kozaka Kiyū, "Shingi hensen no teiryū (1)," SK 5 (4/1963), 123–29.

of this distinctive ideology as well as that of later, especially Japanese, sectarian consciousness, we may have exaggerated the extent to which the classical Ch'an tradition was isolated from the larger Buddhist community and its practice uninfluenced by the standard texts of the common Buddhist canon. Until the Sung, that canon contained no works of the Chinese Meditation school, but it did contain a wealth of material on how to practice meditation. If the great Ch'an masters of the T'ang were not often in the habit of quoting from the many "meditation *sūtras*" or recommending the technical methods of Yogācāra or T'ien-t'ai, this in itself does not mean that they did not resort to the common lore of Chinese Buddhist contemplative tradition.

Tsung-tse himself reminds us of this possibility when he calls our attention to several earlier accounts of meditation on which he could draw. In a passage of the *Tso-ch'an i* warning against the "doings of Māra" (*mo shih*), which can afflict the higher stages of meditation practice, he advises his reader seeking further information to consult the *Śūraṅgama-sūtra*, T'ien-t'ai's *Chih-kuan*, and Kuei-feng's *Hsiu-cheng i*. Of these, the first presumably refers to the T'ang text in ten rolls traditionally attributed to Paramiti; this work, which was quite popular with Tsung-tse's Sung contemporaries, contains a detailed discussion of fifty demoniacal states of mind into which the practitioner may fall.[14] Apart from this particular discussion, there is nothing in the *Śūraṅgama* text that would serve as a basis for Tsung-tse's description of meditation; but such is not the case with the other two works, which clearly have more intimate connections with his own manual.

We cannot say with certainty which text Tsung-tse intends by his reference to the *Chih-kuan*. One thinks first of the famous *Mo-ho chih-kuan*, by T'ien-t'ai Chih-i, a work that includes two lengthy sections on the various morbid and demoniacal states to which the meditator is susceptible.[15] Similar discussions, however, appear in other of Chih-i's meditation texts, and a more likely candidate here may be the so-called *T'ien-t'ai hsiao chih-kuan*. Not only does this popular work contain an explanation of *mo shih*, but, more importantly, it provides a concrete description of the preparation for, and practice of, meditation; several of the elements of this description are reflected in the *Tso-ch'an i*. Moreover, it is the basis for the discussion of

---

14. *Shou-leng-yen ching*, T.19:147a–155a. This work is now generally thought to be of Chinese origin. (See Mochizuki Shinkō, *Bukkyō kyōten seiritsu shi ron* [1946; repr., 1978], 493–508; Paul Demiéville, *Le Concile de Lhasa* [1952], 43–52, n. 3.) Sekiguchi Shindai suggests that the reference here is to the earlier *Śūraṅgama-samādhi-sūtra* (*Shou-leng-yen san-mei ching* [T. #642]), translated by Kumārajīva (see his *Tendai shikan no kenkyū* [1969], 323); but this text, though it contains a discussion of Māra, does not provide explicit information on his obstructions of meditation. Kagamishima et al., *Yakuchū Zen'en shingi*, 282, appears to have the two *sūtras* confused.

15. T.46:106c–111c, 114c–117a.

meditation practice in the *Hsiu-cheng i*, the other work to which Tsung-tse refers.[16]

The *Yüan-chüeh ching tao-ch'ang hsiu-cheng i*, by the important Hua-yen and Ch'an scholar Kuei-feng Tsung-mi (780–841), represents an extended explication of Buddhist practice according to the Chinese *Sūtra of Perfect Enlightenment* (*Yüan-chüeh ching*). It consists of three major divisions that deal with the conditions for practice, the method of worship, and the method of meditation. Large sections of the text, especially of the first and third divisions, are taken directly from the *Hsiao chih-kuan*; indeed when these sections are assembled and rearranged, it appears that Tsung-mi has quoted Chih-i's work almost in toto. It is passages from these same sections, in which the *Hsiu-cheng i* is relying on the *Hsiao chih-kuan*, that have parallels in our text.[17]

Sekiguchi Shindai, in his several influential studies of the *Hsiao chih-kuan*, has called attention to its parallels in the *Tso-ch'an i* and has emphasized the degree to which not only Tsung-tse's work but subsequent meditation manuals of Ch'an and Zen—including Dōgen's *Fukan zazen gi*—have relied, at least indirectly, on Chih-i. Such emphasis is but an extension of this Tendai scholar's long-running argument for the T'ien-t'ai influence on the Ch'an tradition.[18] Though his argument does not itself extend to the general issue of the Ch'an uses of non-Ch'an sources, it does alert us to the need for greater sensitivity to this issue. Yet Sekiguchi's approach does not really help us very much in understanding either the *Tso-ch'an i* or, as we shall see, the idiosyncratic character of the Ch'an treatment of (or silence on) the techniques of meditation.

We are not likely to have found very much when we find parallels

---

16. For the *Hsiao chih-kuan* discussion of *mo shih*, see *Hsiu-hsi chih-kuan tso-ch'an fa-yao*, T.46:470b–472b. This work, in one (or two) rolls, summarizes Chih-i's earlier, and much longer, *Shih ch'an po-lo-mi tz'u-ti fa-men* (T.#1916; see Sekiguchi Shindai, *Tendai shō shikan*, Iwanami bunko, 33-309-3 [1974], 203–7.) The *Taishō* text is based on the vulgate version; another, widely variant text, entitled *Lüeh-ming k'ai-meng ch'u-hsüeh tso-ch'an chih-kuan yao-men*, is preserved in Japan. For a study and comparison of all extant versions, see Sekiguchi, *Tendai shō shikan no kenkyū* (1954; repr., 1961).
17. See Sekiguchi, *Tendai shō shikan no kenkyū*, 29–32. The text of the *Hsiu cheng i* can be found at ZZ.2B,1:361–498; for a summary of its contents, see Kamata Shigeo, *Shūmitsu kyōgaku no shisō shi teki kenkyū* (1975), 499–521. Tsung-mi also quotes extensively from the *Hsiao chih-kuan* in his *Yüan-chüeh ching ta-shu ch'ao* (ZZ.1,14:454aff). Sekiguchi, *Tendai shō shikan no kenkyū*, 285–302, provides a table comparing the "Cheng hsiu" section of the *Hsiao chih-kuan* with the *Hsiu-cheng i*, the *Ta-shu ch'ao*, and Chih-i's *Ch'an-men yao-lüeh* (ZZ.2,4:35–37); Kamata, *Shūmitsu*, 524–608, gives a similar table of the first three of these works covering the first and third divisions of the *Hsiu-cheng i*.
18. Sekiguchi's argument goes back at least to his *Tendai shō shikan no kenkyū* (1954) and *Daruma daishi no kenkyū* (1957; rev. ed., 1969); he has reviewed many of the points of the argument in *Tendai shikan no kenkyū*, 271–81. This last work (328–35) provides an elaborate table comparing the relevant sections of the *Hsiao chih-kuan* and *Hsiu-cheng i* with parallel passages in the *Tso-ch'an i*, *Ch'ih-hsiu Po-chang ch'ing-kuei*, *Kōzen gokoku ron*, (vulgate) *Fukan zazen gi*, and Keizan's *Zazen yōjin ki*.

between Chih-i and Tsung-tse. The *T'ien-t'ai hsiao chih-kuan*, as Sekiguchi has emphasized, probably represents the first popular primer of meditation available to the Chinese. Although it draws on material from several Indian and Chinese sources, it differs from earlier works in being expressly intended to introduce the practi, e of seated meditation to the beginning student.[19] Except for a brief final section, therefore, the *Hsiao chih-kuan* omits discussion of the kind of technical T'ien-t'ai doctrine characteristic of most of Chih-i's writings and emphasizes instead concrete description of the actual techniques of mental and physical discipline, including what is probably the first explicit account of some of the details of the *tso-ch'an* posture.[20] Because of its attention to practical detail, the *Hsiao chih-kuan*—and especially its "T'iao-ho" chapter on the control of body, breath, and mind—could serve as a handy, nonsectarian guide to the basics of Buddhist contemplative practice; in fact not only Tsung-mi but many Buddhist writers, from Tao-hsüan (596–667), Shan-tao (617–81), and Fa-tsang (643–712) on, referred to this chapter in their own presentations of seated meditation.[21] It is hardly surprising, therefore, that by the Northern Sung, a brief text like Tsung-tse's *Tso-ch'an i*, itself intended as a meditation primer, should reflect something of this popular guide. Yet such reflection should not blind us to the fact that, unlike the *tso-ch'an* section of Tsung-mi's *Hsiu-cheng i*, Tsung-tse's manual is essentially a new work, original in both its language and the focus of its treatment.

The *T'ien-t'ai hsiao chih-kuan*'s discussion of meditation practice is divided into ten chapters that cover, in addition to the morbid and demoniacal states, such topics as control of the desires and abandonment of the obstacles (*nivaraṇa*), development of the good roots (*kuśula-mūla*), practice of calming

---

19. See Chih-i's introduction, Sekiguchi, *Tendai shō shikan no kenkyū*, 322. There is a tradition that the work was composed for Chih-i's brother, the layman Ch'en Chen, who had been diagnosed as terminally ill; after he practiced the repentence recommended in the book, his health was fully restored. (For a discussion, see Sekiguchi, *Tendai shō shikan no kenkyū*, 51–62.)

20. Excluding, of course, Chih-i's own account in the *Tz'u-ti ch'an-men* (T.46:489bff), from which the *Hsiao chih-kuan* passage is taken. Buddhist authors before Chih-i appear to have been content to leave such details to oral instruction; and, for the most part, earlier accounts tended to be extremely brief and schematic. A standard version was that appearing in Kumāra-jīva's popular *Ch'an pi yao fa ching*:

Spread your mat in a quiet place. Sit with legs crossed. Arrange your robes, straighten your body, and sit erect. Bare your right shoulder; place your left hand on your right hand; close your eyes, and press your tongue against your palate. Stabilize your mind, make it stationary, and do not let it disperse. (T.15:243b.)

For a study of the concrete descriptions of meditation appearing in the Chinese *vinaya* literature, see Hirakawa Akira, "Ritsuzō ni arawareta zen no jissen," in *Shikan no kenkyū*, ed. by Sekiguchi (1975), 51–71. More general accounts of the literature and history of meditation in early Chinese Buddhism can be found in Sasaki Kentoku, *Kan Gi Rikuchō zenkan hatten shi ron* (repr. 1978); and Mizuno Kōgen, "Zenshū seiritsu izen no Shina no zenjō shisō shi josetsu," KDKK 15 (3/1957), 15–54.

21. For a list of early texts affected by the *Hsiao chih-kuan*, see Sekiguchi, *Tendai shikan no kenkyū*, 343–44.

(*śamatha*) and contemplation (*vipaśyanā*), and so on. Tsung-tse ignores most of this material. As might be expected, there is nothing in his work comparable to Chih-i's concluding chapter on the T'ien-t'ai dogma of the three truths (*san ti*). Even the central practice of *chih-kuan* itself is not mentioned. Of the five chapters devoted to Chih-i's standard list of twenty-five spiritual techniques (*fang-pien*), only the first, on fulfilling the conditions for meditation, and especially the fourth, on regulating physical and mental activities in meditation, find significant parallels in our text. Moreover, aside from certain standard Buddhist admonishments, these parallels are limited almost wholly to the concrete description of the meditation posture. By Tsung-tse's time this material was surely the common lore of Chinese Buddhist monks and precisely of the sort in which one would expect to find the least innovation. Under the circumstances the notion of influence, if it still remains relevant, becomes too vague to sustain much interest.[22]

Thus, while we can assume from Tsung-tse's reference to the *T'ien-t'ai hsiao chih-kuan* that he was familiar with Chih-i's work and may, in fact, have consulted it in the writing of his own, this fact does little to explain either the content or the historical character of the *Tso-ch'an i*. It leaves wide open our question of why Tsung-tse chose to break with centuries of tradition and compose a popular Ch'an meditation manual. Exploration of this question will help us to understand not only the work itself—and, indirectly, the *Fukan zazen gi*—but also the ideological forces in the tradition against which it was in part a reaction. In Chapter 4, I shall pursue this latter topic in more detail, but let us begin here by recalling something of the historical background and significance of the *Tso-ch'an i*.

As a practical primer for the novice meditator, the *T'ien-t'ai hsiao chih-kuan* was in its own day undoubtedly a rather revolutionary work, but it was nevertheless the work of a medieval scholar, probably intended primarily for use within the cloister. If over the centuries the text was read by Buddhists of all persuasions, by Tsung-tse's time, its formal categories and technical language were no longer appropriate vehicles for the broad dissemination of Ch'an meditation. Indeed, whatever inspiration they may have drawn from the precedent of Chih-i's manual, already within a century of its appearance the earliest Ch'an masters had begun to turn their backs on his style and seek new, more popular approaches to both the technique and interpretation of the practice. Some of these approaches had close affinities with Tsung-tse's own, and to that extent his teachings seem to belong to a venerable Ch'an meditation tradition.

As we shall see in Chapter 4, among the eighth-century Ch'an docu-

---

22.   Prior to Sekiguchi's publication of his table of the texts in his *Tendai shikan no kenkyū*, Yamauchi Shun'yū did his own comparison and analysis of the *Hsiao chih-kuan* and *Tso-ch'an i*; he also concludes that Chih-i's influence is largely limited to the description of the meditation posture. ("Zazen gi to Tendai shō shikan," SK 8 [4/1966], 29–50.)

ments from Tun-huang, especially those associated with the East Mountain (Tung shan) tradition of the Patriarchs Tao-hsin (580–651) and Hung-jen (601–674), we find several texts that, if they do not quite constitute meditation manuals, still provide us with explicit instruction on the basic features of certain techniques of concentration, contemplation, and visualization. While there is considerable variety in the specific exercises recommended, at least this early lineage of the school sustained a coherent discourse on meditation and actively sought to promote its practice. Though most of these exercises are familiar from earlier Buddhist *sūtra* and commentarial literature, they are here characteristically simplified and reinterpreted in the spirit of the young Ch'an movement. Like Tsung-tse's own meditation, they are intended for everyman; indeed, some of them seem identical with the technique recommended four centuries later in the *Tso-ch'an i.*

Despite this promising start, the Ch'an meditation literature did not develop; throughout the classic age of the school—the late T'ang, Five Dynasties, and early Sung—we find very little discussion of the actual methods of Ch'an practice. I shall suggest some ideological reasons for this later on, but one reason may have to do with the very success of the school itself. The texts on the East Mountain tradition, like most of the Tun-huang Ch'an materials, were written by men who were striving to promote a new brand of Buddhism that would be attractive to the new society of the mid-T'ang. To this end, they sought, among other things, to articulate a practical approach to Buddhist training accessible to the ordinary man and to advertise that approach as a distinctive asset of the school. By the turn of the ninth century, however, the public promotion of Ch'an was no longer an issue; by then the school was comfortably established as a legitimate institution. Now it could remain ensconced on its famous mountains and wait for its followers to come. It could also revert to the esoteric style of the cloister, where meditation practice was taken for granted and its techniques transmitted orally within the community.

In any case, from the establishment of Ch'an as a separate Buddhist tradition, more than three centuries passed before the school began to discuss its meditation practices in public. By this time Ch'an was a venerable institution—indeed the central monastic institution of Chinese Buddhism. Its writings had now begun to take their place in the orthodox Buddhist canon, and its monks were mingling with the lay political and intellectual elite. This position of prominence gave it considerable influence on Sung society, but it also made it susceptible to influences from that society. In fact, despite its institutional success, the school—if not yet quite on the defensive—already felt the need to redefine itself in terms of the emerging Sung culture and to reform itself in response to the nascent Sung religious revival.

As its ranks swelled and its social, political, and economic responsibilities broadened, Ch'an was forced to turn its attention to the formalization and regulation of its institutions and practices. Confronted with the resurgence of neoclassical Confucian scholarship and its spread through the new medium of printing, it now began to look back to its own classic age and to set about writing the history of its tradition and publishing the teachings of its great masters. Surrounded by a newly vigorous and more modern society, with increased expectations for lay religious activity, Ch'an also began to consider ways in which its monastic practices might be translated into forms accessible to a wider segment of the community. Hence, for the first time in a long time, the school was obliged to recall its basic spiritual techniques and to set about explaining them in public.

At the close of the eleventh century, Tsung-tse stands near the beginning of some of these tendencies that would soon yield the new Ch'an of the Southern Sung. He seems to have been a man of his time, and in several ways his Buddhism both reflects and itself contributes to the emerging reformation. Unfortunately, we know little of his life: though the school's histories make note of him and preserve a few of his sayings, they record no dates and almost no biographical information. For the most part, they simply repeat the brief notice in the *Chien-chung ching-kuo hsü teng lu*, the first of the histories in which he appears. Since this work was compiled during his lifetime by Fo-kuo Wei-po, a fellow disciple of Tsung-tse's first master, Fa-hsiu, what little it does record is no doubt to be trusted. There we are 'told that Tsung-tse was from Yung-nien, in Lo-chou (modern Honan), and that his family name was Sun. As a youth, he excelled in Confucian studies. He was encouraged to study Buddhism by Yüan-feng Ch'ing-man, a Yünmen monk in the lineage of the influential T'ien-i I-huai (993–1064). As we have seen, he subsequently entered the order under I-huai's disciple Fa-yün Fa-hsiu. Thereafter, he studied with another of I-huai's disciples, Ch'ang-lu Ying-fu (dates unknown), under whom he attained a sudden awakening to the way. He was favored with the patronage of the Lo-yang official Yang Wei (fl. 1067–98) and was honored by the court. Fo-kuo identifies him as a monk of the Hung-chi ch'an-yüan in Chen-ting, the monastery where, as we know from its colophon, the *Ch'an-yüan ch'ing-kuei* was composed in 1103.[23]

This is all that the Ch'an histories have to tell us, but Tsung-tse is also remembered in the literature of Pure Land. As early as the *Lo-pang wen-lei*,

---

23. ZZ.2B,9:133c. The *Hsü teng lu* was published in 1101, before the appearance of Tsung-tse's monastic code. There is some uncertainty about Tsung-tse's place of residence. The Chen-ting district is in modern Hopei, but the Hung-chi monastery there has not been identified; the Hung-chi ssu known in Ch'an records is at Ch'ang-lu, in modern Kiangsu. It is sometimes suggested that Tsung-tse moved (back?) to Ch'ang-lu at the end of his life, and Yanagida (Kajitani et al., *Shinjin mei*, 233) has speculated that it was in this last period, after the composition of the *Ch'an-yüan ch'ing-kuei*, that he produced the *Tso-ch'an i*, but the evidence for such a chronology is unclear.

the miscellany of Ching-t'u material published in 1200 by Shih-chih Tsung-hsiao, he is listed as the last of the five great Patriarchs who carried on the tradition of the Lotus Society. A brief notice there informs us that he was given the honorific title Tz'u-chüeh, "compassionate enlightenment" (which also appears in the colophon of the *Ch'an-yüan ch'ing-kuei*), and that he was living at Ch'ang-lu during the Yüan-yu era (1086–93). There he was active in proselytizing, and apparently in 1089, he founded a Lotus Assembly *(lien-hua sheng-hui)* to promote the universal cultivation of the *samādhi* of the recollection of the Buddha *(nien fo san-mei)*. His practice was to seek birth in the Western Pure Land by reciting the name of Amitābha up to ten thousand times a day, recording each recitation with a cross.[24]

P'u-tu's *Lu-shan lien-tsung pao-chien* of 1305 also contains a brief biography, which gives Tsung-tse's place of origin as Hsiang-yang and adds the information that he lost his father as a boy and took vows at the age of twenty-nine. Even as abbot of Ch'ang-lu, we are told here, he remained a deeply filial son and guided his mother in the *nien fo* practice, so that she passed on in beatitude. He is said to have written a *Ch'üan hsiao wen*, a work in 120 sections "promoting filial piety," as well as a *Tso-ch'an chen* [*sic*], or "lancet of meditation."[25] Tsung-hsiao's collection of Pure Land documents, the *Lo-pang i-kao*, also reports on Tsung-tse's *Ch'üan hsiao wen* and provides a short extract; also, the *Lo-pang wen-lei* preserves a few minor pieces by Tsung-tse, including a preface to the *Kuan wu-liang-shou ching*, some verses, and several brief tracts.[26]

Tsung-tse's Pure Land writings seem, in one sense, to present another side of his religion, a side quite different from that of the Ch'an abbot who composed the monastic code and the meditation manual. In these writings, and especially in the piece called "Lien-hua sheng-hui lu wen," apparently written for his *nien fo* congregation, he emphasizes the difficulty of actually practicing monastic Buddhism in this Sahā world and encourages his readers to turn to Amitābha and to call upon Him to take them up to the next world where they may enjoy the purity and bliss of Sukhāvatī. Whereas in the Sahā world, the practitioner is plagued by demons and assailed by sexual and other sensory temptations, in Sukhāvatī he is bathed in the radiance of Amitābha, everything around him proclaims the *dharma*, and his *karma*

---

24. T.47:193c.

25. T.47:324c. P'u-tu goes on to report that Tsung-tse once had a dream in which he was approached by a man named P'u-hui, who sought membership in the Lotus Assembly for himself and his brother P'u-hsien; after awakening, Tsung-tse realized that these were the two *bodhisattvas* who appear in the *Hua-yen ching* (T.10:279bff). The story of the dream is found among Tsung-tse's writings in the *Lo-pang wen-lei*, ibid., 178a–b; the source of the other information here is unknown.

26. *Lo-pang i-kao*, T.47:249; the notice is taken from the *Lung-shu ching-t'u wen*, T.47:271a. Tsung-tse's preface appears at T.47:167a–b; see also his "Lien-hua sheng-hui lu wen" (dated 1089), "Nien-fo fang t'ui fang-pien wen," "Nien-fo hui-hsiang fa-yüan wen," ibid., 177b–178c; and his verses, ibid., 219c–220a.

is purified; there are no demonic experiences there, and there are no women.[27]

In another sense Tsung-tse's Pure Land piety seems of a piece with his approach to Ch'an. As is clear from his regimen of multiple recitations, Tsung-tse was no "protestant" ideologue of pure grace, seeking to deny the efficacy of works. Like other Ch'an masters who sought conciliation with the Ching-t'u teachings, he held that "Amitābha is our own nature, and the. Pure Land our own mind," and that "the cardinal principle [of these teachings] is to think [on Him] without thought (wu nien), and to be born [therein] without birth (wu sheng)."[28] Hence elsewhere he could claim that "nien fo and the study of Ch'an do not interfere with each other: they are but two methods based on the same principle."[29] And, as in his Ch'an writings, so too here it is less the principle than the method of the Pure Land faith—perhaps especially its power to overcome spiritual obstacles—that seems to have most attracted him. He recommends the nien fo practice in particular to beginners, as a means of developing calm (kṣānti), and also to those near death, as a means of relieving pain and settling the mind.[30]

Tsung-tse was apparently a practical and compassionate man. Undistracted by dogmatic niceties, he directly addressed the everyday problems of spiritual cultivation; undaunted by the weight of tradition, he sought to open up the mystery of Ch'an practice and to share with others, both inside and outside the cloister, some of the techniques and institutions that might aid them in that cultivation. To this end, he functioned as both Ch'an prelate and Pure Land pastor. As the former, deploring the confusion and corruption of monastic tradition that accompanied the rapid growth of the school, he tried to rationalize the training of monks by setting out, in his Ch'an-yüan ch'ing-kuei, a detailed code of the bureaucratic structure, administrative procedures, and ritual forms of the Ch'an institution. As the latter, lamenting the isolation of that institution from the Pure Land faith of the lay community, he sought—like his Yün-men predecessors I-huai and Ying-fu—to encourage interaction, bringing Ching-t'u practices into the ritual of his monastery and taking the Ch'an emphasis on mental cultivation out to his nien fo society. Probably as both prelate and pastor, he took it upon himself to make available, for the first time, a practical guide to the procedures of Ch'an meditation.[31]

27. Lo-pang wen-lei, T.47: 177b–178b; the same text is preserved in the Lung-shu ching-t'u wen under the title "Ch'üan ts'an-ch'an jen chien hsiu ching-t'u," T.47: 283c–284c.

28. T.47: 177b23, 178a20.

29. "Nien-fo tsan-ch'an chiu tsung-chih shuo," Lu-shan lien-tsung pao-chien, T.47: 318b25–26.

30. "Lien-hua sheng-hui wen," T.47: 177c; "Nien-fo hui-hsiang fa-yüan wen," ibid., 178c.

31. Tsung-tse's nien-fo practice appears repeatedly throughout the Ch'an-yüan ch'ing-kuei and clearly represented a major element in the ritual of his monastery. His combination of

Tsung-tse may not have left us many profound Ch'an sayings, but what he did leave had a profound impact on subsequent Ch'an and Zen literature. His *Ch'an-yüan ch'ing-kuei* became the inspiration and often the model for a new body of monastic codes. Whereas before its publication there had apparently been no detailed written regulations (if we discount the illusive *Po-chang ch'ing-kuei*), in the centuries following its appearance, there was a steady stream of such texts in both China and Japan. Though some of these—like Dōgen's *Eihei shingi*—would come in time to supplant his own, many of the practices and institutions first set down by Tsung-tse endured. Moreover, though Ch'an and Zen monasteries would change considerably after his day, Tsung-tse's basic principle that they should be governed by written regulations remained a permanent fixture of the school.[32]

Similarly, although the Ch'an tradition had managed to survive for some half a millennium without producing a meditation manual, once Tsung-tse's *Tso-ch'an i* appeared, it seems to have found a ready market and soon spawned a new genre of practical guides to mental cultivation. We have already seen that an abbreviated version of the text was quickly picked up by the layman Ch'en Shih for inclusion in his *Ta-tsang i-lan*, a work intended to make available a digest of the basic teachings of Buddhism for popular consumption. Following the publication of Yü Hsiang's influential edition of the *Ch'an-yüan ch'ing-kuei*, the full text of the manual circulated within the monastic community as well; in 1338, it was incorporated, with only minor variations, in Te-hui's important *Ch'ih-hsiu Po-chang ch'ing-kuei*. This work, compiled by order of the last Mongol emperor, Shun-tsung, became the standard code for the Ch'an monasteries of the Ming. Shortly after its publication, it was—like the *Ch'an-yüan ch'ing-kuei* before it—taken to Japan, where it provided a model for the regulation of the institutions of the official *gozan* system. In this way Tsung-tse's *Tso-ch'an i* spread its influence throughout the lay and clerical communities of both China and Japan and became a basic source for the description of Zen meditation.[33]

The publication and dissemination of Tsung-tse's manual signalled—and no doubt itself helped to inspire—a new interest in Ch'an spiritual

---

Ch'an tradition with Sung popular religion is perhaps nowhere better symbolized than in his saying, "The one word 'filial' [*hsiao*] is the gateway to all mysteries," an expression that gives a homey, ethical twist to Tsung-mi's famous metaphysical dictum, "The one word 'knowing' [*chih*] is the gateway to all mysteries." (Quoted in *Lu-shan lien-tsung pao-chien*, T.47:306c26.)

32. For a brief introduction to the literature of Ch'an and Zen monastic regulations, see Martin Collcutt, "The Early Ch'an Monastic Rule: *Ch'ing kuei* and the Shaping of Ch'an Community Life," in *Early Ch'an in China and Tibet*, ed. by Lewis Lancaster and Whalen Lai, Berkeley Buddhist Studies Series 5 (1983), 165–84.

33. For Te-hui's text of the *Tso-ch'an i*, see T.48:1143a–b. The manual also appears in the *Tzu-men ching-hsün*, a compendium of practical advice for Ch'an monks compiled in 1313 by Yung-chung (dates unknown) (T.48:1047b–c); but since the extant text of this work is a much later, greatly expanded version, we cannot be entirely certain that the *Tso-ch'an i* was included in the original.

technique and new approaches to its discussion. The school had long maintained a tradition of brief poetic and philosophical reflections on the contemplative life, a tradition exemplified in such classic early pieces as the *Hsin-
wang ming* (attributed to the Liang figure Fu Ta-shih), the *Hsin hsin ming*
(traditionally associated with the Third Patriarch, Seng-ts'an), Niu-t'ou
Fa-jung's *Hsin ming*, Yung-chia's *Cheng tao ko*, Shih-t'ou's *Ts'an t'ung ch'i*, the
Pao-ching san-mei ko (ascribed to Tung-shan Liang-chieh), and so on. The
Sung authors carried on this tradition, developing a genre of verse—often
styled "meditation inscriptions" (*tso-ch'an ming*) or, as we have seen, "meditation lancets" (*tso-ch'an chen*)—that celebrated the mysteries of *samādhi*.[34]

The Sung tradition of such literary treatment of Ch'an practice should
not be overlooked in considering the context of Dōgen's own presentation
of meditation: it represents one of the two major strands that seem always
to be interwoven in his work. The other is represented by Tsung-tse's style
of teaching and the practical forms of religious instruction it prefigured. If
the Sung masters continued to write poetry, they also began to explore anew
the mental techniques of Ch'an and to step outside the tradition of literary
appreciations of meditation to develop more explicit prose texts that offered
concrete advice on the actual practice. Indeed the century following the
appearance of the *Tso-ch'an i* is marked by the rise to prominence of the
Yang-ch'i school of Ta-hui Tsung-kao and the growing popularity of its
innovative methods of *kung-an* concentration. If Ta-hui's teaching was often
at odds with that of Tsung-tse, in its concern for the propagation of a simple
Ch'an exercise for the control of the mind, it inherited the new, more
practical spirit of the *Tso-ch'an i*. It was not long before his descendants
began to try their own hands at popular manuals of meditation. This seems
to have been particularly true in Japan, where Zen was just beginning to
make itself felt.

The religious reformation on the continent was mirrored—indeed, mag-
nified—overseas in the Buddhist movements of the Kamakura. As the
breakup of the Heian social and ecclesiastical orders opened new possibilities
for religious experiment and provoked a new sense of religious urgency,
Japanese Buddhists began to cast about for more modern, more accessible
forms of the faith to replace the old scholastic systems imported from the
T'ang. Thus, it is hardly surprising that they fastened on the popular Sung

---

34. At the beginning of the Sung, quite a few of the early Ch'an meditation verses were
collected in an appendix to the *Ching-te ch'uan teng lu*, the first history of the school to be accepted
into the Buddhist canon. Here we also find what is probably the earliest record of a "meditation
lancet," attributed to Wu-yün Chih-feng (909–85). (T.51:459c–460a.) The *Tzu-men ching-
hsün*, which contains quite a few such pieces, includes what may be the earliest example of a
Tso-ch'an ming, attributed to Huai-jang's disciple Ta-te Ta-i (745–818). (T.48:1048b.) The
Chia-t'ai p'u teng lu (ZZ.2B,10:216a–b) preserves a *Tso-ch'an i* in the same general style by
Tsung-tse's younger contemporary Fo-hsin Pen-ts'ai. Other works in this genre have been
collected in the *Ch'an-men chu-tsu-shih chieh-sung* (ZZ.2,21:454–92).

movements of Ch'an and Pure Land, which offered new models for the organization of the spiritual community and new hope of quick salvation to monk and layman alike. Nor is it difficult to see why they should have welcomed popular meditation texts like the *Tso-ch'an i* that provided practical instruction in elementary forms of spiritual cultivation.

The veneration of the accomplished meditātor—the great ascetic, sunk in profound *samādhi* or wielding the psychic powers of *dhyāna*—had long been an important element in popular religious writing and a major source of popular religious authority. The various movements and societies that formed around charismatic figures in the late Heian and Kamakura may be seen in part as a new, communal expression of such veneration. At the same time, of course, these movements offered their adherents direct access to some of the spiritual techniques of the contemplative and a real opportunity to translate their faith into personal participation. But for this to occur, it was first necessary to translate the arcana of professional contemplative tradition into simplified, readily mastered forms. This process had already begun in Japan well before the advent there of Zen.

In his "Senjutsu yurai," Dōgen laments the fact that, prior to his day, no meditation manual had ever been transmitted to the islands. Taken at face value, this would seem to suggest that his own work represented the first Japanese contact with the Buddhist meditation literature. Since, however, he also claims in the same passage that true Buddhism itself, or the *shōbō genzō*, "has never been heard of in our kingdom," his remark probably tells us more about Dōgen and his particular sense of Zen transmission than it does about history. Indeed whatever Dōgen may have thought about the matter—and we shall come back to this question in Part III—we hardly need emphasize that his contemporaries were quite familiar with the major Chinese meditation texts and were the inheritors of a long tradition of *zazen*.

As early as the eighth century, Chih-i's works on meditation, including the *Hsiao chih-kuan*, were already available in Japan.[35] Contact with these works led Saichō (767–822) to undertake the study of Chinese T'ien-t'ai and ultimately to found an independent Tendai institution on Mt. Hiei. Saichō, who is also known to have studied the teachings of early Ch'an, was himself an ardent exponent of meditation and established special cloisters at his monastery for the training of monks in the contemplative exercises described in the *Mo-ho chih-kuan*. Thereafter, with the rise to prominence of

35. Earliest notice of the *Hsiao chih-kuan* in Japanese records appears in 740. (See Sekiguchi, *Tendai shō shikan no kenkyū*, 103. Sekiguchi believes that the work was introduced in 736 by the Chinese monk Tao-hsüan [Dōsen, 702–60], a student of the well-known Northern Ch'an master P'u-chi. Tao-hsüan, we may note, also introduced Fa-tsang's *Ta-sheng ch'i-hsin lun i-chi*, which itself contains a description of meditation taken from the *Hsiao chih-kuan* [T.44:283a–b].) Most of the major works of Chih-i, including the *Mo-ho chih-kuan* and *Hsiao chih-kuan*, were among the books brought to Japan by the famed *vinaya* master Chien-chen (Ganjin, 688–763), who arrived in 754. (See *Tō dai wajō tōsei den*, *Yūhō ki shō*, T.51:993a.)

the Hiei zan Tendai establishment, Chih-i's meditation texts became one of the major sources for Heian Buddhism, and his *shikan* one of its major practices. Dōgen, of course, must have studied at least the rudimentary techniques of *shikan* as a Tendai monk on Mt. Hiei, but in his *Bendō wa* he dismisses them as irrelevant to the meditation he is now introducing from China. In that work he says that no Patriarch of the orthodox transmission of the Buddha seal in India and China has ever combined the T'ien-t'ai exercises with the practice of *zazen*. This early disclaimer notwithstanding, that Dōgen retained considerable respect for Chih-i's meditation texts even in his later years is reflected in the fact that his writings are sprinkled with references to the *Mo-ho chih-kuan* and especially to Chan-jan's detailed commentary on it, the *Chih-kuan fu-hsing*.[36]

In the centuries after Saichō, the Tendai meditation practices began to transcend the confines of the monastic centers to become a feature of the new, more popular forms of later Heian Buddhism. The tradition on Mt. Hiei of the contemplation of the Buddha that Chih-i called "the constant walking *samādhi*" (*jōgyō zanmai*) is often given as a primary stimulus for the devotional exercises of the Pure Land *hijiri* movements of this period. Among those who left the mountain to train and teach independently, there were many known for their cultivation of his Lotus (*hokke*) or "single practice" (*ichigyō*) meditations. The popularization of Tendai contemplative exercises during this time is reflected in texts like the *Shikan zazen ki*, attributed to the famous Tendai prelate and Pure Land Patriarch Genshin (942–1017). This work is based, in part, on the *Hsiao chih-kuan*, but, like some of the contemporaneous literature on the *samādhi* of the recollection of the Buddha (*nenbutsu zanmai*) or the contemplation of the mystic first syllable, "a" (*aji kan*), it represents an attempt to translate the technical practices of monastic tradition into simpler, more easily accessible forms.[37]

---

36. It may be worth noting in this regard that, in his conversations with Ju-ching in the *Hōkyō ki*, Dōgen gives his master a little lecture on his understanding of the various kinds of Chinese Buddhism in which he singles out Chih-i as the best of the scholastic masters (DZZ.2: 381–82); for a discussion of the conspicuous T'ien-t'ai element in the *Hōkyō ki*, see Ikeda Rosan, "Dōgen zenji no nyū Sō denbō," SK 25 (3/1983), 36–42. Dōgen's references to the T'ien-t'ai meditation literature are listed at Kagamishima, *Dōgen zenji to inyō kyōten goroku no kenkyū*, 226–27; for the *Bendō wa* disclaimer, see DZZ.1:741. In his *Zōtan shū*, the eclectic Mujū laments the fact that some of his contemporaries drew a sharp distinction between Zen meditation and *shikan*; the real difference between the two, he says, is merely that, while the techniques of *zazen* had long been available to Japanese Buddhists in Chih-i's *Tz'u-ti ch'an men*, the Tendai scholars only argued over its theory without putting it into practice (Yamada and Miki, *Zōtan shū*, 256–59). A recent argument for the continuity of the Kamakura Zen movement with the earlier *shikan* tradition on Mt. Hiei can be found in Funaoka Makoto, "Shoki zenshū juyō to Hiei zan," in *Zenshū no sho mondai*, ed. by Imaeda Aishin (1979), 57–84; for an interesting piece emphasizing the view that Dōgen's Zen remained deeply indebted to the Lotus tradition of Chih-i, see Yanagida Seizan, "Dōgen to Chūgoku bukkyō," *Zen bunka kenkyū jo kiyō* 13 (3/1984), 7–128.

37. For the *Shikan zazen ki*, see DNBZ.31:267–72. The dissemination of the *nenbutsu zanmai* in late Heian and Kamakura is well known, but we should not overlook the parallel

By the thirteenth century, then, when the *Fukan zazen gi* was composed, interest in, and knowledge of, the basic methods of meditation was widespread, and the practice of writing popular guides to these methods was well established. Indeed, within Dōgen's own lifetime, there were texts such as the *Zazen shidai*, attributed to Myōe Kōben, who also wrote on *aji kan*, and the *Zazen jigi*, by the famed Vinaya master Fukaki Shunjō (1166–1227), who likewise produced a popular tract on the technique of the *nenbutsu zanmai*. Both these men enjoyed the support of powerful laymen inside and out of the court; they were known for their dedication to meditation and—like Tsung-tse—were active at once in the purification of the monastic order and the propagation of the faith. Though they remained in the fold of established Heian schools, both were also interested in the new Zen contemplative tradition being introduced at Kennin ji. And both were no doubt personally known to Dōgen.[38]

In such an environment, then, Tsung-tse's *Tso-ch'an i* appeared in Japan. As is the case with many of the Sung Ch'an materials, we do not know exactly when or how this happened. In later Japanese Zen the work was no

development of the tantric techniques of *aji kan* prevalent in both the Tendai and Shingon schools. While the object of contemplation in this exercise distinguishes it from both the Tendai *shikan* and the *zazen* practices of the Zen school, much of the basic method is of course the same. (For examples of influential descriptions of the practice, see *Wu-wei san-tsang ch'an yao*, T.18:944c; *Aji kan yōjin kuketsu*, T.77:145a.) The practice was popularized in late Heian by Shingon reformers like Kakuban (1095–1143), who was also interested in the *nenbutsu* and who managed—in a piece written for his mother—to reduce the intricacies of the Vajrayāna to the mere intonation of the sacred first syllable itself (see his *Aji kan gi*, found with many of his other popular *aji kan* texts in *Kōgyō daishi senjutsu shū*, ed. by Miyazaka Yūshō, vol. 1 [1977], 226–28; for a discussion of Kakuban's popularization of meditation, see Matsuzaki Keisui, "Kōgyō daishi Kakuban no kangyō ni tsuite," IBK 29, 2 [3/1981], 298–303.) In Dōgen's day the Kōya san monk Dōhan (1178–1252) produced a simplified *aji kan* tract that was to enjoy considerable currency; see his *Dōhan shōsoku*, *Kana hōgo shū*, ed. by Miyazaka Yūshō, *Nihon koten bungaku taikei* 83 (1964), 76–83.

38. Myōe and Shunjō both enjoyed the support of the powerful patron of Zen Kujō Michiie, and both had contact with Yōsai. We have already seen Dōgen participating with Myōe in the opening of Saihō ji immediately following the former's return from China. Shunjō, who himself spent a dozen years on the mainland, stayed at Kennin ji for some time after his own return in 1211 and before he settled at nearby Sennyū ji. There is a Kamakura period document from the tradition of the latter monastery in which Shunjō holds up his "disciple" Buppōbō (i.e., Dōgen) as a model for the etiquette of bowing (*gasshō*), and Notomi Jōten has suggested that, in preparing for his pilgrimage to China, the young Dōgen must have sought out the experienced traveler's intimate knowledge of Sung monastic institutions and of colloquial Chinese language. (See his "Shunjō to Dōgen," IBK 23, 1 [12/1974], 114–21.)

Myōe's *Zazen shidai* is noted in Shiren's *Genkō shakusho* (DNBZ.101:205a), but its content is not known; it may be identical with his *Bukkō kan ryaku shidai*, one of several brief meditation texts that he wrote toward the end of his life. That Dōgen was familiar with these texts is suggested by what appears to be a criticism of Kōben's "Buddha radiance *samādhi*" (*bukkō zanmai*) in the *Zazen shin*. (DZZ.1:96; for discussion of Kōben's *samādhi*, see Robert Gimello, "Li T'ung-hsüan and the Practical Dimensions of Hua-yen," in *Studies in Ch'an and Hua-yen*, ed. by Gimello and Peter Gregory, Studies in East Asian Buddhism 1 [1983], 321–89.) For reference to Shunjō's text, said to have been written for Michie, see *Sennyū ji Fukaki hosshi den*, *Zoku Gunsho ruijū* 9A:56; and *Genkō shakusho*, ibid., 296b.

doubt most widely read—together with the *Hsin hsin ming*, *Cheng tao ko*, and K'uo-an's *Shih niu t'u*—in the popular collection called the *Shibu roku*. Exactly when these texts were first associated—and whether in China or Japan—is not known; but at least the *Hsin hsin ming* and *Cheng tao ko* seem to have circulated together in the Heian period, and it has been speculated that by Dōgen's time they had already been joined with the *Tso-ch'an i*.[39] In any case we know that as early as 1198 extracts from the *Ta-tsang i-lan* version of Tsung-tse's manual had already appeared in Yōsai's important *Kōzen gokoku ron*, a work intended to defend the newly imported Zen school as a legitimate form of Buddhism and promote its practice among the Japanese. Soon thereafter, of course, the full text of the *Tso-ch'an i* was brought to Japan—perhaps by Dōgen himself—in Yü Hsiang's edition of the *Ch'an-yüan ch'ing-kuei*.[40]

If Tsung-tse's manual was well received and continued to enjoy wide readership, it was by no means without competition. Like Dōgen, the other early Japanese Zen teachers—both natives and Chinese missionaries—were not content merely to quote the *Tso-ch'an i* on meditation: they went on to compose their own guides to the practice that reflected the Japanese circumstances and the development of the continental tradition since the days of the Northern Sung. This latter development is already seen in an early manual imported from the mainland, the *Ju-ju chü-shih tso-ch'an i*, attributed to the Yang-ch'i layman Yen Ping (d. 1212?) and now preserved, along with many other Kamakura Zen documents, in the Kanazawa bunko. Yen Ping quotes from the *Tso-ch'an i* but offers his own explanation of meditation, reflecting the *k'an-hua* practice of his forebear Ta-hui. It is likely that this work was introduced to Japan during Dōgen's lifetime, and in fact it may be that he had already seen it while in China.[41]

---

39. See Kajitani et al., *Shinjin mei*, 182–83. Yanagida Seizan notes here that the *Fukan zazen gi* draws passages from all three of these works and goes on to suggest that it may have been the meditation text of this collection, rather than of the *Ch'an-yüan ch'ing-kuei*, that influenced Dōgen. This suggestion, however, ignores the evidence of the "Fukan zazen gi senjutsu yurai." For the *Shibu roku* text of the *Tso-ch'an i*, the earliest extant version of which is a *gozan* printing from the fourteenth century, see Ōmori Sōgen, *Kunchū Zenshū shibu roku* (1962), 10–18.

40. For Yōsai's quotation, see T.80:12a14–17. As Yanagida has pointed out, the fact that Yōsai often quotes the *Ch'an-yüan ch'ing-kuei* but uses the *Ta-tsang i-lan* as his source for the *Tso-ch'an i* provides additional evidence that, when he visited China in 1187, the manual was still not included in Tsung-tse's code. (See Yanagida's additional notes to the *Kōzen gokoku ron*, in Ichikawa Hakugen et al., *Chūsei zenke no shisō*, *Nihon shisō taikei* 16 [1972], 398; and his "Yōsai to Kōzen gokoku ron no kadai," ibid., 471–76.) Apart from the *Ta-tsang i-lan* and *Ch'an-yüan ch'ing-kuei* versions, we know that the *Tso-ch'an i* was also circulating as an independent work in the Kamakura, for we have a manuscript of (a variant form of) the text from this period that belonged to Myōe's Kōzan ji. (See Ishii Shūdō, "Daie Sōkō to sono deshitachi [5]," 291.)

41. Yen Ping's biography does not appear in the Ch'an histories, but he is identified as a follower of Ta-hui's important disciple Hsüeh-feng Hui-jan (*Hsü ch'uan teng lu*, T.51:701a). The 1212 date for his death has recently been proposed by Nagai Masashi, in "Nansō ni okeru ichi koji no seishin seikatsu: Nyonyo koji Ganpei no baai (1)," KDBGR 15 (10/1984), 202–27.

Yen Ping's little tract was only one of a considerable number of similar popular Zen texts that circulated in the Kamakura period—some of the earliest of which had already appeared before Dōgen's death. From Dōgen's contemporary Enni, for example, we have a brief *Zazen ron* in Japanese, said to have been written for his patron, the Regent Kujō Michiie. Enni was one of the most successful of the early pioneers of Japanese Zen. Like Dōgen, he had studied with a disciple of Yōsai and had spent several years on the continent, where he was certified by the influential Yang-ch'i master Wu-chun Shih-fan (1177–1249). After his return to Japan in 1241, he was invited to the capital by Michiie and, as we have seen, was installed at the great new Zen monastery of Tōfuku ji, where he was patronized by both court and shōgunate. Like Yōsai, Enni retained an interest in the native tantric tradition and wrote a commentary on the *Mahā-vairocana-sūtra*, but in his *Zazen ron* he argues that the "Meditation school" (*zazen no shūmon*) transmits the very mind of the Buddha (*busshin*), from which all other practices spring and through which all the exoteric and esoteric traditions must achieve enlightenment.[42] Dōgen may have known of this work, which was composed in the last decade of his life. After Dōgen's death his disciples would criticize the meditation teachings of both Enni and Lan-ch'i Tao-lung as inferior to those of their master.

Lan-ch'i Tao-lung (Rankei Dōryū, 1213–78) was the first Sung Ch'an missionary to the Kamakura. He arrived in 1246 and was soon installed by his patron, Hōjō Tokiyori, as the founding abbot of the new Kenchō ji monastery in Kamakura. Here he firmly established the basis for an independent Zen school in the *bakufu* capital. Like Dōgen, he seems to have put great emphasis on the forms of Zen monastic life and especially the life of the meditation hall (*sōdō*): in his tradition, he said, *zazen* was the very essence of the monastic rule.[43] At the same time Tao-lung publicized Zen practice

His *Tso-ch'an i* corresponds to a text, dated 1194 and entitled *Ch'u-hsüeh tso-ch'an fa*, that is included in a manuscript of the *Ju-ju chü-shih yü lu* preserved at Kyoto University. (See Shiina Kōyū, "Sō Gen ban zenseki kenkyū (4)," IBK 29, 2 [3/1981], 251–54.) The Kanazawa manuscript, which probably dates from the early fourteenth century, has been edited by Ishii Shūdō in *Kanazawa bunko shiryō zensho*, vol. 1, 155–61. Nagai ("Nansō") suggests that the work was among the Zen texts brought into Japan by Enni in 1241. Though the correspondence may merely be a coincidence, it is interesting to note that Dōgen's invocation, in his introduction to the *Fukan zazen gi*, of Śākyamuni's six years of sitting and Bodhidharma's nine years of wall gazing closely parallels a passage in Yen Ping's own introduction (*Kanazawa bunko shiryō zensho*, vol. 1, 157).

42. *Shōichi kokushi hōgo, Zenmon hōgo shū* 2:411–24; the remarks on the superiority of the Meditation school appear at 411. The passage in the text identifying Michiie as the recipient of its teachings may be a later emendation: it does not appear in the earliest extant version, discovered several years ago and published by Sanae Kensei, in "Hōsa bunko bon Shōichi kana hōgo no kenkyū (1): Honbun hen," *Zen bunka kenkyū jo kiyō* 6 (5/1974), 265–94.

43. See his final admonitions recorded in the *Daikaku shūi roku*, DNBZ.95:111b. A like emphasis on *zazen* as the central monastic practice of his master's tradition is expressed by Enni as well. Such remarks remind us of Dōgen's own claims that, in Ju-ching's tradition, all

beyond the monastery. In 1246, immediately upon his arrival in Kyūshū, he wrote a brief *Zazen gi*, the text of which is now preserved in the Kanazawa bunko. Tradition also credits him with a popular *Zazen ron* in the form of answers to basic questions about the theory and practice of Zen meditation. Whether or not Tao-lung was actually received by the government in Kamakura during Dōgen's visit there in 1247–48, the arrival of this first representative of Sung Buddhism must have been the talk of the city at the time. Later Sōtō literature records the texts of correspondence supposed to have passed between the two Zen masters.[44]

Another of Dōgen's contemporaries, Shinchi Kakushin, also wrote a detailed description of Zen mental techniques. Kakushin was a Shingon monk from Kōya san, who became a follower of Yōsai's disciple Gyōyū. After training under several of Yōsai's descendants, including Dōgen, he traveled in 1249 to the Sung, where he studied with the author of the famed *Wu-men kuan*, Wu-men Hui-k'ai (1183–1260). Returning to Japan in 1254, he lived again on Mt. Kōya; eventually, he was given the abbacy of Ganshō's Saihō ji and enjoyed the patronage of several emperors. Like Yōsai, Gyōyū, and Enni, Kakushin seems to have been rather eclectic in his approach to Buddhism and sought to combine the established Japanese tantric tradition with the new continental style of Zen meditation. He has left a brief *Zazen gi* (which does not, in fact, describe meditation technique) and a longer *kana*

Buddhist practices could be reduced to "just sitting.". The similarity of Enni, Tao-lung, and Dōgen on this point was noticed by Mujū, who singles out these three in his *Zōtan shū* as the first in Japan to establish the orthodox Sung monastic style of Ch'an meditation (Yamada and Miki, *Zōtan shū*, 257).

44. Found in the *Kenzei ki* (Kawamura, *Teihon taikō Kenzei ki*, 64). The authenticity of the letters is now usually questioned; see Ōkubo, *Dōgen zenji den no kenkyū*, 272–75; Kagamishima, "Eihei Dōgen to Rankei Dōryū," *Kanazawa bunko kenkyū kiyō* 11 (3/1974), 1–13; reprinted in the same author's *Dōgen zenji to sono shūhen*, 59–77; but cf., Notomi Jōten, "Dōgen no Kamakura kyōke ni tsuite." Tao-lun's *Zazen gi* text is preserved with the manuscript of the *Ju-ju chü-shih tso-ch'an i*; it bears a colophon dated in the fourth year of Kangen (1246). (See Ishii's edition in *Kanazawa bunko shiryō zensho*, vol. 1, 161–68.) His *Zazen ron* (which is in fact a version of the *kana* text of the same title attributed to Enni) can be found at *Kokuyaku zennaku taisei* 23:1–8; it has been translated by Thomas Cleary, in *The Original Face: An Anthology of Rinzai Zen* (1978), 19–41.

Dōgen's writings contain no reference to either Tao-lung or Enni, but the *Shōbō genzō shō*, the commentary by his followers Senne and Kyōgō completed fifty years after his death, includes an attack on the meditation teachings of both these masters—the former for encouraging the practice of *zazen* as a way to "get the point" (*tokushi*) of Buddhism; the latter for recommending it as something to do only after one has got the point. (SSZ.Shūgen,1:348a.) Neither characterization seems to bear much relation to the content of either man's *Zazen ron*, but the attack does show us the antipathy toward these Rinzai teachers (or perhaps their followers) among at least one faction of Dōgen's students. Interestingly enough, Enni's own disciple Mujū has identical criticisms of the misunderstanding of *zazen* among "certain Zen teachers"—those who say one need not do the practice after achieving insight into one's nature (*kenshō*), and those who maintain that practice before such insight is worthless (*itazura goto*); the latter view he finds even among the followers of his master. (Yamada and Miki, *Zōtan shū*, 253, 255, 276. For a discussion of these issues, see Itō Shūken, "Shōbō genzō shō kenkyū nōto (1), SKKKK 11 [8/1979], 6–13.)

hōgo, or vernacular tract, which includes a concrete account of the procedures of *zazen* and recommends concentration on the popular *kōan* of the
"original face" (*honrai menmoku*).[45]

The Zen tradition introduced by these early figures continued to prosper
in the century following Dōgen's death, and the new Zen contemplative
practices were spread through the growing literature of the school. In
addition to explicit meditation tracts, like the well-known *Zazen yōjin ki* and
Sankon zazen setsu, by Dōgen's descendant Keizan Jōkin (1268–1325), or the
so-called *Zazen hōgo* of Keizan's own disciple Myōhō Sotetsu (1277–1350),
the masters of this period produced an abundance of informal writings—
homilies, letters, and so on, often in Japanese—that taught the methods
of Zen to monk and layman alike.[46] The popular *hōgo* texts of influential figures like Wu-hsüeh Tsu-yüan (Mugaku Sogen, 1226–86), Nanpo
Jōmin (1235–1308), Shūhō Myōchō (1282–1337), Ming-chi Ch'u-chün
(Minki Soshun, 1264–1338), Musō Soseki (1275–1351), and so on, all
encourage the cultivation of *zazen* and offer practical advice to the beginner
on how to go about controlling the mind in meditation.

If the rather sudden proliferation of such writings, both in Japan and
on the continent, bears witness to the historical significance of Tsung-tse's
manual in pioneering a new genre of meditation literature, it also suggests
that the authors of these writings were not wholly satisfied with his account
of meditation practice. If Tsung-tse's Buddhism had prefigured, and itself
advanced, the development of a new kind of Ch'an, that development soon
passed it by. His *Ch'an-yüan ch'ing-kuei*, while providing the precedent for the
many codes that were to follow, remained largely innocent of the rituals
associated with the later official monastic system of the Five Mountains. His
appreciation of the Pure Land faith, which led him to advocate the combined practice of Ch'an meditation and Ching-t'u devotion, did not yet yield
the kind of synthesis of the two traditions that was to become so popular in
later China. Similarly, his *Tso-ch'an i*, although it reflected a new concern
for the popularization of simple spiritual exercises, gave no hint of the radical
new technique of *k'an-hua* practice that was soon to capture the attention of
the Ch'an school during the Southern Sung. To this extent, by the thirteenth
century, Tsung-tse's rather conventional meditation teachings must already
have looked somewhat old-fashioned. But there was more to the dissatisfaction with Tsung-tse than this; his teachings posed (or, rather, exposed) real
ideological problems for the tradition. In the next chapter we shall see why
this was so and why Dōgen was by no means alone in harboring doubts
about the sort of Buddhism we find in the *Tso-ch'an i*.

---

45. See *Yura kaizan Hottō kokushi hōgo*, DNBZ.96:213–22, especially "Zazen no koto,"
220–22; Kakushin's *Zazen gi* appears at ibid., 211–12.

46. For Keizan's works, see SSZ.Shūgen,2:423–27, 428–29; Myōhō's text, which is very
similar to the *Sankon zazen setsu*, can be found at *Myōhō kana hōgo*, *Zenmon hōgo shū* 2:523–25.

4

The Sudden Practice and the Ch'an Meditation Discourse

In the preceding chapter I have suggested that, whatever the supposed precedents for the *Tso-ch'an i*, Tsung-tse's manual is best understood as a new kind of Buddhist text, created in a new religious environment and intended for a new audience. Despite what Dōgen and the Zen tradition may have thought, it is probably not based on the Ch'an teachings of Po-chang; contrary to the approach of one prominent modern interpretation, it is not merely the abbreviation of a T'ien-t'ai manual by Chih-i. Still, if we can question the historical premises of these two views, their disagreement over the religious character, or ideological filiation, of the text is not without some reason; in terms at least of our usual notions of sectarian styles, the *Tso-ch'an i* is somewhat difficult to place. It seems to combine a portion of the kind of standard Buddhist material found in the T'ien-t'ai text with a dash of the particular approach to meditation characteristic of some earlier Ch'an writings. Yet the resulting mix—and the simple, colloquial style in which it is served—gives Tsung-tse's Buddhism a very different flavor from Chih-i's sixth-century scholastic version and, at the same time, leaves his meditation teachings with a philosophically conservative, matter-of-fact quality that contrasts with much of the intervening Ch'an literature on the subject.

This freedom from both the technical conventions of traditional scholarship and the philosophical obscurities of classical Ch'an makes Tsung-tse's little manual unusually accessible and may, in fact, have been an important factor in its popularity; but it also makes the work—for all its seeming innocuousness—rather controversial. If the text itself is new, from the perspective of Ch'an in the Sung dynasty, its teachings appear as something of a throwback to an earlier, less theologically developed treatment of Buddhist practice—a treatment in some ways more akin to that of the *Hsiao chih-kuan* than to the received position of the school. Despite the widespread acceptance of the *Tso-ch'an i*, this heterodox character of the work was not entirely lost on its early readers. To see why Dōgen and his contemporaries felt obliged to improve on Tsung-tse's teachings, we shall need to recall the way in which the tradition had dealt with meditation.

In Chapter 5, where I take up the teachings of the *Fukan zazen gi*, we will have an opportunity to examine in some detail Tsung-tse's concrete instructions on the preparation for, and practice of, meditation. We will see certain obvious continuities between Dōgen and Tsung-tse, on the one hand, and between Tsung-tse and Chih-i, on the other. Some important differences among the three will also become apparent. Of these differences, none is more striking nor more central to an understanding of the problematics both of Dōgen's *shikan taza* and of Zen meditation in general than the disagreement over the basic question of how to employ the mind during practice. This disagreement is not merely a matter of differing psychological techniques: it may be that, but it is also closely tied to disparate approaches to some fundamental issues in the interpretation of Buddhism—issues that have been debated in Zen since its inception. As an introduction to this debate, then, let us look here at what Tsung-tse has to say on the central technique of meditation and how it is related to the sort of material we find in a scholastic work like the *Hsiao chih-kuan*.

If some passages in the *Tso-ch'an i* resemble material in the *T'ien-t'ai hsiao chih-kuan*, the brief explanation of the mental technique does not. In his discussion of the basic procedures of meditation, Chih-i follows the description of the posture with an account of the methods for regulating the mind (*t'iao hsin*) so as to avoid the twin obstacles of torpor (*ch'en, laya*) and agitation (*fu, audatya*).[1] In later chapters he goes on to recommend various other mental antidotes for different spiritual problems. But the core of his meditation—what he calls "the practice proper" (*cheng hsiu*)—is, of course, the traditional exercises of calming (*chih, śamatha*) and discernment (*kuan, vipaśyanā*) from which his manual takes its name.

In the chapter devoted to these exercises, Chih-i divides them into five types, depending on the purposes for which they are practiced. Of these exercises, the first, intended to overcome the rough fluctuations of the mind at the outset of meditation, is basic. There are essentially two types of *śamatha* exercises for this purpose. One, which is more or less mechanical, involves

---

1. T.46:466a. As an antidote for the former, the meditator is to fix his attention on the tip of his nose; if the mind becomes agitated, he is to focus his awareness on his abdomen. In addition to this classic Buddhist formula on spiritual imbalance, Chih-i also discusses here antidotes for the slack (*k'uan*) and strained (*chi*) attention.

fixation on an object or conscious suppression of random thoughts. The other exercise, which is intellectual, trains the practitioner to understand as each thought occurs that its object arises from conditions and has no nature of its own. Once the practitioner understands this, his mind will not grasp the object, and deluded thoughts will cease. A somewhat more complicated technique is recommended for the *vipaśyanā* practice: if the meditator has failed to put an end to deluded thoughts through *śamatha*, he should reflect on these thoughts, asking himself whether they exist or not. Chih-i then supplies a set of arguments for this reflection. By rehearsing these arguments, the practitioner can convince himself that neither the mind nor its object can be grasped; thus convinced, the mind will break off discrimination and become still.[2]

These classic Buddhist contemplative exercises, of a sort widely recommended in both Indian and Chinese sources, play no part in Tsung-tse's manual. Instead what he calls "the essential art of *tso-ch'an*" is simply this:

> Do not think of any good or evil whatsoever. Whenever a thought occurs, be aware of it [*nien ch'i chi chüeh*]; as soon as you are aware of it, it will vanish. If you remain for a long period forgetful of objects [*wang yüan*], you will naturally become unified [*i-p'ien*].[3]

This passage has no parallel in the *Hsiao chih-kuan*. If it has any analogue in Chih-i's teachings, it is not in the *chih-kuan* techniques described in his manual but, rather, in the simple mindfulness practice recommended as one of the famous four forms of *samādhi* in the *Mo-ho chih-kuan*—the practice referred to there as "neither walking nor sitting" (*fei hsing fei tso*) and otherwise known as "the *samādhi* of awareness of mental activity" (*chüeh-i san-mei*).

> The master Nan-yüeh [i.e., Chih-i's master, Hui-ssu (515–77)] called this [practice] "following one's own mental activity" [*sui tzu i*]—that is, whenever any mental activity occurs, one is to practice *samādhi* [*i ch'i chi hsiu san-mei*]. The *Pañcaviṃśati* refers to it as "the *samādhi* of awareness of mental activity"—that is, wherever mental activity may be directed, one is to be conscious of, and clear about, it.... "Awareness" [*chüeh*] here means luminous understanding [*chao-liao*]; "mental activity" [*i*] means the mental *dharmas* [*hsin-shu, caitasika*].... In practicing this, whenever a mental *dharma* arises, one reflects on, and contemplates it, without attending to its development—its source or outcome, its point of origin or destination.[4]

---

2. T.46:466c–469b.
3. For this and subsequent passages from the *Tso-ch'an i*, see the translation in my appendices.
4. T.46:14b–c. See also Chih-i's *Chüeh-i san-mei*, T.46:621–27. The interesting interpretation of the term *chüeh-i* (usually *bodhyaṅga*) here is explained at some length in Neal Donner, "The Great Calming and Contemplation of Chih-i" (1976), 352–53, n. 249.

Whatever the ultimate antecedents of Tsung-tse's practice—either in T'ien-t'ai or earlier Buddhist tradition—Chih-i is not the source for our *Tso-ch'an i* passage. Rather, as we shall shortly see, it derives from a standard formula for meditation found in some early Ch'an materials. But before we consider those materials, we should note two general features of Tsung-tse's practice that seem, at least on the surface, to distinguish it from that of the *Hsiao chih-kuan* and many other classical Buddhist treatments of meditation. One of these concerns the apparently passive style of his technique.

In the discernment meditations recommended in the *Hsiao chih-kuan*, as is characteristically the case in the scholastic *vipaśyanā* systems, the practitioner is expected to engage the object actively, contemplating it under the rubric of some Buddhist category until he has brought about a change in the way the object occurs to him, such that it now appears as an instance of that category. In contrast, Tsung-tse's meditation seems to involve no such discursive activity; instead the practitioner is to relinquish judgments and passively observe his thoughts as they come and go. In this sense his practice seems more akin to such common preliminary concentration exercises as following the breath, observing the activities of the body, and so on.[5] The distinction between active and passive styles of meditation is worth noting because the dichotomy is a recurrent theme in Ch'an discussions of the practice and one source of internecine dispute. This theme frequently overlaps with a somewhat similar but separable dichotomy between mental clarity and calm.

The *chih-kuan* practice I have just summarized is expressly recommended for the control of the gross fluctuations of the mind; it is intended to put an end to the stream of deluded thoughts characteristic of ordinary consciousness and to bring about the calm, concentrated state of *samādhi*. Such a state would seem to be the goal of Tsung-tse's meditation as well: the practitioner is to observe his thoughts so that they will cease; he is to continue observing them until they no longer occur and the mind becomes unified. This agreement on the goal of the practice is hardly surprising: no doubt most Buddhists would hold with Tsung-tse here that the unified state of *samādhi*, or *dhyāna*, is indeed the essential art of meditation. They would also hold, however, that this state is not an end in itself: whether or not it is a necessary

---

5. It should be remembered that even in the simpler Buddhist mindfulness practices, the traditional accounts (as opposed, say, to certain modern descriptions of *vipassanā*) usually assume that the meditator will observe the object under some conceptual rubric, such that he can recognize the former as an instance of the latter. So, for example, the classical exercise of *dharma-smṛty-upasthāna*, which otherwise might seem akin to Tsung-tse's bare observation of thoughts, involves the application of a variety of doctrinal formulae: the five hindrances, the six sense fields, the four noble truths, and so on. Similarly, Chih-i's *chüeh-i san-mei* expects the practitioner at the very least to identify each object as characterized by one of the three *karmic* natures (of good, bad, and neutral)—a practice explicitly rejected here by Tsung-tse.

condition for enlightenment, it is not a sufficient one but must be supplemented by the generation of insight, or wisdom. On this point, Chih-i would surely concur, as his entire system of calming and discernment makes quite clear. Whether Tsung-tse would also concur is much less clear, at least from the text of the *Tso-ch'an i*, and his silence on this matter makes it possible to interpret the work as recommending the elimination of thought for its own sake. A tendency toward some such understanding of yogic discipline is probably endemic to Buddhist meditation teachings, from the early *dhyāna* and *samāpatti* systems on, and the religion has repeatedly been obliged to counter it with an emphasis on the need for doctrinal study. Ch'an Buddhism, with its focus on meditation and its characteristic dismissal of theoretical reflection, has been particularly susceptible to this tendency and has often struggled mightily against it. Hence, if only by omission, the *Tso-ch'an i* account of meditation touches a sensitive nerve in the tradition.[6]

In fairness to Tsung-tse, we must point out that he is not entirely oblivious to the question of wisdom. In the opening lines of the *Tso-ch'an i*, he recommends the cultivation of *samādhi* for one who has taken the *bodhisattva* vows and seeks to study *prajñā*. This passage undoubtedly reflects the traditional Buddhist formula of the three disciplines (*san hsüeh, trini-śikṣāṇi*), of ethics, meditation, and wisdom, and suggests that, like most interpreters, Tsung-tse understood the three as a series, such that meditation follows upon ethics and somehow leads to wisdom. Unfortunately, he does not pause to discuss the question of just how it leads to wisdom, but later on he does give us a hint, at least, of what he may have had in mind. Toward the end of his text, in a rather rambling discussion of the benefits of meditation, he seems to offer three: it will make one happy, healthy, and peaceful; it will prepare one to face death; and it will lead to wisdom. This last is expressed by means of a well-known metaphor.

To seek the pearl, we should still the waves; if we disturb the water, it will be hard to get. When the water of meditation is clear, the pearl of the mind will appear of itself. Therefore, the *Perfect Enlightenment Sūtra* [*Yüan-chüeh ching*] says, "Unimpeded, immaculate wisdom always arises dependent on meditation."[7]

---

6. The issue of mental quiescence as a goal of concentration, and the Buddhist ambivalence toward it, is well reflected in the vexed topic of the *nirodha-samāpatti* (*mieh-chin ting*), the state of mental "extinction" that was held to be at once the pinnacle of the *dhyāna* system and a soteriological dead end. (The anomaly was sometimes "handled" by reserving the meditation for the *anāgāmin* and *arhat*—that is, those for whom salvation was no longer an issue.) The famous Ch'an teachings of "no-thought" (*wu-nien*) and "no-mind" (*wu-hsin*) ran the constant risk of identification with mental extinction, and many of the school's warnings against *dhyāna* seem to have something like this state as their object.

7. The metaphor of water and waves is best known in Ch'an from the *Laṅkāvatāra-sūtra* (e.g., T.16:538c); Tsung-tse's line on the pearl here is probably from Tung-shan Liang-chieh (see *T'ien-sheng kuang teng lu*, ZZ.2B,8:353d). The passage from the *Yüan-chüeh ching* occurs at T.17:919a21.

As Tsung-tse uses it, the metaphor itself may have become somewhat opaque, but we can still discern the outlines of the model behind it: like the pearl at the bottom of the sea, wisdom rests deep within the mind, obscured only by the surface fluctuations of thought; once these fluctuations are calmed, wisdom is automatically made manifest. Hence meditation leads to wisdom not in the usual sense that it prepares the mind to undertake the discipline of *prajñā* but in the sense that it uncovers a preexistent *prajñā*, inherent to the mind. Thus it is possible to speak of the calm of meditation, if not as an end in itself, at least as a sufficient condition for that end. The theory behind this way of speaking—the model of the pure, enlightened mind covered over by discursive thinking—is by no means, of course, an uncommon one, not only in Ch'an texts but in Chih-i's writings and other versions of Mahāyāna. Whatever we may say of it as a theory, from the perspective of Buddhist practice, it offered the religion a handy way of dealing with the difficult question of the relationship between *samādhi* and *prajñā* and provided a meaningful rationale for the cultivation of meditation. These virtues notwithstanding, the theory was questioned by some of the most influential figures of the early Ch'an movement—figures whose teachings became the basis for orthodoxy in the later tradition. On this point too, therefore, the *Tso-ch'an i* could raise the eyebrows (if not the hackles) of its more thoughtful readers.

Tsung-tse's approach to Buddhism, then, may not be quite that of sixth-century T'ien-t'ai treatises, but neither is it quite what we are familiar with from the recorded sayings of the great Ch'an masters of the late T'ang and Five Dynasties—sayings so popular among Tsung-tse's Sung contemporaries. If anything, he seems rather to take us back to an earlier phase of the school, when the Ch'an movement was still seeking to articulate its basic doctrinal positions and define a form of religious practice consistent with them. Indeed, of all the preceding Ch'an literature, his manual is perhaps most reminiscent of the kind of material one sometimes finds in the texts associated with the seventh-century Tung shan ("East Mountain") tradition of the Patriarchs Tao-hsin (580–651) and Hung-jen (601–74). It is in the teachings of these men, and those of their immediate successors in the so-called Northern school of the eighth century, that we find the most explicit descriptions of Ch'an meditation prior to the *Tso-ch'an i* itself. It is also in their teachings that we find the beginnings of those doctrines that, in the hands of their rivals in the Southern school, would render Ch'an meditation peculiarly problematic and help to silence for some three centuries the open discussion of its techniques.

This is not the place to explore in detail the history of the early Ch'an meditation literature, which is better left to those more expert in this matter than I. But it is worth recalling here several general features of that literature that help to explain some of the attitudes of the later tradition. Of the East

Mountain corpus, we may take as obvious examples the teachings of Tao-
hsin in the *Leng-ch'ieh shih-tzu chi* and the treatise attributed to Hung-jen
known as the *Hsiu hsin yao lun*.[8] Whether or not this material represents
accurate reports of the Buddhism of the Fourth and Fifth Patriarchs, it does
preserve for us the understanding of those teachings current among influential factions of Ch'an in the eighth century. Both texts are highly practical
in approach and provide fairly concrete instructions on a range of spiritual
techniques. These seem to fall into three general types. One is a contemplation on emptiness roughly of the sort we have seen in Chih-i's meditations.
We find this type, for example, in the Tao-hsin section of the *Leng-ch'ieh
shih-tzu chi*, where it appears in conjunction with the famous practice of
"guarding the one without moving" (*shou i pu i*). Here we are told to
contemplate all *dharmas* of both body and mind—from the four elements
and five aggregates to the *dharmas* of the common man (*pṛthagjana*) and the
Buddhist adept (*ārya*)—recognizing that they are all empty and quiescent,
without origination or cessation, and so on. We should continue this practice
in all activities, day and night, until we can see our own existence as but
a reflection, a mirage, an echo. Should random thoughts intrude on the
meditation, we are to see whatever occurs as ultimately not occurring, as
coming from nowhere and going nowhere; when thoughts are seen thus, the
mind will become stabilized.[9]

More commonly encountered and probably more characteristic of the
tradition are two other types of meditation. One recommends the observation of some symbol of what, for want of a better term, we may call the
ultimate principle. Such, for example, is the popular *samādhi* of one array
(*i-hsing san-mei, ekavyūha-samādhi*), introduced at the outset of the Tao-hsin
section of the *Leng-ch'ieh shih-tzu chi*: here the practitioner is to focus on the
image of a single Buddha, recognizing therein the identity of that Buddha
with the entire *dharma-dhātu* and, as the text goes on to comment, with the
practitioner's own mind.[10] In the Hung-jen section of the same text, we find
a meditation on the numeral one, either projected onto the horizon or
visualized internally; in this meditation the practitioner experiences a sense

8. Both these texts have recently been the subject of detailed studies and translations: for
the latter, see John McRae, "The Northern School of Chinese Ch'an Buddhism" (1983); for
the former, Bernard Faure, "La Volonté d'Orthodoxie: Généalogie et Doctrine du Bouddhisme
Ch'an de l'École du Nord" (1985). Tao-hsin's teachings have also recently appeared in English,
in David Chappell, "The Teachings of the Fourth Ch'an Patriarch Tao-hsin (580–651)," in
Lancaster and Lai, *Early Ch'an in China and Tibet*, 89–129.

9. The *Leng-ch'ieh shih-tzu chi* appears at T.85:1283ff; here I am using the edition in
Yanagida Seizan, *Shoki no zen shi* I, *Zen no goroku* 2 (1971), 248–49.

10. Yanagida, *Shoki no zen shi* I, 186. Tao-hsin is here explicitly following the instructions
of the *Wen-shu shuo pan-jo ching* (T.8:731b). Though Chinese tradition, both within and outside
of Ch'an, tends to interpret the term *i-hsing* as "single practice," it seems clear that here, as in
the *Sūtra* itself, the emphasis is on the original sense of "single array"—that is, the entirety of
the *dharma-dhātu* manifest in the *samādhi*.

of unlimited space analogous to the *dharma-kāya*.[11] Similarly, the *Hsiu hsin yao lun*, which uses the sun as a metaphor for the true enlightened mind within us all, recommends the contemplation of an image of the disk of the sun.[12]

The other type of technique involves some sort of simple concentration exercise. This would seem to be the practical import of Tao-hsin's most basic description of "guarding the one without moving." It is defined simply as maintaining the concentrated observation of one thing (*kuan i wu*) until the mind becomes fixed in *samādhi*. If the mind wanders, it is to be brought back to the object, as the saying goes, like a bird held by a string. Just as the archer gradually narrows his aim to the very center of the target, so too the meditator should learn to focus his attention until the mind remains fixed on its object in each moment, and right mindfulness (*cheng nien*) is present without interruption.[13] Closest, perhaps, to Tsung-tse's description of meditation are some of the accounts of Hung-jen's practice of "guarding the mind" (*shou hsin*) given in the *Hsiu hsin yao lun*. In the most explicit of these accounts we are told to abandon the seizing of objects; to regulate body, breath, and mind; and then to focus gently on the fluctuations of consciousness (*hsin-shih liu-tung*) until they disappear of their own accord. When they do so, they take with them all the obstacles to complete enlightenment.[14]

The distinction among these types of meditation is not always clear, and apparently such catchwords as "the *samādhi* of one array," "guarding the one," or "guarding the mind" could, in practice, denote a variety of contemplative techniques. Whatever their differences, they seem to share a common theoretical context—the characteristic East Mountain doctrine of the pure, radiant consciousness inherent in every mind—and a common purpose— the detachment from, and eventual suppression of, the stream of discursive thoughts that is supposed to obscure this consciousness. Perhaps most significantly, on the basis of these common elements, each of the techniques is typically presented as at once readily accessible to the beginner and yet leading directly to enlightenment.

This abrupt leap from a seemingly rather pedestrian psychophysical exercise to the rarified reaches of the spiritual path is well expressed in a passage from the *Leng-ch'ieh shih-tzu chi* attributed to Tao-hsin. There we are told that, when one first sets out to practice meditation and observe the

---

11. Ibid., 287.

12. *Tsui-shang sheng lun*, T.48: 378a–b. The practice appears as the first of the contemplations recommended in the *Kuan wu-liang-shou ching* (T.12: 342a).

13. Yanagida, *Shoki no zen shi* I, 241. The striking metaphor here of the archer who keeps each of his arrows aloft with another fired into its shaft is probably, as Yanagida notes in his annotation (246), from the *Ta-chih-tu lun* (T.25: 592c, 594b), where it is used in reference not to meditation technique but to the *bodhisattva*'s ability to keep himself from "falling" into *nirvāṇa* until he has completed all the practices leading to Buddhahood.

14. *Tsui-shang sheng lun*, T.48: 379a.

mind, he should seek solitude; sitting erect, he should loosen his robe and belt, relax his body, stretch himself several times, and exhale fully; then he will have a sense of expanding to his true nature and become clear and vacant, tranquil and still. When he has thus regulated body and mind and settled his spirit, his breathing will be calm; as he gradually controls his mind, it will become clear and bright. When his contemplation becomes clear, and both inside and out become empty and pure, the mind itself will be quiescent; when this happens, the *ārya* mind (*sheng hsin*) will appear. The text then goes on to tell us that the nature of this mind, always functioning within us, is the Buddha nature, and that one who experiences this nature is forever released from *saṃsāra* and has transcended this world; he has, as the *Vimalakīrti-sūtra* says, suddenly regained his original mind (*pen hsin*).[15]

Though this passage tells us little about the mental technique involved here, its concrete description of some of the physical elements reminds us of both the *Hsiao chih-kuan* and the *Tso-ch'an i*; indeed the passage has been singled out by Sekiguchi as the first example of a Ch'an description of meditation technique.[16] What is perhaps most striking from a doctrinal perspective is its apparent identification of the calm, clear state of *samādhi* with the attainment of the *ārya* path, and the impression it gives that the beginning meditator, simply by quieting his mind, can in a single sitting attain this *samādhi* and propel himself onto that path. Such hyperbolic praise of meditation is not, of course, unusual in Buddhist literature; in fact, the message here is quite similar to the direct identification of *śamatha* with the attainment of *nirvāṇa* that we sometimes find in the *Hsiao chih-kuan* itself.[17] Nor is the recommendation of a single, simple practice for exclusive cultivation without ample precedent: it is a characteristic of some of the very Mahāyāna *sūtra* literature on which both Chih-i and the Tung shan teachers like to draw for their accounts of meditation. Unlike more conservative interpretations of such literature, the Tung shan teachings tend to ignore the various graded hierarchies of vehicles, paths, stages, and the like that provide the traditional contexts for specific meditations. In effect, then, they seem to reduce the panoply of Buddhist spiritual exercises to a single practice

---

15. Yanagida, *Shoki no zen shi* I, 255.

16. See, for example, his *Tendai shikan no kenkyū*, 346.

17. So, for example, this passage on "*śamatha* through comprehension of the truth" (*t'i-chen chih*):

If the practitioner knows that the mind is without [its own] nature, why should there be reality to the *dharmas* [that arise from the mind]?... Being empty and without substance, they cannot be grasped. If they are not grasped, the mind of deluded thoughts [*wang-nien hsin*] will cease; and, if the mind of deluded thoughts ceases, it is quiescent and unconditioned [*wu-wei*]. This unconditionedness is the original source of all *dharmas*. If one rests his mind in this original source, it is without defilement; and, if the mind is without defilement, then all *karmic* activity of *saṃsāra* ceases. When the *karmic* activity of *saṃsāra* ceases, this is itself *nirvāṇa*. (Translated from Sekiguchi's edition, *Tendai shō shikan no kenkyū*, 339–40.)

and the perpetuity of the *bodhisattva* path to a single experience. In this they are presenting one form of a "sudden" version of Buddhist practice.

The Zen tradition may look to its own Sixth Patriarch for its famous doctrine of sudden enlightenment (*tun wu*), but by his day, notions of a sudden approach to religious practice had been current in Chinese Buddhism for some time. One such notion was basic to the early T'ien-t'ai discussion of meditation and is well expressed in Kuan-ting's oft-quoted introduction to the *Mo-ho chih-kuan*. There we are told that, unlike the gradual (*chien*) cultivation of *śamatha-vipaśyanā*, which proceeds along the spiritual path by overcoming in turn the obstacles characteristic of each of the stages of the *mārga*, the "perfect sudden" (*yüan-tun*) practice takes from the start the ultimate reality of the *dharma-dhātu* itself as the sole object of meditation. Such a practice is based on what T'ien-t'ai considers the highest version of Buddhism—the one Buddha vehicle, in which, as the text says, every sight and every smell is the ultimate middle way, in which ignorance is identical with enlightenment, *saṃsāra* is identical with *nirvāṇa*, and there is no religious path leading from one to the other. In such a practice, *śamatha* is nothing but the quiescence of *dharmatā* itself (*fa-hsing chi-jan*) and *vipaśyanā* is but its constant luminosity (*ch'ang chao*).[18]

Here, as elsewhere throughout the Chinese literature on this complex topic, the distinction between sudden and gradual seems to cover a bewildering array of issues, ranging from practical matters of spiritual technique to theoretical positions on the interpretation of Buddhist doctrine. Read simply in concrete psychological terms, for example, the distinction described here might be seen as one between antidotal meditations, intended to counteract specific spiritual obstacles, and insight meditations, which, like the venerable *nirvedha-bhāgīya* exercises, take the metaphysical doctrines of Buddhism as their theme and lead directly (and, by the very nature of insight, quite abruptly and inexplicably) to an apprehension of the truth of these doctrines. Since Buddhist tradition tends to associate these two types of meditations with such standard polarities as *śamatha* and *vipaśyanā*, or *samādhi* and *prajñā*, respectively, it is possible to read into the concrete distinction more general definitions: that spiritual techniques of calming and concentration are gradual in nature, while those of discernment and wisdom are sudden. Something like these definitions were assumed by many in the Ch'an school; it is hardly surprising, therefore, that, insofar as they claimed to champion the sudden practice, they should have been wary of any techniques that smacked of concentration exercises.

There is more, of course, to the sudden-gradual dichotomy than differences in contemplative exercise: as is clear from our *Mo-ho chih-kuan* passage,

18. T.46:1c–2a.

there is also the broader question of whether it is necessary to master certain preliminary exercises of ethics, meditation, or wisdom before proceeding to more advanced meditations. The sudden practice appears to abandon the various meditative objects and techniques that aid the aspirant in the negotiation of the path and immediately takes up the contemplation of absolute reality itself—a reality that is supposed to transcend all the ethical and metaphysical categories through which Buddhism is taught. It is as though the practitioner is invited to plunge directly into the culmination of the path, the mighty *vajropama-samādhi*, in which the *bodhisattva* vaults in one final moment of trance to the supreme, perfect enlightenment of Buddhahood.

However radical this feature of the sudden practice may seem when encountered out of context, for a scholar like Chih-i, it probably always remained more an interpretive device than a prescription for action. His perfect sudden meditation was the pinnacle of an elaborate classification system that sought to bring order to the diverse theories and practices of the Buddhist tradition, from what he took to be the elementary teachings of the *śrāvaka* vehicle through the more advanced doctrines of the *bodhisattva* path to the ultimate truths of the Buddha vehicle. It is in the context of this last, highest stage of the religion that he can (indeed, under the circumstances, probably must) envision a perfect teaching, with no condescension to the unenlightened understanding, and a sudden practice, no longer impeded by the obstacles to Buddhahood. In terms of the larger system, however, all Buddhist teaching was a single vehicle, and all its practices had their place.

Thus, for his part, Chih-i is ever careful to hedge round his vision of the highest, sudden practice with detailed description of traditional Buddhist training and to find room on his one great vehicle for even the humblest forms of *upāya*. Always the scholar, he never forgets the distinction between theory and practice or the various levels of philosophical discourse and spiritual maturation. Yet for those impatient to taste the fruits of his supreme Buddha vehicle, the prospect of a sudden meditation beyond the old practices of the *bodhisattva-mārga* was too tempting to postpone to the final course. Thus the Ch'an movement was quick to pass over the formal setting of the meditation and seek a means to put it immediately into practice.

This brings us to a final implication of the sudden doctrine without which we cannot understand the rather curious development of the Ch'an discourse on meditation. As the contemplation of the *dharma-dhātu*, the sudden meditation reveals, we are told, a sacred reality in which every phenomenon is the middle way of Buddhism. There is no gap between *saṃsāra* and *nirvāṇa* and, hence, no spiritual defect that must be overcome by religious practice. Such is the vision appropriate to the supreme Buddha vehicle—the path of one for whom, his training complete, no practice remains. In this revelation the ultimate meditation seems to consume itself. In fact in the hands of the Buddhist metaphysician, the sudden practice is no longer merely the best method for the cultivation of the mind or the one method of the ultimate vehicle. If it can be described as such from the outside, from the inside, so to speak, it is no method at all but the very nature of the mind and, indeed, of all things. Thus our T'ien-t'ai text can identify the practice of meditative calm with the ultimate quiescence, or emptiness, of phenomena and the practice of discernment of phenomena with their miraculous manifestation. Thus, too, the Ch'an teachers can describe their practice as no-practice, as nothing more than the inherent state and spontaneous function of the mind.

The problem with this abstract interpretation of the sudden meditation, of course, is that, taken neat, its radical nondualism undermines the rationale for its cultivation and renders philosophically embarrassing any concrete discussion of its techniques. Chih-i's ample Buddhism could easily live with this problem, its catholic embrace of *upāya* allowing him room to discuss the practical methods of even this most mysterious and metaphysical of meditations.[19] Similarly, the early Ch'an movement, though no doubt inspired by the notion of a perfect Buddha vehicle, still tended to operate within a model—of the Buddha nature obscured—that retained the dualistic metaphysics of what T'ien-t'ai would call the relative (*hsiang-tai*) teaching more characteristic of its "distinct" (*pieh*), *bodhisattva* vehicle. Though its vision of meditation may have narrowed to the single, sudden practice that leads directly to enlightenment, it still takes for granted the kind of distinctions—between theory and practice, cause and effect, meditation and wisdom—that allow it to speak frankly of the psychological techniques through which this practice is implemented. But as the movement, perhaps in the heat of sectarian competition, began to focus more and more narrowly on the supreme vehicle (*wu-shang sheng*), the one true teaching (*chen tsung*), the meditation of the Tathāgata Himself (*ju-lai ch'an*), and so on, the metaphysics of the absolute, nondual truth became the norm. Thus the radiant Buddha nature became ever brighter, its obscurations ever emptier, and the resulting contradiction inherent in any description of a psychological method for inducing the sudden practice ever more obvious.

It is this contradiction that so tickled the fancy of the movement known to us as the Southern school and inspired the severe criticisms of meditation that we find in such influential texts as the *Liu-tsu t'an ching* and Shen-hui's *T'an yü* and *Ting shih-fei lun*. The movement began from the premise that, as Shen-hui put it, man's essential nature is the suchness body of all the Buddhas—empty, still, all-pervasive, unattached. His mind is beyond right

---

19. Hence the *Mo-ho chih-kuan*'s detailed presentation of the practice of contemplation of the mind (*kuan hsin*), in which the sudden meditation is effected through the recognition of "the three thousand" *dharmas* in every thought (*i nien san-ch'ien*).

and wrong or coming and going and is without determinate place of abode (*wu chu ch'u*).[20] Taking their stand on this, the uncompromised cardinal principle (*ti-i i*) of the perfection of wisdom alone, the Southern masters delighted in pointing out the falsity of all conventional understanding of mental states and the consequent folly of methods to overcome what was, after all, not really real. Now the sudden practice was to be precisely that which ignores the unreal and abandons all methods—that which, being one with ultimate *bodhi*, was without attributes (*wu hsiang*), without intentionality (*wu wei*), without artifice (*wu tso*), and so on. Since it was without attributes, this practice could not be described; since it was without artifice, nothing could be done about it.

Perhaps the *T'an ching* put the matter most bluntly in its discussion of the so-called "three attributeless disciplines" (*wu-hsiang san hsüeh*). The difference, says Hui-neng, between his own sudden teaching and the gradual approach of his Northern rival, Shen-hsiu, is that the latter still condescends to the conventional understanding and presents ethics, meditation, and wisdom as something to be put into practice. Hui-neng prefers the higher ground of the ultimate nature.

The fact that the basis of the mind [*hsin ti*] is without any wrong is the ethics of one's own nature; the fact that the basis of the mind is without disturbance is the meditation of one's own nature; the fact that the basis of the mind is without ignorance is the wisdom of one's own nature.... When we understand our own nature, we do not set up ethics, meditation, and wisdom.... Since our own nature is without wrong, disturbance, or ignorance, and in every moment of thought *prajñā* illuminates, always free from the attributes of things, what is there to be set up?[21]

In the luminous wisdom of our own true nature there appears no need for religion. In the sudden style of the Southern school it was now enough simply to recognize this fact—simply to recognize, as they said, one's own nature (*chien hsing*)—and leave off misguided attempts to cultivate Buddhism. Meditation, as Buddhist cultivation par excellence (and the forte of the Northern masters), was particularly to be avoided: any effort to control, suppress, or otherwise alter the mind was ipso facto a gradual—and, hence, at best a second-rate—form of Buddhism. In first-rate Buddhism the true meaning of sudden meditation was simply the fact that the mind was inherently calm, inherently without any real thoughts (*wu nien*) that might disturb it. In this way the practical thrust of early Ch'an meditation was overwhelmed by its own logic: religious prescription was sublated in metaphysical description, and *samādhi* was liberated from its earthly burdens to join *prajñā* in the higher realm of pure principle.

---

20. *Nan-yang ho-shang t'an yü*, in Hu Shih, *Shen-hui ho-shang i-chi* (rev. ed., 1970), 237–40.
21. Philip Yampolsky, *The Platform Sutra of the Sixth Patriarch* (1967), end matter, 20.

Thus, by the mid-eighth century, even as the tradition of Bodhidharma was beginning to establish itself as the Meditation school, it was beginning to find itself unable to advocate openly the actual practice of meditation. On the contrary, it was now de rigueur to attack even the simplified contemplative exercises of the earlier movement as gradual methods—methods considered not only theoretically inconsistent with the fashionable doctrine of sudden awakening but actually detrimental to the quick attainment of liberation. The writings of Shen-hui, widely recognized as the chief architect of the Southern doctrine, fairly bristle with such attacks.

At the outset of his *T'an yü*, often held to be his earliest extant teaching, Shen-hui offers a definition of the three "natural" (*wu-tso*) disciplines rather like that we have just seen from Hui-neng. But in the curious passage that follows he goes on to single out *samādhi* as the only one of the three that cannot be attained through artificial means (*yu-tso*).[22] In his *Ting shih-fei lun*, supposed to record the famous debate at Hua-t'ai through which the Southern school first asserted itself as the orthodox lineage of Ch'an, he distinguishes the Buddhism of his own master, Hui-neng, from that of the Northern champion, Shen-hsiu, precisely on the grounds that the latter mistakenly encouraged people to practice meditation, teaching them "to congeal the mind and enter *samādhi*, to fix the mind and observe purity, to arouse the mind and outwardly illumine, to concentrate the mind and inwardly verify."[23]

Shen-hui's arguments against such practices are numerous and varied. Sometimes he argues from history, claiming that none of the orthodox Patriarchs of Ch'an recommended them; sometimes he cites scripture, reminding his audience that Vimalakīrti criticized Śāriputra for practicing meditation.[24] Elsewhere his points are soteriological; the practice of meditation is characteristic of those on the lower vehicles who do not aspire to supreme enlightenment. Their time spent in trance is time wasted—time better spent in practicing the perfection of wisdom, which alone will lead to

---

22. Hu Shih, *Shen-hui ho-shang i-chi*, 228–29. To my knowledge, this little oddity does not occur elsewhere, but it is telling. Telling in a rather different way is the passage just preceding this, which seems to approve of the traditional definition of the three disciplines rejected as gradual by the *T'an ching*.

23. Hu Shih, *Shen-hui ho-shang i-chi*, 285–87. Criticism of the same practices appears in the *T'an yü* as well, where we also find warnings against such techniques as abiding with mind congealed, abiding in direct observation (of the object of contemplation?), abiding with eyes cast down, purposely concentrating the mind, watching over the near and distant (i.e., internal and external objects?) (ibid., 236–37). The four-phrase description of Northern meditative techniques here appears regularly in Shen-hui's texts and was later picked up by Lin-chi as well; see *Lin-chi lu*, in Akizuki Ryōmin, *Rinzai roku, Zen no goroku* 10 (1972), 79.

24. *Ting shih-fei lun*, Hu Shih, *Shen-hui ho-shang i-chi*, 286, 288. The *Vimalakīrti* passage (T.14:539c) is invoked several times by Shen-hui and appears also in the *T'an ching* (Yampolsky, *The Platform Sutra*, end matter, 6).

the realization of enlightenment. Meditation is *karmic* activity, leading only to continued rebirth; it produces no more than a spiritually impotent emptiness (*wu-chi k'ung*), devoid of wisdom and contributing nothing to liberation from the afflictions.[25] Everywhere, however, he returns to the basic charge—or cluster of charges—against meditation that follows from the highest metaphysic: it does not accord with the perfect wisdom; it is an obstruction of inherent *bodhi*; it is based on, and itself contributes to, an attachment to false ideas about the mind, purity and calm, and religion. The only true *samādhi*, says Shen-hui, is the natural stillness and calm of man's original nonabiding mind; to seek an artificial calm through meditation is what he calls "*dharma* bondage," the subtle delusion that shackles this mind with fixed notions of *nirvāṇa*, emptiness, purity, or *samādhi*.[26]

In this way, himself now hemmed in by the highest truth, Shen-hui is left with little ground for cultivation and can only hint shyly at how one might go about practicing his Buddhism. Yet for all its metaphysical ornamentation, what he hints at turns out to be a version of the humble mindfulness technique we have seen in Hung-jen—the same practice that is recommended much later by Tsung-tse.

If true Buddhism is only the *dharma* beyond our fixed notions of the world, then its true practice is only the freedom from such notions—the ongoing realization of no-thought, or the nonabiding mind, in the worldly experience of the Buddhist. In this practice, as the Southern texts repeatedly point out, meditation and wisdom are the same—or more accurately, it would seem, two aspects of the same mental state: wisdom is but the natural experience of the six senses in the absence of deluded thought; meditation is but the nonproduction of such thought in regard to that experience.[27] With this slight shift in the definition of *samādhi*, the school opened a small crack in the system that allowed it to admit the actual cultivation of no-thought. Thus, alongside our metaphysical definitions of meditation and the standard reminders that there is nothing to Buddhist practice but the sudden recognition of one's true nature, we find admonitions to pursue the *prajñā-samādhi*, the *ekavyūha-samādhi*, and so on—all, of course, now defined in one way or another simply as detached awareness of, or nonproduction

---

25. Hu Shih, *Shen-hui ho-shang i-chi*, 229–32, 239–40. So, too, in the *T'an ching*, Hui-neng criticizes the practice of "sitting motionless, removing delusions and suppressing thoughts" as mere insentiency, the practice of "severing thoughts" as leading only to rebirth, and the meditation on emptiness as descent into a neutral emptiness. (Yampolsky, *The Platform Sutra*, end matter, 6–7, 11.)

26. *T'an yü*, Hu Shih, *Shen-hui ho-shang i-chi*, 234, 237–40. In a similar vein Hui-neng criticizes those who seek to "view the mind" (*k'an hsin*) or "view the purity [of the mind]" (*k'an ching*) for setting up an artificial object of contemplation that obscures the inherent nature of the mind. (Yampolsky, *The Platform Sutra*, end matter, 7.)

27. *T'an yü*, Hu Shih, *Shen-hui ho-shang i-chi*, 237–43. Similar discussions appear in several places in Shen-hui and the *T'an ching*.

of thought in regard to, the objects of experience.[28] And in Shen-hui, we even find what looks suspiciously like some practical advice on a psychological technique for achieving no-thought.

In the *Ting shih-fei lun*, when asked about no-thought, Shen-hui replies that it is not thinking about being or nonbeing, about good or evil, *bodhi* or *nirvāṇa*, and so on; it is nothing but the *prajñā-pāramitā*, which is itself the *ekavyūha-samādhi*. He then describes this *samādhi*.

Good friends, for those at the stage of practice, whenever a thought occurs to the mind, be aware of it [*hsin jo yu nien ch'i chi pien chüeh-chao*]. When what has occurred to the mind disappears, the awareness of it vanishes of its own accord. This is no-thought.[29]

Similarly, in the *T'an yü*, in warning against the misguided attempt to purify the mind of delusion, he says:

Friends, when you correctly employ the mind, if any deluded [thought] occurs, and you think about things either near or far, you should not try to constrain it. Why? Because, if the putting forth of a thought is a sickness, the constraint of it is also a sickness.... If any deluded [thought] occurs, be aware of it [*jo yu wang ch'i chi chüeh*]. When awareness and delusion have both disappeared, this is the nonabiding mind of the original nature.[30]

In keeping with his sudden doctrine, Shen-hui seems to be trying here to close the gap between the spiritual exercise and its goal—to offer a unified practice of *samādhi* and *prajñā* and provide an account of this practice that will be no more (and no less) than a description of the enlightened state itself. Since that state is our natural state of mind, and meditation and wisdom are both inherent, clearly only the most passive, most minimal of meditations will do—hence his rejection of formalized contemplation and visualization techniques in favor of a simple mindfulness. Yet for all his doubts about *dhyāna* and suspicions of *samādhi*, his description of practice here still seems to suggest (though he is careful to keep this ambiguous) that no-thought, or the original nature of the mind, is to be discovered when thoughts have been extinguished. In this he is not so different from the earlier tradition or from Ch'ang-lu Tsung-tse. In fact Shen-hui's Buddhism remains rather conservative: while he argues ardently for the Sudden school, he

---

28. So, for example, the *T'an ching* on the *pan-jo san-mei* (Yampolsky, *The Platform Sutra*, end matter, 14), on the *i-hsing san-mei* (ibid., 6), on *wu-nien* (ibid., 7), on *tso-ch'an* and *ch'an-ting* (ibid., 8); or Shen-hui on *wu-nien* and the *se ch'en san-mei*, and so on (*T'an yü*, Hu Shih, *Shen-hui ho-shang i-chi*, 241–43), on *tso-ch'an* (*Ting shih-fei lun*, Hu Shih, op. cit., 286). Note that such definitions always seem to find some way to retain the traditional polarities of calm and discernment, purity and knowledge, and so on.

29. Hu Shih, *Shen-hui ho-shang i-chi*, 308–9.

30. Hu Shih, *Shen-hui ho-shang i-chi*, 249, reading *cheng* for *fei* in line 8 and supplying *wang chü* before *mieh* in line 11.

acknowledges here and there that his sudden awakening, though it launches one directly onto the path, must still be followed by a gradual cultivation of that path.[31] As is well known, Shen-hui's teaching of sudden awakening and gradual practice (*tun wu chien hsiu*) was fixed in its classic form by his self-styled descendant in the fifth generation, the Hua-yen master Kuei-feng Tsung-mi.

Tsung-mi sought to check the Ch'an school's rapid drift toward a radical rejection of works and to steer its practice back onto a more traditional Buddhist course. To this end, he tried to align its teachings with scholastic categories and confine its definition of sudden awakening to the initial insight attained at the early stages of the path.[32] Thus freed from the need for a single, sudden meditation, he could, as we have seen, advocate the frankly gradual techniques of Chih-i's *Hsiao chih-kuan*. Yet, as heir to the supreme vehicle of the Southern school, even Tsung-mi had to bite his tongue. Such techniques belong, after all, only to the very lowest form of Ch'an, that which teaches "the stopping of delusion and cultivation of mind" (*hsi wang hsiu hsin*). As we learn in his *Ch'an-yüan chu-ch'üan chi tu-hsü*, this form of Ch'an, though it recognizes the Buddha nature inherent in all beings, still believes that in ordinary beings the nature is obscured by ignorance, and, therefore, that there is a real difference between *pṛthagjana* and *ārya*. On these grounds, it encourages the contemplation of the mind (*kuan hsin*) in order to wipe away deluded thoughts. Thus it emphasizes techniques for entering *samādhi*, teaching one to "dwell in a quiet place, avoiding the hustle and bustle of the world, to regulate body and breath, to sit in silent meditation with the legs crossed, the tongue pressed against

31. See, for example, *Ting shih-fei lun*:
Our great masters of the six generations have all said [that Buddhist practice is] a single blade entering directly, seeing one's nature in direct comprehension; they have not said there are stages. The student of the way should suddenly see his Buddha nature, gradually cultivate the causes and conditions, and attain liberation without departing this lifetime. Just as when the mother suddenly gives birth to the child, offers it milk and gradually rears it, the child's wisdom grows of its own accord, so for one who has suddenly awakened and seen his Buddha nature, wisdom will gradually grow of its own accord. (Hu Shih, *Shen-hui ho-shang i-chi*, 287.)
   Shen-hui's notion of the path is very difficult to ascertain: sometimes he clearly maintains that the experience of no-thought is itself total enlightenment; sometimes he says only that it "leads to" the wisdom of a Buddha. In one interesting passage in the *T'an yü* (Hu Shih, *Shen-hui ho-shang i-chi*, 247), he seems to suggest that it lifts one directly to the eighth *bodhisattva-bhūmi*. In his debate with Dharma Master Yüan, he himself has completed all ten *bhūmis*, but, when he is quickly asked by his skeptical opponent to demonstrate a few of the supernormal transformations available to one in such an exalted state, he responds that it is possible to become a Buddha in mind while remaining a *pṛthagjana* in body. (*Ting shih-fei lun*, Hu Shih, *Shen-hui ho-shang i-chi*, 269–70, 275–76.)
   32. Hence his distinction (following Ch'eng-kuan) between the "awakening of understanding" (*chieh wu*), which is to be followed by gradual cultivation, and the "awakening of realization" (*cheng wu*), which represents the culmination of the path. (See, for example, his *Yüan-chüeh ching ta-shu ch'ao*, ZZ.14:280b.) The structure here clearly recapitulates the classical progression of the *mārga* from *darśana*, through *bhāvanā*, to *aśaikṣa*.

the palate, and the mind fixed on a single object." Such is the Ch'an of Shen-hui's notorious enemy, the benighted Northern master Shen-hsiu; this master's understanding, says Tsung-mi, may differ somewhat from that of T'ien-t'ai, but his techniques are basically the same.[33]

The highest form of Ch'an, on the other hand, "directly reveals the nature of the mind" (*chih hsien hsin hsing*). Here all *dharmas* are just the true nature, which is without attributes and without conditions, beyond all distinctions of *pṛthagjana* and *ārya*, cause and effect, good and evil, and so on. In this teaching, deluded thoughts are inherently quiescent, and the defilements inherently empty: there is only the numinous knowing (*ling chih*) that is one's own true nature, without thought (*wu nien*) and without form (*wu hsing*). The practice of this Ch'an is simple and, by now, quite familiar.

If one is aware that all attributes are empty, the mind will naturally be without thought [*wu nien*]. Whenever a thought occurs, be aware of it [*nien ch'i chi chüeh*]; as soon as you are aware of it, it will cease to exist. The profound gate of practice lies precisely here. Therefore, although it may cultivate myriad practices, [this school] makes no-thought the essential [*tsung*].[34]

If even Tsung-mi was thus constrained by the sudden doctrine to relegate the meditation teachings of his own *Hsiu-cheng i* to the lowest rank of Ch'an, it is hardly surprising that his more radical contemporaries would be reluctant to associate their Buddhism with meditation. And though his catholic vision would be preserved by men like Yung-ming Yen-shou (904–76) and others who sought to integrate Ch'an and the scholastic systems, already by his day the mantle of the Sixth Patriarch had passed to the radicals. In their style of Ch'an, the Southern notion of inherent practice is taken for granted and the interest shifts, as is sometimes said, from "substance" (*t'i*) to "function" (*yung*)—from the glorification of the calm, radiant Buddha nature latent in every mind to the celebration of the natural wisdom active in every thought. Now, as Tsung-mi complained, the "everyday mind" had become the way, and the Buddhist tampering with that mind a mistake. In such a setting, to talk of sitting calmly in meditation—even if only to be aware of one's thoughts—was in poor taste; on the contrary, one must be ever on his toes, vitally and spontaneously engaged in phenomena. Thus the great masters of the second half of the T'ang—especially those of the dominant Hung-chou school of Tsung-mi's adversary Ma-tsu Tao-i (709–88)—turned their often remarkable energies to the creation of new tech-

---

33. T.48:402b–c. Tsung-mi's *Tu-hsü* has been well translated and studied by Jeffrey Broughton, in "Kuei-feng Tsung-mi: The Convergence of Ch'an and the Teachings" (1975).

34. T.48:403a4–6. This passage is repeated under the section on Shen-hui's Ho-tse school in Tsung-mi's *Zenmon shishi shōshū zu* (**Ch'an-men shih-tzu ch'eng-hsi t'u*), ZZ.2,15:436c. Note that, for all its "higher wisdom," the first sentence here could be used to summarize the description of *śamatha* through comprehension of the truth that we have seen in the *Hsiao chih-kuan*.

niques to draw the student out of his trance and into the dynamic new world
of Ch'an. The old forms of cultivation were superseded—at least in the
imagination of the tradition—by the revolutionary methods of beating and
shouting or spontaneous dialogue, and explicit discussion of no-thought and
sudden practice gave way to suggestive poetry, enigmatic saying, and icon-
oclastic anecdote. In the process the philosophical rationale for, not to
mention the psychological content of, Zen meditation became part of the
great mystery of things.[35]

Despite these developments, probably few Ch'an monks, even in this
period, actually escaped the practice of seated meditation. The Sixth Patriarch himself, in early versions of the *Liu-tsu t'an ching*, leaves as his final
teaching to his disciples the advice that they continue in the practice of
tso-ch'an, just as they did when he was alive. In the *Li-tai fa-pao chi*, the radical
Pao-t'ang master Wu-chu (714–77), whom Tsung-mi saw as negating all
forms of Buddhist cultivation, still admits to practicing *tso-ch'an*. Hui-hai's
Tun-wu ju-tao yao men begins its teaching on sudden awakening by identifying
tso-ch'an as the fundamental practice of Buddhism. Ma-tsu himself, though
he is chided by his master for it, is described by his biographers as having
constantly practiced *tso-ch'an*. According to the "Ch'an-men kuei-shih,"
Po-chang found it necessary to install long daises in his monasteries to
accommodate the monks in their many hours of *tso-ch'an*.[36] Such indications
of the widespread practice of meditation could no doubt be multiplied
several fold. Indeed the very fact that Wu-chu, Huai-jang, Ma-tsu, Lin-chi,
and other masters of the period occasionally felt obliged to make light of the
practice can be seen as an indication that it was taken for granted by the
tradition. We can probably assume that, even as these masters labored to
warn their disciples against fixed notions of Buddhist training, the monks
were sitting with legs crossed and tongues pressed against their palates. But
what they were doing had now become a family secret. As Huai-jang is
supposed to have said to the Sixth Patriarch (in a remark much treasured
by Dōgen), it was not that Ch'an monks had no practice, but that they
refused to defile it.[37]

---

35. The basic theoretical position of this "classical" style of Ch'an is already depicted in
Tsung-mi himself. Thus, for example, in the *Tu-hsü* passage we have just seen, he distinguishes
between two versions of the highest Ch'an: one (the Southern position), based on the true
nature of "numinous knowing" and the cultivation of no-thought; the other (the Hung-chou
position), that identifies the Buddha nature with the totality of human states. According to this
latter view, there is no point in rousing the mind to cultivate the path: true awakening,
cultivation, and verification lie only in the free expression of one's natural mind in all circumstances. (T.48:402c.)

36. *T'an ching*, T.48:345a20–21; *Li-tai fa-pao chi*, T.51:191a1–2; *Tun-wu ju-tao yao men*,
ZZ.2,15:420c14–15; *Ching-te ch'uan teng lu*, T.51:240c18ff; ibid., 251a13.

37. *Ching-te ch'uan teng lu*, T.51:240c. Huai-jang's famous criticism of Ma-tsu's meditation
appears at the same location; for an example of Wu-chu's denial that he enters *samādhi* or abides
in meditation, see *Li-tai fa-pao chi*, ibid., 195a29; for Ma-tsu's celebration of not cultivating and

In one sense, then, the style of classical Ch'an can be seen as the culmination of the efforts of the early movement to liberate Buddhism from its monastic confines and to open the religion to those unequal to, or unattracted by, the rigors of the traditional course of yogic discipline; in another rarely recognized sense classical Ch'an represented the termination of such efforts. In the search for ever simpler, quicker, more direct means to enlightenment, the movement had been led to a radically "protestant" soteriology that denied the efficacy of traditional works and left only the sudden leap of insight into the inherently enlightened nature of the mind. On the face of it such a doctrine would seem to offer equal spiritual opportunity to all, regardless of station or lifestyle; and, in fact, the teachings of the Southern school (and the closely related Oxhead and Pao-t'ang schools) often appear to hold out such an opportunity. Yet the classical Ch'an style of the later T'ang seems to have moved in the opposite direction—toward an elitist, "gnostic" religion.

There are undoubtedly various reasons for this development. As I have already suggested, one reason may be the rapid and considerable success of the school in finding a place among T'ang Buddhist institutions. Other causes may lie in the nature of the sudden doctrine itself. For example, we have already seen the continuing tension between inclusive and exclusive interpretation: if the sudden doctrine was associated with the one great vehicle that proclaimed the universality of enlightenment, it was also the supreme vehicle, the highest understanding and final practice of the religion. As such, in the traditional Buddhist classification of such matters, the practice was reserved for the highest types—for those, as the Sixth Patriarch said, of keen spiritual faculties (*li ken*). From this perspective, we can better understand why the *T'an ching*, which begins with the story of an illiterate, barbarian woodcutter's sudden accession to the Patriarchate of the supreme vehicle, should close with a warning to transmit his teaching only to those of the highest abilities and purest training.[38]

The association of the sudden practice with a spiritual elite is closely related to the doctrine of the ineffability of the highest vehicle. The ultimate teaching cannot be understood by the ordinary mind; it can be communicated only, as the *Lotus Sūtra* said, "from one Buddha to another." Similarly, the true practice, says Shen-hui, is beyond the ordinary teachings of Buddhism; it has been transmitted outside written texts directly from the mind

---

not sitting as the "pure Ch'an of the Tathāgata," see *Ma-tsu yü lu*, Iriya Yoshitaka, ed., *Baso no goroku* (1984), 45; Lin-chi's dismissal of those who "sit motionless with tongue pressed against the palate," appears at *Lin-chi lu*, T.47:501a.

38. Yampolsky, *The Platform Sutra*, end matter, 6, 30. The elitist tendency in the Ch'an movement is probably one of the major factors isolating its doctrinal development and institutional history from that of the Ching-t'u, the other "protestant" movement of the T'ang with which its sudden soteriology has much in common.

of one Patriarch to another.[39] If the theoretical notion of ineffability tended, as I have been at pains to argue, to discourage the public discussion of the techniques of the true practice, the attendant historical claim here of an esoteric tradition outside the public record no doubt tended to encourage the assumption that access to this practice was limited to a select circle of the cognoscenti in direct contact with a living representative of the Patriarchate. The historical claim of a mind-to-mind transmission, of course, became one of the hallmarks of the school, and the extreme emphasis on the enlightened teacher—the cult of the Ch'an master—became one of the most striking features of what was now celebrated as "Patriarchal Ch'an" (*tsu-shih ch'an*).

In sum, then, the Ch'an reformation turned back to the monastic community. While the community probably never long allowed the new sudden theory to interrupt seriously the time-tested practices of the meditation hall, once that sublime theory had become the touchstone of Ch'an orthodoxy, there was little incentive, and probably no little reluctance, to advertise the mundane mechanics of Ch'an mental training. Rather, the focus shifted to the transcendent techniques of the masters—the shouting, beating, riddles, and repartee that celebrated the school's distance from conventional religion and exemplified the mystery of its practice. Within the context of the monastery these techniques undoubtedly served to invigorate the training and inspire the practitioner with a higher sense of its meaning; but outside this context, they offered little clue to how the ordinary Buddhist believer might gather himself spiritually for the leap to *nirvāṇa*. Ironically enough, then, the practical effect of the new doctrine of sudden awakening was to reseal the doors of the meditation hall and reopen the traditional gap between clerical and lay Buddhist practice.

It is this gap, I have suggested, that Tsung-tse sought to bridge. To this end, he looked back to the formative age of Ch'an, when the movement was still interested in promulgating its practice, and reasserted what was probably its most basic and perhaps (though on this point, of course, we cannot be sure) its most common contemplative technique. But from the ideological discourse that had once accompanied and ultimately enveloped that technique, Tsung-tse drew back—perhaps intentionally, lest he once again undermine the rationale for (and his reader's faith in) the practice of meditation. Consequently, whatever attraction it may have had for the uninitiated, for those steeped in the issues of that discourse, his *Tso-ch'an i* must have said at once too much and too little; and it may be no coincidence that the century following its appearance is marked by a sudden revival of the old critique of contemplative practice and a new assertion of the sudden approach to enlightenment.

It is at this point, at the height of the Southern Sung reformulation of

---

39. Hu Shih, *Shen-hui ho-shang i-chi*, 232.

Ch'an and in the midst of its renewed discourse on the theory and practice of meditation, that the young Japanese pilgrim Dōgen visited the continent. By this time the school's theorists had already moved to stop the leak in the one true vehicle and right the alarming list toward *samādhi* that seemed to follow from Tsung-tse's approach. If the twelfth-century Ch'an discussion of meditation opened with his gentle advice on how to calm the mind, it also began with his contemporary Hui-hung's stern reminder that the practice of Bodhidharma should not be confused with the cultivation of *dhyāna* or his tradition with those misguided quietists who would turn the mind into "dead wood and cold ashes" (*k'u mu ssu hui*).[40] These two poles marked out once again the old field within which the new discourse was to be played out.

The famous Southern Sung "debate" on meditation, rather like its T'ang predecessor, was probably not all that it is often cracked up to be. Led on by later, especially Japanese, sectarian accounts, we have been accustomed to imagining a struggle between two distinct camps—represented by the houses of Ts'ao-tung and Lin-chi—that argued back and forth over the theory and practice of Ch'an meditation. Yet, while there is surely good reason to recognize more than one approach to, or style of, Ch'an in twelfth-century China, there is less reason to suppose that the differences ever crystallized into a sustained sectarian dispute, let alone that they reflected mutually exclusive contemplative systems.

If there was a debate, the affair was decidedly lopsided. It is usually portrayed as an argument between the Lin-chi master Ta-hui Tsung-kao, famed exponent of the *kung-an* contemplation (*k'an-hua*), and the Ts'ao-tung figure Hung-chih Cheng-chüeh, who advocated "silent illumination" (*mo-chao*). But to this debate, like that between the Northern and Southern schools, only one side seems to have come, since the entire argument originates almost wholly within Ta-hui's own writings. As we might expect, the description of *mo-chao* there functions as a foil for the author's position and surely tells us more about his Ch'an than it does about the actual teachings of Hung-chih. Indeed we have no clear evidence that these teachings were directly an issue even for Ta-hui himself. For if Hung-chih's writings make no reference to a disagreement with the Lin-chi master, neither do Ta-hui's arguments ever implicate his friend Hung-chih. On the contrary, scholars have recently demonstrated that, if there was a specific object of Ta-hui's criticisms, it was more likely Hung-chih's contemporary Chen-hsieh Ch'ing-liao (1090?–1151).[41]

---

40. *Lin-chien lu*, ZZ.2B,21:295d. Hui-hung's work appeared in 1107; it is unclear whether he knew of the *Tso-ch'an i*.

41. See Yanagida Seizan, "Kanna to mokushō," *Hanazono daigaku kenkyū kiyō* 6 (3/1975), 1–20; Ishii Shūdō, "Daie Sōkō to sono deshitachi (6)," IBK 23, 1 (12/1974), 336–39; ibid. (8), IBK 25, 1 (12/1976), 257–61; ibid., "Daie goroku no kiso teki kenkyū (3)," KDBGKK 33 (3/1975), 151–71.

In any case we do not know whether either Hung-chih or Ch'ing-liao actually recommended the kind of practices that Ta-hui attributes to the false masters of *mo-chao*. Whatever their differences, both these Ts'ao-tung figures belonged to a venerable tradition of Ch'an literary and philosophical interpretation of meditation. They liked to draw on the classic models of substance (*t'i*) and function (*yung*), noumenon (*li*) and phenomenon (*shih*) —or the more stylish Ch'an metaphysical categories of upright (*cheng*) and inclined (*p'ien*), host (*chu*) and guest (*k'e*)—to depict the practice as a return to, or participation in, the inherent calm (*chi*, or sometimes "silence" [*mo*]) and innate wisdom (*chao*) of the Buddha nature. Hung-chih, at least, was an accomplished poet, who has left two famous verses on meditation—the "Inscription on Silent Illumination" (*Mo-chao ming*) and the piece, much admired by Dōgen, known as the "Lancet of Seated Meditation" (*Tso-ch'an chen*):

> Essential function of all the Buddhas,
> Functioning essence of all the Patriarchs—
> It knows without touching things,
> It illumines without facing objects.
> Knowing without touching things,
> Its knowledge is inherently subtle;
> Illumining without facing objects,
> Its illumination is inherently mysterious.
> Its knowledge inherently subtle,
> It is ever without discriminatory thought;
> Its illumination inherently mysterious,
> It is ever without a hair's breadth of sign.
> Ever without discriminatory thought,
> Its knowledge is rare without peer;
> Ever without a hair's breadth of sign,
> Its illumination comprehends without grasping.
> The water is clear right through to the bottom,
> A fish goes lazily along.
> The sky is vast without horizon,
> A bird flies far far away.[42]

Cheng-chüeh celebrates the detached clarity of the state of *samādhi*—the "subtle" and "mysterious" cognition in which the mind has become a boundless space, a limpid pool, through which the object passes effortlessly without a trace. In this he artfully intertwines the two constant desiderata of Buddhist meditation teaching—the calm, unified mind emphasized by Tsung-tse, and the clear, luminous knowledge of the wisdom tradition. He tells us very little about how these desiderata are accomplished. In fact rarely do his writings or those of Ch'ing-liao descend to the level of concrete advice

---

42. *Hung-chih kuang lu*, T.48:98a–b; for the *Mo-chao ming*, see ibid., 100a–b.

on contemplative technique—though, interestingly enough, the latter (who was probably the more active in teaching laymen) is said, in Pure Land sources, to have been an early advocate of the use of the name of the Buddha Amitābha as a *kung-an*.[43]

If these Ts'ao-tung masters leave us in doubt about what, practically speaking, they recommend as Ch'an meditation, Ta-hui is quite explicit about what he means by the practice of silent illumination. The technique freezes the mind and quells thoughts, shuts one's eyes to the world and tries to empty phenomena. Whenever any thought arises, it is quickly eliminated; as soon as the slightest idea occurs, it is immediately suppressed. Silent illumination is one vast darkness, devoid of awareness; the practice is that of a living corpse, the heresy of one fallen into the void.[44]

Ta-hui's rationale for his criticism of the advocates of such practice is a familiar one: they do not recognize the nature of their own minds. They do not realize that their own minds are inherently liberated—like the *maṇi* gem in the mud, forever unstained by sensory defilement, even in the midst of sensory experience. Hence they adopt a practice, based on a nihilistic view (*tuan chien, nitya-dṛṣṭi*) characteristic of the infidels and Hīnayānists, that cuts off (*tuan-mieh*) the inherently luminous nature of the mind and instead clings to an external emptiness and stagnates in the tranquility of *dhyāna*. As a result they make people constrain the mind and sit quietly, without thinking of anything.[45]

Ta-hui's emphasis here and elsewhere throughout his writings on the original nature of the mind—with its inherent calm and innate wisdom— might lead one to suppose that, like Hung-chih and earlier masters of the highest metaphysic, he would shy away from the matter of mental cultivation, lest he fall back into the gradualist heresy. In fact the opposite is the truth: for Ta-hui, the tendency to use Buddhist philosophy (or the sayings of the Ch'an masters) to deny any need for the actual experience of Buddhist practice and enlightenment is one of the most pernicious characteristics of the silent illumination style. The teachers of this style, he complains, like to talk about their Ch'an as the practice beyond *upāya*, the practice of the incomprehensible. They call it the original practice, before the appearance of the primordial Buddha Bhīṣmagarjitasvararāja (*wei-yin no-p'an*), prior to

---

43. See, for example, *Ching-t'u chih-kuei chi*, ZZ.2,13:717b.
44. Such characterizations abound in Ta-hui's writings. I have chosen this example (which appears in a letter to Tsung Chih-ko [*Ta-hui shu*, in *Ta-hui yü lu*, T.47:933b]) because it is, interestingly enough, a quotation from the T'ang figure Hsüan-sha Shih-pei (835–905). (See *Hsüan-sha kuang lu*, ZZ.2,31:190b.) The fact that Ta-hui could use it to describe "the hole in which the false teachers of silent illumination would bury people" reminds us that, whatever the new historical circumstances that may have prompted it, his objection to *mo-chao* is an ancient and generic one. Note that some of the description here is reminiscent of the ultimate (but soteriologically worthless) trance state of the *nirodha-samāpatti*.
45. "Letter to Vice Minister Ch'en," *Ta-hui shu*, T.47:923b.

the age of emptiness and the creation of the world (*k'ung chieh i-ch'ien*). These teachers do not believe that there is such a thing as the actual experience of awakening (*wu*): they say the doctrine of awakening is just a trick; they say it is second-rate (*ti-erh-t'ou*), merely a term used as *upāya*, simply a word used as a teaching device. In this way they deceive and mislead both themselves and others.[46]

If Ta-hui does not like the philosophically naive attachment to particular psychological states, neither does he care for the philosophically sophisticated belittling of all such states. His sudden awakening is not just a theory about the universality of enlightenment but the unique personal experience of the individual's own enlightenment—an experience that, however else we may talk about it, must somehow be brought about through the practice of religion. This focus on the psychological experience of awakening, and the confidence that it is actually accessible to all, gives Ta-hui's Buddhism something of the freshness and vigor of early Ch'an; his willingness to talk directly of concrete methods to bring about the experience makes his Buddhism, for all its emphasis on wisdom and rejection of meditation, heir to the practical contemplative teachings of Tsung-tse's *Tso-ch'an i*.

Having aligned himself with the orthodox wisdom of Ch'an and safely distanced himself from the heretical quietists, Ta-hui is now free to propose his own brand of concentration exercise, the famous *k'an-hua* method. In a letter to one of his followers, he describes the method as follows:

Just once put down the mind of deluded ideas and perverse notions, the mind of thinking and discrimination, the mind that loves life and hates death, the mind of opinion and understanding, the mind that enjoys calm and dislikes bustle. Then where you have put down [such minds], observe this story [*hua-t'ou*]. "A monk asked Chao-chou, 'Does a dog have the Buddha nature?' Chao-chou answered, 'No [*wu*].'" This one word, "no," is a weapon that will crush a multitude of perverse perceptions. Do not try to understand it through having or not having [*yu wu*]; do not try to understand it with reason. Do not rely on the mind to think it through or figure it out; do not be fixated on raising the eyebrows and blinking the eyes. Do not try to make your way on the path of words; do not just float in idleness. Do not simply assent to its source; do not verify it in writings. But all day long, in whatever you are doing, always keep it before you and keep yourself alert to it. "'Does a dog have the Buddha nature?' [Chao-chou] answered, 'No.'" Without leaving your daily activities, try to work at it in this way. In ten days to a month, you will see for yourself.[47]

Whether or not the well-known legend is true that Ta-hui burned the famous *Pi-yen lu kung-an* commentaries of his master, Yüan-wu K'o-ch'in, the story well reflects the fate of the Ch'an wisdom literature in his *k'an-hua*

---

46. "Letter to Tsung Chih-ko," ibid., 933c.
47. "Letter to Councilor Fu," ibid., 921c (reading *te* for *yü* in line 12).

method. Here, and in many similar descriptions of the method throughout his writings, the entire corpus of the old cases, which were the primary source of inspiration for the Sung Ch'an historians and literati, has been reduced to a single conversation. The religious significance of this conversation, which some might expect to lie in the philosophy behind it, has been reduced to the words themselves in their role as an object of mindfulness. In effect, then, Ta-hui seems to do for his own time what the early Ch'an popularizers did for the T'ang—only here the supreme *dharma* of the Buddha vehicle has been embodied in a dog story, and the sudden practice of no-thought, concentrated on the single thought "no." To what extent this represents an advance over the earlier mindfulness technique favored by Tsung-tse is difficult to say.

Ta-hui is justly famous for his formulation of the popular *k'an-hua* exercise, but we should probably not overemphasize its place in his Buddhism. In the thirty fascicles of sermons, interviews, verses, homilies, and epistles of his *Recorded Words*, and in the several fascicles of *kung-an* commentary of his *Chen-fa yen-tsang* and *Ta-hui wu-k'u*, he displays the full range of the accomplished Sung Ch'an author, from stylish verse to vernacular prose, from the classic esoterica of the monastic to the current discourse of the secular elite. It is almost always in his teachings to this latter group—in the letters and lectures to his many prominent lay followers—that we find the emphasis on the simple *k'an-hua* technique. As described earlier, the practice is characteristically recommended to be easy enough to be cultivated even in the midst of a busy life, yet powerful enough to put to rest the nagging doubts and naive ideals of those who see themselves on the margins of the spiritual path.

We probably cannot extend Ta-hui's advocacy of *k'an-hua* much beyond this limited context and assume that the monks who trained under him at Mts. Ching and A-yü-wang abandoned traditional forms of Ch'an practice —including meditation—in favor of the exclusive cultivation of Chao-chou's "*wu.*" There is little call to read into the attack on *mo-chao* a general rejection of contemplative practice. Ta-hui rejects not meditation but a particular approach to, and understanding of, the practice. He puts the matter quite succinctly in a letter to one of his followers.

When you deal [with the world], just deal with it; if you want to practice quiet sitting [*ching tso*], just sit quietly. But when you sit, do not become attached to sitting and make it the ultimate. Recently, a bunch of false teachers has been misleading followers by making silent illumination and quiet sitting the ultimate *dharma*. Unafraid to take them on, I have strongly criticized them, in this way trying to repay the blessings of the Buddha and cure the ills of the final *dharma*.[48]

Ta-hui's calling here is the ancient calling of the Southern school to ward off the evil of attachment to works. Its difficulty was only intensified in his

---

48. "Letter to Vice Minister Ch'en (2)," ibid., 923c.

day by the new demand for, and dissemination of, Ch'an contemplative practice among the laity. And, in fact, if his attack on *mo-chao* was directed against certain unnamed men of the cloth, it was intended especially for the lay community: it typically appears in his letters and public lectures, usually in conjunction with *k'an-hua*, as a warning to lay disciples against false prophets of contemplative calm and misleading models of spiritual cultivation. Yet even here, if the warning is heeded, Ta-hui is not opposed to a little quiet sitting. When one of his correspondents suggests that a little quiet sitting might be good for a beginner, the master quickly rebukes him, points out that in Ch'an there are no levels of practitioners, reminds him that true quiet lies only in the destruction of the mind of *saṃsāra*, and recommends for this purpose the observation of Chao-chou's *kung-an* throughout the course of his ordinary affairs. This said, he goes on to advise,

When you want to practice quiet sitting, light a stick of incense and sit quietly. During sitting, avoid either torpor or agitation, both of which are condemned by the former sages. If, while sitting, you become aware of the presence of either of these maladies, just take up the story that the dog has no Buddha nature. Without your making any special effort to remove them, they will immediately subside.[49]

This little passage well brings out the full range and problematic of Ta-hui's *k'an-hua* Ch'an. Very much like the classical *wu-nien* practice—or the recollection of the Buddha's name (*nien fo*) popular among Ta-hui's contemporaries—his "*wu*" functioned at several levels. As an ideological tool it served as a symbol (and, for Ch'an, an appropriately paradoxical one) of the mystery of universal enlightenment and the transcendental nature of true religion; in this function it necessarily involves a reiteration of the sudden critique of conventional spiritual discipline. At a more practical level it became the core of what seems to be advertised as a complete religious path, in which attention to the *hua-t'ou* alone could, in theory at least, replace or satisfy the traditional disciplines of ethics, meditation, and wisdom; in this role it serves not only as object of the concentration that purifies and focuses the mind but as object of the wisdom that is supposed to discover the meaning of "*wu*." Finally, the *hua-t'ou* could apparently function within the context of, simply as an aid to, traditional contemplative practice; in this context, as exemplified at least in the passage quoted here, the meaning of the story is no longer an issue: the *kung-an* has been stripped of its last vestiges of wisdom and become merely a handy psychological device for avoiding the familiar problems of restlessness and drowsiness in meditation.

Undoubtedly due in part to this great range—from convenient tech-

---

49. "Letter to Councilor Fu," ibid., 922a–b. Ta-hui was also not adverse to recommending the popular practice of *nien fo*; for discussion of this teaching, see Ishii Shūdō, "Daie zen ni okeru zen to nenbutsu no mondai," in *Zen to nenbutsu*, ed. by Fujiyoshi Jikai (1983), 269–301.

nique to ultimate truth—the *k'an-hua* teaching could quickly capture the banner of Ch'an and move to the head of the Sung reformation. Indeed less than a century after the death of Ta-hui, Wu-men Hui-k'ai would begin his famous *Wu-men kuan* by declaring that Chao-chou's "*wu*" was the single gateway to Ch'an, to pass through which was to walk hand in hand with all the Patriarchs of the school. It was enough to doubt this "*wu*" day and night, with every fiber of one's being, until the practice gradually matured, inside and out naturally became unified (*i-p'ien*), and one understood for oneself; it was enough to master this practice in order to meet the Buddha and kill the Buddha, to meet the Patriarchs and kill the Patriarchs, to attain the great freedom in the midst of *saṃsāra* and disport oneself in *samādhi* within the six destinies.[50]

The *Wu-men kuan* was composed in 1228 and presented in the following year to the Emperor Li Tsung on the occasion of his birthday. Though it draws on the earlier genre of literary appreciations of the old Ch'an stories made famous by Yüan-wu's *Pi-yen lu*, in its emphasis on the enlightenment experience and its focus on the utilitarian value of the *kung-an* (perhaps as well in the political circumstances of its publication), Wu-men's work well exemplifies the dynamic new spirit, practical thrust, and popular style of *k'an-hua* Ch'an at the end of the Sung, when Dōgen and his contemporaries were importing Zen to Japan. By this time, of course, whatever it may originally have contributed to the rise of the new movement and still contributed to the dissemination of Ch'an practice, Tsung-tse's account of meditation had been shunted to the side—or worse. In the "Lancet of Ch'an" (*Ch'an chen*) appended to the text of the *Wu-men kuan*, his classical meditation method of no-thought is given its own place along with *mo-chao* in the current list of deluded religious practices, where it is dismissed as mere "toying with the spirit" (*lung ching-hun*) and as leading to "the deep pit" (*shen k'eng*).[51]

This, then, was the environment on the continent when Dōgen set out to write about Zen meditation. Given this environment, it is hardly surprising that he, like his contemporaries, should have felt that Tsung-tse had missed "the understanding beyond words" and failed to transmit the wisdom of the masters. Indeed, while almost all the founders of Japanese Zen (perhaps by necessity) shared Tsung-tse's interest in the dissemination of meditation, few opted to advertise the Buddhism of the *Tso-ch'an i*. Rather,

---

50. T.48:292c–293a.
51. "To keep your mind in clear tranquility is the false Ch'an of silent illumination. To indulge yourself and forget objects [*wang yüan*] is to fall into the deep pit. To be perfectly bright with nothing obscure is to tie yourself in chains and put yourself in pillory. To think of good and think of bad is [to wander between] heaven and hell. To have views of the Buddha and views of the *dharma* is [to be ringed by] the two iron mountains. To be aware of thoughts as soon as they occur [*nien ch'i chi chüeh*] is to be a man who toys with the spirit. To sit fixedly, practicing *samādhi* is [to follow] the lifestyle of a ghost." (Ibid., 299a29–b4.)

they preferred to emphasize the more modern mode, abandoning Tsung-tse's traditional concentration exercise for the new *kung-an* contemplation and replacing his sober treatment of the practice with the livelier literary and philosophic styles current on the continent. This characteristic of the Kamakura Zen literature is well worth remembering when we read the *Fukan zazen gi.*

We have been accustomed to reading Dōgen's work as the original expression of a unique, higher understanding of Zen—an understanding that led its author to reject the kind of teaching found in Tsung-tse and create his own meditation manual. This is, of course, what Dōgen himself suggests in his "Senjutsu yurai." Yet when his manual is read in the context of contemporary discussions of meditation, what stands out is hardly Dōgen's revisions of the *Tso-ch'an i* but rather the degree to which he has remained faithful to it. In fact, of all the original meditation texts produced at this time, only in his work do we find extensive direct reliance on Tsung-tse.

Of course, the *Fukan zazen gi* was one of the first Japanese statements of Zen and (apart from the brief passage in Yōsai's *Kōzen gokoku ron*) the first to attempt a description of Zen meditation. In this respect, it is perhaps not so surprising that it should be more faithful to Tsung-tse's basic, if already dated, treatment than the works that were to follow. Also, if our doubts about the breadth of Dōgen's experience in China hold, he may have been—at least at the beginning of his career—less familiar with the newer styles than some of his contemporaries. In any case, if he too felt the need to modify the teachings of the *Tso-ch'an i* and to introduce some of the more elevated language and ideas of Ch'an literature, Tsung-tse's work still forms the core of Dōgen's manual. Nearly a third of his first version of the *Fukan zazen gi*—includng all of its actual account of *zazen*—is lifted directly from the Chinese text, and much of the rest is clearly derived from it. Though in his later manuals Dōgen moves somewhat further away from that text, he never wholly abandons it as a model. In the next chapter we shall look more closely at the model and what Dōgen does with it.

Part III

Teachings

5

The Essential Art of Meditation and the Authentic Tradition of Enlightenment

The *Fukan zazen gi* is by no means merely a practical manual on the techniques of contemplation: it is also—and perhaps more conspicuously— a theological statement of the Zen approach to Buddhism and a literary appreciation of Zen training. The text falls into three fairly distinct and roughly equal sections. Of these, only the middle section offers concrete advice on the procedures to be followed in meditation. Here, as I have indicated, Dōgen is largely content to follow Tsung-tse's *Tso-ch'an i*—albeit with occasional, sometimes interesting, omissions and additions. In contrast the introductory section, in which Dōgen expounds the rationale of Zen mental cultivation, is wholly new. Similarly, though it retains much of the structure and some of the phrasing of his Chinese model, his conclusion, which constitutes a panegyric on the virtues of meditation and an exhortation to undertake its practice, again departs from Tsung-tse to elaborate Dōgen's own understanding of Zen. These latter two sections, then, most clearly bear Dōgen's stamp and most sharply distinguish his text from Tsung-tse's simple meditation manual.

While the *Fukan zazen gi* may not be merely a practical guide to the techniques of *zazen*, it is such a guide; and while it may not be particularly original in its presentation of these techniques, this in itself does not, of course, detract from its value as a manual or as a source for understanding Zen meditation as it was practiced in thirteenth-century China and Japan. On the contrary, their close correspondences with Tsung-tse's teachings place the practices described in the *Fukan zazen gi* within an established

Buddhist contemplative tradition and give them a universality not always shared by some of Dōgen's more theoretical interpretations of Zen training. To these interpretations, we shall turn in due course; but first let us consider only the central section of the *Fukan zazen gi*, in which Dōgen explains the actual method of *zazen*. This will give us some sense not only of the concrete features of his practice but also of their relationship to the earlier tradition. The literature of this tradition itself is far too vast to explore here, but we can gain at least some perspective by occasionally comparing what Dōgen and Tsung-tse have to say with the classical account of Buddhist meditation given in Chih-i's *T'ien-t'ai hsiao chih-kuan*. For the sake of convenience, I shall generally follow the text of the Tenpuku *Fukan zazen gi* here, referring to Dōgen's other writings only where they help to amplify a topic. The major revisions of the vulgate edition will be discussed in Chapter 6.[1]

Broadly speaking, the practical explanation of *zazen* describes two sorts of activities: (1) seated meditation itself, traditionally treated under the three aspects of body, breath, and mind; and (2) certain ancillary techniques that support the meditation. These latter may range from general considerations of lifestyle and attitude to specific mental and physical preparations for the practice proper. Though scholastic treatises like the *Hsiao chih-kuan* or Tsung-mi's *Hsiu-cheng i* devote considerable space to such topics, their treatment in the *Fukan zazen gi*, like that of the *Tso-ch'an i* from which it is taken, is extremely brief: we are told simply to seek quiet quarters, be moderate in our eating habits, and abandon involvement in worldly activities.

Avoidance of the extremes of self-indulgence and deprivation is, of course, a basic principle of the Buddhist ethic of the middle way, but it is also common Buddhist practical advice to the meditator. The admonition here on the need for moderation in food and drink appears as the first of the five kinds of self-regulation recommended by the *Hsiao chih-kuan*: food, sleep, body, breath, and mind. The *Fukan zazen gi* follows Tsung-tse in mentioning only the amount consumed; but Chih-i adds a warning against eating improper foods, and elsewhere Dōgen himself records an interesting list of such foods said to have been proscribed by his master, Ju-ching.[2] Tsung-tse also recommends the second member of Chih-i's list, the regulation of sleep, but for some reason Dōgen omits it. In his Japanese *zazen gi*, however, he offers at this point in the discussion what appears to be a commentary on the topic by encouraging his reader not to waste time but to throw himself into meditation practice with the urgency of one "brushing a fire from his head." In this same text we also learn a bit more about the physical

1.   For translations of the *Tso-ch'an i* and *Fukan zazen gi*, as well as Dōgen's later manuals, see Document 2; the following discussion refers to the section of the Tenpuku text beginning, "For studying Zen, one should have quiet quarters," and ending, "This is the full realization of the way."

2.   *Hōkyō ki*, DZZ.2:373–74; for Chih-i's comments, see T.46:465b–66c.

preparations for the *zazen* exercise: Dōgen advises that the place of practice be properly maintained; that it be sheltered from drafts and vapors, rain and frost; that it be kept bright both day and night, and of moderate temperature in both winter and summer.[3] The *Fukan zazen gi* itself does not linger over such preliminary matters but follows the text of the *Tso-ch'an i* directly to the explanation of *zazen* posture. One is first to prepare a proper seat, consisting of a cushion placed on top of a mat. The purpose of the cushion (*futon*), as Dōgen explains in his Japanese *zazen gi*, is to raise the level of the torso above that of the knees, which are to rest on the mat. This seating arrangement, he remarks there, was used by all the Buddhas and Patriarchs; and, in fact, one can still observe it among Sōtō meditators today. Other sources, however, do not reveal to what extent it was the common practice of the tradition; the fact that Dōgen goes out of his way to cite precedent for his arrangement itself suggests that it was not the only or even the most popular style. For his part, Tsung-tse recommends simply spreading a single mat (*tso wu*), a custom probably encountered more often both in Buddhist texts and in modern Zen practice throughout the Far East.[4]

In any case, having prepared the spot, one is to take his seat in the classic yogic cross-legged position (*kekkafu za, paryaṅka*) or in the variant semi-cross-legged position (*hankafu za, adhaparyaṅka*). For the former position the right foot is placed on the left thigh and the left foot on the right thigh, with (as the *Shōbō genzō* manual explains) the toes resting along the thighs; for the latter, the left foot is simply placed on the right thigh. Dōgen's description here follows Tsung-tse, but there is clearly considerable difference of opinion within the Buddhist tradition on exactly what to do with the legs in medita-

---

3. Both the warning against drafts and the simile of the burning head also appear in the *Hōkyō ki* (DZZ.2 : 380, 386). Dōgen's manuals do not discuss the best time of day for *zazen*, but his *Bendō hō* indicates that he expected his monks to keep the schedule of four periods (*shiji*) of meditation a day: evening (*kōkon*), night (*goya*), morning (*sōshin*), and afternoon (*hoji*). (DZZ.2 : 313–14, 317–18.) This schedule is not yet mentioned in the *Ch'an-yüan ch'ing-kuei* but does appear in Yōsai's *Kōzen gokoku ron*. The exact times in question are not clear from Dōgen's references, but from other sources we might estimate roughly 4 P.M., 8 P.M., 4 A.M., and 8 A.M.

4. By Tsung-tse's day, the sitting mat (*niṣīdana, tso chü*) that was a standard part of the Indian monk's equipment had become a simple cloth—still seen today—used primarily for bowing. Whether or not it is exactly the same article, Dōgen's rush cushion does appear in earlier Ch'an sources. (See, e.g., *Lin-chi lu*, T.47:504b6; Menzan's commentary on the *Fukan zazen gi* points out several examples in the Buddhist literature of the use of some such cushion [SSZ.Chūkai,3 : 14b–15b].) Keizan's *Zazen yōjin ki*, which also emphasizes the need for such a cushion, gives its diameter as one *shaku*, two *sun* (roughly fourteen inches) (SSZ.Shūgen,2 : 426b). For his part, Chih-i (T.46:465c12) recommends meditation on the traditional cord bench (*sheng ch'uang*), found in Indian texts (see, e.g., *Shih sung lü*, T.23:77a) and—in some variation at least—in Ch'an records as well (see, e.g., *Lin-chi lu*, T.47:504a19). In the more formal Ch'an monasteries, the ordinary monk presumably sat (as he still does in Japan today) on the long dais (*ch'ang lien ch'uang*), reported to have been a feature of Po-chang's meditation hall (see "Ch'an-men kuei-shih," *Ching-te ch'uan teng lu*, T.51:251a11). In Dōgen's hall, of course, the monks sat on the dais facing the wall (*menpeki*), in commemoration, it is often said, of Bodhidharma's nine years of sitting before a wall (see *Bendō hō*, DZZ.2 : 313); the head monk (*shuso*) faced the edge of the dais, while the abbot sat on a chair facing the monks.

tion. Chih-i's account of the full position recommends the opposite form, in which the right leg is crossed over the left; and, while Indian sources are not explicit on this point, the same preference appears in Buddhist iconography and in texts attributed to Indian missionaries to the T'ang.[5] Though Tsung-tse's style seems to have been the more common in the Zen tradition, both forms were probably widely practiced by Dōgen's contemporaries. Perhaps Ju-ching is closest to the historical experience of the *zazen* posture when he kindly remarks, in the *Hōkyō ki*, that the position of the legs may be reversed if they become painful after long sitting.[6]

Once the legs are positioned and the robes loosened and arranged, the practitioner assumes the traditional meditation *mudrā* of the *dharma-dhātu* (*hokkai jōin*): the hands resting open on the lap, drawn back against the abdomen, left on top of right, with palms upturned and thumb tips touching. According to Tsung-tse (and to Dōgen in his later manuals), at this point, one should stretch the torso up and forward and swing it back and forth to the left and right. One then straightens his body and sits erect, with, as the formula goes, the ears in line with the shoulders and the nose in line with the navel. The tongue is placed against the front of the palate, and the lips and teeth are closed; the eyes are to remain open.[7]

On the question of the eyes, Dōgen simply repeats the advice of the *Tso-ch'an i* without comment, but Tsung-tse himself is adamant: he goes out

---

5. *Hsiao chih-kuan*, T.46:465c15–16; see also *Hsiu ch'an yao chüeh*, attributed to Buddhapāli (ZZ.2,15:418b); and *Wu-wei san-tsang ch'an yao*, attributed to Śubhakarasiṃha (T.18:944c). The form of sitting in which the right leg is placed on top of the left is sometimes referred to in the literature as the *chi-hsiang* position; the opposite form, as the *hsiang-mo* position. The *I-ch'ieh ching ying-i* (T.54:353b–c), from the turn of the ninth century, identifies the latter with the Ch'an tradition and the former with Yogācāra and Tantra. Similar disagreement can be found in descriptions of the semi-cross-legged posture and of the positioning of the hands. These and other aspects of the *zazen* posture have been treated in considerable detail by various scholars: see, for example, Sekiguchi, *Tendai shikan no kenkyū*, 137–47; Ōtani Tetsuo, "Chūgoku shoki zenkan jidai ni okeru za no keitai," SK 12 (3/1970), 198–211; Yamauchi Shun'yū, "Shūzen yōketsu ni okeru zahō ni kōsatsu," SK 13 (3/1971), 25–34; Yamauchi, "Zenrin shōki sen narabi ni Chokushū Hyakujō shingi sae ni okeru zazen no chūshaku ni tsuite," KDBGKK 29 (3/1971), 14–31; Tagami Taishū, *Zen no shisō* (1980), 107–31.

6. DZZ.2:386. Tsung-tse's style is followed, for example, by the *Ju-ju chū-shih tso-ch'an i* (*Kanazawa bunko shiryō zensho*, vol. 1, 158) and by Kakushin's "Zazen no koto" (*Hottō kokushi hōgo*, DNBZ.96:220b); but it should be noted that the *Ta-tsang i-lan* version of the *Tso-ch'an i* departs from the standard text here to recommend the *chi-hsiang* form (*Shōwa hōbō sō mokuroku* 3:1305b2).

7. In the *Hōkyō ki* (DZZ.2:386), Ju-ching advises Dōgen that one may either press his tongue against the palate or the front teeth. Though for some reason the Tenpuku manuscript ignores Tsung-tse's advice on swinging the body, Dōgen does include it in both the vulgate *Fukan zazen gi* and the *Bendō hō*. Keizan's *Zazen yōjin ki* explains that one should swing the body seven or eight times, gradually reducing the length of the arc; the process is reversed before one rises after the completion of meditation. (SSZ.Shūgen,2:427a.) Whether or not this exercise, still seen today, actually corresponds exactly to Chih-i's practice, it undoubtedly reflects his rather obscure recommendation, in the *Hsiao chih-kuan*, that one "stretch [? *t'ing-tung*] the torso and limbs seven or eight times, as in the massage technique [*an-mo fa*]." (T.46:465c19–20.)

of his way here to cite the precedent of past meditation adepts who always practiced with their eyes open and to quote his own teacher, Fa-yün, who criticized the practice of meditation with the eyes closed as "the ghost cave of the Black Mountain [*ho shan kuei k'u*]." Not only, he says, does the opening of the eyes ward off drowsiness, but it can serve to enhance the power of *samādhi*. The emphatic nature of these comments leads one to suspect that Tsung-tse was attacking a common practice; in fact this is another point on which the *Tso-ch'an i* differs from the teaching of Chih-i, who recommends that the eyes be closed. Other manuals from this time tend to agree with Tsung-tse and Dōgen, but again Ju-ching may have the last word here when he says simply that, while experienced meditators, not susceptible to drowsiness, may sit with eyes closed, beginners should keep them open.[8]

After adopting the proper posture of *zazen*, one is to regulate his breathing. Neither the *Tso-ch'an i* nor the Tenpuku text tells us how to do this; but in his later manuals, Dōgen does give some hints. We are to begin the practice by taking a breath and exhaling fully (*kanki issoku*); during meditation the breath should pass through the nose and should be neither rasping (*fū*) nor restricted (*sen*), neither too long (*chō*) nor short (*tan*), neither too weak (*kan*) nor forced (*kyū*). Here Dōgen seems to be echoing Chih-i, who recommends that, before settling into meditation, one expel all the "foul air" (*cho ch'i*) through the mouth, and that one aim at a fine (*hsi*) type of breathing and avoid the rasping (*feng*), the restricted (*ch'uan*), and the course (*ch'i*) types.[9]

---

8. *Hōkyō ki*, DZZ.2:386. Not surprisingly, perhaps, Dōgen reiterates his warning against closing the eyes in his discussion of night *zazen* in the *Bendō hō*, DZZ.2:314. Yen Ping's *Tso-ch'an i* recommends that the eyes remain partially open, with the gaze cast down across the tip of the nose to a spot not more than one or two *hsin* in front (*Kanazawa bunko shiryō zensho*, vol. 1, 159). In his *Hsiao chih-kuan* (T.46:465c27), Chih-i says that the eyes should be closed "just enough to cut off the light from outside" (*ts'ai ling tuan wai kuang erh i*). Sekiguchi Shindai has suggested that this statement does not recommend completely closing the eyes, and that there is no real difference between Tsung-tse and Chih-i on this point (*Tendai shikan no kenkyū*, 338–42); but after some experiment, it remains difficult to see how one could shut out the light without fully closing his eyes. Rather, as is suggested in the *Ch'an-men k'ou-chüeh* (T.46:581b6), Chih-i's point here would seem to be that one should close his eyes gently, without pressing the lids together (*wu ling yen-lien ta chi*). In any case, Tsung-tse was hardly original in this matter: meditation with the eyes open is recommended as well by no less an orthodox Indian authority than Kamalaśīla, in his third *Bhāvanākrama*. In fact this latter text's entire passage on the posture of *samatha* is remarkably similar to Tsung-tse's own. (See Giuseppe Tucci, *Minor Buddhist Texts*, Part 3: *Third Bhāvanākrama*, Serie Orientale Roma XLIII [1971], 4.) Tsung-tse's reference to the precedent of the eminent monk of the past is probably to the sixth-century figure Hui-ch'eng (like Chih-i, a disciple of Hui-ssu), who is said to have spent every night for fifteen years sitting in meditation with his eyes open. His biography in the *Hsü kao-seng chuan* contrasts him with those lesser types who can only attain clear contemplation with their eyes closed and lose it as soon as they open them. (T.50:557a–b; reading *yen* for *k'ou* at b4.)

9. T.46:465c. The "translations" of these four types here is based on Chih-i's definitions. On the general matter of breathing techniques, see Ōtani Tetsuo, "Chūgoku shoki zenkan no kokyū hō to yōjō setsu no yōki ni tsuite," IBK 17, 1 (12/1968), 142–43; Ōtani, "Chūgoku ni okeru chōsoku hō," SK 11 (3/1969), 67–72; Yokoi Kakudō, "Fukan zazen gi goshinpitsu bon ni tsuite (2)," SK 12 (3/1970), 19–30.

There is one other place in Dōgen's corpus where we find information on the topic of breathing—in a formal lecture (*jōdō*) given at Eihei ji and preserved in the *Eihei kōroku*. Though the passage is rather long, it is worth quoting here, not only for the light it throws on Dōgen's practice but also as an example of a broader issue to which I shall shortly turn: the tendency of his writings to link the technique of meditation to its theory and to embed the practice of meditation in its sectarian tradition.

When a monk sits in meditation, he should first straighten his body and sit erect and then control his breathing and his mind. In the case of the Hīnayāna, there are basically two methods [for such control]: the counting of the breath and [the contemplation of] the impure [*fujō*]. Hīnayānists use the counting of breath to control the breathing, but the pursuit of the way of the Buddhas and Patriarchs is very different from that of the Hīnayāna. A Buddhist Patriarch has said, "Though you produce the mind of a mangy fox, do not practice the self-regulation of the two vehicles." These "two vehicles" are represented by such schools as the Shibun ritsu or Kusha schools current today. The Mahāyāna also has a method for regulating the breath: it is to know [when the breath is long] that this is a long breath, and to know [when it is short] that this is a short breath. The breath reaches the field of cinnabar [*tanden*] and exits again from the field of cinnabar; inhalation and exhalation may differ, but they both depend on the field of cinnabar.... My former master, T'ien-t'ung, has said, "The breath enters to the field of cinnabar, but it does not come from anywhere; hence, it is neither long nor short. The breath exits from the field of cinnabar, but it does not go anywhere; hence, it is neither short nor long." This is what my former master said. If someone were to ask me how the master controls the breath, I would simply say to him that it is not [the method of] Mahāyāna, but it is different from Hīnayāna; it is not Hīnayāna, but it is different from Mahāyāna. If he were to ask again just what, after all, it is, I would say that inhalation and exhalation are neither long nor short.[10]

Dōgen's account of the Buddhist breathing exercises here is a rather curious one, because both his "Hīnayāna" practice of counting the breath (*susoku*) and his "Mahāyāna" practice of mindfulness of the length of the breath are widely recommended in the texts of both the Greater and Lesser Vehicles. Indeed his warning against what he considers Hīnayāna practice notwithstanding, the counting of breath is still cultivated by Sōtō meditators today and is recommended by no less than the "Second Founder" of the school, Keizan, in his *Zazen yōjin ki*.[11] In any case Dōgen's interest here is

---

10. DZZ.2:96–97. This saying does not appear in Ju-ching's extant teachings. The "field of cinnabar" here refers to the area in the lower abdomen widely recognized in East Asian physiology as the repository of the vital breath (*ki*).

11. "If the mind becomes dispersed, fix it on the tip of the nose or on the *tanden* and count the breaths as they pass in and out." (SSZ.Shūgen,2:427a–b.) Concentration on the breath is said to be especially effective in counteracting random thoughts, and it often appears, along with the contemplation of the impure, in a standard list of the five meditations (*wu t'ing hsin kuan*) used as antidotes to the various psychological obstacles to meditation. (On these practices, see Ōminami Ryūshō, "Go teishin kan to gomon zen," in *Bukkyō no jissen genri*, ed. by Sekiguchi Shindai [1977], 71–90.)

clearly not in describing the Buddhist literature on breathing—nor even in explaining the techniques themselves—but in promoting his master's higher understanding of the phenomenon of breathing, an understanding that transcends both Hīnayāna and Mahāyāna and mocks our attempts to define the object of the meditation. Though this passage comes from a considerably later date, we shall see something of its style of treatment in other parts of the Tenpuku manual itself.

So far the *Fukan zazen gi* has covered, in a very cursory manner, the first two aspects of *zazen*, those of body and breath. Though they omit a phrase here and there, all these instructions are quoted directly from the *Tso-ch'an i*. Tsung-tse's own text, while it lacks much of the detail and occasionally disagrees on some of the basic features of the practice, still corresponds in outline to the kind of description given in the *Hsiao chih-kuan*. But, as we have seen, when we now come to the third and most important aspect of *zazen*, the control of the mind, Tsung-tse parts company with the T'ien-t'ai work to recommend the practice of forgetting objects. And here again the Tenpuku *Fukan zazen gi* simply follows along with its Chinese model, quoting Tsung-tse's brief description of the practice without comment.

Given what we know of the contemporaneous Zen discourse on meditation and of Dōgen's own later writings, the retention here of Tsung-tse's passage on his concentration technique seems quite surprising and rather difficult to explain. As we have seen, aside from its use in Yōsai's *Kōzen gokoku ron*, this technique was not favored by the other early Japanese accounts of meditation. Neither does it appear in any of the texts attributed to Ju-ching or in any of Dōgen's own reports of his master's teaching. Indeed it is not to be found anywhere else in Dōgen's corpus and has been expunged from all his revised manuals.[12] In the next chapter, when we look at the vulgate revision, I shall come back to some of the problems this brief passage raises for our understanding of Dōgen's meditation; but, at this point, we may simply note that Dōgen gives no hint here of his contemporaries' doubts about "forgetting objects" and "becoming unified" or their enthusiasm for the newer technique of *kōan* concentration.

As we shall shortly see, the *Fukan zazen gi* does offer elsewhere some thoughts on the meaning of its meditation exercise—thoughts that differ somewhat in emphasis from Tsung-tse's approach. In this middle section, though, the text does not pause to amplify or justify the mental technique it recommends. Instead, like the *Tso-ch'an i*, it simply moves on to praise the

---

12. Nevertheless, that Dōgen was probably still teaching something like Tsung-tse's concentration exercise in 1237 is suggested by a line in the *Tenzo kyōkun*, a work that draws heavily throughout on the *Ch'an-yüan ch'ing-kuei*: pointing out that our thoughts fly about like wild birds and emotions race around like forest monkeys, Dōgen advises, "If you once make these birds and monkeys reverse their course and reflect back [*taiho henshō*], you will naturally become unified [*ippen*]." (DZZ.2:297.)

practice, calling it "the *dharma* gate of ease and joy" (*anraku hōmon*) and claiming that, when rightly performed, it will relax the body, invigorate the spirit, and make one calm, pure, and joyful. The enlightened practitioner, we are told, takes to it "like a dragon to the water or a tiger to the mountains." [13] Finally, both texts conclude their instructions on the practice with the admonition that, after completing *zazen*, one should arise slowly and calmly and at all times should try to maintain the power of concentration (*jōriki, samādhi-bala*). [14]

This is all that the Tenpuku manual has to say on the actual method of what Dōgen claims is the essential—indeed, the only necessary—spiritual practice of Buddhism. His text adds almost nothing in the way of concrete instructions to the description provided by the *Tso-ch'an i*; on the contrary, it is even shorter and more schematic than Tsung-tse's own abbreviated account and limits itself only to the most basic features of the practice. Clearly Dōgen does not intend this text to provide a full explanation of his meditation method; in fact as we have seen, if we look in his later manuals and elsewhere, we occasionally discover material that supplements the rather meager fare offered here. This discovery serves not only to remind us that the *Fukan zazen gi* rests on a rich oral tradition of practical contemplative technique but to call our attention to the limits of the text as a source for the reconstruction of Dōgen's *zazen* practice.

At the conclusion of his "Fukan zazen gi senjutsu yurai," Dōgen remarks that the teachings of his meditation manual represent merely a substitute for what is transmitted from mind to mind. Implicit here is a warning, made explicit elsewhere, that a full understanding of the Zen practice described in the manual is dependent on direct contact with a Zen master. [15] That meditation should be studied not simply from books but in consultation with a teacher is, of course, a constant refrain of Buddhist contemplative tradition; indeed, as I have tried to emphasize, so dominant was the role of oral

---

13. The reference to "ease and joy" (*anraku, sukha*) invokes the "Sukhavihāra" chapter of the *Lotus Sūtra* (quoted later on in Tsung-tse's manual), in which it is said that the *bodhisattva's* life of ease (*an-lo hsing*) consists in always enjoying *tso-ch'an* (*pratisaṃlayana*), retiring from the world to practice the control of his mind (T.9:37b10). Dōgen gives this claim a more concrete sense in his *Bendō wa*, where he turns it into a justification of the superiority of the seated posture itself (DZZ.1:737).

14. Advice, incidentally, that parallels the *Hsiao chih-kuan* at T.46:466b. At various places in his *Bendō hō*, Dōgen gives concrete guidelines for how the monk can maintain concentration after *zazen*: he is, for example, to turn away from the wall slowly and quietly (to the right, in the traditional Buddhist clockwise direction) and descend from the dais without rustling his robes; he is to walk with hands folded across his chest (in the posture known as *shashu*), with eyes cast down to the floor; he is to begin walking with his right foot, and so on. When moving about the hall during meditation periods, monks were expected to maintain the slow gait known as *kinhin*, in which each pace advanced only the length of the foot. (Though Dōgen makes no mention of it here, Sōtō practice combines this exercise with concentration on the breath, such that each step corresponds to one inhalation and exhalation.)

15. See, for example, *Bendō wa*, DZZ.1:731, 734.

instruction in the classical Ch'an tradition that the appearance of an explicit manual like the *Tso-ch'an i* was something of an anomaly. Hence, even where we have such a manual, we must approach it with caution, bearing in mind that it may well represent merely the tip of an iceberg of meditation lore submerged in the oral tradition. This point is probably so obvious that it need hardly be emphasized; what does need to be emphasized—because it has often been ignored—is the corollary that we cannot argue from the *Fukan zazen gi*'s silence on a given technique that Dōgen did not, in fact, recommend its use. We simply do not know what concrete meditation instruction passed between Dōgen and his students in what he calls the mind's expression, but we do know that there is more to his *zazen* than what we have in the *Fukan zazen gi*. This point raises difficult questions for our current interpretation of Dōgen's meditation practice, and we shall need to refer to it again later.

If the brevity of Dōgen's description here of *zazen* thus leaves us in doubt about some of the concrete features of his practice, this fact in itself tells us something of the character of his text and its approach to meditation instruction. Indeed there is a sense in which what is most interesting about his manual, at least for those accustomed to the classical Buddhist meditation literature, is what it does not say. Unlike more traditional sources, Dōgen's manual shows almost no concern for defining either the contemplative lifestyle that provides the ethical context for meditation or the numerous mental states and objects that determine its psychological content. On the contrary, even where the text does touch on some of the categories employed by such sources, the tendency is not simply to abbreviate but to reinterpret in less concrete, less technical ways.

We have noted, for example, that neither Tsung-tse nor Dōgen shows much interest in the practical and psychological preparations for meditation. Traditional treatments of such preparations characteristically describe, often in considerable detail, a context for the practice that clearly presupposes an ascetic life of renunciation and withdrawal modelled on the ancient ideal of the *sannyāsin*. Chih-i's *Hsiao chih-kuan*, though it is offered as a textbook for beginners, still inherits this character. Indeed Chih-i devotes almost half his manual to this context, including chapters explaining the need to suppress the five sense desires, to overcome the five mental obstacles to meditation, and to cultivate the five psychological means conducive to spiritual progress.[16] In addition to such mental preparations, in his opening chapter he lays out the five practical preconditions (*wu yüan*) for contemplative life: purity in keeping the precepts, provision of food and clothing,

---

16. T.46:463b–65b, 466c. These are all traditional Buddhist categories for the discussion of religious practice. The five obstacles (*nivaraṇa*) are desire, aversion, sloth, restlessness, and doubt; Chih-i's five means (*upāya*) correspond to the five faculties (*indriya*) or powers (*bala*): determination, vigor, mindfulness, concentration, and wisdom.

retirement to a quiet place, cessation of worldly activities, and contact with good friends. Such preconditions are commonly assumed in Buddhist discussions of meditation; in fact two of them—the third and fourth—have found their way into our two manuals, but they appear there in rather altered form.

Chih-i defines a "quiet place" (*ching ch'u*) as any of the three types of environments traditionally considered appropriate for meditation: a mountain fastness, an isolated forest retreat, and a pure monastery. "Worldly activities" (*yüan wu*) are defined as occupational pursuits, social intercourse with laymen, arts and sciences, and scholarship.[17] Both Tsung-tse and Dōgen ignore such standard definitions, and their silence here leaves open the question of whether the meditator need actually withdraw from the secular world to a life of renunciation. Instead they seem to prefer a somewhat different emphasis. Tsung-tse offers at this point what appears to be a comment on the notion of "discontinuing affairs": be unified in body and mind, he says, whether in action or at rest. Such unification is presumably intended to indicate a state of concentrated attention that allows one to maintain his detachment from extraneous, or "wordly," influences even when he is in the midst of action.[18]

Dōgen follows Tsung-tse's lead here but goes on to develop the psychological sense of renunciation even further:

Cast aside all involvements and discontinue all affairs. Do not think of good or evil; do not deal with right or wrong. Halt the revolutions of mind, intellect, and consciousness [*shin i shiki*]; stop the calculations of thoughts, ideas, and perceptions [*nen sō kan*].

Whatever the exact sense of Dōgen's recommendation here to stop thinking, we should probably not understand this passage as teaching a technique of meditation in which the mind is brought to a halt. We are here dealing with the preparation for *zazen*; given its context, the passage should probably be viewed as a Zen comment on the true meaning of suspending worldly affairs. That is, worldliness is within, and what must be relinquished, therefore, is not merely the external ties to the secular world but those internal mechanisms that lead one to experience and believe in such a world. At the same time, of course, the passage serves as a warning, often repeated

---

17.   T.46:462c–63b. Similar definitions appear in discussions of such traditional formulae as the four "stocks of the *ārya*" (*ārya-vaṃśa*), the ten "impediments" (P.: *palibodha*) to meditation, and so on. Chih-i's other preconditions also assume that the practitioner will have "gone forth" from the home: his clothes, for example, should be cast-off rags or traditional Buddhist robes; his food should be gathered in the forest, obtained through begging, or provided by the monastery (463a–b).

18.   Similarly, the *Hsiao chih-kuan*: "Even when you are not in meditation—whether you are walking or standing, moving or still—you should be fully conscious of all your activities, both in motion and at rest" (T.46:465c).

by Ch'an and Zen masters, that the practice is not to be approached through the understanding but begins with a suspension of our ordinary ways of thinking. In a closely related passage in his *Gakudō yōjin shū*, probably written less than a year after the Tenpuku text, Dōgen remarks that, despite the many dedicated practitioners of Buddhism, few have actually awakened to the way for the following reason.

It is extremely difficult to regulate the mind. Intelligence is not a primary factor; learning is not primary; mind, intellect, and consciousness are not primary; thoughts, ideas, and perceptions are not primary: without employing any of these, one must regulate body and mind and by this enter the *buddha-mārga*.... When the two attributes of action and rest are perfectly clear and do not arise, this is the regulation [of body and mind].[19]

Here Dōgen has explicitly extended the discussion from the ethical topic of renunciation to the psychological problem of the regulation of the mind (*chōshin*); yet in doing so, he has simultaneously elevated this latter problem to the domain of Zen metaphysics. His final sentence seems to make the theoretical connection between Tsung-tse's advice to maintain a unified consciousness in both action and rest and Dōgen's recommendation to give up thinking: regulation of the mind, or single-minded attention to the practice, occurs when the two characteristics of action and rest are clearly seen "not to arise"—that is, are seen to be empty categories. Presumably, then, because our ordinary thinking does not see action and rest in this way, our thinking represents an obstacle to the practice and must be suspended. In any event we have here come well beyond Chih-i's original suggestion that the meditator avoid involvement in the secular world: we have apparently come to the very gates of the Zen world of no-thought and sudden awakening. Indeed our *Fukan zazen gi* passage is strongly reminiscent, both in content and language, of a classical teaching on sudden awakening attributed to Po-chang Huai-hai.

A monk asked, "What is the sudden awakening teaching of the Mahāyāna (*ta-sheng tun wu fa-men*)?" Po-chang replied, "You should first stop all involvements and discontinue all affairs. Do not bear in mind, do not think of, any *dharma*—whether good or bad, mundane or transmundane. Cast aside body and mind and set them free.[20]

---

19. DZZ.2:257. There has been some controversy over the dating of the *Gakudō yōjin shū*, but most scholars now accept the traditional date of 1234. The close parallels in phrasing here and elsewhere with the 1233 *Fukan zazen gi* would seem to provide some internal evidence that the two texts were composed around the same time.

20. *Ching-te ch'uan teng lu*, T.51:250a17–20. Generally speaking, all the expressions in Dōgen's passage represent variations on the basic Ch'an message of no-thought. "Do not think of good or evil" (*fu shi zen aku*), borrowed from Tsung-tse's text, is a popular injunction probably first appearing in Shen-hui's *T'an yü* (Hu Shih, *Shen-hui ho-shang i-chi*, 236; Tsung-tse's version follows the form attributed to Hui-neng at *Ching-te ch'uan teng lu*, T.51:236a20). "Do not deal with right or wrong" (*maku kan zehi*) is from a line by Li Tsun-hsü (d. 1038) (*Chia-t'ai*

Dōgen's preference for the "sudden" treatment of renunciation here exemplifies two important—and, in some ways, conflicting—characteristics of the *Fukan zazen gi* that we have seen in the tradition as a whole. On the one hand, in its avoidance of the technical descriptions of meditation and the meditative lifestyle, his text, like the *Tso-ch'an i*, seems to escape the confines of the cloister and to offer a simple spiritual practice for all. On the other hand, the very dearth of description leaves many details of the practice open to question and, consequently, seems to limit the work's effectiveness as an adequate guide for the untutored meditator. In this latter characteristic Dōgen goes beyond the *Tso-ch'an i*; for whatever else it may do, his tendency to substitute Zen ideology for Tsung-tse's straightforward psychological advice only adds to the mystery of *zazen*.

These two characteristics—the avoidance of the technical language of meditation and the movement toward more theoretical interpretations—can be seen again in Dōgen's treatment of the notion of *samādhi*. In his presentation of meditation Chih-i makes a basic distinction, common to many discussions of yoga, between "external techniques" (*wai fang-pien*), which can be practiced outside the state of *samādhi*, and "internal techniques" (*nei fang-pien*), which presuppose that state. Thus his so-called "twenty-five techniques" (*erh-shih-wu fang-pien*), discussed in the *Hsiao chih-kuan* and elsewhere—including those that deal with the regulation of body, breath, and mind—all belong to the former category; into the latter category fall his discussions of *chih-kuan* proper, the fruits of the five contemplations, the overcoming of demonic phenomena, the therapeutic uses of meditation, and so on.[21]

According to this classification, then, the account of *zazen* in the *Fukan zazen gi* is almost entirely limited to the external techniques; like the *Tso-ch'an i*, the description breaks off precisely at the point where the meditator has attained concentration, and one looks in vain for an explanation of what happens next. As we have seen, Tsung-tse does at least warn us against the

---

p'u teng lu, ZZ.2B,10:155a14; also quoted at *Tenzo kyōkun*, DZZ.2:300). The idiom "mind, intellect, and consciousness" (*hsin i shih*, in technical writing, representing *citta, manas,* and *vijñāna*) regularly functions as equivalent to *nien*, "[deluded] thought"; and the Ch'an texts repeatedly admonish one to practice Buddhism "without *hsin i shih*" (see, e.g., Shen-hui's *T'an yü*, 232; Tung-shan Shih-ch'ien's biography, *Lien-teng hui yao*, ZZ.2B,9:401a). The expression *nien hsiang kuan*, translated here as "thoughts, ideas, and perceptions," is rather less common and somewhat ambiguous. It is best known from the "Prajñā-pāramitā-stotra," quoted in the *Ta-chih-tu lun* (T.25:190b20–21), where it probably indicates *vikalpa*, or discriminative cognition; but tradition also associates the three component terms with contemplative exercises (see, e.g., Chih-i's *Chüeh-i san-mei*, T.46:626a29), and there may well be an undercurrent in our passage of the Ch'an dismissal of traditional meditation practice.

21. T.46:466c–72b. The *Hsiao chih-kuan* itself does not explicitly introduce the categories of internal and external; but see, for example, Chih-i's *Tz'u-ti ch'an-men*, T.46:483c–84a. The five contemplations (*wu t'ing hsin kuan*) are the popular preliminary *śamatha* meditations on breathing, impurity, compassion, dependent origination, and the Buddha (or, in some systems, the eighteen elements [*dhātus*]).

psychophysical disorders resulting from the improper cultivation of trance; he then goes on to recommend that the practitioner, after he has come out of *samādhi*, should use techniques (*fang-pien*) to maintain his concentration at all times in order to develop the ability to enter *samādhi* at will (*ting li, samādhi-bala*). Dōgen's text abbreviates even these simple instructions: it drops the topic of aberrant trance states and, though it retains the basic notion of maintaining *samādhi* power, substantially alters its context. Dōgen omits Tsung-tse's references to "emerging from *samādhi*" and "employing *upāya*"; hence, his passage ignores the basic distinction between the state of *samādhi* achieved in *zazen* and the cultivation of the power of concentration practiced outside that state. He also omits Tsung-tse's suggestion that the goal of this cultivation is the development of the ability to enter trance states. Instead he offers at this point his own highly abstract and extremely obscure commentary on *samādhi* power: "In studying and investigating it, you transcend its higher workings, without a basis to rely on; in verifying and letting go of it, you are obstructed by the self, wherein you are never impeded. This is the full realization of the way." [22]

Whatever this passage may mean, it clearly implies that *samādhi* power is not, as is usually understood, simply the power of concentration on the object of meditation; rather, it apparently involves a state of spiritual freedom, in which the practitioner is not dependent upon, or arrested by, anything. Moreover, the maintenance of such a state is apparently not a practice intended to improve one's meditation but is an end in itself. Indeed it is said to represent the complete fulfillment of the Buddhist path (*dō shi jūsei*), a characterization that, if we are to take it literally, can only indicate a state of enlightenment. Thus, if this interpretation is correct, the *Fukan zazen gi* passage is identifying the perfection of *samādhi* power with the perfection of *bodhi*, and here there seems to be an intimation of Dōgen's famous doctrine of the unity of *zazen* and enlightenment. Again, practical advice on psychological technique has been elevated to the level of ideological discourse.

This interest in the theoretical treatment of meditation informs the entire text of the *Fukan zazen gi* and distinguishes it most sharply from Tsung-tse's manual. The latter is a remarkably simple and straightforward work. Though it occasionally mentions *prajñā* or *bodhi* as the goal of meditation practice, one searches in vain for those brilliant, often glaring, displays of enlightenment that we, like Dōgen before us, have come to expect from the masters of Ch'an. Instead we find a humble—one is tempted to say honest—work, almost wholly free from spiritual pretension and literary artifice. It is a work intended simply to encourage its reader to undertake the practice of

---

22. A tentative translation. This passage is probably one of the more self-conscious—and least successful—in the *Fukan zazen gi*; Dōgen wisely eliminated it in his revised version.

meditation and to instruct him in its basic features; on the ultimate meaning of the practice and its relation to the spiritual insights of Ch'an tradition, Tsung-tse is content to remain silent. In contrast, it is precisely in this meaning and these insights that Dōgen, like the majority in the tradition, seems most interested.

The gap between the two works becomes obvious when we turn from the central section of the *Fukan zazen gi* to its introduction and conclusion. Here we move from the description of *zazen* to its interpretation; and here, for the most part, we leave Tsung-tse's *Tso-ch'an i* behind. Since these sections constitute two-thirds of the work, their weight gives the *Fukan zazen gi* a very different feeling from that of its Chinese model; indeed passages from these sections are most often cited as evidence of Dōgen's dissatisfaction with Tsung-tse's style of Zen. Yet even here we should not exaggerate the implications of this dissatisfaction, since much of it seems to have to do more with style than with Zen.

The introduction and conclusion of the *Fukan zazen gi* are largely composed in the ornate *shiroku benrei* verse style popular among Dōgen's aristocratic contemporaries; in keeping with this style, they are heavy with allusion to earlier literature and liberally laced with patches of purple that contrast sharply with Tsung-tse's workmanlike prose. The *Tso-ch'an i*, for example, warns us against procrastination in the following terms:

> Even if one devotes himself to the practice his entire life, he may still not be in time; how, then, can one who procrastinates possibly overcome *karma*?

For this passage, Dōgen substitutes:

> Since you have already obtained the proper conjunction for a human body, do not pass your days in vain; when one always bears in mind the appropriate conduct of the way of the Buddha, who can carelessly enjoy the spark from a flint? Verily, form and substance are like the dew on the grass, and the fortunes of life like the lightning flash: in an instant they are emptied; in a moment they are lost.

Similarly, Tsung-tse closes his essay with the advice:

> Friends in Ch'an, go over this text again and again. Benefitting others as well as ourselves, let us together achieve full enlightenment.

The final lines of the *Fukan zazen gi* offer this advice:

> Eminent students [of the *dharma*], long accustomed to groping for the elephant, pray do not doubt the true dragon. Promptly take the right way, which points directly at reality; quickly become the true man, through with learning and free from action.

Careful attention to the relationship between the texts of the *Tso-ch'an i* and *Fukan zazen gi* reveals that many of the innovations of the latter are of the sort exemplified here—that is, largely literary embellishments of themes originating in the Chinese manual. Whether or not one agrees with Dōgen's admirers that the *Fukan zazen gi* is almost without peer in the *kanbun* writings of Japanese Buddhism, one must concede that his stylistic revision of the *Tso-ch'an i* has transformed a technical manual into a literary work. In this revision Dōgen's text probably owes more in spirit and language to the poetic tradition of the *tso-ch'an chen* genre and texts like the *Hsin hsin ming* and *Cheng tao ko* than it does to any Chinese meditation manual.[23] This literary character of the *Fukan zazen gi* should not be forgotten when its teachings are compared with those of the *Tso-ch'an i*. Failure to keep it in mind will lead—and, in fact, probably has led many commentators—to an overemphasis on Dōgen's innovations in the explanation of *zazen*. As a work of Zen literature, the *Fukan zazen gi* may well offer us more than the *Tso-ch'an i*, but this fact alone hardly justifies the conclusion that Dōgen's understanding of *zazen* practice was markedly different from, or deeper than, that of Tsung-tse. We must be careful here to distinguish literary interpretations of meditation from the practice itself and avoid confusing the pointing finger with the moon.

At the same time there is clearly more to the *Fukan zazen gi* than art and more to Dōgen's disappointment with Tsung-tse than literary criticism. Behind the language there is what Dōgen calls, in the "Senjutsu yurai," "the understanding beyond words," his vision of the true meaning of Zen practice. Indeed so penetrating was this vision that it saw through not only the *Tso-ch'an i* but the entire corpus of meditation literature available to the Japanese and led Dōgen, as we have seen, to claim that no *zazen gi* had previously been transmitted to his country. In one sense this claim might be interpreted simply as an expression of its author's pride in being the first to introduce a complete Zen meditation manual. The *Hsiao chih-kuan* and other traditional treatments of the practice, for all their wealth of instruction, did not, after all, come out of the Ch'an tradition Dōgen had studied in China. Yōsai's quotation from the *Ta-tsang i-lan*, though it did belong to that tradition, remained a severely truncated version of the *Tso-ch'an i*, consigned to a series of brief quotations from various Buddhist sources. Consequently, Dōgen, who presumably discovered the full version while in China, might well have felt that his countrymen still lacked the complete transmission of an authentic *zazen gi*. Yet this interpretation, though there may be truth in it, does not seem to go far enough; if it did, one would expect Dōgen to have been content simply to introduce the full text of the *Tso-ch'an i*. That he was not is probably an expression of his particular understanding of *zazen* and, hence, of an authentic *zazen* manual.

In the *Bendō wa*, written just prior to the Tenpuku *Fukan zazen gi*, Dōgen

---

23. We may recall that, in fact, the *Fukan zazen gi* quotes these two poems, and that Dōgen subsequently revised his text on the basis of his work on Hung-chih's *Tso-ch'an chen*.

is asked by his (presumably fictitious) interlocutor to distinguish his own meditation teaching from that of Tendai and Shingon and to explain how his practice differs from the common Buddhist exercises of *dhyāna* and *samādhi*. His response is that his *zazen* is the *shōbō genzō*, the true *dharma* handed down from Śākyamuni through Bodhidharma and the Ch'an Patriarchs. It is, in other words, the realization of the enlightenment of the Buddha himself—or what Dōgen calls in the *Bendō wa*, "the *samādhi* of [the Buddha's] personal enjoyment" (*ji juyū zanmai*)—and it is, therefore, not to be confused with ordinary meditation techniques.[24]

This response may help us to understand why the "Senjutsu yurai" could bluntly dismiss previous meditation literature and boldly claim that Dōgen's own *zazen gi* was without precedent in Japan. An authentic manual of *zazen* must belong to the true tradition of *zazen*, a tradition inseparable from the Zen lineage of the *shōbō genzō*; hence the meditation texts of Tendai and other Buddhist traditions are excluded. At the same time an authentic manual of *zazen* must teach the true meaning of *zazen*, a meditation of perfect enlightenment; thus a work like the *Tso-ch'an i*, which fails to convey the "understanding beyond words," does not count.

These two interlocking themes—a unique understanding of meditation that interprets the practice through the transcendental wisdom of the Buddha and a unique tradition of meditation that is transmitted through the historical lineage of the Patriarchs—both appear in the *Fukan zazen gi* and, indeed, represent the dominant motifs of those sections in which Dōgen goes beyond the *Tso-ch'an i* to express his own style of Zen. The first of these themes in particular is the subject of his introduction.

In the *T'ien-t'ai hsiao chih-kuan*, Chih-i introduces his discussion of the practice of meditation with the following common advice:

The practitioner beginning to study meditation and intending to cultivate the *dharmas* of the Buddhas of the ten directions and three realms should first produce the great vow to lead all beings to liberation and to seek the supreme enlightenment of a Buddha.[25]

As we have seen, a similar admonition appears at the opening of the *Tso-ch'an i*:

The *bodhisattva* who studies *prajñā* should first arouse the thought of great compassion, make the extensive vows, and then carefully cultivate *samādhi*. Vowing to save sentient beings, he should not seek liberation for himself alone.

24. DZZ.1:734-36.
25. T.46:465b. This passage occurs in the vulgate version as the introduction to the "T'iao-ho" chapter, but it seems originally to have represented an introduction to the "Cheng-hsiu" chapter on *śamatha* and *vipaśyanā*. See Sekiguchi, *Tendai shō shikan no kenkyū*, 150–51.

Here Tsung-tse, like Chih-i, seeks to emphasize at the very outset the Mahāyāna ethical context of his meditation practice: *samādhi* is to be cultivated against the background of the vow to win perfect enlightenment and bring about the salvation of all beings. Hence he addresses his treatise to "the *bodhisattva* who studies *prajñā*." Tsung-tse does not pause to discuss the nature of this *prajñā* or its bearing on meditation but proceeds directly to his description of the practice. Yet it is precisely here, in the interpretation of how the Mahāyāna wisdom teaching should inform the *bodhisattva*'s understanding of meditation, that the early masters of Tsung-tse's Ch'an tradition established their characteristic approach to Buddhism; and it is with this approach that Dōgen begins his own manual.

Fundamentally speaking, the basis of the way is perfectly pervasive; how could it be contingent on practice and verification? The vehicle of the ancestors is naturally unrestricted; why should we expend sustained effort? Surely the whole being is far beyond defilement; who could believe in a method to polish it? Never is it apart from this very place; what is the use of a pilgrimage to practice it? And yet, if a hair's breadth of distinction exists, the gap is like that between heaven and earth; once the slightest like and dislike arises, all is confused and the mind is lost.

Here, in both content and language, the *Fukan zazen gi* is clearly harking back to the original message of the Ch'an school: "fundamentally speaking," enlightenment is universal, not the result of individual religious endeavor; "and yet," as long as one clings to the objects of discrimination, he fails to recognize this fact. Like many of the early masters of Ch'an, Dōgen does not seem to feel the need to emphasize here the altruistic aspiration of the *bodhisattva* (or the necessity of cultivating the various salvific techniques through which that aspiration is expressed); rather, taking advantage of the metaphysical notion that all the goals of the *bodhisattva* path are inherent to the mind, he can focus simply on the individual's quest for the recovery of that mind. Again, like the early masters, he goes on later in this introduction to single out discursive thought—what he calls here "reflection" (*gigi*) and "deliberation" (*shōryō*)—as the most serious obstacle to the quest and to urge his reader to "reverse the intellectual practice of investigating words and chasing after talk." Rather than seek the mind in the objects of its understanding, one should "directly accede" (*jikige jōtō*) to inherent Buddhahood by taking "the backward step" (*taiho*) that illumines the original nature of the subject. When he does so, Dōgen concludes here, all attachments to body and mind will drop away (*shinjin datsuraku*) of their own accord, and the "original face" (*honrai menmoku*) of primordial enlightenment will be manifest.

In all this there is little new: it could have been said by virtually any master from the mid-T'ang on. As a matter of fact, except for a turn of phrase here and there, almost all of it had been said; this entire introduction reads like a series of stock expressions from the Ch'an literature. It opens with an allusion to the dialogue, so treasured by Dōgen, between the Sixth Patriarch and Huai-jang on the ultimate nature of practice and enlightenment; it goes on to recall the famous verse from the *Platform Sūtra* on polishing the mirror of the mind; it draws passages from the verse of the *Cheng tao ko* and the *Hsin hsin ming*; it closes with the popular metaphor of the "original face" attributed to Hui-neng; and, throughout, it consistently borrows the standard vocabulary of the recorded sayings of the T'ang masters.[26]

Of course, not only the medium but also the message is familiar here; precisely the insistence on the inherent perfection of the ordinary mind and the consequent reduction of Buddhist practice to the mere recognition of this fact are the ideological hallmarks of the sudden tradition. Nor is the reassertion here of the classic expressions of Ch'an wisdom particularly noteworthy; in one form or another, they are a common feature of much contemporary writing of the school, both in the Sung and in Japan. What is more significant is that, unlike some of his contemporaries, who saw in this wisdom grounds for reiterating as well the old Ch'an doubts about the cultivation of meditation, Dōgen seems to have no qualms here. He states his position unambiguously in the final sentence of his introduction: "If you want such [a state, in which the original nature of the mind becomes apparent], urgently work at *zazen.*" And, as we soon discover in the following section of the text, what he means by such work is the cultivation of Tsung-tse's venerable concentration exercise. Still, the emphasis on Ch'an wisdom in the Tenpuku *Fukan zazen gi* is a presage of things to come, since Dōgen himself will later feel obliged to upgrade Tsung-tse's account of meditation in order to better integrate it with the higher teachings of the school.

The abstract notions of a perfectly pervasive enlightenment and a naturally unrestricted vehicle with which the *Fukan zazen gi* opens take on greater historical concreteness in the concluding section of the text. Here Dōgen is basically following Tsung-tse's discussion of the need for, and benefits of, *dhyāna*, but again his emphasis is rather different. The *Tso-ch'an i* describes the single practice of meditation as our most urgent business: without it, we shall simply drift aimlessly in the sea of *saṃsāra*, at the mercy of death; with it, the surface waves of the mind will subside, and the pearl of liberating wisdom beneath will appear of its own accord. Therefore, Tsung-tse reminds us, the *sūtras* have recommended it; consequently, too, the great sages—those transcending the distinction between "sinner and saint" and possessed of the power to control their death—have all depended

---

26. For these references, see respectively *Lien-teng hui yao,* ZZ.2B,9:243a; *Liu-tsu t'an ching,* T.48:337c; *Cheng tao ko,* ibid., 396b12; *Hsin hsin ming,* ibid., 376b21–22; *T'an ching* (Kōshō ji text), Nakagawa Taka, *Rokuso dankyō, Zen no goroku* 4 (1976), 46.

on *dhyāna* and *samādhi*. We should cultivate this practice without delay, lest *karma* overtake us, and death intervene before its benefits are realized.

For his part, Dōgen agrees that meditation is important—indeed the highest religious practice—but his explanation is less concerned with the waters of *saṃsāra* and the waves of delusion than with the transcendental wisdom of the other shore. He sagely abandons Tsung-tse's problematic metaphor of the static pearl beneath the turbid sea; in its place he prefers the more dynamic, more dramatic images of Patriarchal Ch'an enlightenment.

First taking up one full understanding and then turning over one half verification [—such Zen teachings] belong solely to this *dharma* [of meditation]. Holding up a flower and breaking into a smile, making a bow and attaining the marrow [—such Zen transactions] represent the great freedom attained through accession to its benevolent power. How could *bodhisattvas* who study *prajñā* fail to follow and accord with it?

In the same vein Dōgen expands on Tsung-tse's reference to the power over life and death that flows from *dhyāna* and *samādhi*. If, as the *Tso-ch'an i* puts it, the masters of meditation can "shed [this body] while seated and flee [this life] while standing," how much more mysterious their everyday methods of expressing enlightenment:

Turning the opportunity with a finger, a pole, a needle or a mallet, and verifying the accord with a whisk, a fist, a staff or a shout [—these Zen teaching devices] are not to be understood through the discriminations of thinking, much less can they be known through the practice and verification of supernormal powers. They represent conduct beyond sound and form; how could they fail to provide a standard prior to our knowledge and understanding?

The move here from Tsung-tse's sober concern with overcoming *karma* and death to Dōgen's exuberant celebration of the enlightened life—like the parallel move from the former's still, luminous pearl to Dōgen's fist and shout—almost seems to recapitulate in microcosm the development we have seen in the early tradition from the contemplative teachings of the East Mountain to the "Patriarchal Ch'an" of the later T'ang. Like that development, the focus has shifted from cause to effect; and, like that development, if the shift is supposed to represent an ascent to a higher perspective, it is also in some sense a descent from the abstract issue of the possibility of Buddhist enlightenment to its concrete manifestation in the reality of Ch'an history. The way to express what cannot be understood through the discriminations of thinking and to gauge the standard that precedes our knowledge is less to imagine innate wisdom with Tsung-tse than to cite specific instances of its workings in the tradition—to hold up Chü-chih's finger and take up Lin-chi's staff. Similarly, the way to justify meditation is less to quote scripture with Tsung-tse than to invoke the precedent of its centrality in the tradition. And, in fact, the *Fukan zazen gi* goes on here to follow up its historical examples of the fruits of the practice with an explicit appeal to precedent.

Both in our world and the other quarters, the *buddha-dharma* has no other *dharma* [than this Zen practice]; from the Western Heavens [i.e., India] to the Eastern Earth [i.e., China], the Patriarchal gate opened five gates. All equally maintain the Buddha seal, while each enjoys its own style of teaching.[27]

This passage brings us to our second major theme, the emphasis on the lineage of *zazen* that emerges in the *Fukan zazen gi*'s repeated references and allusions to the tradition of the Ch'an Patriarchs. In terms of style, as we have seen, whereas Tsung-tse is content to present his teachings in straight-forward, unadorned language, Dōgen's text is self-consciously literary and strives throughout to emulate the classic literature of Ch'an. Indeed so steeped in this literature is the *Fukan zazen gi* that, not only in its introductory remarks but throughout those passages original to Dōgen, there is hardly a sentence that does not in some way invoke the sayings of the masters. Whatever else we may say of such style, it means that the reader cannot but be reminded at every turn of the sectarian affiliation of its author. Yet beyond this, Dōgen goes out of his way to associate his meditation teaching explicitly with the Chinese Ch'an tradition and to encourage his reader to enter into that tradition. In his introduction he cites the precedent of Bodhidharma's nine years of "wall gazing." In his conclusion, as we have just seen, he alludes to the first transmission of the *shōbō genzō* to Mahā-kāśyapa and Bodhidharma's transmission to the Second Patriarch, Hui-k'o, and then goes on to invoke the famous liberating techniques of the T'ang masters and to identify his practice with the one *buddha-dharma* passed down through the Patriarchs of the "five houses" of the school. Finally, he closes his treatise with the claim that his *zazen* accords with the Ch'an institutes of Po-chang and carries on the Ch'an heritage of Shao-lin, the monastery of Bodhidharma.

On all these points Tsung-tse's *Tso-ch'an i* is silent; except for one or two passing references to Ch'an, his text makes no mention of the school or allusion to its lore. For Tsung-tse, of course, and his Sung readers, Ch'an was a long-established tradition; moreover, it was a tradition not in serious competition with other Buddhist schools. On the contrary, Tsung-tse him-self, like many of his contemporaries, did not limit his interests to Ch'an but sought to combine its teachings and practices with those of the popular Pure Land Buddhism. For him, the issue was hardly how to advertise the unique tradition of the school but how to revitalize the tradition and make it relevant to a wider religious audience.

---

27. The "five gates" here, of course, refer to the five "houses" (*wu chia*) into which the Sung historians commonly divided the Ch'an lineages.

In Kamakura Japan, needless to say, the situation was quite different. There the religious scene had long been dominated by other schools of Buddhism. Moreover, these Japanese schools were not merely spiritual or ideological traditions but distinct ecclesiastical bodies with independent economic status and all the political consciousness that status implies. Particularly in Dōgen's day, faced as they were with the economic and political uncertainties attendant upon the decline of the Heian aristocracy and the rise of new centers of temporal power, these established churches inevitably reacted strongly—and in some cases violently—to the recent proliferation of schismatic movements and the sudden introduction of new Buddhist traditions from the mainland.

Zen, of course, was such a new tradition, and under these circumstances it is small wonder that Dōgen, like other Buddhist leaders of the period, succumbed to the heavy atmosphere of sectarian struggle. He had before him the recent examples of men like Hōnen and Shinran, who had been persecuted and driven into exile for their Pure Land teachings. Closer to home, his own predecessor in Zen Dainichibō Nōnin had, as we have seen, similarly run afoul of the dominant Tendai organization; and even Yōsai, whom Dōgen considered his spiritual forebear, despite the fact that he remained within the Tendai fold, was forced to defend his Zen teachings against charges of heresy and antinomianism.

Yōsai and some of the other early Japanese Zen advocates achieved acceptance through compromise with the established traditions of Tendai and Shingon; Lan-ch'i and most of the Chinese Zen missionaries gained direct access to the centers of temporal power as official guests of the shōgunate. Dōgen did neither. Instead he turned his back on Yōsai's monastery and sought to establish his own independent Zen institution not far from the capital. Such a move would hardly have gone unnoticed by the Tendai headquarters on Mt. Hiei; in fact, we know that Dōgen eventually came under attack by the monks of the mountain. We do not know whether and to what extent he was already embroiled in sectarian politics in 1233, but it is hardly surprising that the *Fukan zazen gi*, written as it was just after the move to his new monastery, is already sensitive to the issue of sectarian affiliation. His final remarks in the manual are a poignant sign of the hostile reception he could expect for his mission: "Do not trouble yourself," he advised his followers, "over the winds that assail the ear nor be upset by the sounds of the wagging tongue."

Dōgen's close identification with the Ch'an tradition was surely as much cause as it was effect of his political isolation, since his sectarianism was by no means merely defensive. He had studied in the Great Sung, a fact of which he seems to have been fiercely proud, and was one of the few active teachers of his day personally acquainted with the new Buddhism of the continent. He was privy to the esoterica of the Sung Ch'an literature, a literature not yet widely disseminated in Japan and composed in a new idiom largely unfamiliar to Japanese Buddhists; his *Fukan zazen gi* and, indeed, the entire corpus of his writings reflect his fascination with this idiom and his delight in having made it his own. Most importantly, he seems to have felt himself the sole Japanese inheritor of the orthodox tradition (*shōden*) of the *buddha-dharma*, a tradition hitherto unknown on the islands.

We have seen that in his earliest extant work, the *Bendō wa*, Dōgen uses the notion of the historical tradition of the Buddhas and Patriarchs to distinguish his Zen meditation from other forms of Buddhist practice. In fact the entire work is dominated by an acute sense of this tradition and of the historical significance of its transmission to Japan. In his introduction to the text Dōgen recites the legend of the transmission of the "Buddha mind seal" (*busshin'in*), from Śākyamuni to the five houses of Ch'an. This tradition represents the "orthodox transmission" (*shōden*), the "authentic *buddha-dharma*" (*shinjitsu no buppō*), the "unadulterated *buddha-dharma*" (*jun'ichi no buppō*), brought to the East by the First Patriarch, Bodhidharma, and spread there by the Sixth Patriarch, Hui-neng. Buddhist texts had circulated in China since the later Han, but no one, Dōgen says, had understood their import; it was only with the transmission of the Patriarchal tradition that the "brambles" of misunderstanding were cut away and the unadulterated religion began to flourish there.[28]

The Patriarchal tradition, of course, is the tradition of *zazen*, the Buddhas' "*samādhi* of personal enjoyment" (*ji juyū zanmai*). The *Bendō wa* goes on to claim that all the Buddhas and Patriarchs of both India and China have relied on this practice to attain awakening (*satori*); it is the "mystic art" (*myōjutsu*), the "true arcanum" (*shinketsu*), secretly passed down from master to disciple. It is the one "orthodox gate" (*shōmon*) to the *buddha-dharma* because it is on the basis of this practice that Śākyamuni, all the Tathāgatas of the three times, and all the Patriarchs of the Western Heavens and the Eastern Earth attained the way. According to the orthodox tradition, this *dharma*, directly transmitted through the Patriarchs, is the very pinnacle of the supreme teaching. Here there is no longer need for other forms of practice—incense offerings, obeisance to the Buddha, recitation of His name, repentence or *sūtra* study; here it is enough simply to sit and slough off body and mind (*shinjin datsuraku*).[29]

This Patriarchal tradition of *zazen*, Dōgen goes on, is not yet recognized in Japan. Though Buddhism has been known since the reigns of the em-

---

28. DZZ.1:730.

29. DZZ.1:730–33, passim. Dōgen compares the study of *sūtras* here to reading a prescription without taking the medicine; recitation has no more spiritual efficacy than "the constant croaking of frogs in the spring paddies" (733–34). Later on in the text, he rejects *mantra* (*shingon*) and *śamatha-vipaśyanā* (*shikan*) as well: neither of these practices was ever cultivated by any of the Patriarchs of India or China who correctly transmitted the seal of the Buddha (741).

perors Kinmei (r. 539–71) and Yōmei (r. 585–87), its doctrines and practices are in rank confusion and the practice of *zazen* has not been transmitted. Until now the time was not ripe: previous Japanese pilgrims to China failed to understand this *dharma* and, as a consequence, transmitted only empty dogma. Kegon, Tendai, and Shingon teachers may talk about the ultimate Mahāyāna, but they are just "word-counting scholastics," "the blind leading the blind"; they are not on a par with the enlightened masters revered in the orthodox tradition of the Buddhas and Patriarchs. It is only under such a master that one can hope to learn the true practice of Buddhism.[30]

Now the Japanese have such a master. The *Bendō wa* opens with an account of the author's personal quest for the supreme *buddha-dharma*, his study of the five houses in the great Sung, and his enlightenment at Mt. T'ien-t'ung. Having returned to Japan, he has taken pity on those sincere students who are being led astray by heterodox teachers (*jashi*) and have nowhere else to turn for the truth. It is in order to instruct them in the orthodox Buddhist *dharma* that he is now recording the "true arcanum"— the "customs and rules of the Zen groves" that he himself directly experienced and the "dark decrees of the good friends" that he himself received in the land of the Great Sung.[31]

The text closes on a similar note. The Japanese, says Dōgen, are a barbarian people (*ban'i*), lacking in benevolence and wisdom, weak in intelligence, and prone to desires for fame and profit; yet, even in this benighted land, so distant in both space and spirit from the great civilizations of India and China, it is possible, when the time is ripe, for the orthodox *dharma* of the Tathāgatas to spread. Unfortunately, the essential message of *zazen* has not yet been transmitted; therefore, Dōgen has now collected what he experienced abroad and recorded the true arcanum of the enlightened masters. He has taken it upon himself thus to spread the *buddha-dharma* in the land without awaiting the order of the king, because he knows that all the kings and ministers are themselves under order of the Buddha to defend and maintain the *dharma*.[32]

Behind the final sentence here, we cannot help but sense the lonely and defiant spirit of the young Dōgen's mission to the Japanese. Indeed, despite the persistent modern fiction that his religion somehow transcended the sectarian bickerings of his contemporaries, the entire text is ablaze with a sectarian fervor so intense that it would seemingly lay sole claim to the true

---

30. DZZ.1:734–45, passim.
31. DZZ.1:729–30. Japan's lack of true teachers—those who have obtained the "seal of verification" (*inshō*) from a true teacher—is also lamented in the *Gakudō yōjin shū*, written shortly after the *Bendō wa*; there, interestingly enough, Dōgen advises those readers who would study the supreme Buddha path to seek out "good friends" in the distant Sung. (DZZ.2: 255–56.) Later, of course, he will reject these same friends as heretics.
32. DZZ.1:744–46. The *Bendō wa* concludes with the colophon, "by the śramaṇa Dōgen, pilgrim to the Sung and transmitter of the *dharma*."

teaching of the Buddha and, by implication at least, relegate the competing schools of Japanese Buddhism to heterodoxy. This is a radical claim indeed, and its implications for other Buddhists could hardly be missed even by blind, word-counting scholastics. In the *Fukan zazen gi* and in most of his other works, Dōgen prudently avoids dwelling on these implications and refrains from the sort of explicit attacks on specific Japanese schools and individuals that we find, say, in his contemporary, the notorious sectarian polemicist Nichiren. Nevertheless, it is quite clear from both his words and his deeds that, already by the time he wrote the *Bendō wa* and *Fukan zazen gi*, he was exclusively committed to his own brand—or, as he would have it, the Buddha's own brand—of Buddhism, and that he fully intended to establish it as a separate and institutionally independent religion. It is small wonder, then, that he eventually provoked the wrath of Hiei zan and was forced to seek refuge in Echizen. But by this time, as we have earlier seen, Dōgen's attention had already begun to turn from spreading the true *dharma* to training the true believers. In the process his approach to both the theoretical and the historical interpretation of Zen meditation would become more specialized and more radical.

6

Nonthinking and the Practice of the Seated Buddha

If the autograph manuscript of the *Fukan zazen gi* already displays some of the characteristic flavor of Dōgen's Zen, the vulgate text, to which I want to turn in this chapter, is vintage Dōgen. Written a decade or more after the original, Tenpuku version, it is a more mature expression of his writing. Generally speaking, the style has been somewhat refined, and one or two of the more self-conscious passages have been omitted. Also omitted are several passages—some of them quite important—that had been taken over in the original work from the *Tso-ch'an i*. In their place has been added some new material, emphasizing a doctrine and couched in a technical language familiar to us from the *Shōbō genzō* and other of Dōgen's works written in the years separating the two versions of the *Fukan zazen gi*. Taken together, these revisions result in a text still further in tone from Tsung-tse's manual and unmistakably bearing the characteristic stamp of Dōgen's later approach to Zen. While we need not consider here all the minor revisions, several passages are of particular interest as representative of both the language and the doctrine of Dōgen's mature teachings.

We have seen that the *Fukan zazen gi* differs most conspicuously from the *Tso-ch'an i* in the attention it devotes to the wisdom tradition of Ch'an. In the vulgate revision of the text this character of the work becomes even more pronounced as Dōgen introduces several pregnant passages reflecting the sayings and writings of the masters. The contrast with Tsung-tse is obvious in the section just following the description of meditation. There, we may recall, the *Tso-ch'an i* offers some general remarks on the effects of the practice. Meditation, we are told, is the "*dharma* gate of ease and joy." Although if improperly practiced, it can be injurious to the health, when correctly performed, it will be beneficial for both body and mind. The enlightened man takes to it quite naturally; and even the ordinary, unenlightened man, if he simply gives himself over to the spirit of the practice, will find it easy. At the same time the meditator should expect to face various demonic obstructions; he can prepare himself by reading their description in the Buddhist literature, and he can overcome them by maintaining right thought.

In his earlier draft of the *Fukan zazen gi* Dōgen significantly abbreviated this passage, dropping the references to the possibility of illness, the practice of the unenlightened man, and the occurrence of demonic obstructions.[1] As a result his version tended to advertise only the positive mental and physical effects of the practice. In his later revised text he goes considerably further and completely eliminates all discussion of the worldly benefits of *zazen*. Instead he introduces a totally new perspective.

> *Zazen* is not the practice of *dhyāna*: it is just the *dharma* gate of ease and joy. It is the practice and verification of ultimate *bodhi*. The *kōan* realized, baskets and cages cannot get to it.

Gone here are Tsung-tse's gentle encouragements and practical warnings for the novice embarking on the contemplative life; in their place is a strong doctrinal statement on the true nature of Zen meditation. Gone here are "ease and joy" in the sense of mental and physical pleasure; in their place are the ultimate ease and joy of *nirvāṇa*. *Zazen* here is no longer presented as a psychophysical exercise for the improvement of body and mind, or even for the attainment of Buddhist wisdom; it has itself become the actualization of complete enlightenment.

Dōgen's opening statement here that *zazen* is not the practice of *dhyāna* (*shūzen*) undoubtedly derives from an interesting passage on Bodhidharma, to which I have already referred, in Chüeh-fan Hui-hung's *Lin-chien lu*.

> When Bodhidharma first went to Wei from Liang, he proceeded to the foot of Mt. Sung, where he stopped at Shao-lin. There he just sat facing a wall. This was not the practice of *dhyāna* [*hsi ch'an*], but after a while others, unable to fathom what he was doing, held that Dharma practiced *dhyāna*. This *dhyāna* [*ch'an-na*] is but one among various practices; how could it suffice to exhaust [the practice of] the sage [*sheng jen*]? Nevertheless, people of the time understood [Dharma's practice] in this way; the historians followed this [understanding] and recorded him with those that practiced *dhyāna*, thus making him a confederate of the partisans of "dead wood and

---

1. Note that Dōgen's text here has reduced the problem of the demonic "doings of Māra" (*maji*), which Tsung-tse seems to have taken quite seriously, to the relatively simple matter of dull and agitated states of mind (*konsan*).

cold ashes" [*k'u mu ssu hui*]. Be that as it may, [the practice of] the sage does not stop at *dhyāna*, and yet it does not differ from it: it is like change [*i*], which is beyond *yin* and *yang* and yet does not differ from them.[2]

Whatever the exact implications of the enigmatic simile in his last sentence here, Hui-hung clearly is making several closely related points, all of which should by now be familiar to us: Bodhidharma's legendary nine years of sitting before a wall should not be understood as nine years of meditation, nor (by implication) should the *ch'an* of Bodhidharma's Ch'an school be confused with the *ch'an* of the traditional Buddhist exercise of *ch'an-na*, or *dhyāna*. The latter is only one, finite spiritual technique; moreover, it is a technique that serves to deaden the mind. But Bodhidharma's sitting is the practice of the enlightened sage, a practice that—if it fulfills the obligatory calm concentration of *dhyāna*—transcends the mere cultivation of trance.

The historical point here—that Bodhidharma's tradition of meditation represents a unique form of Buddhism, distinct from (and superior to) ordinary versions of the religion—is, as we know, particularly dear to Dōgen's heart. We have seen it strongly emphasized already in his earliest work, the *Bendō wa*, and it regularly reappears in the subsequent essays of the *Shōbō genzō*. Indeed so sensitive does Dōgen become to this point that he is eventually led to dismiss, somewhat paradoxically, the very notion that Zen represents a distinct Buddhist school. Particularly in the *Butsudō* fascicle of his *Shōbō genzō*, he quotes Hui-hung's passage in full and goes on to argue vehemently against the appellation "Zen school" (*zenshū*). This term, he maintains (with some historical accuracy), appears only in the later literature; it is not found in the early Chinese Patriarchs, let alone their Indian predecessors. Its adoption is the result of a misunderstanding of Buddhism; indeed it was invented by those who "secretly wish to destroy the *dharma*." It is a "demonic appellation" (*mahajun no shō*), and those who use it are themselves demons. There is no such thing, properly speaking, as a "Zen school," a "[Bodhi]dharma school" (*daruma shū*), a "Buddha mind school" (*busshin shū*); and the currency of such expressions in contemporary China is an indication of the decline of the *dharma* there. Properly speaking, there is only "the way of the Buddha" (*butsudō*), "the great way correctly transmitted from Buddha to Buddha" (*butsu butsu shōden no daidō*). This way, of course, is the *shōbō genzō*, the religion of the seven primordial Buddhas,

---

2. ZZ.2B,21:295d. The reference to "the historians" here is undoubtedly to Tao-hsüan (596–667), whose *Hsü kao-seng chuan* includes Bodhidharma's biography in the section on *dhyāna* practitioners (*hsi ch'an*) (T.50:551b). According to the *Hōkyō ki*, Hui-hung's *Lin-chien lu* was recommended to Dōgen by Ju-ching, and in fact the *Shōbō genzō* shows considerable influence from the text: see Mizuno Yaoko, "Rinkan roku kara Shōbō genzō e," in *Bukkyō no rekishi teki tenkai ni miru sho keitai: Furuta Shōkin hakase koki kinen ronshū* (1981), 811–22.

handed down on Vulture Peak from Śākyamuni to Mahākāśyapa and thence through the Patriarchal lineage to Bodhidharma and Hui-neng.[3]

In this same discussion in the *Butsudō*, Dōgen reiterates Hui-hung's point on the limitations of *dhyāna*: this practice, as he says, is not exhaustive of the enlightenment of the Seven Buddhas and Twenty-eight Indian Patriarchs, nor is it by any means the essence of the *buddha-dharma*. He does not go on here with Hui-hung to criticize the practice itself, but elsewhere in the *Shōbō genzō* texts from this period he does show an increased awareness of the ancient and persistent Ch'an attack on the cultivation of trance. Though earlier, in his *Fukan zazen gi*, he had himself encouraged his readers to become unified (*ippen*) by letting thoughts vanish ([*nen*]*shitsu*) and forgetting objects (*bōen*), now he joins in the Sung criticism of such practice. In his *Shōbō genzō tashin tsū*, he explicitly warns against the practice of "cutting off considerations and forgetting objects" (*zetsuryo bōen*). In the *Hotsu mujō shin*, he criticizes the ignorant monks of Hīnayānist leanings who neglect the aspiration for *bodhi* and advocate "suspending considerations and freezing the mind" (*sokuryo gyōshin*). In the *Sanjūshichi hon bodai bunpō*, he attacks Sung Buddhism as dominated by those heretics (*janin*) who share what he identifies as the Hindu view that truth lies in "silence and stillness" (*jakumoku gyōnen*), not in speech and action.[4]

In a similar vein, in his *Zazen shin*, Dōgen dismisses the "stupid illiterates" (*orokanaru zuzan*), so common in the Sung, who think that *zazen* aims at a state of peace and calm (*heion chi*) attained through mental vacuity (*kyōkin buji*). This understanding of meditation does not compare with the views of the Hīnayāna scholastics and is inferior even to the pre-Buddhist vehicles of men and gods (*ninten jō*).[5] Later in the text he attacks the Sung authors of the *Ching-te ch'uan teng lu* and *Chia-t'ai p'u teng lu* for admitting into their Ch'an histories various "Lancets of Meditation" or "Inscriptions on Meditation" that are nothing but "models for reverting to the source and returning to the origin [*gengen henpon*], vain programs for suspending considerations and freezing in tranquility [*sokuryo gyōjaku*]." Such teachings, he complains, do not even approach the basic stages of *anāsrava-dhyāna* or the traditional path of the *bodhisattva*; how could they transmit the meditation of the Buddhas and Patriarchs? These texts were written by men who do

---

3. DZZ.1:376–79. Dōgen quotes Hui-hung's passage elsewhere as well: see *Shōbō genzō gyōji* (2), DZZ.1:142; *Eihei kōroku*, DZZ.2:129. The use of the term *ch'an tsung* seems to have begun sometime during the latter half of the eighth century. It appears probably for the first time in Ch'an literature in the *Tun-wu ta-sheng cheng li chüeh* (Paul Demiéville, *Le Concile de Lhasa*, planches 1, 2, 9); see Yanagida Seizan, *Shoki zenshū shisho no kenkyū*, 454–55.

4. DZZ.1:516. In a remarkable switch from the usual Zen understanding, he identifies this mistake here with the silence of the layman Vimalakīrti. For the *Tashin tsū*, see DZZ.1:589; for the *Hotsu mujō shin*, DZZ.1:526.

5. DZZ.1:91.

not understand *zazen*, who have never experienced its true practice and do not participate in its unique transmission (*tanden*).[6]

It is no doubt in part as an expression of this quickened sense of the need to distance his *zazen* from the heretical quietism so despised by the tradition that, in revising the *Fukan zazen gi*, Dōgen chose to replace Tsung-tse's discussion of the benefits and dangers of trance with a sharp reminder that *zazen* is not *dhyāna*. Indeed he goes on here to purge the following section of his text of almost all its original references to the virtues of concentration— its passages on the importance of the "power of *samādhi*" (*jōriki*), on the "single gate of *dhyāna*" (*zenjō ichimon*) as the supreme teaching, on the "condition of *dhyāna*" (*jōen*) and the "power of *samādhi*" as the bases of enlightenment.[7] It is hardly surprising, therefore, that in this version of Dōgen's manual we no longer find any mention of Tsung-tse's troubling technique of "forgetting objects." I shall come back to this point later, but first we need to pursue the *Fukan zazen gi* passage at which we are looking here and consider Hui-hung's second reason for distinguishing Ch'an from *dhyāna*—that Bodhidharma's sitting is the transcendental practice of the enlightened sage.

If Dōgen joins in the traditional Ch'an criticism of yogic concentration, his real interest, as is suggested by our passage, lies less in the defects of *dhyāna* than in the perfections of *zazen*. *Zazen* is not mere *dhyāna* but the teaching of ease and joy, the practice and verification of ultimate enlightenment (*gūjin bodai shi shushō*). Here, of course, we have a version of Dōgen's famous doctrine of the unity of practice and enlightenment (*shushō ittō*)—a doctrine found in one form or another throughout his writings. Its first and un-doubtedly most famous statement appears already in the *Bendō wa*. There, in response to the question of whether his Zen meditation is appropriate for advanced adepts no less than beginners, he replies:

To think that practice and verification are not one is the view of infidels [*gedō*]. In the *buddha-dharma*, practice and verification are the same [*shushō kore ittō nari*]. Because it is practice based on verification, the beginner's pursuit of the way is the whole substance of original verification [*honshō no zentai*]. Therefore, in giving instruction on what to be careful of in the practice, we teach not to expect verification outside of practice, for [the practice] is itself original verification. Since it is the verification of practice, verification has no limit; since it is the practice of verification, practice has no beginning.[8]

Whatever the peculiarities of Dōgen's use of this doctrine (and we shall come to some of these soon enough), his basic position here that Zen is the

6. DZZ.1:97.
7. Note that, in his haste to eliminate these terms, Dōgen has left the pronoun *shi*, in his phrase *ichi nin shi riki*, with no intelligible antecedent.
8. DZZ.1:737.

practice of enlightenment should not surprise us. In the same *Bendō wa*
passage he himself bolsters this position with the claim that all the great
Buddhist masters, from Śākyamuni and Mahākāśyapa through Bodhidharma and the Sixth Patriarch, have recognized his "enlightened practice"
(*shōjō no shu*); and, if we might be hard pressed to demonstrate the full
historical claim, it is not very difficult to read Dōgen's famous doctrine as a
corollary flowing directly from the classical Ch'an dogma of the supreme,
Buddha vehicle. Since that vehicle is supposed to express the Buddha's own
spirituality, its practice is by definition the expression of His perfect enlightenment. Put somewhat differently, since that vehicle defines its meditation simply as a feature of the inherently enlightened mind, the practice of
its meditation is by definition the act of such a mind. As we know, quite a
few curiosities can be generated from this basic Ch'an position; and, like the
tradition as a whole, Dōgen is quick to take advantage of the transcendental
mysteries of the supreme, sudden teaching. Indeed much of the power of his
Shōbō genzō commentaries derives from the extraordinary skill with which
he seems able, again and again, to spring to the high ground of classical
Ch'an interpretation and, from that elevated vantage, discover the various
paradoxical permutations and unexpected implications of the doctrine of
enlightened practice.

This practice, Dōgen often refers to as "undefiled practice and verification" (*fuzenna no shushō*), an expression he borrows from a famous saying
attributed to the Sixth Patriarch's disciple Nan-yüeh Huai-jang (667–744).

The [Sixth] Patriarch asked [Nan-yüeh], "Where do you come from?" Nan-yüeh
answered, "From Mt. Sung." The Patriarch said, "What is it that comes like this?"
Nan-yüeh replied, "To say anything would be wrong." The Patriarch said, "Then
is it contingent on practice and verification (*hsiu-cheng*)?" Nan-yüeh said, "Practice
and verification are not nonexistent; they are not to be defiled." [9]

This little conversation is one of Dōgen's favorites and appears in many
places throughout his writings. We have seen it alluded to, in fact, in the
opening words of the *Fukan zazen gi*: "Fundamentally speaking, the basis of
the way is perfectly pervasive; how could it be contingent on practice and
verification?" It is reintroduced in the conclusion of the *Kōroku* text in the
line, "Practice and verification are by nature undefiled"; and it appears in
Dōgen's Japanese meditation manual as a substitute for our *Fukan zazen gi*
passage: "*Zazen* is not the practice of *dhyāna*: it is the *dharma* gate of great
ease and joy; it is undefiled practice and verification." Dōgen undoubtedly
appreciates the conversation because it captures so neatly the secret of the
sudden practice.

In one sense the dictum that practice is undefiled (*akliṣṭa*) can be read

9. *Lien-teng hui yao*, ZZ.2B,9:243a. The story has several variants; this version seems
closest to the text in Dōgen's *kōan* collection, *Shōbō genzō sanbyaku soku*, DZZ.2:219.

as a commonplace of Buddhist dogma, which regularly defines the spiritual path of the adept (*ārya*) as free from the psychic effluence (*āsrava*) that sullies the ordinary consciousness. But clearly Huai-jang has something more in mind here—something supposed to put an end to dogma and defy definition. Just as the true nature of the one who "comes like this" cannot be expressed, so too his cultivation of the path can be described only as "not nonexistent." If Bodhidharma's sitting, as Hui-hung would say, is the practice of the enlightened sage, it must be as enigmatic as enlightenment itself—beyond our grasp, incomprehensible, ineffable: it cannot be defined by our ordinary understanding of spiritual discipline. The ethical correlate of this, of course, is that it must not—indeed, properly speaking, cannot— be "defiled" by any intention to grasp the practice and put it to use as a means to an end. If *zazen*, as the *Bendō wa* informs us, is the practice of original enlightenment, it must be as natural as the Buddha nature itself—free from artifice, untrammeled by goals, unsullied by expectations: it must not be approached through our usual notions of spiritual utility.

The mystery—both intellectual and ethical—of the practice and verification of ultimate *bodhi* is embodied in the final line of our *Fukan zazen gi* passage: "The *kōan* realized, baskets and cages cannot get to it." The "baskets and cages" (*rarō*) here, of course, refer to the categories of human understanding by which we try to snare the world and in which, instead, we are ourselves entrapped. The "realized *kōan*" (*genjō kōan*)—in more metaphysical moods, perhaps better read "the *kōan* of realization"—is another of Dōgen's favorite technical terms, one of the most famous in his vocabulary. It is the title theme of one of his earliest, most celebrated, philosophical essays; the expression (or, as here, its verbal form, *kōan genjō*) appears in many of the *Shōbō genzō* texts. The term probably derives originally from a saying attributed to the T'ang figure Tao-ming (dates unknown): "If you have realized the *kōan* (*hsien-ch'eng kung-an*), I'll spare you thirty blows." Whatever Tao-ming may have meant by it, in Sung times his remark was a popular vehicle, among cultured authors like Hung-chih Cheng-chüeh and perhaps especially Ta-hui's master, Yüan-wu K'o-ch'in, for expressing the realization (both psychological and ontological) of the universal Buddhahood.[10] Though in his *Genjō kōan* essay and elsewhere Dōgen often emphasizes its metaphysical dimension, here in the *Fukan zazen gi* the expression clearly plays a more religious role. This is one of the places where the vulgate text shows the influence of a passage in the *Shōbō genzō zazen shin*.

Be it known that, for studying the way, the established [means of] investigation is pursuit of the way in seated meditation [*zazen bendō*]. The essential point that marks

---

10. For Tao-ming's saying, see *Ching-te ch'uan teng lu*, T.51:291b17. Yüan-wu seems to have been particularly fond of the term, and we find it throughout his *Yü lu* and *Pi-yen lu*; for examples of his treatment, see the former, T.47:769a–70a.

this [investigation] is [the understanding] that there is a practice of a Buddha [*gyōbutsu*] that does not seek to make a Buddha [*sabutsu*]. Since the practice of a Buddha is not to make a Buddha, it is the realization of the *kōan* [*kōan genjō*]. The embodied Buddha [*shinbutsu*] does not make a Buddha; when the baskets and cages are broken, a seated Buddha [*zabutsu*] does not interfere with making a Buddha. At just such a time—from one thousand, from ten thousand ages past, from the very beginning—we have the power to enter into Buddha [*hotoke ni iri*] and enter into Māra. Walking forward or back, its measure fills the ditches and moats.[11]

These remarks are offered in the *Zazen shin* as a corrective to two misunderstandings of meditation Dōgen finds current in the Sung. One, as we have seen, is the notion that *zazen* is a technique for calming the mind; the other is the view, common among "a bunch that calls itself a branch of Lin-chi," that *zazen* is a technique only for beginners, transcended by those who realize that (in the words of the *Cheng tao ko*) "walking is Zen, sitting is Zen; in speech and silence, motion and rest, the substance is at ease." This bunch, comments Dōgen, lacking as it does the orthodox transmission of the *buddha-dharma*, does not realize that Zen recognizes no distinction between beginner and adept. With these words, he suddenly ascends to the supernal plane of the true *dharma* and delivers the teachings just quoted. In its technical vocabulary, striking images, clever word play, and surprising turns of thought, the passage represents rather well the transcendent style of Dōgen's *Shōbō genzō* essays. Since this style can be rather obscure, let me hazard a more pedestrian paraphrase of what strikes me as a revealing statement of Dōgen's approach to meditation theory.

Zazen is the orthodox practice of Buddhism. At the same time this *zazen* is not merely a utilitarian device for producing a perfected state of enlightenment (*sabutsu*) but the expression of a more fundamental perfection inherent in all things (*gyōbutsu*). When we understand it in this way, the practice of *zazen* itself becomes the actualization of the ultimate truth (*kōan genjō*), and the practitioner, just as he is, becomes the embodiment of perfect enlightenment (*shinbutsu*). This higher understanding—beyond the mundane categories of cause and effect, universal and particular, and so on—gives true *zazen* (*zabutsu*) its power to produce the experience of enlightenment (*sabutsu*) in the practitioner. In this experience we recognize that our own *zazen* is nothing but the primordial activity of all things—always present even before we recognize it, always perfected even in our most benighted states, always functioning throughout the world around us.

Here we begin to see more clearly the characteristic direction in which Dōgen likes to move from his starting point in the unity of practice and enlightenment. This movement follows the well-trod path upward, toward

---

11. DZZ.1:91. A slightly different version of this same passage occurs in the *Himitsu Shōbō genzō* text of the *Butsu kōjō ji* (DZZ.1:233-34), where it serves to define what Dōgen calls there "studying [the *buddha-mārga*] with the body" (*mi shite narafu*).

the sublation of meditation in the nondualistic metaphysics of the perfection of wisdom. As always, to negotiate this path, Dōgen must pick his way between the two poles of *samādhi* and *prajñā*, calm and insight, stasis and activity. Along the way he must avoid the twin pitfalls of Zen he points out in the *Zazen shin*: one that clings to meditation and seeks the nondual goal in the suppression of thought, the other that clutches at wisdom and mistakes the sublation of meditation for its denial. The gate is strait, and whether or not he has successfully passed through may be subject to dispute; but there is no doubt that the way he has chosen—the way of the practicing Buddha, the sitting Buddha, and so on—leads through a novel religious landscape, perhaps never so fully explored by the tradition.

The particular character of Dōgen's approach to meditation becomes more apparent as we make our way through the *Zazen shin*. The passage I have quoted occurs toward the beginning of the text, as an introduction to a famous *kōan* about *zazen*.

During the K'ai-yüan era [713–41], there was a certain *śramaṇa*, [Ma-tsu] Tao-i, who lived at the Ch'uan-fa hermitage and practiced seated meditation [*tso-ch'an*] all day. The Master [Nan-yüeh Huai-jang], knowing that he was a vessel of the *dharma*, went to him and asked, "Virtuous one, what are you figuring to do, sitting there in meditation?" Tao-i replied, "I'm figuring to make a Buddha." The Master there-upon took up a tile and began to rub it on a stone in front of Tao-i's hermitage. Tao-i said, "Master, what are you doing?" The Master replied, "I'm polishing this to make a mirror." Tao-i said, "How can you make a mirror by polishing a tile?" [The Master answered,] "How can you make a Buddha by sitting in meditation?" Tao-i said, "What should I do?" The Master said, "If a man is driving a cart that won't go, should he beat the cart or beat the ox?" Tao-i had no answer. The Master went on, "Are you studying seated Ch'an [*tso-ch'an*] or are you studying seated Buddha [*tso-fo*]? If you're studying seated Ch'an, Ch'an is not sitting still; if you're studying seated Buddha, Buddhahood is not a fixed form. In a nonabiding *dharma*, there should be no grasping or rejecting. If you're [studying] seated Buddha, you're killing the Buddha; if you're attached to the form of sitting, you're not reaching its principle." [12]

This is another of Dōgen's favorite stories, alluded to in many of his essays. Indeed we find its words introduced into the revision of the *Fukan zazen gi* itself, where, in his discussion of the renunciation of worldly affairs, Dōgen supplements his original recommendation to abandon all thinking with the further admonition that one "not intend to make a Buddha, much less be attached to sitting still." In their context in the *Fukan zazen gi* the words clearly seem to amplify the religious implications of the topic of renunciation: when approaching meditation, one must not only abandon ideas of the secular world but also surrender attachments to the spiritual

---

12. *Ching-te ch'uan teng lu*, T.51:240c18–28. This story, too, has several versions; the one translated here is similar to Dōgen's text at *Shōbō genzō sanbyaku soku*, DZZ.2:202.

life—to its results and to its forms. To this extent Dōgen's use of the words here seems in keeping with Huai-jang's familiar warning that the higher wisdom is not the product of mental purification nor the true practice embodied in fixed religious forms.

Yet there is rather more to Dōgen's use of Huai-jang than is immediately apparent in the *Fukan zazen gi*. In the *Zazen shin* he subjects the dialogue to an extended commentary, taking it apart sentence by sentence, sometimes phrase by phrase. The result is a remarkable tour de force of Zen hermeneutics, which turns the text inside out to reveal the secret wisdom hidden in every line and stands the teaching on its head to uncover the profound meditation buried beneath the words. We cannot follow the entire discussion here (which in any case the reader can consult in my translation in Document 3, later in this book), but some samples should suffice to give us a sense of both its method and its message.

In his very first comments Dōgen warns us not to take the words of our story for granted: "rather than love the carved dragon," he says, "we should go on to love the real dragon" behind it. (And then, in case we have taken his own words for granted, he remarks that the carved dragon is no less efficacious than the real.)[13] Hence, a little later on, he holds up Ma-tsu's question, "What are you doing?" as a model for Buddhist study: though it is quite apparent that his master was polishing a tile, Ma-tsu asked for the true meaning of the act; so too we should "avoid deciding that what we see is what we see" and recognize that there is an essential meaning' (*shūshi*) behind everything. (Thus, we learn here, for example, that the essential meaning behind [the act of asking] "What are you doing?" is [that the question is itself an instance of] the constant, universal Buddhist practice of "polishing a tile.")[14]

The real dragon can be startling, and the essential meaning can be quite different from what we see. When Ma-tsu asks what he should do, Dōgen takes apart the simple four-word interrogative to show that (if I have seen the essential meaning of this obscure passage) it is really a declaration of the ultimate truth of suchness.[15] When Ma-tsu fails to respond to the metaphor of the cart, Dōgen warns us not to violate his silence, since it is really an expression of his perfect understanding.[16] Hence we should not be surprised to learn that Huai-jang is indeed going to make a mirror from his tile: "There is definitely reason in his polishing [a tile] to make a mirror: there is the realized *kōan*; this is no mere empty contrivance." In fact, says Dōgen, the "old mirror" (*kokyō*) is always produced by polishing a tile. Lest we think we see what we see here, he quickly goes on to agree with Ma-tsu that

---

13. DZZ.1:91–92.
14. DZZ.1:92–93.
15. DZZ.1:93.
16. DZZ.1:94.

polishing a tile will not make a mirror. "And even if it does make a mirror," he concludes slyly, "it must be quick about it [*sumiyaka narubeshi*]." [17]

This little passage seems a good example of the way in which Dōgen artfully plays his own tune on the antique instruments of Ch'an tradition. His "old mirror," of course, is the venerable metaphor for the inherent Buddha mind, by definition unproduced, and by standard Ch'an account quite unaffected by polishing. The "quickness" with which his tile becomes this mirror invokes the identification of cause and effect, ordinary consciousness and Buddhahood, that is characteristic of the classic sudden teaching. The tile cannot become the mirror because it is the mirror; yet—and this is the crucial point—there is no mirror apart from the act of polishing the tile. For, as Dōgen makes explicit in his *Shōbō genzō kokyō*, this act is the very essence of enlightenment, "the bones and marrow of the ancient Buddhas."

The *Kokyō*, written a few months before the *Zazen shin*, is devoted to several of the many Ch'an sayings on the mirror, including our tile story. There Dōgen complains that for centuries people have thought that Huai-jang's polishing was simply a heuristic device intended to provoke Ma-tsu. But this interpretation has missed a more basic point: if the great sages had no real method of polishing a tile, how could they possess such heuristic techniques for helping others (*inin no hōben*)? Since these techniques are the very "bones and marrow of the Buddhas and Patriarchs," we know that the practice of polishing a tile to make a mirror preserves the very essence of the ancient Buddhas. In this practice, "when the polishing of the tile becomes a mirror, Ma-tsu makes a Buddha; and when Ma-tsu makes a Buddha, Ma-tsu quickly becomes Ma-tsu. When Ma-tsu becomes Ma-tsu, *zazen* quickly becomes *zazen*." [18]

In the final lines here we recognize the familiar moves of the sudden style, in which the practitioner is identified with his inherent perfection ("when Ma-tsu makes a Buddha, Ma-tsu quickly becomes Ma-tsu") and the practice is subsumed in that identification ("when Ma-tsu becomes Ma-tsu, *zazen* quickly becomes *zazen*"). What is more remarkable about the passage is that it combines these moves with what amounts to a standard argument for the traditional *bodhisattva* path: whether or not he recognizes his inherent perfection, the *bodhisattva* must cultivate the various practices of the path in order to master the salvific techniques (*upāya*) through which a Buddha expresses his compassion. If Dōgen's argument sidesteps the old gradualist heresy, it does so only because his Buddhahood is nothing but the cultivation of the path itself. Clearly the static metaphor of the mirror has been pushed to its limits here, and the real focus has shifted to the dynamic model of polishing.

---

17. DZZ.1:93.
18. DZZ.1:187–88.

The same shift in focus is apparent throughout the *Zazen shin* commentary. When Huai-jang asks Ma-tsu what he is figuring (*t'u*) to do by sitting in meditation, Dōgen immediately fastens on the notion of "figuring" as the key issue and blows it into a symbol of enlightened practice: "figuring to make a Buddha" is the essence of *zazen*, whether before, during, or after Buddhahood; it is the "vines and creepers" (*kattō*) [of discursive thought] that entangle every instance of Buddhahood, the "sloughing off" (*datsuraku*) [that liberates every instance of practice].[19] Similarly, when Huai-jang asks whether it is better to beat the cart or the ox, while Ma-tsu expresses his enlightenment by silence, Dōgen is quick to recommend the beating of the cart (and just as quick to remind us that, in any case, when we beat the "iron ox" of enlightenment, it is "the fist beating the fist and the ox beating the ox").[20] Again, when Huai-jang poses his unacceptable alternatives of "seated meditation" and "seated Buddha," Dōgen praises him as "a scion of true descent," who recognizes that "the study of seated meditation is itself the study of a seated Buddha." In a playful little argument he turns to his own ends Huai-jang's principle that Buddhahood is no fixed mark (*hi jō sō*): since the Buddha has no fixed mark, [He cannot be distinguished from the non-Buddha; hence,] our seated meditation is [indistinguishable from] a seated Buddha. From this, he goes on to praise the practice of the seated Buddha for its virtue of "killing the Buddha," and to recommend "attachment to the form of sitting" as a good way to transcend "reaching its principle."[21]

Finally, Dōgen concludes his commentary on the *kōan* with a strong assertion of the orthodoxy of the meditation of the seated Buddha.

Know this, that it is the seated Buddha that Buddha after Buddha and Patriarch after Patriarch have taken as their essential function [*yōki*]. Those who are Buddhas and Patriarchs have employed this essential function, while those who are not have never even dreamt of it. To say that the teaching of the Buddha has been transmitted from the Western Heavens to the Eastern Earth implies the transmission of the seated Buddha; for it is the essential function [of that teaching]. And where the teaching of the Buddha is not transmitted, neither is seated meditation. What has been inherited by successor after successor [in this transmission] is just this message of seated meditation; one who does not participate in the unique transmission of this message is not a Buddha or a Patriarch.[22]

Taken together, these comments on the famous *kōan* of polishing a tile reveal an interpretation of the basic Ch'an notion of enlightened practice that—for all its continuity with earlier tradition—clearly has its own

---

19. DZZ.1:91–92.
20. DZZ.1:94.
21. DZZ.1:95.
22. DZZ.1:96.

particular thrust. Like the masters of the Southern school, Dōgen draws from the basic notion the conclusion that Zen religious practice must be beyond the machinations of the deluded mind of the practitioner: it must be, as he says, "the practice of an embodied Buddha that does not make a Buddha." Yet more important for him apparently is another conclusion, less conspicuous in the classical sudden teaching, that Zen enlightenment must be expressed in the religious practices of the tradition: it must be "a seated Buddha that does not interfere with making a Buddha." Unlike the famous Ch'an teachings that emphasize the spontaneous, unintentional character of the practice and tend to reduce it—at least in theory—to a sudden return to, or recognition of, the original nature of the mind, Dōgen prefers to stress what might almost be called the intentionality of enlightenment and to interpret Buddhahood as the ongoing commitment to make a Buddha.

Something of the contrast between these two styles is suggested in several of his revisions of the *Fukan zazen gi*. We may recall, for example, that Dōgen ended his original introduction to the text with the admonition, "If you want such [a state, in which the original nature of the mind becomes apparent], urgently work at *zazen*." In his *Kōroku* text, he gives us a doctrinally upgraded version: "If you want such a thing [*inmo ji*], urgently work at such a thing." The new phrasing here is clearly intended to remind us of a well-known line by the T'ang figure Yün-chü (d. 902): "If you want such a thing [*jen-mo shih*], you must be such a man [*jen-mo jen*]; if you are such a man, why do you worry about such a thing?"[23] Yün-chü's line neatly expresses the spiritual bind into which the sudden teaching seeks to put us: only a Buddha can cultivate the Buddha vehicle of supreme enlightenment; yet it is precisely the Buddha who no longer needs any religious cultivation. To recognize this bind and abandon deluded efforts to cultivate religion is itself to awaken to the principle of the sudden practice. Yet Dōgen prefers a slightly different reading. In his *Shōbō genzō* commentary on the line, written just after the *Zazen shin*, he emphasizes that the aspiration for supreme enlightenment is itself "such a thing" and the act of "such a man." Indeed it is precisely "such a man," rather than the deluded man we think we are, who worries about "such a thing" and undertakes religious cultivation.[24]

On these grounds, then, Dōgen can revalidate the effort of the spiritual life and shift the thrust of the sudden practice from the epistemological question of recognition to the ethical issue of participation. We see traces of the shift in the conclusion of the *Fukan zazen gi* as well. In his Tenpuku text he remarks that success in the practice of *zazen* does not depend on the mental abilities of the meditator; the reason is that "If you let go of the six

---

23. *Ching-te ch'uan teng lu*, T.51:335c19.
24. *Shōbō genzō inmo*, DZZ.1:162–63.

senses, you see and turn the whole path [*kenten zendō*]; if you do not produce a single thought, you sit and cut off the ten directions [*zadan jippō*]." [25]

Here Dōgen is clearly echoing classical Ch'an doctrine: true meditation practice is simply nonattachment to sense objects and nonproduction of deluded thoughts, and this in itself is the enlightened state. In his *Kōroku* revision, however, he substitutes a different reason: "Single-minded exertion [in *zazen*] [*sen'ichi kufū*] is itself pursuit of the way [*bendō*]. Practice and verification are by nature undefiled. Advancement [to enlightenment] is just an everyday affair."

In this version, while the unity of practice and enlightenment remains constant, the emphasis is less on avoidance of deluded discrimination than on wholehearted participation in enlightened practice. This same emphasis appears in many of the *Shōbō genzō* essays, in which the immaculate wisdom of the Buddhas is regularly expressed through the undefiled practice of the Patriarchs, and the abstract ideal of practicing enlightenment becomes embodied in the concrete observances (*igi, anri*) of the Zen monastic lifestyle and the historical examples of the heroic ascesis (*gyōji*) of the Zen masters. [26] Indeed, as we have seen earlier, Dōgen's concern for the actual forms of practicing Buddhahood only increases over the years, until he becomes preoccupied with the rites and rituals of his spiritual community. I shall come back to this point in my general concluding remarks; but here we need to complete our look at the vulgate text of the *Fukan zazen gi* to see what the theory of the seated Buddha might mean for the actual practice of seated Zen.

The interest in the Ch'an wisdom tradition that informs the revision of the *Fukan zazen gi* is nowhere more conspicuous than in the new account of the actual technique of *zazen*. In his original version Dōgen seemed largely content to leave his theology out of this section of the text and simply to quote Tsung-tse's practical advice. In his revised version as well, he makes little effort to alter or expand the concrete description of the preparations for, and posture of, *zazen*. But when he comes to the passage on the mental technique, he can no longer hold back and substitutes an entirely new statement of his practice.

Sitting fixedly [*gotsugotsu chi*], think of not thinking [*fu shiryō tei*]. How do you think of not thinking? Nonthinking [*hi shiryō*]. This is the essential art of *zazen*.

This passage, easily the most famous of the text, occurs in all three of Dōgen's later *zazen* manuals. It is another of the places in which the vulgate

25. Here, as elsewhere in his writings, Dōgen is playing with the term *zadan* (usually better read simply as "cut off"); on this usage, see Nakamura Toshiyuki, "Zadan to iu go ni tsuite," SK 21 (3/1979), 179–84.

26. For these latter notions, see, for example, the *Shōbō genzō gyōbutsu igi*, DZZ.1:46–58, esp. 46–47; *Shōbō genzō gyōji*, DZZ.1:122–61, esp. 122–23.

Fukan zazen gi reflects the *Zazen shin*. That essay opens with a story about the Ch'an master Yüeh-shan Wei-yen (751–834).

Once, when the Great Master Hung-tao of Yüeh shan was sitting [in meditation], a monk asked him, "What are you thinking, [sitting there] so fixedly?" The master answered, "I'm thinking of not thinking." The monk asked, "How do you think of not thinking?" The master answered, "Nonthinking." [27]

Unfortunately, Dōgen's brief commentary following the story is not very helpful in interpreting Wei-yen's conversation, let alone in determining just how one might go about his nonthinking. Both Wei-yen's "thinking" and his "not thinking" express, we are told, the very "skin, flesh, bones, and marrow [of Bodhidharma]." The function of nonthinking, Dōgen says, is "crystal clear," but it is what we use to think of not thinking. In this nonthinking, both we who are sitting fixedly and the act of fixed sitting itself are not what we think; indeed fixed sitting cannot be gauged by any measure of human understanding. Wei-yen's practice of sitting fixedly, thinking of not thinking, is the orthodox tradition of Buddhism, correctly transmitted to him through thirty-six generations of Patriarchs, beginning with Śākya-muni himself. [28]

Given the topic of these comments, perhaps we should not think that Dōgen owes us something more substantial to think about here, but clearly he has no interest in demystifying what he calls the essential art of *zazen*. On the contrary, it is precisely the unthinkable mystery of nonthinking—and the orthodox transmission of fixed sitting—that seems to attract him. In fact he moves directly from these remarks to an attack on those Ch'an monks, all too prevalent in the Sung, who understand neither the transcendental wisdom nor the historical tradition of *zazen*. Elsewhere in his writings as well, although Wei-yen's words appear with some frequency, there is little to enhance our human understanding. In the *Eihei kōroku*, for example, we learn—hardly to our surprise—that nonthinking is neither the ordinary mind (*ushin*) nor unconsciousness (*mushin*). [29] In the *Shōbō genzō sanjūshichi hon bodai bunpō*, nonthinking is identified with the traditional Buddhist virtue of

---

27. This version is translated from the *Zazen shin*, DZZ.1:90. The story appears in the *Ching-te ch'uan teng lu*, at T.51:311c; and in Dōgen's *Shōbō genzō sanbyaku soku*, DZZ.2:225. Wei-yen, one of the most famous T'ang masters of Ts'ao-tung and a favorite of Dōgen, seems to have enjoyed such talk about meditation. His biography preserves another conversation, with his teacher, the great Shih-t'ou Hsi-ch'ien (700–90).
One day when the master [Wei-yen] was sitting [in meditation], Shih-t'ou saw him and asked, "What are you up to here?" [Wei-yen] said, "I'm not doing anything [*i-ch'ieh pu wei*]." Shih-t'ou said, "That sort of thing is idle sitting [*hsien tso*]." [Wei-yen] said, "If it were idle sitting, it would be doing something." Shih-t'ou said, "This 'not doing' you speak of is not doing what?" [Wei-yen] said, "Even the thousand sages don't know." (*Ching-te ch'uan teng lu*, T.51:311b.)
28. DZZ.1:90–91.
29. DZZ.2:88.

right thought (*shō shiyui, samyak-saṃkalpa*); but, lest we think we have here found a way to gauge it, Dōgen immediately defines "right thought" as "sitting until one has broken the meditation cushion." [30] Here again we have circled back to fixed sitting; while this movement itself is interesting and probably expresses an important religious characteristic of Dōgen's *zazen* teaching, it offers little direction to the mental mechanics of meditation practice.

Whether or not Dōgen's practice of fixed sitting inherits the true transmission of the Buddhas, his preference here for metaphysical mystery over mental mechanics succeeds to the orthodox tradition of the Patriarchs, at least from the Sixth Patriarch on. Indeed there seems little to choose between Wei-yen's "nonthinking" (*fei ssu-liang*) and the Patriarch's "no-thought" (*wu-nien*). Here and elsewhere in the literature the term seems to operate much like its more famous cousin to express the inexpressible state of enlightened cognition. Where the Southern school texts like to define their "no-thought" as nondiscriminatory thought of suchness, Wei-yen chooses to describe his "nonthinking" as thinking of not thinking. Where Dōgen identifies the "right thought" of the nondeluded mind with nonthinking, a classical author like Hui-hai prefers to call it no-thought. To this extent the essential art of *zazen* seems to have become, in the vulgate *Fukan zazen gi,* nothing more (nor less) than fixed sitting in sudden enlightenment.[31]

Given the profound appreciation for the literature of the classical tradition and the extreme sensitivity to the nuances of its higher philosophy that we find throughout Dōgen's essays from this period, it is hardly surprising that he should have abandoned Tsung-tse's rude passage on concentration for a more sophisticated, more theologically refined (and therefore more mysterious) expression of Zen. This is by no means to say that he has simply plugged into his *Fukan zazen gi* a handy bit of Zen esoterica; for, as we have seen throughout his *Zazen shin,* there is considerable religious thinking behind Dōgen's nonthinking. But the fact is that Wei-yen's conversation, like most of classical Patriarchal Ch'an, does not tell us how to practice meditation. Whatever flavor it may have added to his text or whatever subtlety it may have brought to his doctrine, Dōgen's decision to substitute it for Tsung-tse's advice here recapitulates the old move from practical pre-

---

30. DZZ.1:511.

31. For Hui-hai's definition, see *Tun-wu yao men,* ZZ.2,15:421c. For the Southern School definitions of no-thought, see *Shen-hui yü lu,* Hu Shih, *Nan-yang ho-shang i-chi,* 129; *Liu-tsu t'an ching,* Yampolsky, *The Platform Sutra of the Sixth Patriarch,* end matter, 7. For the definition of *fei ssu-liang* as the "unconditioned" (*wu-wei*), "inconceivable" (*pu-ssu-i*) character of the Buddha's cognition, see Bodhiruci's *Wen-shu-shih-li so shuo pu-ssu-i fo ching-chieh ching* (**Acintya-buddha-viṣaya-nirdeśa*), T.12:108a–b. (Note that, in the same passage in his *Ta pao chi ching* [*Ratnakūṭa*], Bodhiruci has substituted *wu-nien* for *fei ssu-liang* [T.11:566b20].) In Wei-yen's day, Ch'an Buddhists were already reading of "nonthinking" in the popular *Hsin hsin ming* (T.51:457b17).

scription to higher description and renders opaque what had once seemed fairly clear. Obviously, when he rewrote the *Fukan zazen gi*, Dōgen knew the secret of Zen meditation.

To many of Dōgen's interpreters who share the classical preference for the higher wisdom of the supreme vehicle, the very mystery of this passage on nonthinking is one of the major virtues of the *Fukan zazen gi*, since it is a necessary (though one trusts not in itself a sufficient) sign that its *zazen* is indeed the ancient practice of the Patriarchs, the enlightened practice of "just sitting," with "body and mind sloughed off." Much as Hui-hung sees Bodhidharma's sitting as the transcendental practice of the sage that sublates the dichotomies of ordinary Buddhism, so Dōgen's nonthinking is regularly praised as the ultimate thinking, as thinking beyond thinking, the transcendental state that represents, through its higher synthesis of thinking and not thinking (read realism and nihilism), the fulfillment of what amounts to the fundamental dialectic of the *dharma*.[32]

Yet for the unenlightened practitioner who comes to the text for guidance in meditation, the question will surely arise whether this is really all there is to it. And for the unreconstructed historian who would like to use the text to reconstruct Dōgen's meditation, the question will naturally remain whether, and in what way, the passage is related to the practice. In short, one cannot help but wonder whether Dōgen is still teaching (or assuming) a particular contemplative technique in his new *Fukan zazen gi* and, if so, what that technique might be. At the very least, it would not seem overly forward to ask whether or not the practice of the new nonthinking is different from the old practice of forgetting objects.

This simple question is rarely asked in the considerable literature on the *Fukan zazen gi* and its famous teaching of *hi shiryō*. Insofar as that literature is still inspired—even if often only unconsciously—by the spirit of the Patriarchs, the lack of curiosity is hardly surprising; the question clearly ignores the basic premises, and undermines the religious power, of the sudden practice. And even for the uninspired historian, the question—at least in the short run—is not very promising; by its very design, Dōgen's

---

32. We see this style of interpretation already in Menzan's *Fukan zazen gi monge*, where the *zazen* of thinking about not thinking is said to be the true wisdom that transcends both our ordinary thinking about thinking and [transic states of] not thinking about thinking (SSZ.Chūkai,3: 19. Menzan is no doubt borrowing here the *ushin-mushin* dichotomy of the *Eihei kōroku*). For an extended example of the modern treatment of *hi shiryō*, see Kishizawa Ian's commentary on the *Shōbō genzō zazen shin, Shōbō genzō zenkō*, vol. 11 (1973). Within the Sōtō exegetical tradition the dialectical explanation is often combined with a sudden style, in which the four lines of Wei-yen's conversation all become a direct expression of the highest truth. Thus the esoteric reading of the *kōan* comes out something like this:

(1) The thinking that takes place in fixed sitting is [only describable as] "what" [*somo*]. (2) Such thinking is not thinking. (3) But not thinking [here is not merely not thinking; it] is "how" [*ikan*] thinking, (4) the thinking of the [ultimate] "nullity" [*hi*]. (For an example of this style of interpretation, see *Zengaku dai jiten*, s.v. "Yakusan fu shiryō tei.")

teaching of nonthinking does not permit a final answer. Still, we cannot conclude our study of the *Fukan zazen gi* without at least mentioning the possibilities and noting the problems they raise for the interpretation of Dōgen's famous meditation practice of *shikan taza*.

Though Dōgen's *zazen* of just sitting is generally assumed to be somehow superior to Tsung-tse's concentration technique, the *Fukan zazen gi* passage on nonthinking that is regularly given as the "content" of this *zazen* may be nothing more than an elevated way of talking about the Chinese abbot's classic exercise of watching thoughts until the mind becomes unified. Arguments for difference in practice will carry little weight if they are based, as they often seem to be, simply on differences in style or focus of presentation. If we want to read Dōgen's passage simply as a distinctive description of the mind in proper Zen meditation, there seems prima facie no reason why such a description should imply a distinctive practice. On the other hand, if we assume that the *Kōroku Fukan zazen gi*, whatever else it may do, is also recommending a particular meditation practice, we shall read the passage on nonthinking not only as a description of the state of mind achieved in the practice but also as a directive on what to do to achieve that state: apparently we **are** supposed to use something called nonthinking to achieve what is described **as** thinking of not thinking. Of course, in keeping with the sudden style, what we are to do and what we are to achieve should be the same. In fact we have seen that the old sudden notion of no-thought had precisely this ambiguity: it was at once the description of the original nonabiding nature of the mind and the program, of watching thoughts without attachment, through which that nature was discovered. The cultivation of this no-thought was Tsung-tse's program and the program of Dōgen's original version of the *Fukan zazen gi*. If there is little to choose between the notions of no-thought and nonthinking as states of mind, then if we take the sudden teaching (or Dōgen's notion of enlightened practice) seriously, there should be no more to choose between them as practices.

Such an interpretation would mean that the two versions of the *Fukan zazen gi* represent but two ways of talking—one in terms of method, the other emphasizing result—about the same venerable Zen exercise. It would lend some support—though surely not quite the type he would have liked— to Dōgen's claim that his practice is the ancient way of the Patriarchs. It would allow us to take seriously the evidence of the Tenpuku manuscript, which is, after all, our only explicit source on Dōgen's contemplative technique. And it would eliminate what is for some ideologically embarrassing task of explaining why Dōgen taught two different forms of meditation —one just sitting, the other not. But it would also mean that his vaunted *shikan taza*, when stripped of its theoretical trappings, is a rather unremarkable concentration exercise.

This interpretation is based on the content of the *hi shiryō* passage, either as description of, or prescription for, meditation. It may be, however, that we have attended too narrowly to the famous term "nonthinking," and that the referent of this term—whether theoretical or psychological—is less significant here than the fact that it occurs in the context of a famous *kōan* about *zazen*. If we widen our vision to this context, we can see the passage as itself a vehicle for meditation, in which Wei-yen's characterization of the exercise itself becomes the theme of contemplation. There is a certain elegance to the notion that Dōgen meant his monks to practice nonthinking through the contemplation of "nonthinking," and to study the meaning of "fixed sitting" by sitting fixedly. Like the *kanna* method in general, such a practice would neatly resolve the ancient feud between the two Buddhist disciplines of meditation and wisdom by making the *zazen* exercise itself the investigation of the wisdom embodied in the words of the *watō*; but it would do so in the particularly artful way of making the mystery of enlightened *zazen* itself the theme of the exercise. In such a practice, as Dōgen would say, studying seated Zen would indeed be studying "a seated Buddha."

This reading of the vulgate *Fukan zazen gi* would seem to fit snugly into what we already know about the historical circumstances of its composition: that it was probably written at a time when its author was less concerned with pursuing Tsung-tse's dissemination of Zen meditation than in educating an elite core of experienced religious; that this education was carried out primarily through the study of the classical Ch'an wisdom literature; and that the *Fukan zazen gi* was revised in the light of this study to cleanse it of any suggestion of dubious meditation doctrine and upgrade it with material from the old cases that were the primary focus of Sung Ch'an. In such a setting, it would at least not be surprising if Dōgen, like most of his contemporaries, had chosen to replace (or supplement) Tsung-tse's concentration exercise with a practice that focused on a *kōan*. This would mean, of course, that, at different times or perhaps to different students, Dōgen taught more than one method of "just sitting"—a traditional mindfulness exercise and a more modern *kanna* technique.

Whatever their relative strengths and weaknesses, both these readings of the vulgate *Fukan zazen gi* are speculative. Whether or not its realized *kōan* can be grasped through the old *kōan* of nonthinking, the actual technique by which this is done manages in the end to elude our baskets and cages. But, if we are thus left empty-handed, we should note that this fact will now leave the burden of proof with those who would maintain that Dōgen's practice of just sitting is a unique form of meditation, distinct from both the pedestrian concentration exercise of Tsung-tse and the despised *k'an-hua* method of Ta-hui. For historical and ideological reasons the burden will no doubt seem particularly heavy in the case of the latter distinction; hence, it may be worth adding a few words here on this issue.

The notion that Dōgen's unique *shikan taza* might have involved a form of *kanna* practice is not, of course, favored by the mainstream of Sōtō tradition and would quickly be dismissed by most Dōgen scholarship. This scholarship tends to be guided by two sets of assumptions that require a sharp distinction between "just sitting" and "looking at a saying." One of these is historical. It begins from the fact that the Sōtō school, at least in modern times, has distinguished itself from, and argued strongly against, the Rinzai tradition precisely on the basis of such a distinction; it then projects the same argument back on the founder of the school, Dōgen. Noting that he too was highly critical of Sung Lin-chi and especially of its famed representative Ta-hui, and that Ta-hui was famed especially for his *k'an-hua* practice, it assumes that Dōgen rejected this practice and taught his Zen of just sitting as an alternative.

The other kind of assumption is conceptual. Following in the tradition of modern Zen polemics, it understands the two terms *shikan taza* and *kanna* as referring to mutually incompatible techniques of mental training—one that abandons all fixed objects of concentration and all conscious striving for *satori* and simply abides in the undefiled awareness of the Buddha nature, the other that focuses the mind on the *watō* and intentionally strives to break through the "great doubt" (*daigi*) in a sudden experience of awakening. Once again it projects this understanding on history and assumes that *kōan* study for Dōgen would have been in conflict with both the theory and the practice of his *zazen*.

Although these assumptions tell us much about modern Japanese Zen, they do not help us much to understand the actual character of Dōgen's meditation. The distinction between the practices of Rinzai and Sōtō is not nearly so clear in premodern times as it becomes in the hands of Menzan and his successors. Even in his own day Menzan had to struggle against Rinzai heresies within the bosom of his Sōtō school; and before his day, in the centuries separating him from Dōgen, if Rinzai monks continued to read Tsung-tse's *Tso-ch'an i* and practice his *zazen*, Dōgen's successors persisted in reading Ta-hui and studying *kōan*. In fact, as we have seen, Dōgen's own leading disciples, for all his harsh criticism of Ta-hui, continued to treasure their Daruma school roots and transmit the heritage of Ta-hui's Yang-ch'i tradition. No less than Keizan Jōkin, chief among Dōgen's descendants and "Second Founder" of Sōtō Zen, considered himself a successor to that tradition and, like so many of its other members, advocated its popular *kanna* technique in his manuals of *zazen*.[33]

---

33. See *Sankon zazen setsu*, SSZ.Shūgen,2:428a. Here Keizan distinguishes three levels in the understanding of *zazen* (corresponding to the three traditional Buddhist disciplines): the lowest emphasizes the ethical character of the practice; the middling, the psychological character; the highest, the philosophical. The second, he describes as "abandoning the myriad affairs and halting the various involvements," making unflagging effort to concentrate on breathing or consider a *kōan*, until one has gotten clear about the truth. (In the highest *zazen*, of course, this truth is already quite clear.) In his influential *Zazen yōjin ki* as well—though he

If this blurring of what are now often taken to be crucial sectarian differences was common in medieval Japan, how much more was this the case in Sung China, where lineage was less linked to institutional structure, and the houses of Ch'an were not in direct competition for patronage. Ta-hui may have attacked the practice of silent illumination, but we have no evidence that he considered it characteristic of the Ts'ao-tung house as a whole; his own practice of *k'an-hua* may have become popular, but we cannot conclude from this that it ever obviated the cultivation of more traditional forms of *tso-ch'an* in the routine of Lin-chi monks. Indeed, if it had, either in China or Japan, we could hardly explain the persistence of the *Tso-ch'an i* in the monastic codes used by those monks in both countries. Similarly, Dōgen's Ts'ao-tung master, Ju-ching, may (or may not) have taught that Ch'an practice was just sitting, but this did not seem to inhibit him, as we have seen, from advocating the contemplation of Chao-chou's *"wu."* Nor, for that matter, did either of these teachings prevent him from proposing others; even in Dōgen's own *Hōkyō ki* he encourages the study of Tsung-tse's meditation manual and recommends the practice of sitting with the mind focussed in the palm of the left hand, a technique he describes as nothing less than "the method correctly transmitted by the Buddhas and Patriarchs." [34] Thus, even where—as in the case of Dōgen—we find a strong assertion of sectarian tradition, we should be wary of easy extrapolation from the modern Japanese experience and suspicious of the notion of a distinctive Sōtō meditation practice.

There is no doubt that Dōgen saw himself as the inheritor of a unique tradition of meditation, and that, at least in his later writings, he came to associate this tradition with the Ts'ao-tung lineage of Ju-ching. In these same writings he also professes disappointment with the understanding of

repeats the *Fukan zazen gi* passage on nonthinking—Keizan recommends the practice of *kanna* as an antidote to mental agitation in *zazen* (ibid. 427b).

Menzan's prejudice against the *kōan* inherits and develops the position of Dōgen's Heian disciples Senne and Kyōgō, whose *Shōbō genzō kikigaki* and *Shōbō genzō shō* include several comments against "a bunch calling themselves Zen masters" who advocate "simply bearing in mind a *kōan*" (SSZ.Chūkai, 1 : 223a; see also 543b and 2 : 459b–460a. For a discussion of the passages, see Itō Shūken, "Kōan to shikan taza," SK 22 [3/1980], 101–6.), but theirs was hardly the prevailing view in the subsequent literature of the school. In fact, whatever we may say of his interpretation of Dōgen, Menzan's version of the pristine tradition of *shikan taza* has had a disastrous effect on the historical understanding of medieval Sōtō; for it led him and his epigones to dismiss as unworthy of serious attention the considerable corpus of esoteric *kōan* manuals (*monsan*) the secret initiation into which formed one of the most characteristic features of Muromachi Sōtō religion. Perhaps the earliest such text, known as the *Himitsu shōbō genzō shō*, is based on a collection of ten cases probably put together by Keizan himself. (See Ishikawa Rikizan, "Himitsu Shōbō genzō saikō," SK 21 [3/1979], 173–78. Ishikawa has been a leader in the recent rediscovery of the medieval Sōtō esoteric literature [styled *kirigami*] initiated by Sugimoto Shunryū's *Zōtei Tōjō shitsunai kirigami oyobi sanwa kenkyū* [1941]. For some bibliography on the Sōtō vernacular *kōan* commentaries known as *kana shō*, see Hiwatari Noboru, "Hōon roku shohon to sono honbun o megutte," SK 24 [3/1982], 58–64.)

34. DZZ.2:386–87.

meditation current in the Sung. We have already seen specific reasons for this disappointment in the *Zazen shin*, and later on in the text we find it expressed in a more general lament.

At present in the "mountains" of the Great Sung, many of those who are heads of the principal monasteries do not understand, and do not study, seated meditation. There may be some who have clearly understood it, but not many. Of course, the monasteries have fixed periods for seated meditation; the monks, from the abbot down, all take seated meditation as their basic task; and, in leading their students, [the abbots] encourage its practice. Nevertheless, there are few abbots who understand it.[35]

Insofar as it was the Lin-chi house that dominated the Ch'an monasteries of the Sung, we can assume that the abbots mentioned here were members of this house. And, as we have seen, not only the *Zazen shin* but other *Shōbō genzō* texts from this time are often critical of the Lin-chi tradition—of its founder, I-hsüan, its contemporary representatives, and especially its most noted recent figure, Ta-hui. Although these texts often lament the long-term decline of Buddhism in the centuries since the T'ang, Dōgen probably held Ta-hui and his followers partly responsible for the impoverished understanding of meditation he encountered in the Sung. Yet it is much less clear that their fault lay in the advocacy of the use of the old cases as a vehicle for spiritual training.

Dōgen criticizes Ta-hui for his lack of sincerity, worldly ambition, ignorance of Buddhist tradition, and neglect of Buddhist training. He rejects Ta-hui's thought as tending toward the pagan belief in the fallacy of naturalism (*jinen ken*), which ignores the basic Buddhist doctrine of cause and effect that is the rationale for religious cultivation. He dismisses Ta-hui's spiritual attainments as nothing more than the memorization of a few passages of scripture by a student who was unworthy of his teacher. Yet surprisingly enough for one supposed to have been so set against *kanna*, in all this he never finds fault with the practice for which Ta-hui was most famous. On the contrary, he attacks the master of the *kung-an* in his own terms, as a man who throughout his entire life never understood a single case—who himself never produced "the great doubt" and never "broke through" to an awakening. In fact, not only in his discussions of Ta-hui but throughout the ten fascicles of his recorded sayings and the entire corpus of his more than one hundred works, we do not read any criticism of the popular technique of *kanna*.[36]

One interesting passage is regularly cited as evidence that Dōgen himself drew a sharp distinction between his *shikan taza* and the *kanna* practice of

---

35. DZZ.1:96–97.
36. For the remarks on Ta-hui's understanding of *kōan*, see *Jishō zanmai*, DZZ.1:557, 559. I have summarized Dōgen's criticisms in my "Recarving the Dragon," 36–38.

Rinzai. This comes not from Dōgen's own corpus but from Ejō's record of his master's early teachings, the *Shōbō genzō zuimon ki*. In the last section of the work, Ejō raises the question of the relative value of *zazen* practice and the study of the *kōan* and recorded sayings. Dōgen replies,

We may seem to get some understanding by looking at the stories of the *kōan*, but this will actually lead us away from the path of the Buddhas and Patriarchs. If we just pass the time in upright sitting, with nothing to be gained and nothing to be realized, this is the Patriarchal path. The ancients may have recommended both looking at words and just sitting, but still it was sitting that they especially recommended. And while there have been those who achieved awakening through a story, this too was made possible by virtue of their sitting. The real virtue lies in the sitting.[37]

The apparent implication here that one who is committed to the Patriarchal path ought to avoid studying the records of the Ch'an masters' teachings seems so clearly at variance with Dōgen's own practice that it has led one prominent scholar to dismiss the entire text of the *Zuimon ki* as the later product of certain elements among the descendants of Ejō.[38] Yet, whatever else we may say about the authenticity of the text, this little passage hardly seems capable of bearing the kind of weight it has been given by both defenders and critics of its message. Read dispassionately, it is clearly akin to the standard warnings found throughout Ch'an and Zen literature against the notion that study of the records of the religion can serve as a substitute for "the backward step" that leads to the realization of one's own mind. To be sure, for Dōgen, such realization occurs only within the cultivation of the traditional monastic practices of the Patriarchs; to that extent he will necessarily reject not only the sort of literary Zen criticized as well by Ta-hui but also the suggestion fostered by Ta-hui's letters that laymen need not cultivate meditation but can merely go about their business with "*wu*" in mind till they suddenly see their natures.[39] Yet, while Dōgen may have been particularly strict in this regard, his basic position no doubt simply makes explicit what was surely the actual assumption of almost all Ch'an and Zen teachers of whatever persuasion: that *kōan* study, whether by monk or layman, was to be carried out within the larger context of Buddhist spiritual

---

37. DZZ.2:494. (See also ibid., 448, for similar sentiments.) The passage appears in fascicle 5 of the vulgate text but represents the very last section of the early Chōen ji manuscript. For a discussion of the possible linkage of the passage to Ejō's own approach to Zen, see Ishikawa Rikizan, "Shōbō genzō zuimon ki to Nihon Daruma shū," SK 24 (3/1982), 37–43; 25 (3/1983), 43–48.

38. See Imaeda Aishin, *Dōgen: Zazen hitosuji no shamon*, 177–83. Cf. the response of Itō Shūken, in "Shōbō genzō to Shōbō genzō zuimon ki to no aida no mujun," IBK 27, 1 (12/1978), 343–46.

39. See Dōgen's criticism of those "self-styled Ch'an monks" who curry favor with laymen by denying any difference between lay and clerical life (*Shōbō genzō sanjūshichi hon bodai bunpō*, DZZ.1:511–12), and his rejection of the notion he finds current in the Sung that the *buddha-dharma* could be reduced to merely "seeing one's nature" (*kenshō*) (*Shōbō genzō shizen biku*, DZZ.1:708).

life—a context that included contact with a master, moral cultivation, ritual observances, and some form of the mental discipline of meditation that Dōgen took to be the key to the religion.

When thus integrated into the larger religious life, the *kōan* stories clearly had a central role to play in the revelation of what Dōgen saw as the Patriarchal path. Indeed, if they did not, we could hardly make sense of the path taken by his own teaching—his many years spent in detailed explication of the old cases, and his repeated admonitions throughout the commentaries of his *Shōbō genzō* and the lectures of his *Eihei kōroku* to take up the words and deeds of the past masters, to attend to them carefully, reflect upon them quietly, investigate them thoroughly, and penetrate their deepest meanings.[40] That this kind of thinking could contribute directly to the experience of not thinking should hardly surprise us; if, as the *Fukan zazen gi* itself claims, the enlightened acts of the sages all issue from the state of *zazen*, then these acts could well serve as the signs leading us back to that state. That they played some such role in Dōgen's meditation instruction seems clear from the way he repeatedly uses allusion to them in a work like the *Shōbō genzō zazen shin* to point us toward the meaning of Zen meditation. Perhaps particularly enlightening in this regard is his treatment, at the end of the work, of the verse on meditation by Hung-chih from which the *Zazen shin* takes its name.

Hung-chih's "Lancet of Seated Meditation" is a highly abstract ode to the subtle, mysterious "illumination" of *samādhi*, in which the mind "knows without touching things" and "comprehends without grasping" its object. Dōgen introduces this verse by the foremost Sung representative of the Ts'ao-tung house as a work without peer in the literature of *zazen*. Yet, for all his praise of the piece, the spirit of his own commentary on it is in sharp contrast to the cool, philosophical detachment of the original. Where the verse evokes the calm clarity of seated meditation by moving in carefully balanced phrases through the abstract vocabulary of Buddhist epistemology, like many Sung commentators, Dōgen prefers to dramatize each passage of the movement with one or another striking image drawn from the famous sayings of the past masters. For example, the title of the poem is "explained" by Kuei-shan's saying, "the juncture before your parents were born," or Tung-shan's remarkable "head of three feet and neck of two inches"; the line "It knows without touching things" becomes in the commentary P'u-hua's enigmatic, "When they come in the light, I hit them in the light; when they come in the dark, I hit them in the dark"; while to be, in Hung-chih's words, "ever without discrimination" means for Dōgen that "you do not meet a single person" on Tung-shan's "way of the birds";

---

40. Nor could we easily make peace with those passages in the latter text that seem to record instances in which Dōgen worked privately with students on the old cases; see DZZ.2: 152–53; 155–56.

and so on.[41] Whether (and in what sense) such commentary succeeds in "explaining" the Chinese verse may be open to debate, but there is no doubt that the effect of the whole here is continually to interrupt the reader's experience of the unwavering luminosity of Hung-chih's *samādhi* with the sharp flashes of the ancients' insight, and to bind up his understanding of Hung-chih's meditation with the effort to grasp the meaning of the old cases.

Modern Sōtō writing commonly makes a distinction between the "*kōan* of the old cases" (*kosoku kōan*)—the historical precedents used in *kanna* training—and the "*kōan* of realization" (*genjō kōan*)—the "absolute presence" of things that is supposed to be the only proper content of Dōgen's *shikan taza*. Whatever useful functions such a distinction may serve, it suffers from the implication that Dōgen saw the sacred history of the *shōbō genzō* that is preserved in the old cases as divorced from the sacred presence revealed in meditation. But by now we have seen ample evidence that such was simply not the case: the past casts light on the nature and significance of just sitting even as the present practice of nonthinking illumines the meaning of the historical record. This is why Dōgen can say, for example, in his *Shōbō genzō daigo,*

Taking up the three realms, [the Buddhas and Patriarchs] have the great awakening; taking up the hundred grasses, taking up the four elements, they have the great awakening; taking up the Buddhas and Patriarchs, taking up a *kōan*, they have the great awakening. In all cases, they have taken up the great awakening, and then had the great awakening. The moment in which they have done this is our present moment.[42]

The penultimate sentence here is undoubtedly intended to remind us of Dōgen's constant refrain that the Patriarchal practice is not merely something that makes a Buddha but is itself always based on the great awakening (*daigo*) of Buddhahood; and in fact toward the end of this text he rebukes those "shavepates" (*tokusu*) in the recent Sung who, because they are not "illumined by the radiance of the Buddhas and Patriarchs," misunderstand this point and "vainly wait for awakening" (*itazura ni taigo su*).[43] But for those who are thus illumined, the practice of the great awakening of the ancients will be present in everything they take up, whether it be the *kōan* of the past masters or the hundred grasses of the world around them.

The possibility of this coalescence of the cultural record of the past and the natural world of the present in the contemplative experience of the practitioner is put to practical use in one section of Dōgen's *Gakudō yōjin shū*. Here, in an essay written even before the bulk of his *kōan* commentaries (and

---

41. For these references, see my translation, Document 3.
42. DZZ.1:83. The "hundred grasses" here refers to the multiplicity of the phenomenal world, as in the saying, "The intention of the Patriarchs is in the tips of the hundred grasses." (*P'ang chü-shih yü lu*, Iriya Yoshitaka, *Hō koji goroku, Zen no goroku* 7 [1973], 185.)
43. DZZ.1:86.

his criticisms of Ta-hui), he celebrates the mysterious conduct (*anri*) of the Ch'an Patriarchs—conduct that, like Hung-chih's *samādhi*, transcends all attachments and all ordinary judgments. To help the reader realize the meaning of this conduct, he offers a familiar story:

A monk asked Chao-chou, "Does a dog have the Buddha nature?" Chao-chou answered, "No." Can you gauge this word, "no" [*muji*]? Can you contain it? There is no place at all to grasp its nose. Please try letting it go. Let it go and just look. What about your body and mind? What about your conduct? What about life and death? What about the *dharma* of the Buddha, the *dharma* of the world? What about, after all, the mountains, rivers and great earth, the men, beasts, houses and dwellings? If you keep looking and looking, the two attributes of motion and rest will naturally become perfectly clear, without arising. Yet, when these [attributes] do not arise, this does not mean that one becomes rigidly fixed [*ganzen*]. There are many people who fail to realize this and are confused about it. Students, you only attain it when you are still half way; when you are all the way, do not stop. Press on, press on.[44]

Surely there is nothing here that could not have been said by the chief advocate of Chao-chou's "*wu*"; the entire passage reads quite like one of Ta-hui's letters. The mystery of the T'ang master's cryptic "no" becomes a symbol of the larger mystery of Zen and, indeed, of things in general. If we just keep looking (*kan rai kan kyo*) at this mystery long enough, we will naturally achieve the calm clarity beyond motion and rest that we have earlier seen to be the deeper meaning of the regulation of body and mind in meditation. To put this practice of looking to work in *zazen* would seem to require nothing more than a cushion.

In his *Shōbō genzō soshi seirai i*, Dōgen suggests how we might fit a *kōan* on a cushion. Taking up Hsiang-yen's famous problem of the man, hanging by his teeth over a great precipice, who is asked the meaning of Bodhidharma's advent, he complains that, while this enlightening case (*innen*) has been the subject of much discussion and commentary, it has rarely been well clarified. "Nevertheless," he goes on,

When we take up not thinking, or take up nonthinking, and think [about the case], we will naturally be making concentrated effort on the same cushion [*ichi zafu*] as old Hsiang-yen. And once we are sitting fixedly on the same cushion as old Hsiang-yen, we should go on to study the particulars of his case before he has opened his mouth. We should steal old Hsiang-yen's eyes and look into [*shoken*] [the case] with them; nay, we should take out the treasury of the eye of the true *dharma* from the Buddha Śākyamuni Himself and look right through [*shoha*] [the case] with it.[45]

---

44. DZZ.2:259.
45. DZZ.1:522. Note that allusion to Hsiang-yen's case also figures in Dōgen's commentary on the practice of "figuring" in the *Zazen shin* (DZZ.1:92).

If old Hsiang-yen can sit so comfortably on our cushion and his classic case fit so neatly into our nonthinking, we may have difficulty seeing why we are obliged to continue in our assumption that the investigation of the *kōan* is somehow inherently incompatible with Dōgen's just sitting. In fact the assumption is probably based on a caricature of both these practices—a caricature that reduces the former practice to an ideologically naive striving for experience and inflates the latter practice to a psychologically dubious absence of it. Whether or not we can recognize these two tendencies in the history of Ch'an and Zen, the models will be difficult to apply to Ta-hui and Dōgen. If one can find in the writings of the former a practical, utilitarian approach to mental training, one can also find much that is easily as sensitive to the transcendental character of Ch'an practice as any of the wisdom literature Dōgen so enjoys. Even within his letters to laymen, Ta-hui is careful to warn against "waiting for an awakening" (*tai wu*) and quick to dismiss the ordinary mind as the agent of *k'an-hua*. "Do not," as he says in a hauntingly familiar instruction, "think or conjecture [about the *kung-an*]: just think [*ssu-liang*] of the unthinkable [*pu k'o ssu-liang*]." [46] By the same token, if Dōgen preferred just to sit, thinking of what cannot be thought, he spent much of his thinking on *kōan*, and he had no more use than Ta-hui for the "ghost cave" of mental vacuity.

In modern times the expression *shikan taza* has tended to operate as a technical term and to indicate the particular objectless meditation practice that is supposed to distinguish Sōtō from Rinzai; but there is almost nothing in Dōgen's own usage of the expression to support this. For him, it seems to denote little more than "seated meditation" (*zazen*). If it has a connotation of its own, it is only the now familiar claim that Zen practice and enlightenment can be reduced to "just sitting" in meditation. It does not follow from this claim—nor does Dōgen use the term to mean—that Zen meditation can somehow be reduced to a particular mental exercise called "just sitting." In the end, then, the discrimination of Dōgen's meditation technique from that of Ta-hui (or of Tsung-tse) pretends to a knowledge of the psychological content—as opposed to the theological context—of his *shikan taza* that we simply do not have.

Some readers may well find it ludicrous that we have come this far in our study of the *Fukan zazen gi* only to admit that we cannot finally determine just what it is that this famous Zen meditation manual wants us to do—or just what it was that its author himself did to earn his reputation as one of the foremost Zen meditation masters. But this is, after all, the secret of Zen meditation, and it may be that Dōgen's real genius lies precisely in his uncanny ability to talk about the secret openly and at length without ever

---

46. "Letter to Interior Gentleman Lü," *Ta-hui yü lu*, T.47:930c.

giving it away. Still, while his talk has not quite allowed us to put our finger on the actual technique of just sitting, it has permitted us to recognize something of the religious setting for the practice. In closing, therefore, I want to add one or two words about this wider setting and how it affects our interpretation of Dōgen's Buddhism.

Conclusion

In my discussion of the *Fukan zazen gi* I have pointed to two general
themes in Dōgen's approach to the teaching of meditation that seem to
distinguish his style from that of Tsung-tse: like many in the Ch'an tradition,
he is careful always to bind his practice with its theory and present it as an
expression of the higher wisdom of the supreme vehicle; perhaps more than
most in the tradition, he is concerned to ground his practice in history and
identify it with the orthodox transmission of the Buddhas and Patriarchs.
The emphasis on these two themes—and the particular ways in which they
are combined—is probably what determines the characteristic thrust of
Dōgen's meditation teachings, and the interpretation of these themes is
likely to decide how we understand his practice of just sitting.

The linkage of the religious exercise with its theory and historical tradition is, of course, by no means unique to Dōgen and does not in itself imply
a unique form of practice; but, if the theory and tradition in question are
themselves taken as somehow unique, then the stronger the link, the more
likely the practice will follow along. If we take the theory of the supreme
vehicle to exclude the less sublime teachings of ordinary Buddhism, we shall
want its expression in practice to be different from ordinary Buddhist
techniques; and, if we see the orthodox lineage of meditation as distinct from
certain historical forms of Buddhism, we shall not want such meditation to
overlap too far with those forms. As we have seen, Dōgen himself asserted
the uniqueness of his theory and his tradition, and this assertion has undoubtedly tended to foster an interpretation of his *zazen* that seeks to isolate
it, on both theoretical and historical grounds, from other common contemplative exercises. It is not the *dhyāna* of Tsung-tse's concentration technique
nor is it the *kanna* of Rinzai's *kōan* practice; it is *shikan taza*, the Sōtō practice
of just sitting.

Whatever ideological advantages may derive from the isolation of *shikan taza* practice, they would seem to be more than offset by the damage that must follow to the traditional theoretical and historical validation of Dōgen's *zazen*. Insofar as *shikan taza* is viewed as a unique spiritual exercise (rather than as an interpretation of the exercise), the evidence of the autograph *Fukan zazen gi* poses a painful dilemma for the Sōtō doctrinal system. On the one horn, if the system seeks to maintain its crucial historical claim that *shikan taza* is the sacred *shōbō genzō* handed down on Mt. T'ien-t'ung from Ju-ching to Dōgen, then the system must assume that the latter had already acquired this meditation when he wrote his Tenpuku manual, and that he recognized the description in Tsung-tse's *Tso-ch'an i* as an adequate statement of its technique. This will mean, of course, that *shikan taza* is rather less special than we have been led to believe—that it was transmitted even to a Yün-men monk who lacked "the understanding beyond words," and that, whatever we may say about such transcendental understanding, as a technique, Dōgen's *shōbō genzō* is a simple concentration exercise not easily distinguishable from the sort of practices long criticized in Ch'an.

If, on the other horn, the interpretation wants to emphasize the link between theory and practice and claim that *shikan taza* is nothing more than just sitting, with body and mind sloughed off, in the enlightened state of nonthinking, it will have to dismiss Tsung-tse's meditation as a mistake and admit that Dōgen's first efforts at describing what he had learned from Ju-ching were inadequate. The question will then naturally arise why Dōgen, who is supposed to have "sloughed off body and mind" and inherited the enlightened practice of *shikan taza* in China, should have taught a different, mistaken practice after his return to Japan. For the orthodox tradition the question represents a subdilemma: either Dōgen only discovered (or invented) his inheritance long after he had left Ju-ching and written his first meditation manual, or, in that first manual, he purposely denied his inheritance and advocated a form of meditation he himself knew to be out of keeping with the true tradition of the Buddhas and Patriarchs.

Those unburdened by the need for orthodoxy, of course, can slip through these horns quite easily, simply by loosening the rigid definitions of the practice (and the history) of Dōgen's *shōbō genzō* and allowing his famous teaching of enlightened *zazen* to float free as philosophy. Thus unburdened, we can accept a range of religious techniques within a single religious vision (or, more likely, within a complex, developing vision) and appreciate the image of the seated Buddha as a powerful and creative response to the ancient theory of the sudden practice of enlightenment. If this seems easy, however, we should recognize that the Sōtō assertion of a unique, enlightened practice is but a particular instance of the traditional Ch'an claim to the exclusive cultivation of the supreme vehicle, and that, in making a distinction between the theory and its actual cultivation, we are seriously compromising the characteristic Ch'an approach to the sudden practice. As I have been at pains to argue, it is precisely the claim to transcend this distinction that separated the early school from more traditional forms of Buddhism, and that rendered any description of its practice so problematic. One cannot help but feel sympathy for those who struggled to maintain and justify such a description within the intolerable rules set by the tradition.

For those, like Ta-hui and Dōgen, who sought to operate within the rules of the nondual *dharma*, I have suggested that the tradition offered two basic models for explaining religious practice. As the supreme vehicle, both models had to accept the premises that man already possesses the Buddha mind, that true religious practice is nothing more than the natural functioning of this mind, and that, therefore, practice and enlightenment, or meditation and wisdom, occur simultaneously. One conclusion drawn from these premises tended to collapse the religion into its proper understanding, to argue that there was nothing to Ch'an practice save the insight into the truth of the Ch'an premises themselves. This "protestant" tendency, then, dismissed contemplative and other spiritual exercises as mere expedients (or worse) and called simply for the direct experience of a sudden awakening, or radical conversion, to the supreme *dharma*. Alongside this approach— which we might call a "recognition" model—so common in statements of the sudden practice, we find an alternative interpretation that emphasized the opposite member of the practice-enlightenment equation. Under this view—let us call it an "enactment" model—the goal of enlightenment was reduced to the ongoing recapitulation of the clarity and detachment of the inherent Buddha mind in the actual experience of the practitioner. Here the positing of a spiritual goal (whether it be a contemplative state or a special knowledge) beyond the immediate expression of the true mind was taken to be a denial of the basic premises of Ch'an and a misunderstanding of the sudden teaching.

In one form or another these two models of the sudden teaching—one that sought to reduce the practice to the enlightenment experience itself, the other that preferred to expand the practice to encompass enlightenment— can be found together, often within the same texts, throughout the history of Ch'an in both its early and classical phases. Taken alone, each seems inherently unstable and probably requires the support of some version of the other; but, like the ancient Buddhist tension between meditation and wisdom—of which they can no doubt be seen as a Ch'an reworking—they are not easily resolved into a single balanced system that does not lean toward one position or the other. It is hardly surprising, therefore, that, when in the reformations of the Sung and Kamakura, men like Ta-hui and Dōgen tried to articulate their school's religious practice, they found themselves pulling in different directions.

There is an obvious sense in which Dōgen's emphasis on the actual cultivation of enlightenment—on spiritual work (*kufū*) in pursuit of the way (*bendō*)—puts him in company with the Sung reformation movement of *k'an-hua* Ch'an. Like Ta-hui, he is clearly concerned to guard the faith from the inherent inertia of the ultimate, nondual *dharma* and put the sudden teaching back in service as a working religious vehicle. His Buddha may have no fixed mark, but the fact remains—as he says in a *Zazen shin* passage that Ta-hui would surely have liked—all men may sit, but they are not all seated Buddhas.[1] Still, it is just as clear that Dōgen has his own way of salvaging the faith. For whereas Ta-hui—at least in his letters to laymen— tends to justify his practice on psychological grounds, reasserting the classical Ch'an experience of awakening (*wu*) and insight (*chien*) and warning against the mere metaphysics of the original mind, Dōgen prefers the high road of reason (*dōri*), appealing to the venerable Ch'an theory of undefiled practice to infuse the path with its goal and idealize the actual conduct of the religious life.

This preference for theory and ideal often makes Dōgen's way of talking about practice sound more like Ta-hui's *mo-chao* opponents than like Ta-hui himself; and, in fact, though he himself never explicitly enters the argument between *mo-chao* and *k'an-hua*, he is clearly impressed by Hung-chih's philosophical understanding of meditation and just as disappointed by Ta-hui's failure to take the practice more seriously. It is understandable, therefore, that later interpreters—both friend and foe alike—who sought the Chinese precedents for Dōgen's Zen would link it with silent illumination and debate it in the metaphysical and psychological terms favored by Ta-hui and his contemporaries. Yet in the end such terms do not quite seem to fit. Although we can, as I have tried to do here, profitably explore Dōgen's doctrine of enlightened practice through the classical Ch'an philosophy of the Buddha nature and the sudden teaching and discuss his thinking of not thinking through the standard Buddhist psychological vocabulary of concentration and insight, passive and active mental states, and the like, we soon discover that such categories have not yet got at what is probably the most striking single feature of Dōgen's meditation teaching—the extraordinary religious significance he attaches to the historical fact and concrete act of *zazen*. In the end, to appreciate this feature fully, we may have to step outside the Chinese Ch'an meditation tradition so beloved by Dōgen and incorporate other models for his religion.

Dōgen was an uncompromising exponent of pure Zen, who focussed almost exclusively on the lineage of Bodhidharma and had little use for the competing forms of Buddhism that surrounded him in Japan; yet this very exclusivity expresses an approach to religion common to many of his con-

---

1. DZZ.1:95.

temporaries in the other Buddhist movements of the Kamakura reformation. Dōgen taught his religion through the language and lore of Chinese
Ch'an; yet in many ways the structure of his religion reflects familiar
patterns in the soteriological strategies of Japanese writers like Shinran
and Nichiren. This is hardly surprising, since many of the same issues
that determined the rules of Ch'an discourse in China—the theory of the
supreme, Buddha vehicle and the perfect, sudden practice appropriate to
it—had long been at work in the dominant Tendai system in Japan, the
system that initially educated Dōgen, Shinran, Nichiren, and other leaders
of the reformation. Despite their obvious differences, in very broad terms,
the ideologies of all three of these famous religious thinkers can be seen as
an attempt to define the true practice of the Tendai Buddha vehicle—a
sudden practice to be based solely on the absolute truth of Buddhahood
itself, not on the *upāya* of the relative teachings and gradual practices.

Already during the Heian period the notion had grown up within
Tendai itself that the theory of the perfect teaching could best be put into
practice through the three mysteries (*sanmitsu*) of *mikkyō*—in which the
physical, verbal, and mental acts of the practitioner were identified with the
body, speech, and mind of the Buddha—and that the traditional methods
of the *bodhisattva-mārga* could be superseded by the esoteric techniques of the
Vajrayāna, handed down in the lineage of the tantric masters. Such techniques were sudden both in theory and in fact: they were based throughout
on the principle of the identity of man and Buddha, and they were intended
to bring about the full realization of the identity in this very existence. In
this sense *mikkyō*, which itself of course originated as a Mahāyāna reform
movement, had strong affinities with Zen and the other Kamakura schools;
and it is not surprising that elements of it played a significant role in their
development. Still, the regnant esoteric systems of Shingon and Taimitsu
were themselves formulated in highly technical theologies and practiced
through a graded series of complicated initiations, meditations, and rituals.
To this extent, they were not in themselves an adequate vehicle for the
expression of the new spirit of the Kamakura reform.

The spirit of the new Kamakura schools is often summarized by the
expression "selective" (*senjaku*) Buddhism. This term, taken especially from
Pure Land theology, refers first to the selection from a multiplicity of
spiritual exercises (*shogyō*) of one practice for exclusive cultivation (*senju*).
In Pure Land itself, of course, this practice was the recitation of Amitābha's
name (*nenbutsu*); for Nichiren, it was "discerning the mind" (*kanjin*), understood now in its esoteric sense as the recitation of the title of the *Lotus Sūtra*
(*daimoku*). For Dōgen, it was just sitting. In one obvious sense the selection
can be seen as a simplification of Buddhism and a reduction of its practice
to a single, uncomplicated exercise accessible to all. Historically speaking,
such simplification was no doubt linked to the new social conditions of

Kamakura Buddhism and served as an important factor in the subsequent popularity of the new schools. Yet this historical view should not blind us to the fact that, for the founders of these schools themselves, the practices they selected were not merely easy ways to salvation but the only true ways to express the highest teaching of the one vehicle. As such, they were not merely *upāya*—expedient exercises based on man's imperfection—but sudden practices derived from the principle of a higher perfection. For Shinran, of course, this principle was given in the universal grace of the Buddha Amitābha; for Nichiren, it was founded in the eternality of the Buddha Śākyamuni. For Dōgen, it lay in the Buddhahood built into the very structure of consciousness. However it was defined, the practices derived from the principle did not, ultimately speaking, lead to anything: they were supposed rather to be the expression in the act of the practitioner of his acceptance of, and commitment to, the principle. In this expression the goal of the practice was already achieved. As Dōgen would say, practice and its verification were not different.

This radically sudden approach to Buddhist practice stands at the ideological heart of the exclusivity and sectarianism that we find in Dōgen and other Kamakura reformers. Their selection of the one practice was not merely a decision to specialize in a particular religious exercise but a commitment to the highest vehicle alone and a rejection of all other teachings as incompatible with it. Thus unlike classical Tendai—which sought to justify and embrace all versions of Buddhism as the expedient expressions of the one Buddha vehicle—Shinran, Nichiren, and Dōgen, like the Ch'an reformers of the T'ang before them, tended to see the one vehicle as exclusive: the highest *dharma* alone was true; all else was false (or at least religiously irrelevant) and was to be abandoned. Indeed it was precisely in the abandonment of the false (or irrelevant) and the single-minded commitment to the true—the abandonment (in Shinran's terms) of religion based on one's own power (*jiriki*) and reliance on Amitābha's grace (*tariki*), or the abandonment (as Nichiren would say) of the provisional teachings (*gon*) and adherence to the real (*jitsu*)—that the believer's doubts about the principle of perfection were wiped away, and he found himself actually participating in the sudden practice.

The transition from Heian to Kamakura was a time of radical historical change, and Dōgen's contemporaries were aware of their historical situation in a way and to a degree that probably no generation before them had been. For many Buddhists it was the long-predicted age of the end of the *dharma* (*mappō*), in which the human condition had sunk to a state no longer equal to the successful negotiation of the *bodhisattva* path. For Buddhists in such an age, the search for the single, sudden practice of the final vehicle was by no means merely an exercise in defining a form of spiritual discipline theoretically consistent with the highest teaching: it was before all else the expression of a real impatience with impotent theory and empty definition, and of a real need to recreate the religion in the immediate experience of the contemporary practitioner. The touchstone of the new faith, then, was this practitioner—the concrete, historically determined man. The supreme teaching was to be the one that directly addressed this man, and the true practice the one that actually worked for him. It is not surprising, therefore, that thinkers like Shinran and Nichiren found the meaning of Buddhist metaphysics and the key to Buddhist soteriology deeply embedded in history. What justified the faith was not merely the eternal nature of things but the facts of history—the fact of the historical vow of the *bodhisattva* Dharmākara that sinners would be taken up to his Sukhāvatī, the fact of the historical promise of the Buddha Śākyamuni that *bodhisattvas* would appear to preach the *Saddharma-puṇḍarīka* for the salvation of the last age.

Dōgen did not resort to the doctrine of the last age: as we have seen, he had little use even for the mild historical relativism implicit in the creation of new forms of Ch'an in the Sung. For him, there was no compromise with history. There was only the one *dharma*—true for Śākyamuni and true for all time and all men. Hence, while Dōgen certainly shared the concern for the historical experience of the contemporary practitioner, the issue for him was not which form of Buddhism constitutes the right vehicle for the present age but whether the one, true vehicle is actually accessible to this age. The answer, of course, was yes. The one vehicle was nothing but the enlightened practice of the Buddha himself that validated the entire tradition: where that practice was present, there was true religion. And the practice was present in the present age, since "the eye of the true *dharma*" had been handed down by the Buddha through the lineage of the Patriarchs of India and China to Dōgen himself. To accede (*jōtō*) to this lineage was itself to participate in the one vehicle.

In this extreme emphasis on the lineage of the Patriarchs, Dōgen seems even more dependent on historical tradition for the justification of his faith than either Pure Land or Nichiren. An emphasis on lineage, of course, was a characteristic feature of the new Kamakura schools, as it had been of the earlier reform movements of the T'ang and Sung on which they drew. The lineage established a precedent for the new interpretation and an identity for the new community; it provided the historical vehicle to which the practitioner actually committed himself as a member. The importance placed on such lineages is clearly seen in Shinran's devotion to the Pure Land masters, and in Nichiren's identification with the mystical transmission of Viśiṣṭacāritra. Yet for these men the final authority for the true practice remained scripture. The selection of the one practice derived from the commitment to one *sūtra*, indeed, to one crucial passage or section of that *sūtra*—for Shinran, the eighteenth vow of the *Sukhāvatīvyūha*; for Nichiren, the *honmon* section of the *Lotus*. The shared recognition of the true implications of such passages, and the commitment to them, established the identity and ensured the superiority of the tradition.

As we have noticed, Dōgen did not favor the style of Ch'an that asserted a "separate transmission outside scripture": there was only a single true *dharma*, and, if one read with the enlightened "eye of the way" (*dōgen*), he could see that *dharma* in all the scriptures. Nevertheless, the opening of this eye was not the work of scripture itself: it could come about only through contact with a master who preserved the *shōbō genzō* and transmitted the "mind seal." Thus, for Dōgen, no text or set of texts determined the orthodox understanding; this was done only by the enlightenment of the Buddha and the historical continuity of the tradition with that enlightenment. This continuity—what Dōgen sometimes called "the vital artery of the Buddhas and Patriarchs" (*busso no meimyaku*)—sustained the life of the true *dharma* and guaranteed the validity of his religion. Dōgen was justified in his selection of *zazen* as the ultimate expression of enlightened practice by—above all else—the historical fact that each generation of the tradition—from the Seven Buddhas to his own master, Ju-ching—had practiced seated meditation.

Though the notion that true Zen practice is itself enlightenment can be derived from the classical Ch'an metaphysics of the mind, the idea that such practice is only (or even best) fulfilled through the exercise of seated meditation probably cannot be so derived; it must rest in the end on historical demonstration. And, in fact, throughout his writings, Dōgen returns again and again to these historical grounds for his selection of *zazen*. In his introduction to the *Fukan zazen gi*, he reminds his readers of Śākyamuni's meditation under the Bodhi tree and of Bodhidharma's nine years of sitting before a wall; in his conclusion to the vulgate text, he goes on to claim that throughout the history of Buddhism from India to China all the Patriarchs "devoted themselves only to sitting." Through the practice of *zazen*, then, we "accord with the *bodhi* of all the Buddhas and succeed to the *samādhi* of all the Patriarchs."

Similarly, in the *Bendō wa*, *zazen* is called the orthodox gateway to the *buddha-dharma* precisely because it was through this practice that all Buddhas of the three periods and all Patriarchs of India and China had attained the way.[2] Again, in his *Shōbō genzō zanmai ō zanmai*, Dōgen points out that the Buddha sat cross-legged (*kafu za*) under the Bodhi tree, that he passed myriad *kalpas* in such sitting, that he preached the *dharma* while sitting; this practice, he passed on to his disciples and taught to men and gods alike: it is the "mind seal" correctly transmitted by the Seven Buddhas (*shichi butsu shōden no shin'in*). This same sitting was practiced by Bodhidharma at Shaolin; it represents the entirety of the vital artery of the First Patriarch (*shoso*

---

2. DZZ.1:732-33.

no meimyaku).[3] In the *Eihei kōroku*, we are told flatly that "the true *dharma* correctly transmitted by the Buddhas and Patriarchs is nothing but sitting [*taza*]," that "sitting is itself the treasury of the eye of the true *dharma* and the mystic mind of *nirvāṇa*" transmitted from Śākyamuni to Mahākāśyapa.[4]

There is certainly ample historical and doctrinal evidence for the view that, in one form or another, meditation has always been a central feature of (at least the monastic forms of) the Buddhist religion; needless to say, the case is much weaker for the more radical view that Buddhists—even in the lineage of Dōgen's Patriarchs—have generally equated their religion with sitting. Indeed the case is so weak that it is probably fair to say that the view is no less in need of justification than sitting itself. In the end the selection of *zazen* as the one true practice is an act of faith in a particular vision of sacred history. When Dōgen summons us to slough off body and mind and just sit, he is, in effect, calling on us to abandon other readings of Buddhist tradition and commit ourselves to his. In religious terms, then, the act of sitting becomes the sign of our faith in the historical reality of the tradition of enlightened practice and our acceptance of participation in it. Or, to put the matter in terms closer to Dōgen's own, to devote ourselves to the exclusive practice of *zazen* is itself to realize the *shōbō genzō* and accede to the lineage of the Buddhas and Patriarchs.

In the *Shōbō genzō zanmai ō zanmai*, Dōgen distinguishes three aspects of cross-legged sitting: the sitting of the body (*shin no kekkafu za*), the sitting of the mind (*shin no kekkafu za*), and the sitting of body and mind sloughed off (*shinjin datsuraku no kekkafu za*).[5] Needless to say, he understands his *zazen* as encompassing all three—what we may call the physical, psychological, and philosophical aspects of Zen practice corresponding to the three traditional Buddhist disciplines of ethics, meditation, and wisdom. He shares, of course, with the classical tradition as a whole a preference for the last and a tendency to obscurity on the second; what is most remarkable about his vision of the sacred history of *zazen* is the weight he gives to the first. Though the cultivation of meditation would seem to be the psychological practice par excellence, in Dōgen's formulation of it, it seems to have to do with more the body than the mind. And, in fact, this is what he himself says. There are two ways, he says, to study the *buddha-mārga*—with the mind and with the body. To engage in seated meditation as the practice of the Buddha, without seeking to make a Buddha, is to study with the body (*mi shite narafu*).[6] Hence, in the *Zanmai ō zanmai*, he can advance the striking claim that the cross-

---

3. DZZ.1:540–41.
4. DZZ.2:77.
5. DZZ.1:540.
6. *Butsu kōjō ji, Himitsu Shōbō genzō* text, DZZ.1:233. A similar association of *zazen* with "attaining the way with the body" rather than the mind is recorded in Ejō's *Shōbō genzō zuimon ki*, where Dōgen explicitly links his *shikan taza* with enlightenment through the physical senses. (DZZ.2:458.)

legged posture of *kekkafu za* is itself "the king of *samādhis*" and the entrance into enlightenment (*shōnyū*).[7]

The ancient "mind seal" (*shin'in*) transmitted by the Buddhas and Patriarchs seems here to have become a seal (*mudrā*) of a distinctly corporeal sort. Clearly we are moving here from the world of wisdom to the realm of ritual, a realm to which we have seen Dōgen himself move in the latter half of his career. Whatever philosophical curiosities may follow from the identification of ultimate enlightenment with the seated posture, the move can no doubt be seen as an interesting extension of the old enactment model of the sudden practice, in which the enlightened mind was to be directly expressed within the concrete world of form. In the *Fukan zazen gi* itself, Dōgen explicitly links his *zazen* with the tradition that every act of the Ch'an master—whether holding up a finger or beating a student—represents the enlightened behavior of a Buddha, free from discrimination and beyond understanding. The irony, of course, is that, while the basic shift from inward quest to outward expression may have remained constant, what was in the classical style intended precisely to celebrate Ch'an's freedom from traditional forms (especially contemplative forms) of Buddhist cultivation has here become frozen in the ritual reappropriation of the tradition of cross-legged sitting.

In any case we have here gone well beyond the classical theoretical discourse on Buddha nature and sudden practice to a treatment of meditation that is less concerned with cognitive states than with religious action, less concerned with the Buddha as symbol of pure consciousness than as example of liberated agent. If the model for Zen practice here is still the enactment of enlightenment, it is no longer simply the psychological accord of the practitioner's consciousness with the eternally enlightened mind; it is now the physical reenactment by the practitioner of the deeds of the historical exemplars of enlightened behavior.

---

7. DZZ.1 : 540. The claim occurs as a commentary on (Dōgen's emendation of) a passage from the *Ta-chih-tu lun* (T.25 : 111b).

Documents

Document 1

"On the Origin of the 'Principles of Seated Meditation'"

The original manuscript of this note, thought to be in Dōgen's own hand, is untitled. The text appears at DZZ.2:6 under the title supplied by Ōkubo Dōshū: "Fukan zazen gi senjutsu yurai." It has previously been translated into English in Waddell and Abe, "Dōgen's Fukanzazengi and Shōbōgenzō zazengi." Bold type here indicates phrases, undecipherable in the manuscript, that are translated from Ōkubo's reconstruction.

The treasury of the eye of the true *dharma*, separately transmitted outside scripture, has never been heard of in our kingdom, much less has any "Principles of Seated Meditation" been transmitted to us. When I returned to my country from the land of the Sung during the Karoku era [1225–27], there were students [of the *dharma*] who asked me **to compose such a "Principles of Seated Meditation"**; and so, I felt obliged to go ahead and compose one.

In ancient days the Ch'an master Po-chang built a long hall with extended daises [for seated meditation] and transmitted the style of Shaolin. [This style] is not the same as the preceding vines and creepers **and old nests** [of scholastic Buddhism], and students should realize this and not confuse them.

In the *Ch'an-yüan ch'ing-kuei* there is a *Tso-ch'an i*. Though it follows Po-chang's original intention, it adds several new clauses by master I. For this reason, it is filled with many mistakes and misunderstandings. [Its author] knows nothing of the understanding beyond words; who could fail to realize this?

Now I gather the true arcana I have myself seen and heard, [offering them] merely as a substitute for what is received in the mind's expression.

Documents 2 : A–E

"Principles of Seated Meditation": A Comparative Translation of Dōgen's Meditation Manuals

This table compares (B) the Tenpuku version of the *Fukan zazen gi* (FKZZG [1]) with the following:

A. CYCK: Tsung-tse's *Ch'an-yüan ch'ing-kuei Tso-ch'an i*
C. FKZZG (2): *Kōroku Fukan zazen gi*
D. SBGZ: *Shōbō genzō zazen gi*
E. BDH: *Bendō hō*, "zazen hō" section

For convenience of comparison, the following conventions have been used:

Boldface: a. in CYCK, passages common to FKZZG (1)
           b. in other texts, passages common to CYCK
Italics: a. in FKZZG, passages not common to (1) and (2)
           b. in other texts, passages not common to FKZZG

Fukan zazen gi (2) has been translated into English several times; for a good example, see Waddell and Abe, "Dōgen's Fukanzazengi and Shōbō genzō zazengi," which, as its title indicates, also includes a translation of Document D. *Fukan zazen gi* (1) has been rendered into German by Heinrich Dumoulin, in "Allgemeine Lehren zur Förderung des Zazen von Zen-Meister Dōgen," *Monumenta Nipponica* 14 (1958): 429–36. For English versions of the *Bendō hō*, see Yokoi Yūhō, *Regulations for Monastic Life by Eihei Dōgen: Eihei-genzenji-shingi* (1973), 27–39; Jiyu Kennett, *Zen Is Eternal Life* (1976), 112–23. My translation of Document A has appeared as an appendix to my "Ch'ang-lu Tsung-tse's Tso-ch'an i and the 'Secret' of Zen Meditation."

CYCK

The Bodhisattva who studies prajñā should first arouse the thought of great compassion, make the extensive vows, and then carefully cultivate samādhi. Vowing to save sentient beings, he should not seek liberation for himself alone.

FKZZG (1)

Fundamentally speaking, the basis of the way is perfectly pervasive; how could it be contingent on practice and verification? The vehicle of the ancestors is naturally unrestricted; why should we expend sustained effort? Surely the whole being is far beyond defilement; who could believe in a method to polish it? Never is it apart from this very place; what is the use of a pilgrimage to practice it? And yet, if a hair's breadth of distinction exists, the gap is like that between heaven and earth; once the slightest like or dislike arises, all is confused and the mind is lost. *You should know that repeated migrations through eons of time depend on a single moment's reflection; losing the way in this world of defilement derives from the failure to stop deliberation. If you wish to transcend to the extreme beyond, just directly accede [to the way].*

FKZZG (2)

Fundamentally speaking, the basis of the way is perfectly pervasive; how could it be contingent on practice and verification? The vehicle of the ancestors is naturally unrestricted; why should we expend sustained effort? Surely the whole being is far beyond defilement; who could believe in a method to polish it? Never is it apart from this very place; what is the use of a pilgrimage to practice it? And yet, if a hair's breadth of distinction exists, the gap is like that between heaven and earth; once the slightest like or dislike arises, all is confused and the mind is lost.

FKZZG (1)

Though you are proud of your understanding and replete with insight, getting hold of the wisdom that knows at a glance, though you attain the way and clarify the mind, giving rise to the spirit that assaults the heavens, you may have gained the precincts of the entrance and still be missing the path of liberation. Even in the case of *that old one, Śākyamuni,* innately wise though he was, *there remains* the mark of his six years sitting erect; even *the great master Bodhidharma,* though he succeeded to the mind seal, *left the trace* of his nine years facing the wall. When even the ancient sages were like this, how could men today dispense with pursuing [the way]? Therefore, *reverse* the intellectual practice of investigating words and chasing after talk; *take* the backward step of turning the light and shining it back. Of themselves body and mind will drop away, and your original face will appear. If you want such [a state], urgently work at *zazen.*

FKZZG (2)

Though you are proud of your understanding and replete with insight, getting hold of the wisdom that knows at a glance, though you attain the way and clarify the mind, giving rise to the spirit that assaults the heavens, you may *loiter* in the precincts of the entrance and still lack *something* of the *vital* path of liberation. Even in the case of *the one of Jetavana,* innately wise though he was, *we can see* the traces of his six years sitting erect; and in the case of *the one of Shao-lin,* though he succeeded to the mind seal, we *still hear of the fame* of his nine years facing the wall. When even the ancient sages were like this, how could men today dispense with pursuing [the way]? Therefore, *stop* the intellectual practice of investigating words and chasing after talk; *study* the backward step of turning the light and shining it back. Body and mind will drop away of themselves, and your original face will appear. If you want such a state, urgently work at *such a state.*

CYCK

Then cast aside all involvements and discontinue all affairs. Make body and mind one, with no division between action and rest. **Regulate food and drink,** so that you take neither too much nor too little; adjust sleep, so that you neither deprive nor indulge yourself.

FKZZG (1)

For studying Zen, **one should have quiet quarters. Be moderate in food and drink. Then cast aside all involvements and discontinue all affairs. Do not think of good or evil;** do not deal with right or wrong. Halt the revolutions of mind, intellect, and consciousness; stop the calculations of thought, ideas, and perceptions.

FKZZG (2)

For studying Zen, **one should have quiet quarters. Be moderate in food and drink. Cast aside all involvements and discontinue all affairs. Do not think of good or evil;** do not deal with right or wrong. Halt the revolutions of mind, intellect, and consciousness; stop the calculations of thoughts, ideas, and perceptions. *Do not intend to make a Buddha, much less be attached to sitting still.*

SBGZ

Studying Zen is zazen. For zazen, **one should have a quiet place. Spread a thick mat.** *Do not let in drafts or vapors, rain or frost; secure and maintain the place where you practice. There are examples from the past of those who sat on a vajra or a rock; they all put down a thick layer of grass to sit on. The place where you sit should be bright, both day and night; and it is wise to keep it warm in winter and cool in summer.* **Cast aside all involvements and discontinue all affairs. Good is not thought of; evil is not thought of.** *It is not* mind, intellect or consciousness; *it is not* thoughts, ideas or perceptions. Do not intend to make a Buddha; *slough off* sitting still. **Be moderate in food and drink.** *Hold dear the passing time, and take to zazen as though brushing a fire from your head. Thus did the Fifth Patriarch on Huang-mei shan devote himself solely to zazen, to the exclusion of all other activities.*

CYCK

When you sit in meditation, **spread a thick mat in a quiet place. Loosen your robe and belt, and assume a proper demeanor. Then sit in the full cross-legged position. First place your right foot on your left thigh; then place your left foot on your right thigh.** Or you may **sit in the half cross-legged position: simply rest your left foot on your right** foot.

FKZZG (1)

When you sit, **spread a thick mat** and use a cushion on top of it. **Then sit in either the full cross-legged or half cross-legged position.** For the full position, **first place your right foot on your left thigh; then place your left foot on your right thigh.** For the half position, **simply rest your left foot on your right** thigh.

FKZZG (2)

In the place where you regularly sit, **spread a thick mat** and use a cushion on top of it. **Sit in either the full cross-legged or half cross-legged position.** For the full position, **first place your right foot on your left thigh; then place your left foot on your right thigh.** For the half position, **simply rest your left foot on your right** thigh.

SBGZ

When you sit in meditation, *you should wear your surplice.* Put down a cushion. *The cushion should not be placed completely under your legs but only under the rear half, so that your crossed legs rest on the mat and your spine on the cushion. This is the way that all the Buddhas and Patriarchs have sat when they did zazen.* **Sit in either the full cross-legged or half cross-legged position.** For the full position, **place your right foot on your left thigh, and your left foot on your right thigh.** *The toes should lie along the thighs, neither extending beyond nor falling short of them.* For the half position, **simply place your left foot on your right** thigh.

BDH

When you sit in meditation, use a cushion. **Sit in the full cross-legged position.** For the full position, **first place your right foot on your left thigh; then place your left foot on your right thigh.** *Or you may* sit in the half cross-legged position: simply rest your left foot on your right *foot.*

CYCK

Next, place your right hand on your left foot, and your left hand on your right palm. Press the tips of your thumbs together. Slowly raise your torso and stretch it forward. Swing to the left and right; then straighten your body and sit erect. Do not lean to the left or right, forward or backward.

FKZZG (1)

Loosen your robe and belt, and arrange them properly. Next, place your right hand on your left foot, and your left hand on your right palm. Press the tips of your thumbs together. Then straighten your body and sit erect. Do not lean to the left or right, forward or backward.

FKZZG (2)

Loosen your robe and belt, and arrange them properly. Next, place your right hand on your left foot, and your left hand on your right palm. Press the tips of your thumbs together. Then straighten your body and sit erect. Do not lean to the left or right, forward or backward.

SBGZ

Loosen your robe and *underwaist,* and arrange them properly. Place your right hand on your left foot, and your left hand on your right *hand.* Press the tips of your thumbs together. *With your hands in this position, place them against your body, so that the joined thumb tips are aligned with your navel.* Straighten your body and sit erect. Do not lean to the left or right, forward or backward.

BDH

Next, place your right hand on your left foot, and your left hand on your right palm. Press the tips of your thumbs together. Straighten your body and sit erect: *align the top of your head and your backbone, so that you are upright and straight.* Do not lean to the left or right, forward or backward.

CYCK

Keep your hips, back, neck, and head in line, making your posture like a stūpa. But do not strain your body upward too far, lest it make your breathing forced and unsettled. **Your ears should be in line with your shoulders, and your nose in line with your navel. Press your tongue against the front of your palate, and close your lips and teeth. The eyes should remain** slightly **open,** in order to prevent drowsiness. If you attain samādhi [with the eyes open], it will be the most powerful. In ancient times, there were monks eminent in the practice of meditation who always sat with their eyes open. More recently, the Ch'an master Fa-yün Yüan-t'ung criticized those who sit in meditation with their eyes closed, likening [their practice] to the ghost cave of the Black Mountain. Surely this has a deep meaning, known to those who have mastered [meditation practice].

FKZZG (1)

Your ears should be in line with your shoulders, and your nose in line with your navel. Press your tongue against the front of your palate and close your lips and teeth. The eyes should always **remain open.**

FKZZG (2)

Your ears should be in line with your shoulders, and your nose in line with your navel. Press your tongue against the front of your palate and close your lips and teeth. The eyes should always **remain open.** *Breathe gently through the nose.*

SBGZ

Your ears should be in line with your shoulders, and your nose in line with your navel. Press your tongue against the front of your palate. Breathe through the nose. **Close your lips and teeth. The eyes should be kept open,** *neither too widely nor too narrowly.*

BDH

Your ears should be in line with your shoulders, and your nose in line with your navel. Press your tongue against the front of your palate, and close your lips and teeth. The eyes should be *properly* **open,** *neither too widely nor too narrowly. Do not let your eyelids cover your pupils, nor your neck deviate from [the line of] your back. Let your breath pass through your nose; do not pant or rasp, nor make your breath too long or too short, too gentle or too forced.*

CYCK

Once you have settled your posture and regulated your breathing, you should relax your abdomen. **Do not think of any good or evil whatsoever. Whenever a thought occurs, be aware of it; as soon as you are aware of it, it will vanish. If you remain for a long period forgetful of objects, you will naturally become unified. This is the essential art of tso-ch'an.** Honestly speaking, **tso-ch'an is the dharma gate of ease and joy.** If there are many people who become ill [from its practice], it is because they do not take proper care.

FKZZG (1)

Once you have settled your posture, you should regulate your breathing. *Whenever a thought occurs, be aware of it; as soon as you are aware of it, it will vanish. If you remain for a long period forgetful of objects, you will naturally become unified.* **This is the essential art of zazen. Zazen is the dharma gate of** *great* **ease and joy.**

FKZZG (2)

Once you have regulated your posture, *take a breath and exhale fully.* **Swing to the left and right.** *Sitting fixedly, think of not thinking. How do you think of not thinking? Nonthinking.* **This is the essential art of zazen. Zazen is** *not the practice of dhyāna: it is just* **the dharma gate of ease and joy.** *It is the practice and verification of ultimate bodhi. The kōan realized, baskets and cages cannot get to it.*

SBGZ

Having thus regulated body *and mind,* take a breath and exhale fully. Sitting fixedly, think of not thinking. How do you think of not thinking? Nonthinking. **This is the art of zazen. Zazen is** not the practice of dhyāna: it is **the dharma gate of** great **ease and joy.** *It is undefiled practice and verification.*

BDH

Having regulated body *and mind,* **raise your torso** and exhale fully *several times.* **Relax** *both inside and out.* **Swing to the left and right** *seven or eight times.* Sitting fixedly, think of not thinking. How do you think of not thinking? Nonthinking. **This is the essential art of zazen.**

CYCK

If you grasp the point of this [practice], the four elements [of the body] will become light and at ease, the spirit will be fresh and sharp, thoughts will be correct and clear; the flavor of the dharma will sustain the spirit, and you will be calm, pure, and joyful. One who has already achieved clarification [of the truth] may be likened to the dragon gaining the water or the tiger taking to the mountains. And even one who has not yet achieved it, by letting the wind fan the flame, will not have to make much effort. Just assent to it; you will not be deceived. Nevertheless, as the path gets higher, demons flourish, and agreeable and disagreeable experiences are manifold. **Yet if you just keep right thought present,** none of them can obstruct you. The *Śūraṅgama-sūtra*, T'ien-t'ai's *Chih-kuan*, and Kuei-feng's *Hsiu-cheng i* give detailed explications of these demonic occurrences, and those who would be prepared in advance for the unforeseen should be familiar with them.

FKZZG (1)

If you grasp the point of this [practice], *the four elements [of the body] will become light and at ease, the spirit will be fresh and sharp, thoughts will be correct and clear; the flavor of the dharma will sustain the spirit, and you will be calm, pure, and joyful.* Your *daily life will be [the expression of] your true natural state.* **Once you achieve clarification [of the truth], you may be likened to the dragon gaining the water or the tiger taking to the mountains.** You should realize that **when right thought is present,** dullness and agitation *cannot intrude.*

FKZZG (2)

If you grasp the point of this [practice], you are like the dragon gaining the water or the tiger taking to the mountains. You should realize that **when right thought is present,** dullness and agitation are, *from the start, struck aside.*

CYCK

When you come out of samādhi, **move slowly and arise calmly; do not be hasty or rough.** After you have left samādhi, **always** employ appropriate means to **protect and maintain the power of samādhi,** as though you were protecting an infant. Then your samādhi power will easily develop. **This one teaching of meditation** is our most urgent business. If you do not practice meditation and enter dhyāna, then when it comes down to it, you will be completely at a loss. Therefore, to seek the pearl, we should still the waves; if we disturb the water, it will be hard to get. When the water of meditation is clear, the pearl of the mind will appear of itself. Therefore, the *Perfect Enlightenment Sūtra* says, "Unimpeded, immaculate wisdom always arises dependent on meditation." The *Lotus Blossom Sūtra* says, "In a quiet place, he practices the control of the mind, abiding motionless like Mt. Sumeru."

FKZZG (1)

When you arise from sitting, **move slowly and arise calmly; do not be hasty or rough. At all times protect and maintain the power of samādhi.** *In studying and investigating it, you transcend its higher workings, without a basis to rely on. In verifying and letting go of it, you are obstructed by the self, wherein you are never impeded. This is the full realization of the way. Truly* **this one teaching of meditation** *is the highest, the supreme. First taking up a full understanding and then turning over a half verification—such belongs solely to this dharma. Holding up a flower and breaking into a smile, making a bow and attaining the marrow—such represents the great freedom gained through the power of its grace. How could* **bodhisattvas who study prajñā** *fail to follow and accord with it?*

FKZZG (2)

When you arise from sitting, **move slowly and arise calmly; do not be hasty or rough.**

BDH

When you arise from sitting, **arise slowly.**

CYCK

Thus, **transcending the profane and surpassing the holy are always contingent on the condition of dhyāna; shedding [this body] while seated and fleeing [this life] while standing are** necessarily dependent on **the power of samādhi.**

FKZZG (1)

Considering the past, we see that **transcending the profane and surpassing the holy** *are always contingent on the condition of dhyāna;* **shedding [this body] while seated and fleeing [this life] while standing are** fully subject to **the power** *of samādhi.* Surely, then, turning the opportunity with a finger, a pole, a needle or a mallet, and verifying the accord with a whisk, a fist, a staff or a shout—these are not to be understood through the discriminations of thinking; much less can they be known through the practice and verification of supernormal powers. They must represent conduct beyond sound and form; how could they fail to provide a standard prior to our knowledge and understanding?

FKZZG (2)

Considering the past, we see that **transcending the profane and surpassing the holy, shedding [this body] while seated and fleeing [this life] while standing are** totally subject to *this* **power.** Surely, then, *to grasp* the turning of the opportunity through a finger, a pole, a needle or a mallet, and *to present* the verification of the accord with a whisk, a fist, a staff or a shout—these are not to be understood through the discriminations of thinking; much less can they be known through the practice and verification of supernormal powers. They must represent conduct beyond sound and form; how could they fail to provide a standard before knowledge and understanding?

FKZZG (1)

Therefore, it does not matter whether one is very smart or very stupid; there is no distinction between those of sharp and dull faculties. *If you let go of the six senses, you see and turn the whole path; if you do not produce a single thought, you sit and cut off the ten directions.* Both in our world and the other quarters, *the Buddha dharma originally has no other dharma*; from the Western Heavens to the Eastern Earth, *the Patriarchal gate eventually opens five gates.* All equally maintain the Buddha seal, while each enjoys its own style of teaching. They devote themselves only to *single transmission and direct pointing; they engage solely in reversing the body and turning the head.* Though they speak of a thousand differences and ten thousand distinctions, they only *delight in the full investigation of the homeward course.*

FKZZG (2)

Therefore, it does not matter whether one is very smart or very stupid; there is no distinction between those of sharp and dull faculties. *Single-minded exertion is itself pursuit of the way. Practice and verification are by nature undefiled. Advancement [to enlightenment] is just an everyday affair.* In our world and the other quarters, from the Western Heaven to the Eastern Earth, all equally maintain the Buddha seal, while each enjoys its own style of teaching. They devote themselves only to *to sitting; they are obstructed by fixedness.* Though they speak of ten thousand distinctions and a thousand differences, they only *study Zen and pursue the way.*

CYCK

Even if one devotes himself to the practice his entire life, he may still not be in time; how then could one who procrastinates possibly overcome karma? Therefore, an ancient has said, "Without the power of samādhi, you will meekly cower at death's door." Shutting your eyes, you will end your life in vain; and just as you are, you will drift [in saṃsāra].

FKZZG (1)

Why leave behind the seat in your own home to wander in vain through the dusty regions of another land? If you make one false step, you miss what is right before you. Since you have already attained *the proper conjunction* for a human body, do not pass your days in vain; when one *always bears in mind the appropriate conduct* of the way of the Buddha, who can carelessly enjoy the spark from a flint? Verily form and substance are like the dew on the grass, and the fortunes of life like the lightning flash: in an instant they are emptied, in a moment they are lost.

FKZZG (2)

Why abandon the seat in your own home to wander in vain through the dusty regions of another land? If you make one false step, you miss what is right before you. Since you have already attained the *functioning essence* of a human body, do not pass your days in vain; when one *takes care of the essential function* of the way of the Buddha, who can carelessly enjoy the spark from a flint? Verily form and substance are like the dew on the grass, and the fortunes of life like the lightning flash: in an instant they are emptied, in a moment they are lost.

CYCK

Friends in Ch'an, go over this text again and again. Benefitting others as well as ourselves, let us together achieve full enlightenment.

FKZZG (1)

Eminent students [of the dharma], long accustomed to groping for the elephant, pray do not doubt the true dragon. *Promptly take* the *right* way, which points directly at reality; *quickly become* the *true* man, through with learning and free from action. *Then will you comply with the rule of Po-chang and everywhere convey the circumstances of Shao-lin. Do not trouble yourself over winds that offend the ear nor be upset by sounds of the wagging tongue. Just directly open* your own treasure store and use it as you will.

FKZZG (2)

Eminent students [of the dharma], long accustomed to groping for the elephant, pray do not doubt the true dragon. *Apply yourselves to* the way that points directly at reality; *honor* the man who is through with learning and free from action. *Accord with the bodhi of all the Buddhas; succeed to the samādhi of all the Patriarchs. If you act this way for a long time, you will be this way.* Your treasure store *will open of itself*, and you will use it as you will.

Document 3

"Lancet of Seated Meditation"

This translation of Dōgen's *Shōbō genzō zazen shin* is based on the edition published at DZZ.1:90–101, which generally follows the text of an early manuscript, preserved at Kōfuku ji, in Kumamoto, thought by some to be in Dōgen's own hand. (See Mizuno Yaoko, "Shōbō genzō no shohon sono ta ni tsuite," in the introduction to *Shōbō genzō Shōbō genzō zuimon ki*, ed. by Nishio Minoru et al., *Nihon koten bungaku taikei* 81 [1965], 51–52. The manuscript has been published in *Dōgen zenji shinseki kankei shiryō shū* [1980], 421–34.) Such minor variants as exist in other texts are noted in the DZZ edition and are not repeated here. Other English versions of this work have appeared in Nishiyama Kōsen, *Shōbōgenzō*, vol. 4 (1983), 47–56; in Yokoi Yūhō, *The Shōbō-genzō* (1985), 133–47; and (in part) in Hee-jin Kim, *Flowers of Emptiness: Selections from Dōgen's Shōbōgenzō* (1985), 157–65. Terms and passages in bold type here represent material from the root texts on which Dōgen is commenting; square brackets indicate my interpolations.

LANCET OF SEATED MEDITATION

Kannon Dōri Kōshō Hōrin ji[1]

Once, when the Great Master Hung-tao of Yüeh shan was sitting [in meditation], a monk asked him,

"What are you thinking, [sitting there] so fixedly?"
The master answered, "I'm thinking of not thinking."

---

1. The monastery, in Fukakusa (present Fushimi ward, Kyoto), where Dōgen lived from 1233 to 1243. The DZZ text carries the additional title, "Treasury of the Eye of the True Dharma, Number 12," but this designation does not appear in the Kōfuku ji manuscript; it reflects rather the work's location in the 75-fascicle redaction of the *Shōbō genzō*. The *Zazen shin* is not included in either the 60- or 28-fascicle redactions.

The monk asked, "How do you think of not thinking?"
The master answered, "Nonthinking." [2]

Verifying that such are the words of the Great Master, we should study and participate in the correct transmission of fixed sitting. This is the investigation of fixed sitting transmitted in the way of the Buddha. Although he is not alone in **thinking fixedly**, Yüeh-shan's words are singular: he is **thinking of not thinking**. [These words express] what is the very skin, flesh, bones and marrow of **thinking** and the very skin, flesh, bones and marrow of **not thinking**.

The monk asked, "How do you think of not thinking?" Indeed, though [the notion of] **not thinking** may be old, here it is [the question], **how do you think** of it? Could there be no **thinking** [in sitting] **fixedly**? In [sitting] **fixedly**, how could we fail to penetrate [this]? [3] If we are not the sort of fool that despises what is near, we ought to have the strength—and the **thinking**—to question [sitting] **fixedly**. [4]

The master answered, "Nonthinking." Although the employment of **nonthinking** is crystal clear, when we **think of not thinking**, we always use **nonthinking**. There is someone in **nonthinking**, and this someone maintains us. Although it is we who are [sitting] **fixedly**, [our sitting] is not merely **thinking**: it presents itself as [sitting] **fixedly**. Although [sitting] **fixedly** is [sitting] **fixedly**, how could it **think** of [sitting] **fixedly**? Therefore, sitting **fixedly** is not the measure of the Buddha, not the measure of awakening, not the measure of comprehension. [5]

---

2.   Great Master Hung-tao is the posthumous title of Yüeh-shan Wei-yen (751–834), disciple of the important figure Shih-t'ou Hsi-ch'ien. This conversation appears in the former's biography in the *Ching-te ch'uan teng lu*, T.51:311c26ff. For discussion of the terms here and Dōgen's treatment of them, see Chapter 6.

3.   *Gotsugotsu chi no kōjō nani ni yorite ka tsūzezaru*. A tentative translation. Some interpreters would read *gotsugotsu chi no kōjō* here as referring to a state "beyond [sitting] fixedly." Throughout this discussion, Dōgen is treating the adverb *gotsugotsu chi* ("fixedly," also "toweringly") as a nominal expression equivalent to *gotsuza* ("fixed sitting")—hence, my rather awkward "[sitting] fixedly."

4.   From the old Chinese saying, "The ordinary man values what is distant and despises what is near." Here, as later, the translation loses Dōgen's play on *ryō* ("measure"), in the expressions *shiryō* ("thinking") and *rikiryō* ("strength").

5.   This is one of the more obscure "arguments" in the text. I understand the passage to say something like the following. Although nonthinking is an enlightened activity, free from all obstructions to knowledge (as in the Zen expression, "all eight sides are crystal clear [*hachimen reirō*]"), it is a distinct act of cognition, with its own agent (the enlightened "someone" [*tare*] who is present in all our cognitive states). But the activity of nonthinking in meditation is not merely a matter of cognitive states: it is the identification with the act of "sitting fixedly" itself. When one is thus fully identified with the act, it is beyond what can be thought of or measured, even through the notions of Buddhahood or awakening.

My rather clumsy phrase, "It presents itself as [sitting] **fixedly**," attempts to preserve something of the grammatical play in Dōgen's *gotsugotsu chi... gotsugotsu chi o kotō su*. The invocation here of the "someone" that sustains us in our nonthinking may remind some of traditional Buddhist discussions of what mental factor it is that continues during states of mental cessation. "Measure of the Buddha" (*butsuryō*) can be taken as "what is validated on the authority of the Buddha (*buddha-pramāṇa*)"; here again, Dōgen is playing with the graph *ryō* in *shiryō*.

The single transmission of this [sitting **fixedly**] by Yüeh-shan represents the thirty-sixth generation directly from the Buddha Śākyamuni: if we trace back from Yüeh-shan thirty-six generations, we come to the Buddha Śākyamuni. And in what was thus correctly transmitted [from the Buddha] there was already [Yüeh-shan's] **thinking of not thinking**.[6]

Recently, however, some stupid illiterates say, "Once the breast is without concerns, the concentrated effort at seated meditation is a state of peace and calm." This view does not compare with that of the Hīnayāna scholastics; it is inferior even to the vehicles of men and gods. How could one [who holds such a view] be called a man who studies the teaching of the Buddha? At present, there are many such practitioners in the Great Sung. How sad that the path of the Patriarchs has become overgrown.[7]

Then there is another type [which holds] that to pursue the way through seated meditation is a function essential for the beginner's mind and the late student, but it is not necessarily an observance of the Buddhas and Patriarchs. Walking is Zen, sitting is Zen; whether in speech or silence, motion or rest, the substance is at ease.[8] [Therefore, they say,] do not adhere solely to the present concentrated effort [of seated meditation]. This view is common among those calling themselves a branch of the Lin-chi [lineage]. It is because of a deficiency in the transmission of the orthodox lineage of the teaching of the Buddha that they say this. What is the "beginner's mind?" Where is there no beginner's mind? Where do we leave the beginner's mind?

Be it known that, for studying the way, the established [means of] investigation is pursuit of the way in seated meditation. The essential point that marks this [investigation] is [the understanding] that there is a practice of a Buddha that does not seek to make a Buddha. Since the practice of a Buddha is not to make a Buddha, it is the realization of the *kōan*. The embodied Buddha does not make a Buddha; when the baskets and cages are broken, a seated Buddha does not interfere with making a Buddha. At just such a time—from one thousand, from ten thousand ages past, from

---

6. Wei-yen is listed as the thirty-sixth Patriarch in the lineage of Ju-ching in Dōgen's *Shōbō genzō busso*, DZZ.1:456.

7. The "vehicles of men and gods" (*ninten jō*) are the "pre-Hīnayāna" approaches to religion, the lowest of the traditional five vehicles. "Illiterates" renders Dōgen's *zuzan*, literally "Tu authors (or compositions)"—that is, those who, like Tu (most often identified as the Sung poet Tu Mo), are ignorant of classical precedents; one of Dōgen's favorite insults. "Without concerns" (*buji*), an expression made famous by Lin-chi, was used at one time in Ch'an literature as a virtue, but by Dōgen's day it had tended to become identified with the vice of quietism. The exact source of the illiterates' opinion here is unclear; the same view is criticized in Ta-hui's *Letters*, where he takes to task those who make concentrated effort (*kung-fu*) in a quiet place: "If they happen to achieve a state in which the breast is without concerns [*hsiung chung wu shih*], they think this is the ultimate ease and joy. They do not realize it is simply like a stone pressing down grass." ("Letter to Councilor Fu," *Ta-hui yü lu*, T.48:921c.)

8. From the *Cheng tao ko*, *Ching-te ch'uan teng lu*, T.51:460b16.

the very beginning—we have the power to enter into Buddha and enter into Māra. Walking forward or back, its measure fills the ditches and moats.[9]

When the Ch'an master Ta-chi of Chiang-hsi was studying with the Ch'an master Ta-hui of Nan-yüeh, after intimately receiving the mind seal, he always sat in meditation. Once Nan-yüeh went to Ta-chi and said, "Worthy one, what are you figuring to do, sitting there in meditation?"[10]

We should calmly give concentrated effort to the investigation of this question. Does it mean that there must be some **figuring** above and beyond **seated meditation**? Is there no path to be **figured** outside of **seated meditation**? Should there be no **figuring** at all? Or does it ask what kind of **figuring** occurs at the very time we are practicing **seated meditation**? We should make concentrated effort to understand this in detail. Rather than love the carved dragon, we should go on to love the real dragon. We should learn that both the carved and the real dragons have the ability [to produce] clouds and rain. Do not value what is far away, and do not despise it; become completely familiar with it. Do not despise what is near at hand, and do not value it; become completely familiar with it. Do not take the eyes lightly, and do not give them weight. Do not give weight to the ears, and do not take them lightly. Make your eyes and ears clear and sharp.[11]

Chiang-hsi said, "I'm figuring to make a Buddha."

We should clarify and penetrate the meaning of these words. What does it mean to speak of **making a Buddha**? Does it mean to be **made a Buddha** by the Buddha? Does it mean to **make a Buddha** of the Buddha? Does it mean that one or two faces of the Buddha emerge? Is it that **figuring to**

---

9. For my interpretation of this difficult passage, see Chapter 6. "Entering into Māra [The Evil One] (*ma ni iru*)" is used to express the spiritual freedom of advanced Zen practice, as in the saying, "You can enter into Buddha, but you cannot yet enter into Māra." (*Tsung-men wu-k'u*, T.47:950a15.) A similar freedom is celebrated in the expression, "filling the ditches and moats (*mizo ni michi tani ni mitsu*)," as in the saying, "When we vainly expend concentrated effort, we build a cart to fit the ruts; when we are fundamentally without any skills, it clogs the moats and fills the ditches." (*Hung-chih kuang lu*, T.48:22c18.)

10. Ch'an Master Ta-chi is the posthumous title of the famous Ma-tsu Tao-i (709–88); Ch'an Master Ta-hui is Nan-yüeh Huai-jang (677–744), reputed disciple of the Sixth Patriarch. Their conversation can be found at *Ching-te ch'uan teng lu*, T.51:240c18ff; but note that Dōgen's introduction to the conversation here (as in his *Sanbyaku soku*, DZZ.2:202) includes elements from Ma-tsu's biography (*Ching-te ch'uan teng lu*, T.51:245c26f) to make it appear—as the original version does not—that he had already received his master's certification when the conversation took place. For a translation of the *Ching-te ch'uan teng lu* version and my discussion of Dōgen's treatment of this story, see Chapter 6.

11. From the old Chinese saying, "To give weight to the ears and take the eyes lightly is the constant failing of the common man." The "carved dragon" is from the ancient story of the Duke of She, who loved the image of the dragon but was terrified of the real thing. Commentators since Kyōgō have sought to identify the "carved dragon" here with meditation practice and the "real dragon" with its fruit (*Shōbō genzō chūkai zensho* 4:89), but the passage might better be seen simply as advice on how to read a Zen text.

make a Buddha is sloughing off [body and mind], and [that what is meant here is] a **figuring to make a Buddha** as [the act of] sloughing off? Or does **figuring to make a Buddha** mean that, while there are ten thousand ways to **make a Buddha**, they become entangled in this **figuring**?[12]

It should be recognized that Ta-chi's words mean that **seated meditation** is always **figuring to make a Buddha**, is always the **figuring** of **making a Buddha**. This **figuring** must be prior to **making a Buddha**; it must be subsequent to **making a Buddha**; and it must be at the very moment of **making a Buddha**. Now what I ask is this: How many [ways of] **making a Buddha** does this one **figuring** entangle? These entanglements themselves intertwine with entanglements. At this point, entanglements, as individual instances of the entirety of **making a Buddha**, are all direct statements of that entirety and are all instances of **figuring**. We should not seek to avoid this one **figuring**: when we avoid the one **figuring**, we destroy our body and lose our life. When we destroy our body and lose our life, this is the entanglement of the one **figuring**.[13]

At this point, Nan-yüeh took up a tile and began to rub it on a stone. At length, Ta-chi asked, "Master, what are you doing?"

Who could fail to see that he was **polishing a tile**? Who could see that he was **polishing a tile**? Still, **polishing a tile** has been questioned in this way: **"What are you doing?"** This **"What are you doing?"** is itself always **polishing a tile**. This land and the other world may differ, but the essential message of **polishing a tile** never ceases. Not only should we avoid deciding that what we see is what we see, we should be firmly convinced that there is an essential message to be studied in all the ten thousand activities. We should know that, just as we may see the Buddha without knowing or

---

12. "Sloughing off [body and mind]" (*shinjin datsuraku*) is Dōgen's famous term for Zen enlightenment. "Entangled" here renders *kattō* [*su*], Dōgen's verbal form of the "vines and creepers" used in Zen to express the spiritual complications of language—including the language of Zen discourse on the basis of which the meditator "figures to make a Buddha."

13. From the famous problem, posed by Hsiang-yen, of the man hanging by his teeth over a thousand-foot cliff who is asked the meaning of Bodhidharma's coming from the West: "If he opens his mouth to answer, he will destroy his body and lose his life." (*Ching-te ch'uan teng lu*, T.51:284b23ff.) The notion of intertwining entanglements is probably from a saying of Ju-ching, that the bottle gourd vine intertwines with itself (*Nyojō goroku*, T.48: 128b20), a remark praised as unprecedented by Dōgen in his *Shōbō genzō kattō* (DZZ.1:331). There he interprets *kattō* as succession to the *dharma* (*shihō*) and claims that true Zen practice is not merely, as is usually thought, to cut off the roots of entanglements but to intertwine entanglements with entanglements. I do not pretend to have figured out all the twists in this tangled passage, but one way of paraphrasing what seems to be the point here is this: the effort to practice, and achieve the goal of, Buddhism "entangles" us in the *dharma*; yet complete entanglement in the *dharma*—both in its discourse and its cult—is itself the goal of Buddhism; hence, the practice of "figuring" is completely "entangled" in the goal of "making a Buddha." Dōgen is clearly enjoying himself here with the multivalent notion of *kattō*—as the constricting language within which we ordinarily "figure," as the liberating language of the Zen *kōan*, and as the interdependence of the two in Zen study.

understanding Him, so we may see rivers and yet not know rivers, may see mountains and yet not know mountains. The precipitate assumption that the phenomena before one's eyes offer no further passage is not Buddhist study.

Nan-yüeh said, "I'm polishing this to make a mirror."

We should be clear about the meaning of these words. There is definitely a principle in **polishing [a tile] to make a mirror**: there is the *kōan* of realization; this is no mere empty contrivance. A **tile** may be a **tile** and a **mirror** a **mirror**, but when we exert ourselves in investigating the principle of **polishing**, we shall find there are many examples of it. The old mirror and the bright mirror—these are **mirrors** made through **polishing a tile**. If we do not realize that these **mirrors** come from **polishing a tile**, then the Buddhas and Patriarchs have nothing to say; they do not open their mouths, and we do not perceive them exhaling.

Ta-chi said, "How can you produce a mirror by polishing a tile?"

Indeed, though [the one who is] **polishing the tile** be a man of iron, who borrows no power from another, **polishing a tile** is not **producing a mirror**. And, even if it is **producing a mirror**, it must be quick about it.[14]

Nan-yüeh replied, "How can you make a Buddha by sitting in meditation?"

This is clearly understood: there is a principle that **seated meditation** does not await **making a Buddha**; there is nothing obscure about the essential message that **making a Buddha** is not connected with **seated meditation**.

Ta-chi asked, "Then, what is right?"

These words resemble a simple question about this [practical matter of **what** to do], but they are also asking about that [final] **rightness**. You should realize [that the relationship between **what** and **right** here is like], for example, the occasion when one friend meets another: the fact that he is my friend means that I am his friend. [Similarly, here the meanings of] **what** and **right** emerge simultaneously.[15]

---

14. For a discussion of this passage on the mirror, see Chapter 6. The "old mirror" (*kokyō*) and "bright mirror" (*meikyō*) are, of course, venerable symbols for the Buddha nature, or Buddha mind. The "man of iron" (*tekkan*) is the accomplished Zen practitioner.

15. Ma-tsu's question here (*ikan sokuze*) might be more naturally put, "What should I do?" But Dōgen seems to be suggesting that the question "what" (*ikan*) is itself what is "right" (*sokuze*), or that, like the relationship between "figuring" and "making a Buddha," they are interdependent. As should be apparent from the amount of interpolation in the translation, the passage is highly elliptical.

Nan-yüeh replied, "When a man is driving a cart, if the cart doesn't go, should he beat the cart or beat the ox?"

Now, when we say **the cart doesn't go**, what do we mean by the cart's **going** or **not going**? For example, is the cart **going** [analogous to] water flowing, or is it [analogous to] water not flowing? [There is a sense in which] we can say that flowing is water's **not going**, and that water's **going** is not its flowing. Therefore, when we investigate the words, **the cart doesn't go**, we should approach them both in terms of **not going** and in terms of not **not going**; for it is a question of time. The words, **if [the cart] doesn't go**, do not mean simply that it does not go.[16]

Should he beat the cart or beat the ox? Does this mean there is a **beating of the cart** as well as a **beating of the ox**? Are **beating the cart** and **beating the ox** the same or not? In the world, there is no method of **beating the cart**; but, though ordinary men have no such method, we know that on the path of the Buddha there is a method of **beating the cart**, and this is the very eye of [Buddhist] study. Even though we study that there is a method of **beating the cart**, we should give concentrated effort to understanding in detail that this is not the same as **beating the ox**. And even though the method of **beating the ox** is common in the world, we should go on to study the **beating of the ox** on the path of the Buddha. Is this **ox-beating** the water buffalo, or **ox-beating** the iron bull or the clay ox? Is this beating with a whip, with the entire world, the entire mind? Is this to beat by using the marrow? Should we beat with the fist? The fist should beat the fist, and the ox beat the ox.[17]

Ta-chi did not reply.

---

16.   Dōgen is here doubtless alluding to the Buddhist doctrine of impermanence, according to which we cannot step in the same water twice. The notion of water's nonflowing is best known from the line attributed to Fu Ta-shih, "The bridge flows and the water doesn't" (*Ching-te ch'uan teng lu*, T.51:430b7); Dōgen explores this and other notions of water in his *Shōbō genzō sansui kyō* (DZZ.1:258–67). Huai-jang's metaphor of the cart and ox probably reflects a story in the *Ta chuang-yen lun ching* (T.4:266a), where the terms indicate body and mind, respectively.

17.   My barbarous "ox-beating" here tries to retain something of the double accusative in forms such as *suikogyū o dagyū su*. References to these various bovines appear frequently in Zen literature; we may take Dōgen's use of them here simply as an evocation of the rich spiritual resonance of his root text. My sentence on the "marrow" is tentative. Dōgen is clearly playing with the colloquial verbal marker *ta* ("to beat"), but I have not found the precedent for his *tahei zui*, and commentarial opinion on the interpretation of the predicate *hei* here is widely divided: Menzan (*Shōbō genzō chūkai zensho* 4:118) likes the primary sense "to scatter" (Morohashi entry 38929)—hence, his "to cause to gush forth"; Kishizawa (*Shōbō genzō zenkō*, vol. 11, 328) prefers the sense "to put together" (Morohashi 746)—hence, "the whole"; given the context, I follow Kyōgō (*Shōbō genzō chūkai zensho* 4:118) in reading "to make use of" (Morohashi 12236).

We should not miss [the import of] this. In it, there is throwing out a tile to take in a jade; there is turning the head and reversing the face. By no means should we do violence to his silence.[18]

Nan-yüeh went on, "Are you studying seated meditation or are you studying seated Buddha?"

Investigating these words, we should distinguish the essential activity of the Patriarchal ancestors. Without knowing what the full reality of **studying seated meditation** is, we do know here that it is **studying seated Buddha**. Who but a scion of true descent could say that **studying seated meditation** is **studying seated Buddha**? We should know indeed that the **seated meditation** of the beginner's mind is the first **seated meditation**, and the first **seated meditation** is the first **seated Buddha**. In speaking of this **seated meditation**, [Nan-yüeh] said,

"If you're studying seated meditation, meditation is not sitting still."[19]

The point of what he says here is that **seated meditation** is **seated meditation** and is not **sitting still**. From the time the fact that it is not **sitting still** has been singly transmitted to us, our unlimited **sitting still** is our own self. Why should we inquire about close or distant familial lines? How could we discuss delusion and awakening? Who would seek wisdom and eradication?[20] Then Nan-yüeh said,

"If you're studying seated Buddha, Buddha is no fixed mark."

Such is the way to say what is to be said. The reason the **seated Buddha** is one or two Buddhas is that He adorns Himself with **no fixed mark**. When [Nan-yüeh] says here that **Buddha is no fixed mark**, he is describing the mark of the Buddha. Since He is a Buddha of **no fixed mark**, the **seated Buddha** is difficult to avoid. Therefore, since it is adorned with this [mark of] **Buddha is no fixed mark**, if you're studying **seated meditation**,

---

18. To "throw out a tile and take in a jade" (*hōsen ingyoku*) is a polite way to ask for a capping verse for your poem; here it no doubt refers to the give and take of Ch'an repartee. "Turning the head and reversing the face" (*kaitō kanmen*) suggests the notions both of a (spiritual) reversal and of the inseparability of awakening and delusion—or, as probably in this case, of master and disciple.

19. *Zaga*, usually "sitting and lying down," is here probably better taken simply as "sitting."

20. Close and distant "familial lines" (*meimyaku*) here probably refers to the logical relationship between (our human) sitting and (the Buddha's) seated meditation; "wisdom and eradication [of the spiritual defilements]" (*chidan*) are the two primary factors that separate a Buddha from an ordinary man. The argument here would seem to be that (a) seated meditation is (the act of) a seated Buddha, not mere human sitting; (b) yet, once we recognize why this is so, we recognize that (higher) self—or inherent Buddhahood—that is present even in our human sitting; (c) in the light of this recognition, the distinction between our sitting and the Buddha's meditation, or between ignorance and enlightenment, is no longer ultimate.

you are a **seated Buddha. In a nonabiding** *dharma*, [as Nan-yüeh goes on to say,] who would **grasp or reject** [something] as not the Buddha? Who would **grasp or reject** it as the Buddha? It is because **[seated meditation]** has sloughed off all **grasping and rejecting** that it is a **seated Buddha.**[21] Nan-yüeh continues,

> **"If you're studying seated Buddha, this is killing Buddha."**

This means that, when we investigate further [the notion of] **seated Buddha**, [we find] it has the virtue of **killing Buddha**. At the very moment that we are a **seated Buddha** we are **killing Buddha**. Indeed, when we pursue it, [we find] that the [thirty-two] marks and [eighty] signs and the radiance of **killing Buddha** are always a **seated Buddha**. Although the word, **kill**, here is identical with that used by ordinary people, [its meaning] is not the same. Moreover, we must investigate in what form it is that a **seated Buddha** is **killing Buddha**. Taking up the fact that it is itself a virtue of the Buddha to **kill Buddha**, we should study whether we are killers or not.[22]

> **"If you grasp the mark of sitting, you're not reaching its principle."**

To **grasp the mark of sitting** here means to **reject the mark of sitting** and to touch **the mark of sitting**. The principle behind this is that, in being a **seated Buddha**, we cannot fail to **grasp the mark of sitting**. Since we cannot fail to **grasp it**, though our **grasping the mark of sitting** is crystal clear, we are **not reaching its principle**. This kind of concentrated effort is called "sloughing off body and mind."[23]

Those who have never sat do not talk like this: [such talk] belongs to the time of sitting and the man who sits, to the **seated Buddha** and the

---

21. Dōgen is here alluding to a sentence from Nan-yüeh's answer to Ma-tsu that he does not bother to quote: "In a nonabiding *dharma*, there should be no grasping or rejecting." The discussion of the "mark" (*sō*, *lakṣaṇa*) of the Buddha here and later is based on the famous doctrine of emptiness in the perfection of wisdom (*prajñā-pāramitā*) literature, where—as in the *Diamond Sūtra* so popular in Zen—we are told that the true mark of the Buddha is not His thirty-two major and eighty minor physical marks of spiritual excellence but precisely His freedom from all marks. Nan-yüeh's "nonabiding *dharma*" (*mujū hō*) derives from the closely cognate doctrine that all phenomena are without enduring natures. Dōgen's argument here can be seen as an amplification of his conclusion in the preceding paragraph.

22. We may recall here one of the most famous sayings of Zen: "If you meet the Buddha, kill the Buddha; if you meet a Patriarch, kill the Patriarch." (*Lin-chi lu*, T.47:500b22.) Dōgen's treatment of *setsubutsu*, "to kill the Buddha," here plays on the syntactical parallel with *zabutsu*, "seated Buddha," to suggest that the Buddha is subject as well as object of the predicate.

23. In his commentary on this difficult passage, Nishiari Bokusan advises us to take the verb "grasp" (*shū*) here to mean complete identification with seated meditation, and to understand the expression "not reaching its principle" to mean "has already reached its principle." (*Shōbō genzō keiteki*, ed. by Kurebayashi Kōdō, vol. 2 [1965], 574.) He is probably right that, to make sense of this passage, we must assume that here again Dōgen wants to give a positive connotation to both clauses of Nan-yüeh's sentence, though clearly in this case we shall have to reach quite far for his principle.

study of the **seated Buddha**. The sitting that occurs when the ordinary man sits is not [the sitting of] the **seated Buddha**. Although a man's sitting naturally resembles a **seated Buddha**, or a Buddha's sitting, the case is like that of a man's **making a Buddha**, or the man who makes a Buddha: though there are men who make Buddhas, not all men make Buddhas, and Buddhas are not all men. Since all the Buddhas are not simply all men, man is by no means a Buddha, and a Buddha is by no means a man. The same is true of a **seated Buddha**.

Here, then, in Nan-yüeh and Chiang-hsi we have a superior master and a strong disciple: Chiang-hsi is the one who verifies **making a Buddha** as a **seated Buddha**; Nan-yüeh is the one who points out the **seated Buddha** for **making a Buddha**. There was this kind of concentrated effort in the congregation of Nan-yüeh and words like the above in the congregation of Yüeh-shan.

Know this, that it is the seated Buddha that Buddha after Buddha and Patriarch after Patriarch have taken as their essential activity. Those who are Buddhas and Patriarchs have employed this essential activity, while those who are not have never even dreamt of it. To say that the *dharma* of the Buddha has been transmitted from the Western Heavens to the Eastern Earth implies the transmission of the seated Buddha, for it is the essential function [of that *dharma*].[24] And where the *dharma* of the Buddha is not transmitted, neither is seated meditation. What has been inherited by successor after successor [in this transmission] is just this message of seated meditation; one who does not participate in the unique transmission of this message is not a Buddha or a Patriarch. When one is not clear about this one *dharma*, he is not clear about the ten thousand *dharmas* or about the ten thousand practices. And without being clear about each of these *dharmas*, he cannot be said to have a clear eye. He has not attained the way; how could he represent the present or past [in the lineage] of the Buddhas and Patriarchs? By this, then, we should be firmly convinced that the Buddhas and Patriarchs always transmit seated meditation.

To be illumined by the radiance of the Buddhas and Patriarchs means to concentrate one's efforts in the investigation of this seated meditation. Some fools, misunderstanding the radiance of the Buddha, think it must be like the radiance of the sun or moon or the light from a pearl or a fire. But the light of the sun and moon is nothing but a mark of action within [the realm of] transmigration in the six destinies; it is not to be compared with the radiance of the Buddha. The radiance of the Buddha means receiving and hearing a single phrase, maintaining and protecting a single *dharma*,

---

24. The "Western Heavens" and the "Eastern Earth" (*saiten tōchi*) refer to India and China, respectively.

participating in the single transmission of seated meditation. So long as one is not illumined by the radiance [of the Buddha], he is not maintaining, nor has he accepted, [the Buddha's *dharma*].²⁵

This being the case, [throughout history] there have been few who understood seated meditation as seated meditation. And at present, in the [Ch'an] mountains of the great Sung, many of those who are heads of the principal monasteries do not understand, and do not study, seated meditation. There may be some who have clearly understood it but not many. Of course, the monasteries have fixed periods for seated meditation; the monks, from the abbot down, take seated meditation as their basic task; and, in leading their students, [the teachers] encourage its practice. Nevertheless, there are few abbots who understand it.

For this reason, although from ancient times to the present there have been one or two old worthies who have written [texts known as] "Inscriptions on Seated Meditation," "Principles of Seated Meditation," or "Lancets of Seated Meditation," among them there is nothing worth taking from any of the "Inscriptions on Seated Meditation," and the "Principles of Seated Meditation" are ignorant of its observances. They were written by men who do not understand, and do not participate in, its unique transmission. Such are the "Lancet of Seated Meditation" in the *Ching-te ch'uan teng lu* and the "Inscription on Seated Meditation" in the *Chia-t'ai p'u teng lu*.²⁶ What a pity that, though [the authors of such texts] spend their lives passing among the [Ch'an] groves of the ten directions, they do not have the concentrated effort of a single sitting—that sitting is not their own, and concentrated effort never encounters them.²⁷ This is not because seated meditation rejects their bodies and minds but because they do not aspire to the true concentrated effort and are precipitately given over to their delusion. What they have collected [in their texts] is nothing but models for

---

25. The "radiance of the Buddha" (*butsu kōmyō*) refers to both the "physical" aureola said to emanate from His body and the inner effulgence of His perfect wisdom that "illumines" the world. In his *Shōbō genzō* commentary on *kōmyō* (DZZ.1:116–17), Dōgen identifies this radiance with the spiritual tradition of Bodhidharma and, as here, criticizes those who think of it as visible light. In this, he may well have had in mind the mystical visualization of such light (*bukkō zanmai*) popularized in his day by the Kegon master Kōben (for which, see Chapter 3). The "six destinies" (*rokudō*) are the several states—from hell to heaven—that together constitute the mundane realm of *saṃsāra*; the Buddha, of course, is by definition beyond this realm. In Zen parlance, "a single phrase" (*ikku*) usually suggests an expression of enlightenment.

26. The last roll of the *Ch'uan teng lu*, compiled in 1004, includes a "Tso-ch'an chen" by Wu-yün (Chih-feng) Ho-shang (909-85) (T.51:459c–60a); the *Chia-t'ai p'u teng lu*, compiled in 1204, records a "Tso-ch'an ming" by Fo-yen (Lung-men Ch'ing-) Yüan Ch'an-shih (1067–1120) (ZZ.2B,10:214b). For more on such texts, see Chapter 3.

27. *Taza sude ni nanji ni arazu kufū sara ni onore to sōken se[zu].* A tentative translation of a passage variously interpreted. I take the point to be simply that they never properly sit and hence do not engage in true practice; some would prefer to read the second clause to mean that, in their practice, they never encounter their (true) selves. Note that here and in the following sentence Dōgen has personified Zen practice as a ⌐ ₋scious agent that encounters and chooses us.

reverting to the source and returning to the origin, vain programs for suspending considerations and congealing in tranquility. [Such views of meditation] do not approach the stages of observation, exercise, infusion, and cultivation, or the understandings of [those on the path of] the ten stages and the equivalence of enlightenment; how, then, could they be the single transmission of the seated meditation of the Buddhas and Patriarchs? The Sung chroniclers were mistaken to record [these texts], and later students should cast them aside and not read them.[28]

Among the "Lancets of Seated Meditation," the only one that is [an expression of] the Buddhas and Patriarchs is that by the Reverend Cheng-chüeh, the Ch'an Master Hung-chih of the Ching-te Monastery at T'ien-t'ung, renowned Mt. T'ai-po, in the district of Ching-yüan in the Great Sung.[29] This one is a [true] "Lancet of Seated Meditation." This one says it right. It alone radiates throughout the surface and interior of the realm of the *dharma*. It is [the statement of] a Buddha and Patriarch among the Buddhas and Patriarchs of past and present. Prior Buddhas and later Buddhas have been lanced by this "Lancet"; present Patriarchs and past Patriarchs appear from this "Lancet." Here is that "Lancet of Seated Meditation":

LANCET OF SEATED MEDITATION

by Cheng-chüeh
by imperial designation the Ch'an Master Hung-chih[30]

Essential function of all the Buddhas,
Functioning essence of all the Patriarchs—

---

28. The terms, "reverting to the source" and "returning to the origin" (*gengen henpon,* more often in reverse order, *henpon gengen*) both suggest a notion of spiritual practice as the process of recovering the "original mind"; the expression is best known in Zen as the title of the ninth of K'uo-an's famous "Ten Oxherding Pictures" (see *Jūgyū zu*, Kajitani, *Shinjin mei*, 134). "Suspending considerations" and "congealing in tranquility" (*sokuryo gyōjaku*) suggest calm transic states free from all thinking; a similar expression, "suspending considerations and forgetting objects (*hsi lü wang yüan*)," appears in Wu-yün's "Tso-ch'an chen" (T.51:459c27), though the text itself also warns against attachment to the cultivation of *samādhi*. "Observation, exercise, infusion, cultivation" (*kan ren kun ju*): a list of terms for the various "undefiled" (*wu-lou, anāsrava*) meditations; they are identified by Chih-i as the second of his three levels of meditation —the "transmundane" (*ch'u shih-chien, lokottara*) practices that rank above the "mundane" but below the "supreme (*shang-shang*) transmundane" (see, e.g., his *Fa-hua hsüan i*, T.33:719bff). "The ten stages and the equivalence of enlightenment" (*jūji tōgaku*) refer to the final phases of the *bodhisattva* path, the latter being the penultimate state, just preceding, but virtually equivalent to, Buddhahood.

29. Hung-chih Cheng-chüeh (1091–1157) was originally from present-day Shansi. He entered the order at the age of eleven and, after studying with various masters, succeeded to the *dharma* of Tan-hsia Tsu-ch'un (1064–1117). In 1129, he became abbot of T'ien-t'ung, where for the remainder of his life he was active in restoring the monastery and teaching his many students. He was famed as a man of letters and produced the collection of verses on one hundred old cases that became the core of the *Tsung-jung lu* (T. #2004). His biographical notice appears at *Hsü ch'uan teng lu*, T.51:579a; his recorded sayings, in nine rolls, are found at T.48:1.

30. The text appears in the *Hung-chih kuang lu*, T.48:98a29–b5. Cheng-chüeh received his title, "Ch'an Master Spacious Wisdom," from the Sung emperor Kao Tsung.

It knows without touching things,
It illumines without facing objects.
Knowing without touching things,
Its knowledge is inherently subtle;
Illumining without facing objects,
Its illumination is inherently mysterious.
Its knowledge inherently subtle,
It is ever without discriminatory thought;
Its illumination inherently mysterious,
It is ever without a hair's breadth of sign.
Ever without discriminatory thought,
Its knowledge is rare without peer;
Ever without a hair's breadth of sign,
Its illumination comprehends without grasping.
The water is clear right through to the bottom,
A fish goes lazily along.
The sky is vast without horizon,
A bird flies far far away.

The **lancet** in this **lancet of seated meditation** means the manifestation of the great function, the comportment beyond sight and sound; it is the juncture before your parents were born. It means you had better not slander the Buddhas and Patriarchs; you do not avoid destroying your body and losing your life; it is a head of three feet and a neck of two inches.[31]

Essential function of all the Buddhas,

The **Buddhas** always take the **Buddhas** as their **essential function**: this is the **essential function** that is realized here; this is **seated meditation**.

Functioning essence of all the Patriarchs—

My master had no such saying—this principle is [what is meant here by] **the Patriarchs**. [It is in this that] the *dharma* and the robe are transmitted. The faces [that are reversed] when we turn the head and reverse the face are **the essential function of all the Buddhas**; the heads [that

---

31.   A series of classical allusions to Zen expressions of enlightenment. "Manifestation of the great function" (*daiyō genzen*): see Yüan-wu's commentary to the *Pi-yen lu*, T.48:142c5. "Comportment beyond sight and sound" (*shōshiki kōjō igi*): after a line by Hsiang-yen Chih-hsien (d. 898), *Lien-teng hui yao*, ZZ.2B,9:283c8. "Juncture before your parents were born" (*fubo mishō zen*): after a question to Chih-hsien by his master Kuei-shan, ibid., 283b15. "You had better not slander the Buddhas and Patriarchs" (*maku bō busso kō*): here probably after a remark of Kuang-hsiao Hui-chüeh (dates unknown), *Lien-teng hui yao*, ZZ.279a16. "Do not avoid destroying your body and losing your life" (*mimen sōshin shitsumyō*): again from Chih-hsien (see n. 13); also see *Lin-chi lu*, T.47:496c26. "A head of three feet and a neck of two inches" (*zuchō sanjaku keitan nisun*): from Tung-shan Liang-chieh (807–69), *Ching-te ch'uan teng lu*, T.51:323a8.

turn] when we reverse the face and turn the head are **the functioning essence of all the Patriarchs.**[32]

It knows without touching things,

Knowing here, of course, does not mean perception; for perception is of little measure. It does not mean understanding; for understanding is artificially constructed. Therefore, this **knowing** is **not touching things**, and **not touching things** is **knowing.** [Such **knowing**] should not be measured as universal knowledge; it should not be categorized as self-knowledge. This **not touching things** means, when they come in the light, I hit them in the light; when they come in the dark, I hit them in the dark. It means sitting and breaking the skin born of mother.[33]

It illumines without facing objects.

This **illumining** does not mean the **illumining** of luminosity or of spiritual illumination: it means simply **without facing objects.** [In this meaning,] the **illumining** does not change into the **object**, for the **object** itself is **illumining. Without facing** means it is never hidden throughout the world, it does not emerge when you break the world. It is **subtle**; it is **mysterious**; it is interacting while not interacting.[34]

Its knowledge inherently subtle,
It is ever without discriminatory thought;

Thought is itself **knowing**, without dependence on another's power. **Its knowing** is its form, and its form is the mountains and rivers. These mountains and rivers are **subtle**, and this **subtlety** is **mysterious**. When we put it to use, it is brisk and lively. When we make a dragon, it does not matter whether we are inside or out of the Yü Gate. To put this single **knowing** to the slightest use is to take up the mountains and rivers of the entire world and **know** them with all one's power. Without our intimate

---

  32. "My master had no such saying" (*senshi mu shi go*): that is, the true Patriarchate lies beyond words; again, from a remark of Hui-chüeh, *Lien-teng hui yao*, ZZ.2B,9:279a16. "Essential function" and "functioning essence" translate *yōki* and *kiyō*, respectively. As binomes, both terms mean roughly what is pivotal, or essential; but it seems clear from his association of them with the head and face (for which, see n. 18) that Dōgen wants to understand the two component graphs in each as expressing the classical metaphysical categories of "substance" (head) and "function" (face), or essence and expression—hence, my rather forced translation.

  33. *Zaha jō shō hi*: that is, (sitting and) transcending the physical body. "When they come in the light... " is from a saying attributed to the Ch'an monk P'u-hua in the *Lin-chi lu* (T.47:503b20); though its interpretation is much debated, we may take it to suggest here the detached spontaneity of the mind in meditation.

  34. *Ego fu ego*: that is, (subject and object) are both independent and interdependent; from a line in the *Tsan t'ung ch'i*, of Shih-t'ou Hsi-ch'ien (700–791), *Ching-te ch'uan teng lu*, T.51:459b10. "Never hidden throughout the world" (*henkai fu zō zō*): that is, (the object) is always manifest; from a saying of Shih-shuang Ch'ing-chu (807–88), *Ching-te ch'uan teng lu*, T.51:321a4.

knowing of the mountains and rivers, we do not have a single knowing or a half understanding. We should not lament the late arrival of **discriminatory** thinking: the Buddhas of previous **discrimination** have already been realized. **Ever without** here means "previously"; "previously" means "[already] realized." Therefore, **ever without discrimination** means you do not meet a single person.[35]

> Its illumination inherently mysterious,
> It is ever without a hair's breadth of sign.

A hair's breadth here means the entire world; yet it is **inherently mysterious**, inherently **illumining**. Therefore, it is as if it is never brought out. The eyes are not to be doubted, nor the ears to be trusted. You should clarify the essential meaning apart from the sense; do not look to words to grasp the rule—this is [what is meant by] **illumining**. Therefore, it is **without peer**; therefore, it is **without grasping**. This has been preserved as being **rare** and maintained as **comprehending**, but I have doubts about it.[36]

> The water is clear right through to the bottom,
> A fish goes lazily along.

The water is clear: the **water** that has to do with the sky does not get **right through to the bottom** of [what is meant here by] **clear water**; still less is that which forms clear, deep pools in the vessel world the **water** [intended by the expression] **the water is clear**. That which has no shore as its boundary—this is what is meant by **clear water** penetrated **right**

---

35. *Fuhō ichinin*: from Tung-shan Liang-chieh's "definition" (*Ching-te ch'uan teng lu*, T.51:322c22) of the trackless path of his famous "way of the birds" (*niao tao*), on which one is said not to "meet anyone." The "Yü Gate" refers to the point on the Yellow River beyond which the climbing carp is said to change into a dragon; here, presumably a metaphor for the point of awakening. (The translation, "brisk and lively," loses the piscine imagery of Dōgen's *kappatsupatsu*, an onomatopoetic expression for the leaping of the fish.) I interpret this rather obscure passage to mean something like the following. The "subtle knowing" of the Buddhas clearly discriminates every phenomenon. We should not think that this (higher) "discriminatory thinking" is something for which we must wait; for it is "already realized" in each mind's inherent power of discrimination ("the Buddhas of previous discrimination" *isō funbetsu naru butsubutsu*). Cheng-chüeh's "ever without (*sōmu*) [discriminatory thought]" refers to this inherent (*isō*) power, which is "realized" (*genjō*) even in ordinary perception. The spiritual practice of one who understands this power is as free as Tung-shan's "way of the birds."

36. Dōgen's "doubts" (*gijaku*) here are probably best taken in the sense, "there is more to this than meets the eye," a common Zen usage seen, for example, in Lin-chi's response to the P'u-hua story cited earlier (q.v.). Cheng-chüeh's "sign," or "portent" (*chō*), suggests an indication of what is to come; his mysterious illumination, then, can be seen as knowledge of that which "precedes" all things. I take Dōgen's remarks to mean that, since this illumination is "inherent," or spontaneous (*jishō*), it is not brought about (*shōrai se[zu]*): it is to be found in ordinary sensory experience ("do not doubt the eyes"), if we but know where to look for it ("do not trust the ears"); we should look for it in the "meaning" (*shū*) that lies beyond the literal "sense" (*shi*) of Zen teaching.

through to the bottom. If a **fish** goes through this **water**, it is not that it does not **go**; yet, however many tens of thousands the degree of its progress, its **going** is immeasurable, inexhaustible. There is no shoreline by which it is gauged; there is no sky to which it ascends, nor bottom to which it sinks. And therefore there is no one who can take its measure. If we try to discuss its measure, [all we can say is that] it is only **clear water** penetrated **right through to the bottom**. The virtue of seated meditation is like the **fish going**: who can calculate its degree in thousands or tens of thousands? The degree of the **going** that penetrates **right through to the bottom** is [like that on] the path of the bird along which the body as a whole does not **go**.[37]

The sky is vast without horizon,
A bird flies far far away.

[The expression,] **the sky is vast**, here has nothing to do with the heavens: the **sky** that has to do with the heavens is not the **vast sky**. Still less is that [space] which extends everywhere here and there the **vast sky**. Neither hidden nor manifest, without surface or interior—this is what is meant by the **vast sky**. When the **bird** flies this **sky**, it is the single *dharma* of **flying** the **sky**. This conduct of **flying** the **sky** is not to be measured: **flying** the **sky** is the entire world, for it is the entire world **flying** the **sky**. Although we do not know how far this **flying** goes, to express what is beyond our calculation, we call it **far, far away**. This is [equivalent to the saying], you should go off without a string beneath your feet. When the **sky** flies off, the **bird** flies off; when the **bird** flies off, the **sky** flies off. To express the investigation of this flying off, we say, "It is just here." This is the lancet of [sitting] fixedly: through how many tens of thousands of degrees does it express this "it is just here."[38]

Such, then, is the Ch'an Master Hung-chih's "Lancet of Seated Meditation." Among the old worthies throughout all the generations, there has never been another "Lancet of Seated Meditation" like this one. If the

---

37. *Kotai no fugyō chōdō*: an allusion to Tung-shan's remark that "[the original face] does not follow the path of the bird" (*Ching-te ch'uan teng lu*, T.51:322c26). The "vessel world" (*kikai, bhājana-loka*) refers to the natural world, seen as the container of sentient beings. Dōgen's commentary here takes advantage of Cheng-chüeh's expression, *tettei*, which conveys both a literal and a figurative sense of "getting to the bottom" of something.

38. *Shi zai shari*: from Dōgen's version of the conversation between Po-chang and Ma-tsu over a passing flock of wild geese. When Ma-tsu asked where the birds were going, Po-chang said they had flown past; Ma-tsu twisted his nose and said, "You say they've flown past, but from the beginning they're just here." (*Shōbō genzō sanbyaku soku*, DZZ.2:233. Dōgen's text seems to conflate the original story [see *Lien-teng hui yao*, ZZ.2B,9:247b] with the interlinear comments in the *Pi-yen lu* [T.48:187c21].) "You should go off..." (*jiki shu sokka mu shi ko*): from Tung-shan's "explanation" (*Ching-te ch'uan teng lu*, T.51:322c23) of how one is to follow his "path of the bird"; usually interpreted to mean one should go without leaving a trace (of his sandal strings). Cheng-chüeh's term for "sky," *kū*, is of course the same graph used by the Buddhists for their "emptiness."

stinking skin bags throughout all quarters were to attempt to express a "Lancet of Seated Meditation" like this one, they could not do so though they exhaust the efforts of a lifetime or two. This is the only "Lancet" in any quarter; there is no other to be found. When he ascended the hall [to lecture], my former master often said, "Hung-chih is an old Buddha." He never said this about any other person. When one has the eye to know a man, he will know as well the voice of the Buddhas and Patriarchs. In truth, we know that there are Buddhas and Patriarchs in [the tradition of] Tung-shan.[39]

Now, some eighty years and more since [the days of] the Ch'an Master Hung-chih, reading his "Lancet of Seated Meditation," I compose my own. The date is the eighteenth day of the third month in [the cyclical year] Mizunoetora, the third year of Ninji [1242]; if we calculate back from this year to the eighth day of the tenth month in the twenty-seventh year of [the Southern Sung era of] Shao-hsing [1157, when Hung-chih died], there are just eighty-five years. The "Lancet of Seated Meditation" I now compose is as follows:

LANCET OF SEATED MEDITATION

Essential function of all the Buddhas,
Functioning essence of all the Patriarchs—
It is present without thinking,
It is completed without interacting.
Present without thinking,
Its presence is inherently intimate;
Completed without interacting,
Its completion is inherently verified.
Its presence inherently intimate,
It is ever without any stain or defilement;
Its completion inherently verified,
It is ever without the upright or inclined.
Intimacy ever without stain or defilement,
Its intimacy sloughs off without discarding;
Verification ever without upright or inclined,
Its verification makes effort without figuring.
The water is clear right through the earth,
A fish goes along like a fish.
The sky is vast straight into the heavens,
A bird flies just like a bird.[40]

---

39. That is, in Hung-chih's (and Dōgen's) Ts'ao-tung lineage. Dōgen's appeal to his former master Ju-ching's appreciation of Hung-chih is repeated in the *Shōbō genzō ō saku sendaba* (DZZ.1 : 595); in the context there, it seems clear that Dōgen had in mind in particular a remark in the *Nyojō goroku* (T.48: 127a25). Hung-chih, of course, had been the most famous abbot of Ju-ching's T'ien-t'ung monastery.

40. Dōgen manages to work into his verse many of the familiar terms of Zen teaching: "present" and "completed" here represent the two elements of the binome, *genjō*, translated

It is not that the "Lancet of Seated Meditation" by the Ch'an Master Hung-chih has not yet said it right, but it can also be said like this. Above all, descendants of the Buddhas and Patriarchs should study seated meditation as the one great concern. This is the orthodox seal of the single transmission.[41]

---

earlier as "realization"; "intimate" and "verification" come from the term, *shinshō*, "intimate verification," an expression for enlightened understanding much favored by Ta-hui; "stain or defilement" translates *senna*, famous in the saying, "The way does not depend on cultivation; only don't defile it"—words often directed against meditation (as by Ta-hui, at *Ta-hui yü lu*, T.47:b2); "upright or inclined" (*shōhen*) are the terms for absolute and relative used in the famous schema of five ranks (*wu wei*) developed by Tung-shan and Ts'ao-shan (on which Hung-chih wrote an appreciative verse [*Hung-chih kuang lu*, T.48:99a]).

41.   The DZZ text ends with the following colophon, which does not appear in the Kōfuku ji manuscript:

Treasury of the Eye of the True Dharma 12: Lancet of Seated Meditation.

Recorded at Kōshō Hōrin ji, eighteenth day, third month, Mizunoetora, third year of Ninji [i.e., April 19, 1242].

Presented to the assembly at Yoshimine shōja, Yoshida district, Esshū, eleventh month, winter of Mizunotou, fourth year [of Ninji; i.e., December 1243–January 1244].

Glossary of Chinese and Japanese Names and Terms

Ch'ing-liao. *See* Chen-hsieh Ch'ing-liao
Ching shan   徑山
Ching-te ssu   景德寺
Ching-t'u   淨土
Ch'ing-yüan   慶元
Chōen ji   長圓寺
Ch'uan-fa   傳法
Chü-chih   俱胝
Chüeh-fan Hui-hung   覺範慧洪

Daibutsu ji   大佛寺
Daikatsu Ryōshin   大歇了心
Dainichibō Nōnin   大日房能忍
Daruma shū   達磨宗
Dōgen   道元
Donki   曇希
Dōun ji   洞雲寺

Eihei ji   永平寺
Ejō. *See* Koun Ejō
Ekan   懷鑑
Enni (Ben'en)   圓爾辯圓

Fa-hsiu. *See* Fa-yün Fa-hsiu
Fa-tsang   法藏
Fa-yün Fa-hsiu   法雲法秀
Fa-yün Yüan-t'ung   法雲圓通
Fo-chao Te-kuang   佛照德光
Fo-yen Yüan Ch'an-shih   佛眼遠禪師
Fu   富
Fujiwara no Teika   藤原定家
Fukaki Shunjō   不可棄俊芿
Fukakusa   深草
Fuke   普化
Fushimi   伏見
Fu Ta-shih   傅大士

Ganshō   願性
Gentō Sokuchū   玄透即中
Gien   義演

Giin	義伊
Gijun	義準
Gikai	義介
Giun	義雲
Gokuraku ji	極樂寺
Guzei in Jikan	弘誓院慈觀
Gyōyū. *See* Taikō Gyōyū	
Hakuin Ekaku	白隱慧鶴
Hakusan	白山
Hatano Yoshishige	波多野義重
Heisen ji	平泉寺
Hiei zan	比叡山
Hōjō Masako	北條政子
Hōjō Tokiyori	北條時賴
Hōnen	法然
Hongaku	本覺
Ho-tse	荷澤
Hsiang-yang	襄陽
Hsiang-yen	香嚴
Hsiang-yen Chih-hsien	香嚴智閑
Hsing-sheng ssu	興聖寺
Hsü-an Huai-ch'ang	虛庵懷敞
Hsüan-sha Shih-pei	玄沙師備
Hsüeh-feng Hui-jan	雪峰慧然
Huai-hai. *See* Po-chang Huai-hai	
Huai-jang. *See* Nan-yüeh Huai-jang	
Hua-t'ai	滑台
Huang-lung	黃龍
Huang-mei shan	黃梅山
Hua-yen	華嚴
Hui-ch'eng	惠成
Hui-chüeh. *See* Kuang-hsiao Hui-chüeh	
Hui-hung. *See* Chüeh-fan Hui-hung	
Hui-k'o	慧可
Hui-neng	慧能
Hung-chi ch'an-yüan	洪濟禪院
Hung-chih Cheng-chüeh	宏智正覺
Hung-chi ssu	洪濟寺
Hung-chou	洪州

Hung-jen	弘忍
Hung-tao	弘道
I	頤
I-huai. *See* T'ien-i I-huai	
I-yüan	義遠
Ju-ching. *See* T'ien-t'ung Ju-ching	
Jufuku ji	壽福寺
K'ai-yüan	開元
Kakuan	覺晏
Kakuban	覺鑁
Kakushin. *See* Shinchi Kakushin	
Kanazawa bunko	金沢文庫
Kangen	寛元
Kannon Dōri in	觀音導利院
Karoku	嘉禄
Katei	嘉禎
Katsurayama Kagetomo	葛山影倫
Kegon. *See* Hua-yen	
Keizan Jōkin	瑩山紹瑾
Kenchō ji	建長寺
Kenkon in	乾坤院
Kennin ji	建仁寺
Kenzei	建撕
Kippō ji. *See* Yoshimine dera	
Kōben. *See* Myōe Kōben	
Kōfuku ji	興福寺
Kōfuku ji	廣福寺
Koga	久我
Kohitsu Ryōhan	古筆了伴
Kōin	公胤
Kōkoku ji	興國寺
Komu	虚無
Kongō Zanmai in	金剛三昧院
Kōshō Chidō	光紹智堂
Kōshō Hōrin ji	興聖寶林寺
Kōshō ji	興聖寺
Koun Ejō	孤雲懷奘

Kōun ji	耕雲寺
Kōya san	高野山
Kōzan ji	高山寺
Kuang-hsiao Hui-chüeh	光孝慧覺
Kuan-ting	湛頂
Kuei-feng Tsung-mi	圭峰宗密
Kuei-shan	潙山
Kujō Michiie	九條道家
Kujō Noriie	九條教家
Kyōgō	經豪
Lan-ch'i Tao-lung	蘭溪道隆
Lin-chi	臨濟
Lin-chi I-hsüan	臨濟義玄
Li Tsun-hsü	李遵勗
Lü	呂
Manzan Dōhaku	卍山道白
Ma-tsu Tao-i	馬祖道一
Menzan Zuihō	面山瑞方
Michiie. *See* Kujō Michiie	
Minamoto no Michichika	源通親
Minamoto no Michitomo	源通具
Minamoto no Sanetomo	源實朝
Minamoto no Yoriie	源頼家
Ming-chi Ch'u-chün	明極楚俊
Mizunoetora	壬寅
Mizunotou	癸卯
Monkaku	門鶴
Mujaku Dōchū	無著道忠
Mujū Dōgyō	無住道曉
Murakami Genji	村上源氏
Musō Soseki	夢窓疎石
Myōe Kōben	明惠高辨
Myōzen	明全
Nanpo Jōmin	南浦紹明
Nan-yüeh Huai-jang	南嶽懷讓
Nan-yüeh Hui-ssu	南嶽慧思
Nan-yüeh Ta-hui	南嶽大慧
Nichiren	日蓮

Nihon Daruma shū	日本達磨宗
Ninji	仁治
Nishiari Bokusan	西有穆山
Nobuko	信子
Nōnin. *See* Dainichibō Nōnin	
Onjō ji	園城寺
P'an-shan Ssu-cho	盤山思卓
Pao-ch'ing	寳慶
Pao-lin ssu	寳林寺
Pao-t'ang	保唐
Po-chang Huai-hai	百丈懷海
Po-chang shan	百丈山
P'u-chi	普寂
P'u-hsien	普賢
P'u-hua	普化
P'u-hui	普慧
Rinzai. *See* Lin-chi	
Rokuhara	六波羅
Rurikō ji	瑠璃光寺
Ryūzen	隆禪
Saichō	最澄
Saihō ji	西方寺
Sanetomo. *See* Minamoto no Sanetomo	
Senne	詮慧
Sennyū ji	泉涌寺
Shan-tao	善導
Shao-hsing	紹興
Shao-lin	少林
Shen-hsiu	神秀
Shen-hui	神會
Shigetsu	指月
Shih-shuang Ch'ing-chu	石霜慶諸
Shih-t'ou Hsi-ch'ien	石頭希遷
Shinchi Kakushin	心地覺心
Shingon	眞言
Shinran	親鸞

Shōbō ji	正法寺
Shōkaku	正覺
Shūhō Myōchō	宗峰妙超
Shunjō. *See* Fukaki Shunjō	
Sōji ji	總持寺
Sosan	祖山
Sōtō. *See* Ts'ao-tung	
Sun	孫
Sung shan	嵩山
Ta-chi. (Hsiang-hsi Ta-chi)	大寂(江西大寂)
Ta-hui Tsung-kao	大慧宗杲
Taikō Gyōyū	退耕行勇
Taimitsu	台密
T'ai-po shan	太白山
Taira no Kagekiyo	平景清
Tan-hsia Tsu-ch'un	丹霞子淳
Tao-hsin	道信
Tao-hsüan	道宣
Tao-hsüan	道璿
Tao-i. *See* Ma-tsu Tao-i	
Tao-lung. *See* Lan-ch'i Tao-lung	
Tao-ming	道明
Tendai. (T'ien-t'ai)	天台
Tenkei Denson	天桂傳尊
Tenpuku	天福
T'ien-i I-huai	天衣義懷
T'ien-t'ai Chih-i	天台智顗
T'ien-t'ai shan	天台山
T'ien-t'ung Ju-ching	天童如淨
T'ien-t'ung shan	天童山
Tōdai ji	東大寺
Tōfuku ji	東福寺
Tokiyori. *See* Hōjō Tokiyori	
Tōnomine	多武峰
Ts'ao-shan	曹山
Ts'ao-tung	曹洞
Tse	賾
Tsung Chih-ko	宗直閣
Tsung-mi. *See* Kuei-feng Tsung-mi	

Tsung-tse. *See* Ch'ang-lu Tsung-tse
Tu Mo   杜默
Tung shan   東山
Tung-shan Liang-chieh   洞山良价
Tung-shan Shih-ch'ien   洞山師虔
Tz'u-chüeh   慈覺

Wan-nien ssu   萬年寺
Wan-shou ssu   萬壽寺
Wei-yen. *See* Yüeh-shan Wei-yen
Wu-chi Liao-p'ai   無際了派
Wu-chu   無住
Wu-chun Shih-fan   無準師範
Wu-hsüeh Tsu-yüan   無學祖元
Wu-men Hui-k'ai   無門慧開
Wu-yün Ho-shang   五雲和尚

Yamashi bu   禪師峰
Yang-ch'i   楊岐
Yang Wei   陽畏
Yen-tang shan   雁蕩山
Ying-fu. *See* Ch'ang-lu Ying-fu
Yō Kōshū   楊光秀
Yōsai   榮西
Yoshida   吉田
Yoshimine dera   吉峰寺
Yoshimine shōja   吉峰精舍
Yoshishige. *See* Hatano Yoshishige
Yü   禹
Yüan-feng Ch'ing-man   元豐清滿
Yüan-tzu   元蕭
Yüan-wu K'o-ch'in   圜悟克勤
Yüan-yu   元祐
Yüeh shan   藥山
Yüeh-shan Wei-yen   藥山惟儼
Yü Hsiang   虞翔
Yün-chü   雲居
Yung-ming Yen-shou   永明延壽
Yung-nien   永年

Yung-p'ing	永平
Yün-men	雲門
Yura	由良

TERMS

aji kan	阿字觀
ango	安居
an-lo hsing	安樂行
an-mo fa	按摩法
anraku	安樂
anraku hōmon	安樂法門
anri	行履
ban'i	番夷
bendō	辨道
bodai ji	菩提寺
bōen. *See* wang yüan	
buji	無事
bukkō zanmai	佛光三昧
busshin	佛心
busshin'in	佛心印
busshin shū	佛心宗
busso no meimyaku	佛祖の命脈
butsu butsu shōden no daidō	佛佛正傳の大道
butsudō	佛道
butsugyō	佛行
butsu kōmyō	佛光明
butsuryō	佛量
ch'ang chao	常照
ch'ang lien ch'uang	長連床
ch'an-na	禪那
ch'an-ting	禪定
ch'an tsung	禪宗
chao	照
chao-liao	照了
ch'en	沈
cheng	正
cheng hsiu	正修

cheng nien　　　　　　　　　正念

cheng wu　　　　　　　　　　證悟

chen tsung　　　　　　　　　　眞宗

chi　　　　　　　　　　　　　急

chi　　　　　　　　　　　　　寂

ch'i　　　　　　　　　　　　氣

chidan　　　　　　　　　　　智斷

chieh wu　　　　　　　　　　解悟

chien　　　　　　　　　　　　漸

chien　　　　　　　　　　　　見

chien hsing　　　　　　　　　見性

chih　　　　　　　　　　　　止

chih　　　　　　　　　　　　知

chih hsien hsin hsing　　　　　直顯心性

chih-kuan　　　　　　　　　　止觀

chi-hsiang　　　　　　　　　　吉祥

ching ch'u　　　　　　　　　　靜處

ching tso　　　　　　　　　　靜坐

chō　　　　　　　　　　　　　長

chō　　　　　　　　　　　　　兆

cho ch'i　　　　　　　　　　濁氣

chōshin. *See* t'iao hsin

chu　　　　　　　　　　　　主

ch'uan　　　　　　　　　　　喘

chüeh　　　　　　　　　　　　覺

chüeh-i　　　　　　　　　　　覺意

chüeh-i san-mei　　　　　　　覺意三昧

ch'u shih-chien　　　　　　　出世間

daigi　　　　　　　　　　　　大疑

daigo　　　　　　　　　　　　大悟

daiichi za　　　　　　　　　　第一座

daimoku　　　　　　　　　　題目

daiyō genzen　　　　　　　　大用現前

daruma shū　　　　　　　　　達磨宗

datsuraku　　　　　　　　　　脫落

dōgen　　　　　　　　　　　道眼

dōri　　　　　　　　　　　　道理

dō shi jūsei　　　　　　　　道之十成

ego fu ego	回互不回互
erh-shih-wu fang-pien	二十五方便
fa-hsing chi-jan	法性寂然
fang-pien	方便
fei	非
fei hsing fei tso	非行非坐
fei ssu-liang	非思量
feng	風
fu	浮
fū. *See* feng	
fubo mishō zen	父母未生前
fuhō ichinin	不逢一人
fujō	不淨
fu shiryō tei	不思量底
fu shi zen aku	不思善惡
futon	蒲團
fuzenna no shushō	不染污の修證
ganzen	頑然
gasshō	合掌
gedō	外道
gege	解夏
geju	偈頌
gengen henpon	還源返本
genjō	現成
genjō kōan. *See* hsien-ch'eng kung-an	
gigi	擬議
gijaku	疑著
gogai	五蓋
gon	權
gongai shi ryōran	言外之領覽
gotsugotsu chi	兀兀地
gotsugotsu chi no kōjō nani ni yorite ka tsūzezaru	兀兀地の向上なにによりてか通ぜざる
gotsugotsu chi o kotō su	兀兀地を舉頭す
gotsuza	兀坐
goya	後夜
goyoku	五欲

gozan. *See* wu shan

gūjin bodai shi shushō 究盡菩提之修證

gyōbutsu 行佛

gyōji 行持

hachimen reirō 八面玲瓏

hankafu za 半跏趺坐

hattō 法堂

heion chi 平穩地

henkai fu zō zō 遍界不曾藏

hi 非

hijiri 聖

hi jō sō 非定相

hi shiryō. *See* fei ssu-liang

hōben. *See* fang-pien

hōgo 法語

hoji 晡時

hokkai jōin 法界定印

hokke 法華

honmon 本門

honrai menmoku 本來面目

honshō myōshu 本證妙修

honshō no zentai 本證の全體

hōsen ingyoku 抛塼引玉

ho shan kuei k'u 黑山鬼窟

hōza 法座

hsi 息

hsiang-mo 降魔

hsiang-tai 相待

hsiao 孝

hsi ch'an 習禪

hsien-ch'eng kung-an 現成公案

hsien tso 閑坐

hsi lü wang yüan 息慮忘緣

hsin i shih 心意識

hsin jo yu nien ch'i chi pien chüeh-chao 心若有念起即便覺照

hsin-shih liu-tung 心識流動

hsin-shu 心數

hsin ti 心地

hsiu-cheng 修證

hsiung chung wu shih	胸中無事
hsi wang hsiu hsin	息妄修心
hsün	尊
hua-t'ou	話頭
i	意
i	易
i ch'i chi hsiu san-mei	意起即修三昧
i-ch'ieh pu wei	一切不爲
ichigyō	一行
ichi nin shi riki	一任此力
ichi zafu	一坐蒲
igi	威儀
i-hsing	一行
i-hsing san-mei	一行三昧
ikan	如何
ikan sokuze	如何即是
ikku	一句
i nien san-ch'ien	一念三千
inin no hōben	爲人の方便
inmo ji. *See* jen-mo shih	
innen	因緣
inshō	印證
i-p'ien	一片
ippen. *See* i-p'ien	
ishin denshin	以心傳心
isō	已曾
isō funbetsu naru butsubutsu	已曾分別なる佛佛
itazura ni taigo su	いたづらに待悟す
jakumoku gyōnen	寂默凝然
janin	邪人
jashi	邪師
jen-mo jen	恁麼人
jen-mo shih	恁麼事
ji juyū zanmai	自受用三昧
jikige jōtō	直下承當
jiki shu sokka mu shi ko	直須足下無絲去
jinen ken	自然見
jiriki	自力

jishō	自照
jishu	示衆
jitsu	實
jōdō	上堂
jōen	靜緣
jōgyō zanmai	常行三昧
jōriki. *See* ting li	
jōtō	承當
jo yu wang ch'i chi chüeh	若有妄起即覺
jūji tōgaku	十地等覺
juko	頌古
ju-lai ch'an	如來禪
jun'ichi no buppō	沌一の佛法
kafu za	跏趺坐
kaisho	楷書
kaitō kanmen	回頭換面
kan	卷
kan	緩
kana	假名
kana hōgo	假名法語
kana shō	假名抄
kanbun	漢文
k'an ching	看淨
k'an hsin	看心
k'an-hua	看話
kanjin. *See* kuan hsin	
kanki issoku	欠氣一息
kanna. *See* k'an-hua	
kan rai kan kyo	看來看去
kan ren kun ju	觀練薰修
kaō	花押
kappatsupatsu	活鱍鱍
kattō	葛藤
k'e	客
kekkafu za	結跏趺坐
kenshō. *See* chien hsing	
kenten zendō	見轉全道
keshin minchi	灰心泯智
ki. *See* ch'i	

kikai	器界
kinhin	經行
kirigami	切紙
kiyō	機要
kōan. *See* kung-an	
kōan genjō	公案現成
ko i	古意
kōkon	黄昏
kokuhō	国宝
kokyō	古鏡
kōmyō	光明
konsan	昏散
kōsei	校正
kosoku	古則
kosoku kōan	古則公案
kotai no fugyō chōdō	舉體の不行鳥道
k'ou	口
koza mokushō	枯坐默照
kū	空
kuan	觀
k'uan	寬
kuan hsin	觀心
kuan i wu	觀一物
kufū. *See* kung-fu	
k'u mu ssu hui	枯木死灰
kung-an	公案
k'ung chieh i-ch'ien	空劫已前
kung-fu	功夫
kyōge betsuden	教外別傳
kyōke	教家
kyōkin buji	胸襟無事
kyū	急
li	理
lien-hua sheng-hui	蓮華勝會
li ken	利根
ling chih	靈知
lung ching-hun	弄精魂
mahajun no shō	魔波旬の稱

maji. *See* mo shih

maku bō busso kō   莫謗佛祖好

maku kan zehi   莫管是非

ma ni iru   魔にいる

mappō   末法

meikyō   明鏡

meimyaku   命脈

menpeki   面壁

mieh   滅

mieh-chin ting   滅盡定

mikkyō   密教

mimen sōshin shitsumyō   未免喪身失命

mi shite narafu   身してならふ

mizo ni michi tani ni mitsu   溝にみち壑にみつ

mo   默

mo-chao   默照

mōjin soku butsu   妄心即佛

mokushō. *See* mo-chao

monsan   門參

mo shih   魔事

muji   無字

mujū hō   無住法

mushin   無心

myōjutsu   妙術

nehan myōshin   涅槃妙心

nei fang-pien   内方便

nenbutsu. *See* nien fo

nenbutsu zanmai. *See* nien fo san-mei

nenshitsu   念失

nen sō kan. *See* nien hsiang kuan

niao tao   鳥道

nien   念

nien ch'i chi chüeh   念起即覺

nien fo   念佛

nicn fo san-mei   念佛三昧

nien hsiang kuan   念想觀

ninten jō   人天乘

orokanaru zuzan   おろかなる杜撰

pan-jo san-mei	般若三昧
pen hsin	本心
pieh	別
p'ien	偏
pu k'o ssu-liang	不可思量
pu ssu-i	不思議
rarō	羅籠
rikiryō	力量
rokudō	六道
rufu	流布
ryō	量
sabutsu	作佛
saijō jō	最上乘
saiten tōchi	西天東地
san hsüeh	三學
sanmitsu	三密
san ti	三諦
sanzen	參禪
satori	悟
se ch'en san-mei	色塵三昧
seisho	清書
seiten	聖典
sen. *See* ch'uan	
sen'ichi kufū	專一功夫
senjaku	選擇
senju	專修
senna	染汚
senshi kobutsu	先師古佛
senshi mu shi go	先師無此語
setsu butsu	殺佛
shaku	尺
shang-shang	上上
shashu	叉手
sheng ch'uang	繩牀
sheng hsin	聖心
sheng jen	聖人
shen k'eng	深坑
shi	旨

shichi butsu shōden no shin'in	七佛正傳の心印
shih	事
shihō	嗣法
shiji	四時
shikan. *See* chih-kuan	
shikan taza	只管打坐
shikan zazen	只管坐禪
shinbutsu	身佛
shingon	眞言
shin'in	心印
shin i shiki. *See* hsin i shih	
shinjin datsuraku	身心脱落
shinjin datsuraku no kekkafu za	身心脱落の結跏趺坐
shinjitsu no buppō	眞實の佛法
shinjō	新條
shinketsu	眞訣
shin no kekkafu za	身の結跏趺坐
shin no kekkafu za	心の結跏趺坐
shinpitsu	眞筆
shinshō	親證
shiroku benrei	四六駢儷
shiryō. *See* ssu-liang	
shisho	嗣書
shi zai shari	只在這裏
sho	書
shōbō genzō	正法眼藏
shōden	正傳
shogyō	諸行
shoha	覷破
shōhen	正偏
shōjō no shu	證上の修
shoken	覷見
shōmon	正門
shōnyū	證入
shōrai sezu	將來せず
shōryō	商量
shōsan	小參
shōshiki kōjō igi	聲色向上威儀
shō shiyui	正思惟
shoso no meimyaku	初祖の命脈

shou hsin	守心
shou i pu i	守一不移
shū	取
shū. *See* tsung	
shūgaku	宗学
shūshi	宗旨
shushō kore ittō nari	修證これ一等なり
shushō ittō	修證一等
shuso	首座
shūzen. *See* hsi ch'an	
sō	相
sōdō	僧堂
sokuryo gyōjaku	息慮凝寂
sokuryo gyōshin	息慮凝心
somo	什麼
sōmu	曽無
sōshin	早晨
ssu-liang	思量
suikogyū o dagyū su	水牯牛を打牛す
sui tzu i	隨自意
sun	寸
susoku	數息
ta	打
tahei zui	打逃髄
taigo. *See* tai wu	
taiho	退步
taiho henshō	退步返照
tai wu	待悟
tan	短
tanden	單傳
tanden	丹田
tariki	他力
ta sheng tun-wu fa men	大乘頓悟法門
taza	打坐
taza sude ni nanji ni arazu kufū sara ni onore to sōken sezu	打坐すでになんぢにあらず功夫さらにおのれと相見せず
te	得
tekkan	鐵漢

tettei	徹底
t'i	體
t'iao-ho	調和
t'iao hsin	調心
t'i chen chih	體真止
ti-erh-t'ou	第二頭
ti-i i	第一義
ting li	定力
t'ing tung	挺動
tokushi	得旨
tokusu	禿子
tongo. *See* tun wu	
tonshu	頓修
tōsu	東司
ts'ai ling tuan wai kuang erh i	纔令斷外光而已
tso-ch'an	坐禪
tso-ch'an chen	坐禪箴
tso-ch'an ming	坐禪銘
tso chü	坐具
tso-fo	坐佛
tso wu	坐物
tsung	宗
tsu-shih ch'an	祖師禪
t'u	圖
tuan chien	斷見
tuan-mieh	斷滅
tun wu	頓悟
tun wu chien hsiu	頓悟漸修
ushin	有心
wai fang-pien	外方便
wang chü	妄俱
wang-nien hsin	妄念心
wang yüan	忘緣
watō. *See* hua-t'ou	
wei-yin no-p'an	威音那畔
wu	無
wu	悟

wu chia	五家
wu-chi k'ung	無記空
wu chu ch'u	無住處
wu hsiang	無相
wu-hsiang san hsüeh	無相三學
wu-hsin	無心
wu-hsing	無形
wu ling yen-lien ta chi	勿令眼臉大急
wu-lou	無漏
wu-nien	無念
wu shan	五山
wu-shang sheng	無上乘
wu-sheng	無生
wu t'ing hsin kuan	五停心觀
wu tso	無作
wu wei	無爲
wu wei	五位
wu yüan	五緣
yang	陽
yen	眼
yin	陰
yōki	要機
yü	語
yüan-tun	圓頓
yüan-wu	緣務
yung	用
yu-tso	有作
yu wu	有無
zabutsu. *See* tso-fo	
zadan	坐斷
zadan jippō	坐斷十方
zaga	坐臥
zaha jō shō hi	坐破孃生皮
zazen. *See* tso-ch'an	
zazen bendō	坐禪辨道
zazen gi	坐禪儀
zazen no shūmon	坐禪の宗門

zenjō ichimon   禪定一門

zenshū. *See* ch'an tsung

zetsuryo bōen   絶慮忘縁

zuchō sanjaku keitan nisun   頭長三尺頸短二寸

zuzan   杜撰

Works Cited

Abbreviations appearing here can be found in the section "Abbreviations and Conventions" in the front matter. The authorship of some of the works in the section entitled "Other Premodern Works" is dubious; use here of the traditional attributions (and of reconstructed titles, indicated by *) is simply for convenience of identification. Also for the convenience of those seeking to identify their original Chinese or Japanese graphs, I have included a number of entries (of alternative titles, works not longer extant, and so on) that receive notice in the text but are not cited as sources.

MULTIVOLUME COLLECTIONS OF PREMODERN WORKS (BY TITLE)

Ch'in-ting Ch'uan T'ang wen 欽定全唐文. 20 vols. Taipei: Hua-wen shu-chü, 1965.

Dai Nihon bukkyō zensho 大日本仏教全書. 150 vols. Tokyo: Bussho Kankōkai, 1912–22.

Dai Nihon zoku zōkyō 大日本続蔵経. 750 vols. Kyoto: Zōkyō Shoin, 1905–12.

Dōgen zenji zenshū 道元禅師全集. Ed. by Ōkubo Dōshū 大久保道舟. 2 vols. Tokyo: Chikuma Shobō, 1969–70.

Eihei kōroku chūkai zensho 永平広録註解全書. Ed. by Itō Toshimitsu 伊藤俊光. 3 vols. Tokyo: Eihei Kōroku Chūkai Zensho Kankōkai, 1961.

Eihei Shōbō genzō shūsho taisei 永平正法眼蔵蒐書大成. 25 vols. Tokyo: Taishūkan, 1974–81.

Hakuin oshō zenshū 白隠和尚全集. 8 vols. Tokyo: Ryūmeisha, 1934.

Kōgyō daishi senjutsu shū 興教大師撰述集. Ed. by Miyazaka Yūshō 宮坂宥勝. 2 vols. Tokyo: Sankibō Busshorin, 1977.

Kokuyaku zengaku taisei 国訳禅学大成. 25 vols. Tokyo: Nishōdō Shoten, 1930.

Shōbō genzō chūkai zensho 正法眼蔵註解全書. Ed. by Jinbo Nyoten 神保如天 and Andō Bun'ei 安藤文央. 11 vols. Repr. Tokyo: Nihon Bussho Kankōkai, 1956–57.

Shōwa hōbō sō mokuroku 昭和法宝総目録. 3 vols. Supplement to T. Tokyo: Taishō
  Issaikyō Kankōkai, 1929–34.
Sōtō shū zensho 曹洞宗全書. 20 vols. Tokyo: Kōmeisha, 1929–38.
Taishō shinshū daizōkyō 大正新修大蔵経. 85 vols. Tokyo: Taishō Issaikyō Kankōkai,
  1924–33.
Zenmon hōgo shū 禅門法語集. 3 vols. Rev. ed. Tokyo: Kōyūkan, 1921.
Zoku Gunsho ruijū 続群書類従. 33 vols. Repr. Tokyo: Zoku Gunsho Ruijū Kankōkai,
  1925–28.

PREMODERN WORKS (BY TITLE)

Works by Dōgen

Bendō hō 辨道法. DZZ.2:313–19.
Bendō wa 辨道話. DZZ.1:729–63.
Chiji shingi 知事清規. DZZ.2:320–46.
Eihei Gen zenji goroku 永平元禅師語録. SSZ.Shūgen,2:27–42.
Eihei kōroku 永平廣録. DZZ.2:7–200.
Eihei shingi 永平清規. T.#2584.
Fukan zazen gi 普勧坐禅儀. (Autograph text) DZZ.2:3–5; (vulgate text) in *Eihei
  kōroku*, DZZ.2:165–66.
"Fukan zazen gi senjutsu yurai 普勧坐禅儀撰述由來." DZZ.2:6.
Fu shukuhan pō 赴粥飯法. DZZ.2:248–57.
Gakudō yōjin shū 學道用心集. DZZ.2:253–60.
Gokoku shōbō gi 護國正法義.
"Hatano Yoshishige ate shojō 波多野義重宛書狀." DZZ.2:407.
Himitsu Shōbō genzō 秘密正法眼蔵.
Hōkyō ki 寶慶記. DZZ.2:371–88.
"Ju Kakushin kaimyaku 授覺心戒脈." DZZ.2:291.
Jūundō shiki 重雲堂式. DZZ.2:304–7.
"Kyōge betsuden o eizu 詠教外別傳," in *Dōgen zenji waka shū* 道元禅師和歌集.
  DZZ.2:412.
Nichiiki Sōtō shoso Dōgen zenji shingi 日域曹洞初祖道元禅師清規.
Ryakuroku 略録. See *Eihei Gen zenji goroku*.
Sanbyaku soku. See *Shōbō genzō sanbyaku soku*.
"Shari sōden ki 舍利相傳記." DZZ.2:395–96.
"Shi Ryōnen dōsha hōgo 示了然道者法語." DZZ.2:162.
Shōbō genzō 正法眼蔵. DZZ.1:
  Ango 安居. 568–84.
  Bukkyō 佛教. 306–14.
  Busshō 佛性. 14–35.
  Busso 佛祖. 454–57.
  Butsudō 佛道. 376–88.
  Butsu kōjō ji 佛向上事. 224–39.
  Daigo 大悟. 82–87.
  Den'e 傳衣. 285–300.
  Genjō kōan 現成公案. 7–10.

Gyōbutsu igi 行佛威儀. 46–58.

Gyōji 行持. 122–61.

Hachi dainin gaku 八大人覺. 723–26.

Hotsu mujō shin 發無上心. 525–31.

Inmo 恁麼. 162–68.

Jishō zanmai 自證三昧. 552–60.

Kattō 葛藤. 331–36.

Kesa kudoku 袈裟功德. 623–44.

Kobusshin 古佛心. 78–81.

Kokyō 古鏡. 175–88.

Kōmyō 光明. 116–21.

Maka hannya haramitsu 摩訶般若波羅蜜. 11–13.

Menju 面授. 446–53.

Ō saku sendaba 王索仙陀婆. 594–96.

Sanjūshichi hon bodai bunpō 三十七品菩提分法. 502–18.

Sansui kyō 山水經. 258–67.

Senjō 洗淨. 466–74.

Senmen 洗面. 424–35, 436–45.

Shisho 嗣書. 337–47.

Shizen biku 四禪比丘. 704–16.

Soshi seirai i 祖師西來義. 522–24.

Tashin tsū 他心通. 585–93.

Toki 都機. 206–9.

Zanmai ō zanmai 三昧王三昧. 539–41.

Zazen gi 坐禪儀. 88–89.

Zazen shin 坐禪箴. 90–101.

Zenki 全機. 203–5.

Shōbō genzō sanbyaku soku 正法眼藏三百則. DZZ.2:201–52.

Shōbō genzō zuimon ki 正法眼藏隨聞記. DZZ.2:419–95.

Shukke ryaku sahō 出家略作法. DZZ.2:272–78.

Shuryō shingi 衆寮箴規. DZZ.2:363–66.

Tai taiko goge jari hō 對大己五夏闍梨法. DZZ.2:308–12.

Tenzo kyōkun 典座教訓. DZZ.2:295–303.

"Uji Kannon Dōri in sōdō kenritsu kanjin sho 宇治觀音導利院僧堂建立勸
進疏." DZZ.2:400–401.

"Zazen shin 坐禪箴." In *Eihei kōroku*, DZZ.2:166; in *Eihei Gen zenji goroku*, SSZ.
Shūgen, 2:39b.

Other Premodern Works

Abhidharma-kośa. See *Chü-she lun.*

Aji kan gi 阿字觀義, by Kakuban 覺鎫. *Kōgyō daishi senjutsu shū*, vol. 1, 226–28.

Aji kan yōjin kuketsu 阿字觀用心口訣, by Jitsue 實慧. T.#2432.

Azuma kagami 吾妻鏡. 4 vols. *Shintei zōho Kokushi taikei* 新訂增補国史大系. Repr.
Tokyo: Yoshikawa Kōbunkan, 1983–84.

Bhāvanākrama. Tucci, *Minor Buddhist Texts, Part 3: Third Bhāvanākrama.*

Bukkō kan ryaku shidai 佛光觀略次第, by Kōben 高辨. DNBZ.13:127–30.

"Ch'an chen 禪箴," by Hui-k'ai 慧開. In *Wu-men kuan*, T.48:299.

Ch'an-men chu-tsu-shih chieh-sung 禪門諸祖師偈頌, by Tzu-sheng 子昇 and Ju-yu 如祐. ZZ.2,21:454–92.

Ch'an-men k'ou-chüeh 禪門口訣, by Chih-i 智顗. T.#1919.

"Ch'an-men kuei-shih 禪門規式." In *Ching-te ch'uan teng lu*, T.51:250–51.

Ch'an-men yao-lüeh 禪門要略, by Chih-i 智顗. ZZ.2,4:315–17.

Ch'an pi yao fa ching 禪秘要法經. T.#613.

Ch'an-yüan ch'ing-kuei 禪苑清規, by Tsung-tse 宗賾. Kagamishima et al., *Yakuchū Zen'en shingi*; and see *Chung-tiao pu-chu Ch'an-yüan ch'ing-kuei*.

Ch'an-yüan chu-ch'üan chi tu-hsü 禪源諸詮集都序, by Tsung-mi 宗密. T.#2015.

Cheng-fa yen-tsang 正法眼藏, by Ta-hui 大慧. ZZ.2,23:1–78.

Cheng tao ko 證道歌, by Yung-chia 永嘉. In *Ching-te ch'uan teng lu*, T.51:460–61.

Chia-t'ai p'u teng lu 嘉泰普燈錄, by Cheng-shou 正受. ZZ.2B,10:1–219.

Chien-chung ching-kuo hsü teng lu 建中靖國續燈錄, by Fo-kuo 佛國. ZZ.2B,9:1–217.

Ch'ih-hsiu Po-chang ch'ing-kuei 勅修百丈清規, by Te-hui 德煇. T.#2025.

Chih-kuan fu-hsing 止觀輔行. See *Chih-kuan fu-hsing ch'uan hung chüeh*.

Chih-kuan fu-hsing ch'uan hung chüeh 止觀輔行傳弘決, by Chan-jan 湛然. T.#1912.

Ching-te ch'uan teng lu 景德傳燈錄, by Tao-yüan 道原. T.#2076.

Ching-t'u chih-kuei chi 淨土指歸集, by Ta-yu 大佑. ZZ.2,13:57–99.

Chin-kang ching 金剛經 (*Vajracchedikā-sūtra*). T.#235.

Ch'üan hsiao wen 勸孝文, by Tsung-tse 宗賾.

Ch'uan teng lu. See *Ching-te ch'uan teng lu*.

"Ch'üan ts'an-ch'an jen chien hsiu ching-t'u 勸參禪人兼修淨土," by Tsung-tse 宗賾. In *Lung-shu ching-t'u wen*, T.47:283–84.

Chüeh-i san-mei 覺意三昧, by Chih-i 智顗. T.#1922.

Ch'u-hsüeh tso-ch'an fa 初學坐禪法, by Yen Ping 顏丙.

Chung-tiao pu-chu Ch'an-yüan ch'ing-kuei 重雕補註禪苑清規, by Tsung-tse 宗賾. ZZ.2,16:438–71.

Chü-she lun 俱舍論 (*Abhidharma-kośa*). T.#1558.

Daikaku shūi roku 大覺拾遺錄. DNBZ.95:101–16.

Daruma daishi sanron 達磨大師三論.

Diamond Sūtra. See *Chin-kang ching*.

Dōhan shōsoku 道範消息. Miyazaka, *Kana hōgo shū*, 76–83.

Eihei ji sanso gyōgō ki 永平寺三祖行業記. SSZ.Shiden,1:1–9.

Eiso zazen shin monge 永祖坐禪箴開解, by Menzan 面山. SSZ.Chūkai, 3:33–46.

Fa-hua hsüan i 法華玄義. See *Miao-fa lien-hua ching hsüan i*.

Fukan zazen gi funō go 普勸坐禪儀不能語, by Shigetsu 指月. SSZ.Chūkai,3:47–53.

Fukan zazen gi monge 普勸坐禪儀開解, by Menzan 面山. SSZ.Chūkai,3:1–33.

Genkō shakusho 元亨釋書, by Shiren 師鍊. DNBZ.101:133–513.

Himitsu Shōbō genzō shō 秘密正法眼藏抄.

Hottō Enmyō kokushi no engi 法燈圓明國師の緣起.

Hottō kokushi gyōjitsu nenpu 法燈國師行實年譜, by Shōkun 聖薰. *Zoku Gunsho ruijū*, 9A:346–61.

Hsiao chih-kuan 小止觀. See *T'ien-t'ai hsiao chih-kuan*.

Hsin hsin ming 信心銘, by Seng-ts'an 僧璨. T.#2010.

Hsin ming 心銘, by Fa-jung 法融. In *Ching-te ch'uan teng lu*, T.51:457–58.

Hsin-wang ming 心王銘, by Fu Ta-shih 傅大士. In *Ching-te ch'uan teng lu*, T.51:456–57.

Hsiu ch'an yao chüeh 修禪要訣, by Buddhapāli. ZZ.2,15:417–20.

Hsiu-cheng i 修證義. See *Yüan-chüeh ching tao-ch'ang hsiu-cheng i*.

Hsiu-hsi chih-kuan tso-ch'an fa-yao 修習止觀坐禪法要, by Chih-i 智顗. T.#1915; Sekiguchi, *Tendai shō shikan no kenkyū*, 321–64.

Hsiu hsin yao lun 修心要論, by Hung-jen 弘忍. See *Tsui-shang sheng lun*.

Hsüan-sha kuang lu 玄沙廣錄. ZZ.2,31:176–203.

Hsü ch'uan teng lu 續傳燈錄, by Chü-ting 居頂. T.#2077.

Hsü kao-seng chuan 續高僧傳, by Tao-hsüan 道宣. T.#2060.

Hua-yen ching 華嚴經 (*Avataṃsaka-sūtra*). T.#279.

Hung-chih kuang lu 宏智廣錄. T.#2001.

Hyakujō no zazen gi 百丈の坐禪儀.

Hyakujō zenji zazen gi 百丈禪師坐禪儀.

Hyōhan ki 兵範記.

I-ch'ieh ching ying-i 一切經音義, by Hui-lin 慧琳. T.#2128.

Jōtō shōkaku ron 成等正覺論. *Kanazawa bunko shiryō zensho*, vol. 1, 199–206.

Ju-chung jih-yung ch'ing-kuei 入眾日用清規, by Tsung-shou 宗壽. ZZ.2,16:472–74.

Ju-ju chü-shih tso-ch'an i 如如居士坐禪儀, by Yen Ping 顏丙. *Kanazawa bunko shiryō zensho*, vol. 1, 155–61.

Ju-ju chü-shih yü lu 如如居士語錄.

Keiran shūyō shū 溪嵐拾葉集, by Kōsō 光宗. T.#2410.

Kenshō jōbutsu ron 見性成佛論. *Kanazawa bunko shiryō zensho*, vol. 1, 173–98.

Kenzei ki 建撕記. Kawamura, *Shohon taikō Eihei kaisan Dōgen zenji gyōjō Kenzei ki*; and see *Teiho Kenzei ki*.

Kōroku 廣錄. See *Eihei kōroku*.

Kōzen gokoku ron 興禪護國論, by Yōsai 榮西. T.#2543.

Kuan wu-liang-shou ching 觀無量壽經 (**Amitāyur-buddhānusmṛti-sūtra?*). T.#365.

"*Kuan wu-liang-shou fo ching hsü* 觀無量壽佛經序," by Tsung-tse 宗賾. In *Lo-pang wen-lei*, T.47:167.

Laṅkāvatāra-sūtra. See *Leng-ch'ieh ching*.

Leng-ch'ieh ching 楞伽經 (*Laṅkāvatāra-sūtra*). T.#671.

Leng-ch'ieh shih-tzu chi 楞伽師資記, by Ching-chüeh 淨覺. T.#2837; Yanagida, *Shoki no zenshi*, vol. 1, 49–326.

Li Chiao tsa yung 李嶠雜詠.

"*Lien-hua sheng-hui lu wen* 蓮華勝會錄文," by Tsung-tse 宗賾. In *Lo-pang wen-lei*, T.47:177–78.

Lien-teng hui yao 聯燈會要, by Wu-ming 悟明. ZZ.2B,9:208–475.

Lin-chien lu 林間錄, by Hui-hung 慧洪. ZZ.2B,21:293–324.

Lin-chi lu 臨濟錄. T.#1985; Akizuki, *Rinzai roku*.

Li-tai fa-pao chi 歷代法寶記. T.#2075.

Liu-tsu t'an ching 六祖壇經. T.#2007; Yampolsky, *The Platform Sutra of the Sixth Patriarch*, following 216; Nakagawa, *Rokuso dankyō*.

Lo-pang i-kao 樂邦遺稿, by Tsung-hsiao 宗曉. T.#1969B.

Lo-pang wen-lei 樂邦文類, by Tsung-hsiao 宗曉. T.#1969A.

Lotus Sūtra. See *Miao-fa lien-hua ching*.

Lüeh-ming k'ai-meng ch'u-hsüeh tso-ch'an chih-kuan yao-men 略明開曚初學坐禪止觀要門. See *Hsiu-hsi chih-kuan tso-ch'an fa-yao.*

Lung-shu ching-t'u wen 龍舒淨土文, by Wang Jih-hsiu 王日休. T.＃1970.

Lu-shan lien-tsung pao-chien 廬山蓮宗寶鑑, by P'u-tu 普度. T.＃1973.

Mahā-vairocana-sūtra. See *Ta-jih ching.*

Ma-tsu yü lu 馬祖語錄. In *Szu chia yü lu* 四家語錄, ZZ.2,24:414–19; Iriya, *Baso no goroku.*

Miao-fa lien-hua ching 妙法蓮華經 (*Saddharmapuṇḍarīka-sūtra*). T.＃262.

Miao-fa lien-hua ching hsüan i 妙法蓮華經玄義, by Chih-i 智顗. T.＃1716.

Mo-chao ming 默照銘, by Hung-chih 宏智. In *Hung-chih kuang lu,* T.48:100.

Mo-ho chih-kuan 摩訶止觀, by Chih-i 智顗. T.＃1911.

Mo-ho pan-jo po-lo-mi ching 摩訶般若波羅蜜經 (*Pañcaviṃśati-sāhasrikā-prajñā-pāramitā-sūtra*). T.＃223.

Myōhō kana hōgo 明峰假名法語. In *Zenmon hōgo shū* 2:523–25.

Nan-yang ho-shang t'an yü 南陽和尚壇語, by Shen-hui 神會. Hu Shih, *Shen-hui ho-shang i-chi,* 225–52.

"Nien-fo fang t'ui fang-pien wen 念佛防退方便文," by Tsung-tse 宗賾. In *Lo-pang wen-lei,* T.47:178.

"Nien-fo hui-hsiang fa-yüan wen 念佛迴向發願文," by Tsung-tse 宗賾. In *Lo-pang wen-lei,* T.47:178.

"Nien-fo ts'an-ch'an chiu tsung-chih shuo 念佛參禪求宗旨説," by Tsung-tse 宗賾. In *Lu-shan lien-tsung pao-chien,* T.47:318.

Nyojō oshō goroku 如淨和尚語錄. T.＃2002A.

Orategama 遠羅天釜, by Hakuin 白隱. *Hakuin oshō zenshū* 5:105–209.

Pañcaviṃśati. See *Mo-ho pan-jo po-lo-mi ching.*

P'ang chü-shih yü lu 龐居士語錄. Iriya, *Hō koji goroku.*

Pao-ching san-mei ko 寶鑑三昧歌, by Tung-shan 洞山. In *Tung-shan yü lu,* T.47:515.

Pi-yen lu 碧巖錄, by Yüan-wu 圜悟. T.＃2003.

Po-chang ch'ing-kuei 百丈清規.

"Po-chang kuei-sheng sung 百丈規繩頌," by Tsung-tse 宗賾. In *Ch'an-yüan ch'ing-kuei,* Kagamishima et al., *Kunchū Zen'en shingi,* 340–52.

P'u-t'i-ta-mo nan-tsung ting shih-fei lun 菩提達磨南宗定是非論, by Shen-hui 神會. Hu shih, *Shen-hui ho-shang i-chi,* 258–318.

Sankon zazen setsu 三根坐禪説, by Keizan 瑩山. SSZ.Shūgen,2:428–29.

Sanshū meiseki shi 三州名跡史.

Sennyū ji Fukaki hosshi den 泉涌寺不可棄法師傳, by Shinzui 信瑞. *Zoku Gunsho ruijū,* 9A:45–58.

Shibu roku 四部錄. Ōmori, *Kunchū Zenshū shibu roku.*

Shih ch'an po-lo-mi tz'u-ti fa-men 釋禪波羅蜜次第法門, by Chih-i 智顗. T.＃1916.

Shih niu t'u 十牛圖, by K'uo-an 廓庵. Kajitani et al., *Shinjin mei Shōdō ka Jūgyū zu Zazen gi,* 97–143.

Shih sung lü 十誦律 (*Sarvāstivāda-vinaya?*). T.＃1435.

Shikan zazen ki 止觀坐禪記, by Genshin 源信. DNBZ.31:267–72.

Shōbō genzō kikigaki 正法眼藏聞書, by Senne 詮慧.

Shōbō genzō senpyō 正法眼藏僭評, by Mujaku 無著.

Shōbō genzō shō 正法眼藏抄, by Kyōgō 經豪. SSZ.Chūkai,1:1–2:568.

Shōichi kokushi hōgo 聖一國師法語, *Zenmon hōgo shū* 2:411–22.

Shou-leng-yen ching 首楞嚴經 (*Śūraṅgama-sūtra). T. #945.

Shou-leng-yen san-mei ching 首楞嚴三昧經 (*Śūraṅgama-samādhi-sūtra*). T. #642.

Sukhāvatīvyūha-sūtra. See *Wu-liang-shou ching.*

Sung kao-seng chuan 宋高僧傳, by Tsan-ning 贊寧 et al. T. #2061.

Śūraṅgama-samādhi-sūtra. See *Shou-leng-yen san-mei ching.*

Śūraṅgama-sūtra. See *Shou-leng-yen ching.*

Ta-chih-tu lun 大智度論 (**Mahā-prajñā-pāramitopadeśa*). T. #1509.

Ta chuang-yen lun ching 大莊嚴論經 (*Kalpanāmaṇḍitikā*). T. #201.

Ta-hui shu 大慧書. In *Ta-hui yü lu,* T.47:916–43.

Ta-hui tsung-men wu-k'u 大慧宗門武庫. T. #1998B.

Ta-hui yü lu 大慧語錄. T. #1998A.

Ta-jih ching 大日經 (*Mahā-vairocana-sūtra*). T. #848.

T'an ching 壇經. See *Liu-tsu t'an ching.*

"*T'ang Hung-chou Po-chang shan ku Huai-hai ch'an-shih t'a-ming* 唐洪州百丈山
    故懷海禪師塔銘," by Ch'en Hsü 陳詡. *Ch'üan T'ang wen* 446:4b–7a.

T'an yü 壇語. See *Nan-yang ho-shang t'an yü.*

Ta pao chi ching 大寶積經 (*Ratna-kūṭa*). T. #310.

Ta-sheng ch'i-hsin lun i-chi 大乘起信論義記, by Fa-tsang 法藏. T. #1846.

Ta-tsang i-lan 大藏一覽, by Ch'en Shih 陳實. *Shōwa hōbō sō mokuroku* 3:1253–1415.

Teiho Kenzei ki 訂補建撕記, ed. by Menzan 面山. SSZ.Shiden,2:15–32.

Tendō san Keitoku ji Nyojō zenji zoku goroku 天童山景德寺如淨禪師續語錄.
    T. #2002B.

T'ien-sheng kuang teng lu 天聖廣燈錄, by Li Tsun-hsü 李遵勗. ZZ.2B,8:298–451.

T'ien-t'ai hsiao chih-kuan 天台小止觀, by Chih-i 智顗. See *Hsiu-hsi chih-kuan tso-ch'an
    fa-yao.*

Ting shih-fei lun 定是非論. See *P'u-t'i-ta-mo nan-tsung ting shih-fei lun.*

Tō dai wajō tōsei den 唐大和尚東征傳, by Genkai 元開. In *Yūhō ki shō,* T.51:988–95.

Ts'an t'ung ch'i 參同契, by Shih-t'ou 石頭. In *Ching-te ch'uan teng lu,* T.51:459.

"*Tso-ch'an chen* 坐禪箴," by Chih-feng 志峰. In *Ching-te ch'uan teng lu,* T.51:
    459–60.

"*Tso-ch'an chen* 坐禪箴," by Hung-chih 宏智. In *Hung-chih kuang lu,* T.48:98.

"*Tso-ch'an i* 坐禪儀," by Pen-ts'ai 本才. In *Chia-t'ai p'u teng lu,* ZZ.2B,10:216.

Tso-ch'an i 坐禪儀, by Tsung-tse 宗賾. In *Ch'an-yüan ch'ing-kuei,* ZZ.2,16:460–61;
    Kagamishima et al., *Yakuchū Zen'en shingi,* 279–83.

"*Tso-ch'an ming* 坐禪銘," by Ch'ing-yüan 清遠. In *Chia-t'ai p'u teng lu,* ZZ.2B,10:
    214.

"*Tso-ch'an ming* 坐禪銘," by Ta-i 大義. In *Tzu-men ching-hsün,* T.48:1048.

Tsui-shang sheng lun 最上乘論, by Hung-jen 弘忍. T. #2011.

Tsung-jung lu 從容錄, by Hung-chih 宏智. T. #2004.

Tsung-men wu-k'u. See *Ta-hui tsung-men wu-k'u.*

Tu-hsü. See *Ch'an-yüan chu-ch'üan chi tu-hsü.*

Tun-wu ju-tao yao men 頓悟入道要門, by Hui-hai 慧海. ZZ.2,15:420–26.

Tun-wu ta-sheng cheng li chüeh 頓悟大乘正理決. Demiéville, *Le Concile de Lhasa,* end
    matter, plates 1–32.

Tzu-men ching-hsün 緇門警訓, by Yung-chung 永中. T. #2023.

Tz'u-ti ch'an-men 次弟禪門. See *Shih ch'an po-lo-mi tz'u-ti fa-men.*

Untō shō 雲桃抄, by Unshō Ikkei 雲章一慶.

Vimalakīrti-sūtra. See *Wei-mo ching.*

Wei-mo ching 維摩經 (*Vimalakīrti-sūtra*). T.#475.

Wen-shu-shih-li so shuo pu-ssu-i fo ching-chieh ching 文殊師利所説不思議佛境界經 (*Acintya-buddha-viṣaya-nirdeśa*). T.#340.

Wen-shu shuo pan-jo ching 文殊説般若經 (*Saptaśatikā-prajñā-pāramitā-sūtra*). T.#233.

Wu-liang-shou ching 無量壽經 (*Sukhāvatīvyūha-sūtra*). T.#360.

Wu-men kuan 無門關, by Hui-k'ai 慧開. T.#2005.

Wu-wei san-tsang ch'an yao 無畏三藏禪要. T.#917.

Yabu kōji 藪柑子, by Hakuin 白隱. *Hakuin oshō zenshū* 5:319–40.

Yüan-chüeh ching 圓覺經. T.#842.

Yüan-chüeh ching tao-ch'ang hsiu-cheng i 圓覺經道場修證儀, by Tsung-mi 宗密. ZZ.2B,1:361–498.

Yüan-chüeh ching ta-shu ch'ao 圓覺經大疏鈔, by Tsung-mi 宗密. ZZ.1,14:204– 15:416.

Yüan-wu yü lu 圓悟語錄. T.#1997.

Yūhō ki shō 遊方記抄. T.#2089.

Yura kaizan Hottō kokushi hōgo 由良開山法燈國師法語. DNBZ.96:213–22.

Zazen gi 坐禪儀, by Kakushin 覺心. DNBZ.96:211–12.

Zazen gi 坐禪儀, by Tao-lung (Dōryū) 道隆. *Kanazawa bunko shiryō zensho,* vol. 1, 161–68.

Zazen hōgo 坐禪法語. See *Myōhō kana hōgo.*

Zazen jigi 坐禪事儀, by Shunjō 俊芿.

Zazen ron 坐禪論, by Enni 圓爾. In *Shōichi kokushi hōgo, Zenmon hōgo shū* 2:411–24.

Zazen ron 坐禪論, by Tao-lung (Dōryū) 道隆. *Kokuyaku zengaku taisei* 23:1–8.

Zazen Shidai 坐禪次第, by Kōben 高辨.

Zazen yōjin ki 坐禪用心記, by Keizan 瑩山. SSZ.Shūgen,2:423–27.

Zenmon shishi shōshū zu (**Ch'an-men shih-tzu ch'eng-hsi t'u*) 禪門師資承襲圖, by Tsung-mi 宗密. ZZ.2,15:433–38.

Zōtan shū 雜談集, by Mujū 無住. Yamada and Miki, *Zōtan shū.*

MODERN WORKS

Akishige Yoshiharu 秋重義治. "Fukan zazen gi kō 普勸坐禪儀考." *Tetsugaku nenpō* 哲学年報 14 (1953), 459–80.

Akizuki Ryōmin 秋月龍珉, ed. *Rinzai roku* 臨濟錄. *Zen no goroku* 禪の語錄 10. Tokyo: Chikuma Shobō, 1972.

Bielefeldt, Carl. "Ch'ang-lu Tsung-tse's *Tso-ch'an i* and the 'Secret' of Zen Meditation." In *Traditions of Meditation in Chinese Buddhism,* ed. by Peter Gregory, 129–61. Kuroda Institute Studies in East Asian Buddhism 4. Honolulu: University of Hawaii Press, 1986.

———. "Recarving the Dragon: History and Dogma in the Study of Dōgen." In *Dōgen Studies,* ed. by William LaFleur, 21–53. Kuroda Institute Studies in East Asian Buddhism 2. Honolulu: University of Hawaii Press, 1985.

Broughton, Jeffrey. "Kuei-feng Tsung-mi: The Convergence of Ch'an and the Teachings." Ph.D. diss., Columbia University, 1975.

Chappell, David. "The Teachings of the Fourth Ch'an Patriarch Tao-hsin (580–

651)." In *Early Ch'an in China and Tibet*, ed. by Lewis Lancaster and Whalen Lai, 89–129. Berkeley Buddhist Studies Series 5. Berkeley: University of California, 1983.

Cleary, Thomas. *The Original Face: An Anthology of Rinzai Zen.* New York: Grove Press, 1978.

Collcutt, Martin. "The Early Ch'an Monastic Rule: *Ch'ing-kuei* and the Shaping of Ch'an Community Life." In *Early Ch'an in China and Tibet*, ed. by Lewis Lancaster and Whalen Lai, 165–84. Berkeley Buddhist Studies Series 5. Berkeley: University of California, 1983.

———. *Five Mountains: The Rinzai Zen Monastic Institution in Medieval Japan.* Harvard East Asian Monographs 85. Cambridge, Mass., and London: Harvard University Press, 1981.

Demiéville, Paul. *Le Concile de Lhasa.* Paris: Imprimerie Nationale de France, 1952.

Dōgen zenji shinseki kankei shiryō shū 道元禅師真蹟関係資料集. Supplement to *Eihei Shōbō genzō shūsho taisei.* Tokyo: Taishūkan, 1980.

Donner, Neal. "The Great Calming and Contemplation of Chih-i." Ph.D. diss., University of British Columbia, 1976.

Dumoulin, Heinrich. "Allgemeine Lehren zur Förderung des Zazen von Zen-Meister Dōgen." *Monumenta Nipponica* 14 (1958), 429–36.

Etō Sokuō 衛藤即応. *Shōbō genzō josetsu: Bendō wa gikai* 正法眼蔵序説弁道話義解. Tokyo: Iwanami Shoten, 1959.

Faure, Bernard. "La Volonté d'Orthodoxie: Généalogie et Doctrine du Bouddhisme Ch'an de l'École du Nord." Doctorat d'État, Paris, 1985.

Fukan zazen gi no sankyū 普勧坐禅儀の参究. *Sanshō* 傘松 372 (9/1974); 373 (10/1974).

Funaoka Makoto 船岡誠. "Shoki zenshū juyō to Hiei zan 初期禅宗受容と比叡山." In *Zenshū no sho mondai* 禅宗の諸問題, ed. by Imaeda Aishin 今枝愛真, 57–84. Tokyo: Yūzankaku, 1979.

Furuta Shōkin 古田紹欽. *Nihon bukkyō shisō shi no sho mondai* 日本仏教思想史の諸問題. Tokyo: Shunjūsha, 1964.

———. *Shōbō genzō no kenkyū* 正法眼蔵の研究. Tokyo: Sōbunsha, 1972.

Gendai yaku Shōbō genzō 現代訳正法眼蔵. Ed. by Zen Bunka Gakuin 禅文化学院. Tokyo: Seishin Shobō, 1968.

Gimello, Robert. "Li T'ung-hsüan and the Practical Dimensions of Hua-yen." In *Studies in Ch'an and Hua-yen*, ed. by Gimello and Peter Gregory, 321–89. Kuroda Institute Studies in East Asian Buddhism 1. Honolulu: University of Hawaii Press, 1983.

Hanuki Masai 葉貫磨哉. "Kamakura bukkyō ni okeru Yōsai monryū no ichi: Taikō Gyōyū to sono shūhen 鎌倉仏教に於ける栄西門流の位置退耕行勇とその周辺." *Bukkyō shigaku kenkyū* 仏教史学研究 20, 2 (3/1978), 1–29.

Harada Kōdō 原田弘道. "Nihon Sōtō shū no rekishiki teki seikaku (2): Dōgen zenji to Ryūzen Kakushin to no kōshō o megutte 日本曹洞宗の歴史的性格道元禅師と隆禅覚心との交渉を還って." KDBGR 5 (12/1974), 1–16.

Harada Sogaku 原田祖岳. *Fukan zazen gi kōwa* 普勧坐禅儀講話. Repr. Tokyo: Daizō Shuppan, 1982.

———. *Zazen no shikata* 坐禅の仕方. Tokyo: Chūō Bukkyōsha, 1927.

Hirakawa Akira 平川彰. "Ritsuzō ni arawareta zen no jissen 律蔵に現れた禅の
実践." In *Shikan no kenkyū* 止観の研究, ed. by Sekiguchi Shindai 関口真大,
51–71. Tokyo: Iwanami Shoten, 1975.

Hiwatari Noboru 樋渡登. "Hōon roku shohon to sono honbun o megutte 報恩録諸
本とその本文をめぐって." SK 24 (3/1982), 58–64.

Hōbōgirin: Dictionnaire Encyclopédique du Bouddhisme. Fascicule 1: *A-Bombai.* Tokyo:
Maison Franco-Japonaise, 1929.

Hu Shih 胡適, ed. *Shen-hui ho-shang i-chi* 神會和尚遺集. Rev. ed. Taipei: Hu Shih
Chi-nien Kuan, 1970.

Ichikawa Hakugen 市川白弦 et al., ed. *Chūsei zenke no shisō* 中世禅家の思想. *Nihon
shisō taikei* 日本思想大系 16. Tokyo: Iwanami Shoten, 1972.

Ienaga Saburo 家永三郎. *Chūsei bukkyō shisō shi kenkyū* 中世仏教思想史研究.
Tokyo: Hōzōkan, 1947.

Ikeda Rosan 池田魯参. "Dōgen zenji no nyū Sō denbō 道元禅師入宋伝法." SK
25 (3/1983), 36–42.

Imaeda Aishin 今枝愛真. *Chūsei zenshū shi no kenkyū* 中世禅宗史の研究. Tokyo:
Tōkyō Daigaku Shuppankai, 1970.

———. *Dōgen: Zazen hitosuji no shamon* 道元坐禅ひとすじの沙門. NHK bukkusu
225. Tokyo: Nihon Hōsō Shuppankai, 1976.

Iriya Yoshitaka 入矢義高. *Baso no goroku* 馬祖の語録. Kyoto: Zen Bunka Ken-
kyūjo, 1984.

———. *Hō koji goroku* 龐居士語録. *Zen no goroku* 禅の語録 7. Tokyo: Chikuma
Shobō, 1973.

Ishii Shūdō 石井修道. "Busshō Tokkō to Nihon Daruma shū: Kanazawa bunko
hokan Jōtō shōkaku ron o tegakari toshite 仏照徳光と日本達磨宗金沢文
庫保管成等正覚論をてがかりとして." *Kanazawa bunko kenkyū* 金沢文庫
研究 20, 11 (11/1974), 1–16; 12 (12/1974), 1–20.

———. "Daie goroku no kiso teki kenkyū 大慧語録の基礎的研究 (3)." KDBGKK
33 (3/1975), 151–71.

———. "Daie Sōkō to sono deshitachi 大慧宗杲とその弟子たち (5)." IBK 22,
1 (12/1973), 291–95.

———. "Daie Sōkō to sono deshitachi (6)." IBK 23, 1 (12/1974), 336–39.

———. "Daie Sōkō to sono deshitachi (8)." IBK 25, 1 (12/1976), 257–61.

———. "Daie zen ni okeru zen to nenbutsu no mondai 大慧禅における禅と念
仏の問題." In *Zen to nenbutsu* 禅と念仏, ed. by Fujiyoshi Jikai 藤吉慈海,
269–301. Tokyo: Daizō Shuppan, 1983.

———. "Mana Shōbō genzo no motozuku shiryō ni tsuite 真字正法眼蔵の基ず
く資料について." SKKKK 3 (10/1974), 51–84.

Ishikawa Rikizan 石川力山. "Himitsu Shōbō genzō saikō 秘密正法眼蔵再考."
SK 21 (3/1979), 173–78.

———. "Shōbō genzō zuimon ki to Nihon Daruma shū 正法眼蔵随聞記と日本
達磨宗." SK 24 (3/1982), 37–43; 25 (3/1983), 43–48.

Itō Shūken 伊藤秀憲. "Kōan to shikan taza 公案と只管打坐." SK 22 (3/1980),
101–6.

———. "Shōbō genzō shō kenkyū nōto 正法眼蔵抄研究ノート (1)." SKKKK
11 (8/1979), 6–13.

———. "Shōbō genzō to Shōbō genzō zuimon ki to no aida no mujun 正法眼蔵と正法眼蔵随聞記との間の矛盾." IBK 27, 1 (12/1978), 343–46.

Kagamishima Genryū 鏡島元隆. *Dōgen zenji to inyō kyōten goroku no kenkyū* 道元禅師と引用経典語録の研究. Tokyo: Mokujisha, 1965.

———. *Dōgen zenji to sono shūhen* 道元禅師とその周辺. Gakujutsu sōsho: Zen bukkyō 学術叢書禅仏教. Tokyo: Daitō Shuppansha, 1985.

———. "Eihei Dōgen to Rankei Dōryū 永平道元と蘭渓道隆." *Kanazawa bunko kenkyū kiyō* 金沢文庫研究紀要 11 (3/1974), 1–13; repr. in Kagamishima, *Dōgen zenji to sono shūhen*, 59–77.

———. "Eihei kōroku kō 永平広録考." *Shūkyō gaku ronshū* 宗教学論集 8 (12/1977), 147–60.

———. "Eihei kōroku to Ryakuroku 永平広録と略録." KDKK 15 (3/1957), 55–64.

———. "Hyakujō ko shingi henka katei no ichi kōsatsu 百丈古清規変化過程の一考察." KDBGKK 25 (3/1967), 1–13.

———. "Kanazawa bunko bon Zen'en shingi ni tsuite 金沢文庫本禅苑清規について." *Kanazawa bunko kenkyū* 金沢文庫研究 14, 3 (3/1968), 1–6.

———. Review of Kawamura, *Shohon taikō Eihei kaisan Dōgen zenji gyōjō Kenzei ki*. KDBGR 6 (10/1975), 141–46.

———. *Tendō Nyojō zenji no kenkyū* 天童如浄禅師の研究. Tokyo: Shunjūsha, 1983.

——— et al. *Yakuchū Zen'en shingi* 訳註禅苑清規. Tokyo: Sōtōshū Shūmuchō, 1972.

Kajitani Sōnin 梶谷宗忍 et al., ed. *Shinjin mei Shōdō ka Jūgyū zu Zazen gi* 信心銘証道歌十牛図坐禅儀. *Zen no goroku* 禅の語録 16. Tokyo: Chikuma Shobō, 1974.

Kamata Shigeo 鎌田茂雄. *Shūmitsu kyōgaku no shisō shi teki kenkyū* 宗密教学の思想史的研究. Tokyo: Tōkyō Daigaku Shuppankai, 1975.

Kanazawa bunko shiryō zensho 金沢文庫資料全書. Vol. 1. Yokohama: Kanazawa Bunko, 1974.

Kapleau, Philip. *Three Pillars of Zen*. New York: Harper and Row, 1966.

Karaki Junzō 唐木順三. *Mujō* 無常. Chikuma sōsho 筑摩叢書 39. Tokyo: Chikuma Shobō, 1965.

Kawamura Kōdō 河村孝道. "Kanazawa bunko shozō Shōbō genzō kanken 金沢文庫所蔵正法眼蔵管見." *Kanazawa bunko kenkyū* 金沢文庫研究 17, 11 (11/1971), 1–9; 17, 12 (12/1971), 10–16; repr. in Kawamura and Ishikawa, *Dōgen zenji to Sōtō shū*, 54–74.

———. "Mana Shōbō genzō no kenkyū 真字正法眼蔵の研究." KDBGKK 30 (3/1972), 135–59; 31 (3/1973), 95–138; 33 (3/1975), 41–96; 34 (3/1976), 64–98.

———. *Shohon taikō Eihei kaisan Dōgen zenji gyōjō Kenzei ki* 諸本対校永平開山道元禅師行状建撕記. Tokyo: Taishūkan, 1975.

——— and Ishikawa Rikizan 石川力山, ed. *Dōgen* 道元. *Nihon meisō ronshū* 日本名僧論集 8. Tokyo: Yoshikawa Kōbunkan, 1983.

——— and Ishikawa Rikizan 石川力山, ed. *Dōgen zenji to Sōtō shū* 道元禅師と曹洞宗. *Nihon bukkyō shūshi ronshū* 日本仏教宗史論集 8. Tokyo: Yoshikawa Kōbunkan, 1985.

Kennett, Jiyu. *Zen Is Eternal Life*. Emeryville, Calif.: Dharma Publishing, 1976.

Kim, Hee-jin. *Flowers of Emptiness: Selections from Dōgen's Shōbōgenzō*. Studies in Asian Thought and Religion 2. Lewiston, N.Y. and Queenston, Ont.: The Edwin Mellen Press, 1985.

Kinoshita Jun'ichi 木下純一. "Fukan zazen gi no kenkyū 普勧坐禅儀の研究." SK 7 (4/1965), 132-37.

Kishizawa Ian 岸沢惟安, ed. *Fukan zazen gi teiji roku* 普勧坐禅儀提耳録, by Nishiari Bokusan 西有穆山. Tokyo: Kōmeisha, 1911.

——. *Shōbō genzō zenkō* 正法眼蔵全講. 24 vols. Tokyo: Daihōrinkaku, 1973-74.

Kodera, James. *Dōgen's Formative Years in China: An Historical Study and Annotated Translation of the Hōkyō-ki*. Boulder, Colo.: Prajñā Press, 1980.

Kondō Ryōichi 近藤良一. "Chōro Sōsaku ni tsuite 長蘆宗賾について." IBK 4, 2 (3/1966), 280-83.

——. "Hyakujō shingi to Eihei shingi 百丈清規と永平清規." IBK 13, 1 (1/1965), 297-300.

Kozaka Kiyū 小坂機融. "Shingi hensen no teiryū 清規変遷の底流 (1)." SK 5 (4/1963), 123-29.

——. "Zen'en shingi no hen'yō katei ni tsuite: Kōrai ban Zen'en shingi no kōsatsu o kaishite 禅苑清規の変容過程について高麗板禅苑清規の考察を介して." IBK 20, 2 (3/1972), 720-24.

Kurebayashi Kōdō 樗林皓堂. *Dōgen zen no honryū* 道元禅の本流. Tokyo: Daihōrinkaku, 1980.

——. "Dōgen zen no kihon teki seikaku 道元禅の基本的性格." SK 3 (3/1961); 4 (3/1962); repr. in Kawamura and Ishikawa, *Dōgen*, 76-96.

——, ed. *Shōbō genzō keiteki* 正法眼蔵啓迪, by Nishiari Bokusan 西有穆山. 3 vols. Tokyo: Daihōrinkaku, 1965.

Matsuzaki Keisui 松崎恵水. "Kōgyō daishi Kakuban no kangyō ni tsuite 興教大師覚鑁の観行について." IBK 29, 2 (3/1981), 298-303.

McRae, John. "The Northern School of Chinese Ch'an Buddhism." Ph.D. diss., Yale University, 1983.

Miyazaka Yūshō 宮坂宥勝, ed. *Kana hōgo shū* 仮名法語集. *Nihon koten bungaku taikei* 日本古典文学大系 83. Tokyo: Iwanami Shoten, 1964.

Mizuno Kōgen 水野弘元. "Zenshū seiritsu izen no Shina no zenjō shisō shi josetsu 禅宗成立以前の支那の禅定思想史序説." KDKK 15 (3/1957), 15-54.

Mizuno Yaoko 水野弥恵子. "Hōkyō ki 宝慶記." In *Dōgen no chōsaku* 道元の著作, ed. by Kagamishima Genryū 鏡島元隆 and Tamaki Kōshiro 玉城康四郎, 218-40. *Kōza Dōgen* 講座道元 3. Tokyo: Shunjūsha, 1980.

——. "Hōkyō ki to jūni kan Shōbō genzō 宝慶記と十二巻正法眼蔵." SK 21 (3/1979), 27-30.

——. "Rinkan roku kara Shōbō genzō e 林間録から正法眼蔵へ." In *Bukkyō no rekishi teki tenkai ni miru sho keitai: Furuta Shōkin hakase koki kinen ronshū* 仏教の歴史的展開にみる諸形態古田紹欽博士古稀記念論集, 811-22. Tokyo: Sōbunsha, 1981.

——. "Shōbō genzō no shohon sono ta ni tsuite 正法眼蔵の諸本その他について." In *Shōbō genzō Shōbō genzō zuimon ki* 正法眼蔵正法眼蔵随聞記, ed. by Nishio Minoru 西尾実 et al., 34-56. *Nihon koten bungaku taikei* 日本古典文学大系 81. Tokyo: Iwanami Shoten, 1965.

Mochizuki Shinkō 望月信亨. *Bukkyō kyōten seiritsu shi ron* 仏教経典成立史論. 1946. Repr. Tokyo: Hōzōkan, 1978.

Moriya Shigeru 守屋茂. "Fukakusa Kōshō ji no kaiki Shōkaku ni ni tsuite 深草興聖寺の開基正覚尼について." IBK 26, 1 (12/1977), 55–60.

———. "Dōgen to Minamoto no Sanetomo Hongaku ni no kotodomo 道元と源実朝本覚尼のことども." In Moriya, *Dōgen zenji kenkyū: Kyōto shūhen ni okeru Dōgen to sono shūmon* 道元禅師研究京都周辺における道元とその宗門. Kyoto: Dōmeisha Shuppan, 1984.

Nagahisa Toshio 永久俊雄. "Fukan zazen gi no kenkyū 普勧坐禅儀の研究." SK 5 (4/1963), 9–13.

Nagai Masashi 永井政之. "Nansō ni okeru ichi koji no seishin seikatsu: Nyonyo koji Ganpei no baai 南宋における一居士の精神生活如如居士顔丙の場合 (1)." KDBGR 15 (10/1984), 202–27.

Nakagawa Taka 中川孝. *Rokuso dankyō* 六祖壇経. *Zen no goroku* 禅の語録 4. Tokyo: Chikuma Shobō, 1976.

Nakamura Toshiyuki 中村信幸. "Zadan to iu go ni tsuite 坐断という語について." SK 21 (3/1979), 179–84.

Nakao Ryōshin 中尾良信. "Dainichibō Nōnin no zen 大日房能忍の禅." SK 26. (3/1984), 221–35.

Nishio Kenryū 西尾賢隆. "Sōdai Nitchū bukkyō kōryū shi 宋代日中仏教交流史." *Bukkyō shigaku kenkyū* 仏教史学研究 19, 1 (1/1977), 1–32.

Nishiyama Kōsen, tr. *Shōbōgenzō*. Vol. 4. Tokyo: Nakayama Shobō, 1983.

Notomi Jōten 納富常天. "Dōgen no Kamakura kyōke ni tsuite 道元の鎌倉教化について." KDBGKK 31 (3/1973), 181–203.

———. "Shunjō to Dōgen 俊芿と道元." IBK 23, 1 (12/1974), 114–21.

Ōbora Ryōun 大洞良雲. *Gendai kōwa Fukan zazen gi* 現代講話普勧坐禅儀. Repr. Reimei bukkyō sōsho 黎明仏教叢書 2. Nagoya: Reimei Shobō, 1982.

Ōkubo Dōshū 大久保道舟. *Dōgen zenji den no kenkyū* 道元禅師伝の研究. Rev. ed. Tokyo: Chikuma Shobō, 1966.

———, ed. *Dōgen zenji goroku* 道元禅師語録. Iwanami bunko 岩波文庫 2211–12. Tokyo: Iwanami Shoten, 1940.

———, ed. *Dōgen zenji shingi* 道元禅師清規. Iwanami bunko 岩波文庫 2896–98. Tokyo: Iwanami Shoten, 1941.

———, ed. *Dōgen zenji shinpitsu shūsei* 道元禅師真筆集成. Supplement to DZZ. Tokyo: Chikuma Shobō, 1970.

———, ed. *Zen'en bokka* 禅苑墨華. Vol. 1. 1925; repr. Tokyo: Kokusho Kankōkai, 1974.

Ōminami Ryūshō 大南龍昇. "Go teishin kan to gomon zen 五停心観と五門禅." In *Bukkyō no jissen genri* 仏教の実践原理, ed. by Sekiguchi Shindai 関口真大, 71–90. Tokyo: Sankibō Busshorin, 1977.

Ōmori Sōgen 大森曹玄, ed. *Kunchū Zenshū shibu roku* 訓註禅宗四部録. Kyoto: Kichūdō, 1962.

Ōtani Tetsuo 大谷哲夫. "Chūgoku ni okeru chōsoku hō 中国における調息法." SK 11 (3/1969), 67–72.

———. "Chūgoku shoki zenkan jidai ni okeru za no keitai 中国初期禅観時代における坐の形態." SK 12 (3/1970), 198–211.

———. "Chūgoku shoki zenkan no kokyū hō to yōjō setsu no yōki ni tsuite 中国初

期禅観の呼吸法と養生説の養気について." IBK 17, 1 (12/1968), 142–43.

Ryōso daishi zazen seiten 両祖大師坐禅聖典. Ed. by Sōtōshū Shūmuchō Kyōikubu 曹洞宗宗務庁教育部. Tokyo: Sōtōshū Shūmuchō Kyōikubu, 1959.

Sakai Tokugen 境井徳元. "Zen ni okeru henkō 禅における偏向." SK 2 (1/1960); repr. in Kawamura and Ishikawa, *Dōgen zenji to Sōtō shū*, 22–41.

Sanae Kensei 早苗憲生. "Hōsa bunko bon Shōichi kana hōgo no kenkyū (1): Honbun hen 逢左文庫本聖一假名法語の研究本文篇." *Zen bunka kenkyū jo kiyō* 禅文化研究所紀要 6 (5/1974), 265–94.

Sasaki Kentoku 佐々木憲徳. *Kan Gi Rikuchō zenkan hatten shi ron* 漢魏六朝禅観発展史論. 1935. Repr. Tokyo: Pitaka, 1978.

Sekiguchi Shindai 関口真大. *Daruma daishi no kenkyū* 達磨大師の研究. 1957. Rev. enl. ed. Tokyo: Shunjūsha, 1969.

————. *Tendai shikan no kenkyū* 天台止観の研究. Tokyo: Iwanami Shoten, 1969.

————. *Tendai shō shikan* 天台小止観. Iwanami bunko 岩波文庫 33-309-3. Tokyo: Iwanami Shoten, 1974.

————. *Tendai shō shikan no kenkyū* 天台小止観の研究. 1954. Repr. Tokyo: Sankibō Busshorin, 1961.

Shibata Dōken 柴田道賢. *Zenji Dōgen no shisō* 禅師道元の思想. Tokyo: Kōronsha, 1975.

Shibe Ken'ichi 志部憲一. "Shōbō genzō senpyō no ichi kōsatsu 正法眼蔵僧評の一考察." SK 24 (3/1982), 72–77.

————. "Shōbō genzō senpyō to Edo ki shūgaku no kanren 正法眼蔵僧評と江戸期宗学の関連." SK 25 (3/1983), 246–61.

Shiina Kōyū 椎名宏雄. "Shōshitsu rokumon to Daruma daishi sanron 少室六門と達磨大師三論." KDBGR 9 (11/1978), 208–32.

————. "Sō Gen ban zenseki kenkyū 宋元版禅籍研究 (4)." IBK 29, 2 (3/1981), 251–54.

Shōbo genzō yōgo sakuin 正法眼蔵用語索引. Ed. by Katō Shūkō 加藤宗厚. 2 vols. Tokyo: Risōsha, 1962–63.

Shōwa teiho Sōtō shū gyōji kihan 昭和訂補曹洞宗行持軌範. Tokyo: Sōtōshū Shūmuchō, 1967.

Sugimoto Shunryū 杉本俊龍. *Zōtei Tōjo shitsunai kirigami oyobi sanwa kenkyū* 増訂洞上室内切紙并参話研究. Publisher unknown, 1941.

Sugio Gen'yū 杉尾玄有. "Minamoto no Sanetomo no nyū Sō kito to Dōgen zenji 源実朝の入宋企図と道元禅師." SK 18 (3/1976), 41–46.

Suzuki Daisetsu 鈴木大拙. *Zen shisō shi kenkyū* 禅思想史研究 I. 1943. Repr. *Suzuki Daisetsu zenshū* 鈴木大拙全集, vol. 1. Tokyo: Iwanami Shoten, 1968.

Tagami Taishū 田上太秀. *Zen no shisō* 禅の思想. Tokyo: Tōkyō Shoseki, 1980.

Takahashi Shū'ei 高橋秀栄. "Dainichibō Nōnin to Daruma shū ni kansuru shiryō 大日房能忍と達磨宗に関する資料." *Kanazawa bunko kenkyū* 金沢文庫研究 22, 4 (6/1976), 14–16; 22, 7–23, 1 (combined number, 12/1976–1/1977), 22–33.

Takasaki Jikidō 高崎直道. "Mukyū no butsugyō 無窮の仏行." In *Kobutsu no manabi* (*Dōgen*) 古仏のまなび道元, ed. by Takasaki and Umehara Takeshi 梅原猛. *Bukkyō no shisō* 仏教の思想 11. Tokyo: Kadokawa Shoten, 1969.

Takeuchi Michio 竹内道雄. *Dōgen* 道元. Jinbutsu sōsho 人物叢書 88. Tokyo: Yoshikawa Kōbunkan, 1962.

Tamura Yoshiro 田村芳朗. *Kamakura shin bukkyō shisō no kenkyū* 鎌倉新仏教思想の研究. Kyoto: Heirakuji Shoten, 1965.

Tsugunaga Yoshiteru 嗣永芳照. "Nihon Sōtō shū ni okeru Dainichi Nōnin no Daruma shū no shōchō 日本曹洞宗に於ける大日能忍の達磨宗の消長." *Shoryōbu kiyō* 書陵部紀要 18 (11/1966), 31–42; repr. in Kawamura and Ishikawa, *Dōgen*, 346–64.

Tucci, Giuseppe. *Minor Buddhist Texts, Part 3: Third Bhāvanākrama.* Serie Orientale Roma XLIII. Rome: Is.M.E.O., 1971.

Uchiyama Kōshō 内山興聖. *Shūkyō toshite no Dōgen zen: Fukan zazen gi ikai* 宗教としての道元禅普勧坐禅儀意解. Tokyo: Hakujusha, 1977.

Ui Hakuju 宇井伯寿. *Zenshū shi no kenkyū* 禅宗史の研究. 3 vols. Tokyo: Iwanami Shoten, 1939–43.

Waddell, Norman and Abe Masao. "Dōgen's Fukanzazengi and Shōbōgenzō zazengi." *The Eastern Buddhist*, new series 6, 2 (10/1973), 115–28.

Watsuji Tetsuro 和辻哲郎. "Shamon Dōgen 沙門道元." In *Nihon seishin shi kenkyū* 日本精神史研究, by Watsuji, 156–246. Tokyo: Iwanami Shoten, 1926.

Yamada Kōdō 山田孝道, ed. *Zenshū Sōtō seiten* 禅宗曹洞聖典. 1911. Repr. Tokyo: Kōyūkan, 1929.

Yamada Shōzen 山田昭全 and Miki Sumito 三木紀人, eds. *Zōtan shū* 雑談集. Chūsei no bungaku 中世の文学 1:3. Tokyo: Miyai Shoten, 1973.

Yamauchi Shun'yū 山内舜雄. "Shūzen yōketsu ni okeru zahō no kōsatsu 修禅要訣における坐法の考察." SK 13 (3/1971), 25–34.

———. "Zazen gi to Tendai shō shikan 坐禅儀と天台小止観." SK 8 (4/1966), 29–50.

———. "Zenrin shōki sen narabi ni Chokushū Hyakujō shingi sae ni okeru zazen no chūshaku ni tsuite 禅林象器箋並びに勅修百丈清規左觽における坐禅の註釈について." KDBGKK 29 (3/1971), 14–31.

Yampolsky, Philip. *The Platform Sutra of the Sixth Patriarch.* New York: Columbia University, 1967.

Yanagida Seizan 柳田聖山. *Chūsei hyōhaku* 中世漂泊. Hōzō sensho 宝蔵撰書 8. Kyoto: Hōzōkan, 1981.

———. "Dōgen to Chūgoku bukkyō 道元と中国仏教." *Zen bunka kenkyū jo kiyō* 禅文化研究所紀要 13 (3/1984), 7–128.

———. "Dōgen to Rinzai 道元と臨済." *Risō* 理想 513 (2/1976), 74–89.

———. "Kanna to mokushō 看話と黙照." *Hanazono daigaku kenkyū kiyō* 花園大学研究紀要 6 (3/1975), 1–20.

———, ed. *Shisō dokuhon: Dōgen* 思想読本道元. Kyoto: Hōzōkan, 1982.

———, ed. *Shoki no zen shi* 初期の禅史 I: *Ryōga shiji ki Denbō hōbō ki* 楞伽師資記伝法宝紀. Zen no goroku 禅の語録 2. Tokyo: Chikuma Shobō, 1971.

———. *Shoki zenshū shisho no kenkyū* 初期禅宗史書の研究. Tokyo: Hōzōkan, 1967.

———. "Yōsai to Kōzen gokoku ron no kadai 栄西と興禅護国論の課題." In Ichikawa, *Chūsei zenke no shisō*, 439–86.

———. "Zenseki kaidai 禅籍解題." In *Zenke goroku* 禅家語録, vol. 2, ed. by Nishitani Keiji 西谷啓治 and Yanagida, 445–514. Sekai koten bungaku zenshū 世界古典文学全集 36B. Tokyo: Chikuma Shobō, 1974.

Yokoi Kakudō 横井覚道. "Fukan zazen gi goshinpitsu bon ni tsuite 普勧坐禅儀御真筆本について." SK 11 (3/1969), 78–90.

————. "Fukan zazen gi goshinpitsu bon ni tsuite (2)." SK 12 (3/1970), 19–30.

Yokoi Yūhō, tr. *Regulations for Monastic Life by Eihei Dōgen: Eihei-Genzenji-Shingi (Eiyaku Eihei daishingi* 英訳永平大清規*).* Tokyo: Sankibō Busshorin, 1973.

————. *The Shōbō-genzō.* Tokyo: Sankibō Busshorin, 1985.

Zengaku dai jiten 禅学大辞典. 3 vols. Tokyo: Taishūkan, 1978.

Index

Compositor. Asco Trade Typesetting Ltd.
Text: 10/12 Baskerville
Display: Baskerville

This volume is sponsored by
the Center for Japanese Studies
University of California, Berkeley

Milton Keynes UK
Ingram Content Group UK Ltd.
UKHW040615160224
437942UK00001B/54

9 780520 068353